# Tolley's
# Statutory Residenc

Second Edition

# Tolley's
# Statutory Residence Test

Second Edition

by

**Amanda Hardy QC**
and

**Carolyn Steppler MA DPhil**

**Members of the LexisNexis Group worldwide**

| | |
|---|---|
| United Kingdom | LexisNexis, a Division of Reed Elsevier (UK) Ltd, Lexis House, 30 Farringdon Street, London EC4A 4HH, and London House, 20-22 East London Street, Edinburgh EH7 4BQ |
| Australia | LexisNexis Butterworths, Chatswood, New South Wales |
| Austria | LexisNexis Verlag ARD Orac GmbH & Co KG, Vienna |
| Benelux | LexisNexis Benelux, Amsterdam |
| Canada | LexisNexis Canada, Markham, Ontario |
| China | LexisNexis China, Beijing and Shanghai |
| France | LexisNexis SA, Paris |
| Germany | LexisNexis Deutschland GmbH, Munster |
| Hong Kong | LexisNexis Hong Kong, Hong Kong |
| India | LexisNexis India, New Delhi |
| Italy | Giuffrè Editore, Milan |
| Japan | LexisNexis Japan, Tokyo |
| Malaysia | Malayan Law Journal Sdn Bhd, Kuala Lumpur |
| New Zealand | LexisNexis NZ Ltd, Wellington |
| Poland | Wydawnictwo Prawnicze LexisNexis Sp, Warsaw |
| Singapore | LexisNexis Singapore, Singapore |
| South Africa | LexisNexis Butterworths, Durban |
| USA | LexisNexis, Dayton, Ohio |

© Reed Elsevier (UK) Ltd 2017

Published by LexisNexis

ISBN for this volume: 9780754554097

Printed and bound in Great Britain by Hobbs the Printers Ltd, Totton, Hampshire

**Visit LexisNexis at www.lexisnexis.co.uk**

# About the Authors

**Amanda Hardy QC** was appointed Queen's Counsel in 2015 and is ranked as a Leading Silk for both private client work and corporation tax. Chambers and Partners High Net Worth 2017 states 'Amanda Hardy QC is a "highly respected" tax silk, with a strong litigation and advisory practice'. Amanda has appeared this year in the Supreme Court, the High Court and the First Tier Tribunal and has appeared three times in the House of Lords, eight times in the Court of Appeal, once in the European Court of Justice and twice in the Privy Council as well as a number of appearances before the High Court, First and Upper Tier Tribunal and Special Commissioners during her career. Amanda has recently been involved in litigation in many areas of direct and indirect tax, including trusts (appearing in the High Court in five recent separate applications to vary extremely substantial trusts), capital gains tax, income tax, tax aspects of divorce and international taxation. She has appeared five times in the Ugandan Tax Tribunal in Kampala for a multi-national oil company. Amanda's advisory private client work focuses on offshore trusts, residence and domicile issues and pensions tax. A fellow barrister describes Amanda as 'a standout silk in this area. I think she's extremely good with clients, very clear in her advice and it's very practical advice'. Amanda studied law at King's College London where she also completed her Masters in Tax. She was a visiting Lecturer in the Law of Trusts at King's from 1993-1998. She was a Middle Temple Queen Mother's Scholar at Bar School and did her first six months pupilage in Erskine Chambers. She did her second six months pupilage in what is now Tax Chambers, 15 Old Square where she practises. Amanda is Honorary Secretary of the Chancery Bar Association, a member of the Revenue Bar Association and a Liveryman of the Worshipful Company of Tax Advisors. She was elected a Bencher of the Middle Temple in 2017.

**Carolyn Steppler MA DPhil** is Head of UK Wealth Planning for Credit Suisse AG and is based in Zurich. Previously she was a private client tax partner in the London office of EY, where she specialised in advising non-domiciled individuals and their family structures on their UK tax affairs, including UK residence. She now works with private clients of Credit Suisse AG on structures for their private and business wealth, estate planning and on wealth advisory services in connection with relocation to and from the UK. The residence rules in the UK are often the starting point for a discussion with a client.

# Preface

The statutory residence test was introduced by *Finance Act 2013* with effect from 6 April 2013. Its introduction was at the time arguably one of the most significant changes to personal taxation. For the first time in UK law, residence is determined by reference to a comprehensive statutory code and no longer relies primarily on case law and HMRC guidance. The move to statute-based tests makes the law more prescriptive. However, although the law is now less flexible to a taxpayer's circumstances, once within the tests he can have certainty as to his residence position. Unfortunately, some remaining ambiguities of the test mean that this certainty is not always achieved. With the 2017 changes to domicile and the introduction of a new statutory deemed UK domicile status which depends on years of UK tax residence, the SRT takes on an increased significance.

One of the stated aims of the new regime is to ensure that the residence status of most taxpayers remains unchanged. For this reason, although there are some changes from the case law tests (some fairly significant), much of the old regime has been codified with only minor modification.

This work is based on the law as originally enacted on 17 July 2013, with the minor amendment of FA 2014, and on the updated guidance issued by HMRC in August 2016 (RDR3) and, to a lesser extent, the additional guidance of RDR1 (updated in June 2016). It is noteworthy that, even before the law was enacted, we had over 100 pages of HMRC guidance. The legislation depends on a number of terms which are not always clearly defined and, in consequence, case law is likely to develop over time. We may see additional developments and clarification in the coming years, although the Government has not currently expressed any firm commitment to review the operation of the law in practice over the first few years.

There are a number of people without whom this work would not have been possible. A significant debt is owed to the previous co-author of this book, Jane Scott, the private client specialist in the Tax Knowledge team at EY in the UK and also to Eleanor Meredith who contributed invaluable content to the first edition, particularly in the area of employment tax and the impact of the SRT on employees. There are many others who supported the first edition of this book and we would like to thank again the staff at LexisNexis for their patience. Finally, we should like to acknowledge with gratitude the support of our family and friends during the writing process. Any remaining errors in the text are, of course, our own.

Amanda Hardy QC and Carolyn Steppler MA DPhil
*November 2017*

# Contents

# Contents

# Contents

# List of Abbreviations

| | |
|---|---|
| CGT | Capital Gains Tax |
| CTA 2010 | Corporation Tax Act 2010 |
| FA 2008 | Finance Act 2008 |
| FA 2013 | Finance Act 2013 |
| HMRC | Her Majesty's Revenue and Customs |
| HNWI | High Net Worth Individual |
| IHT | Inheritance Tax |
| IHTA 1984 | Inheritance Tax Act 1984 |
| ITA 2007 | Income Tax Act 2007 |
| ITEPA 2003 | Income Tax (Earnings and Pensions) Act 2003 |
| ITTOIA 2005 | Income Tax (Trading and Other Income) Act 2005 |
| OECD | Organisation for Economic Co-operation and Development |
| OWR | Overseas Workday Relief |
| SRT | Statutory Residence Test |
| TCGA 1992 | Taxation of Chargeable Gains Act 1992 |

# Table of Statutes

All references in the right-hand column are to paragraph numbers. Paragraph numbers printed in **bold** type indicate where an Act is set out in part or in full.

# Table of Statutory Instruments

Paragraph references printed in **bold** type indicate where the Statutory Instrument is set out in part or in full

# Table of Cases

## R

## T

# Chapter 1

# The Statutory Residence Test: historical background

## Introduction

**[1.01]** The Statutory Residence Test (SRT) was introduced by *Finance Act 2013* and came into effect on 6 April 2013. For the first time, the UK has a residence test based on a detailed statutory code, rather than case law and HMRC guidance. The concept of a legislative test for residence has had a long gestation, with the present test taking two years to develop from consultation to legislation. However, the detailed formal consultation is only the last in a long line of more informal proposals and consultations. This opening chapter outlines this journey and sets out the background to the SRT.

## The previous regime

**[1.02]** Prior to the introduction of the SRT, there was no statutory definition of residence. Some legislation existed regarding tax residence for individuals, but the statutory regime was not comprehensive. For example, legislation considered the residence position of an individual leaving the UK for only occasional residence abroad (*s 829, ITA 2007*), and provided that available accommodation in the UK was ignored in determining the residence position of an individual working full-time abroad (*s 830, ITA 2007*); but the only statute which allowed an individual to determine his residence position was found in *s 831* and *s 832, ITA 2007*. These sections provided that, for the purpose of taxing certain non-UK income, any individual in the UK for some temporary purpose would be treated as non-resident if they spent fewer than 183 days in the UK. *Finance Act 2013 (Sch 43, para 50)* repealed the existing law.

The legislation was necessarily supplemented by case law which provided some guidance, but only really where the taxpayer's circumstances were at one with those set out in the specific case.

The statutory regime was therefore limited, and the regime was in practice governed by HMRC published guidance. Some of HMRC's published practice could be traced back to particular cases, although for some areas the origin was more obscure. For example, there were cases such as *Levene v IRC* [1928] AC 217, 13 TC 486, HL, and *Lysaght v IRC* 13 TC 511, [1927] 2 KB 55, CA, in the 1920s which suggested that a commitment to visit the UK for about three months each tax year over a period was enough to make someone tax resident, but none of them suggested that a 91-day averaging test was the appropriate measure.

# Impetus for change

**[1.03]** The complexity and vagueness of the previous regime had long been recognised.

As early as 1936 the Income Tax Codification Committee criticised the limited statutory guidance (ie the rules of what became *ss 829–832, ITA 2007*), concluding that the reliance on case law and the courts 'is intolerable and should not be allowed to continue'. In 1955 the Royal Commission on the Taxation of Profit and Income concluded that statute should lay down the principles of residence. While not requiring an exhaustive definition of residence, the Commission proposed a statutory set of rules to determine residence and ordinary residence and to cover visitors to the UK.

Instead of statute, advisers and taxpayers received HMRC guidance, the last two versions of which were designated as IR20 and, from 6 April 2009, HMRC 6.

For much of the period when IR20 held sway it was accepted as a reasonable basis for determining tax residence, and in some areas it worked well. It was relatively easy to identify someone who had left the UK to work full-time abroad. Typically, international assignees were accompanied by their families, and for that reason it was quite clear when an assignee had left the UK, or had come here on assignment.

In the event, the impetus for change was not primarily any development in tax law but rather social change and improved international transport that made commuting into and out of the UK a more realistic possibility for many more people. It became more acceptable for families to stay put and for one partner to commute, while at the same time it became far easier and cheaper to do so because of the availability of frequent cheap international flights. By the 1990s it was reasonably common for an employee to take a commuter assignment, especially within Europe, while his family remained UK resident. This gave rise to the possibility that an employee might regard himself as working full time abroad while HMRC might question whether his departure from the UK had the required distinct break in the pattern of residence they expected for someone to be regarded as no longer UK tax resident.

For many years after 1936 there was only one important tax case on residence – *Reed (Inspector of Taxes) v Clark* [1986] Ch 1, 58 TC 528 in 1985. However from 2005, starting with *Shepherd v Revenue and Customs Comrs* [2005] STC (STD) 644, there was a flurry of cases which exposed the difficulties for taxpayers seeking to rely on HMRC guidance.

In the late 2000s, three taxpayers, Messrs Davies, James and Gaines-Cooper, sought judicial review on HMRC's application of IR20, claiming that HMRC was not following its own guidance and had changed its approach (*R (on the application of Davies) v Revenue and Customs Comrs, R (on the application of Gaines-Cooper) v Revenue and Customs Comrs* [2010] EWCA Civ 83, [2010] STC 860). The Supreme Court held that HMRC guidance is binding and that HMRC can only change it prospectively. This was of no help to the taxpayers concerned, however, since their Lordships also concluded that they were UK resident under the guidance in the years in question and that there was insufficient evidence to support a change in HMRC's practice. The Supreme Court was none the less critical of the guidance in IR20.

As a result of these cases (and before the final outcome of the above judicial review), IR20 was replaced with HMRC 6 which contained a change to HMRC's approach to determining residence and emphasised to a far greater degree that the booklet provided only general guidance in order to help individuals make a decision about their residence status.

For example, the October 2011 version of HMRC 6 stated:

'This guidance outlines our (H M Revenue & Customs) application and interpretation of legislation and case law. The material is provided for your guidance. It sets out the main factors that are taken into account based on the rulings of the courts. Whether any section of this general guidance is applicable to you depends on your particular facts, as each set of circumstances will be different. It also seeks to give practical examples of what the relevant law means; these are only illustrative examples.

Any practices described in this guidance are subject to periodic review and may subsequently be altered or withdrawn. If practices were to be changed or revoked this would not normally be done retrospectively.'

Concurrently with these court cases came a Government consultation into residence and domicile.

Since 1955 there had been only one formal Government consultation in this area, and that was in 1988, when the Inland Revenue published 'Residence in the United Kingdom, The Scope of UK Taxation for Individuals, A Consultation Document'. The 1988 consultation recognised the complexity of the existing regime and sought to make the residence rules simple and objective. Most interestingly, it proposed an approach based on day counts in the current and two proceeding tax years. Coupled with this were new proposals to reform the remittance basis. However, in 1989 the Government announced that the proposals would not proceed.

In Budget 2002, the Government announced a review of the residence and domicile rules as they affected individuals and invited contributions. The then current regime was described as 'complex and poorly understood' and as not reflecting 'the reality of today's more integrated world'. Any modernising rules should be 'fair, . . . support the competitiveness of the UK economy, and should be clear and easy to operate' (see HMT and IR paper 'Reviewing the Residence and Domicile Rules as they affect the taxation of individuals: A background paper' (April 2003), paras 1.2 and 1.3). There were no formal proposals in the paper and no developments for a number of years. Then, between 6 December 2007 and 28 February 2008, HMT conducted a public consultation on proposals to reform the residence and domicile personal tax rules.

The result of this exercise was a radical reform of the domicile (remittance basis) rules in *Finance Act 2008* and a single change to the residence rules to count days where the individual is present in the UK at midnight (excluding days in transit). This, with the then existing regime, was stated to be 'a more flexible way of determining residence, and . . . therefore preferable to a new statutory test' (a summary of responses to 'Paying a fairer share: A consultation on residence and domicile', para 2.74). This was despite professional bodies such as STEP and the ICAEW calling for a statutory residence test.

Among the *Finance Act 2008* changes to the remittance basis was a new Remittance Basis Charge or RBC that had to be paid by long-term UK tax residents who wished to continue to claim the remittance basis. Liability to the RBC was determined by reference to whether or not the taxpayer had been UK tax resident in at least seven out of the previous nine UK tax years. The point at which someone coming to the UK became tax resident could also therefore determine the tax year in which he would first be required to pay £30,000 in order to claim the remittance basis. It therefore became even more important to be able to establish tax residence status with clarity. Concerns expressed about the *FA 2008* changes led the Exchequer Secretary to the Treasury to make a statement committing to keep the remittance basis law under review and also indicating a willingness on the part of the Government to introduce a comprehensive statutory residence test if all interested parties could agree on what that test should look like.

Informal consultations between the Government and various interested bodies went on for some time but no conclusions were reached. Instead, the issue was left undetermined until, in its first Budget in March 2011, the new coalition Government committed to a formal consultation.

## The consultations leading to Finance Act 2013

**[1.04]** The first of the formal consultation documents was issued in June 2011. Once again, the reasons for proposed change were given as the subjectivity and uncertainty of the existing regime, the reliance on case law that derived from an era before the global economy and changes to technology, travel and working patterns, and the fact that the existing regime was a deterrent to individuals and businesses wishing to come to the UK. The intention was to replace the then existing regime with a new regime that was transparent, objective and simple to use, to enable taxpayers to assess their residence status in a straightforward way. Moreover it was stated that the tax residence status for most individuals would not be affected by the changes ('Statutory Definition of Tax Residence: A consultation', Section 1).

The June 2011 consultation document set out the framework for the three-part test that was eventually adopted (see **CHAPTER 2** for an overview of the test). In very broad terms it used the criteria that would have been taken into account historically in assessing residence status, such as having a UK home, working in the UK and spending a significant number of days in the UK. It also posed a number of consultation questions, asking whether the framework proposed was appropriate, consulting on the proposed definitions and on whether the status of ordinary residence should be retained. The period for consultation ran until 9 September 2011.

It was anticipated that draft legislation would be released in December 2011 with the final version of the law being enacted in *Finance Act 2012*. On 6 December 2011 the Exchequer Secretary to the Treasury instead released a written statement indicating a one-year delay, as explained in the following extract:

'The consultation on tax residence raised a number of detailed issues which will require careful consideration to ensure the legislation achieves its important aim of providing certainty for individuals and businesses. The Government will therefore legislate the statutory residence test in Finance Bill 2013 to take effect from April 2013 rather than April 2012. It will introduce any reforms to ordinary residence at the same time. This will give time to consult thoroughly on the detail of these changes well in advance of implementation.'

There were no further significant developments until the response to the original consultation was released in June 2012. This document included a summary of responses received on the proposals, an overview of the Government's then plans and a first draft of the proposed legislation, which confirmed the broad framework that had previously been suggested. Some further questions for consultation were put forward and some amendments were proposed, including the decision to abolish ordinary residence for income tax and capital gains tax, while retaining a form of overseas workdays relief to encourage expatriates (and their employers) to continue to invest in the UK.

In relation to the above relief, it was decided to continue the requirement that income earned by reference to overseas workdays had to be retained offshore if it was to qualify for relief. This meant that HMRC's then current practice for remittances from expatriates' employment income, Statement of Practice 1/09, needed to be replaced by legislation. Consultation on this continued in parallel (the first consultation was released in October 2012) but separately until the full draft law was released in Finance Bill 2013.

As they are largely now of academic interest, it is not intended to detail here the minutiae of the changes and at which point every amendment to the draft law was made during the consultation process.

The final draft release of the legislation was issued as part of the Finance Bill on 28 March 2013. Some minor changes were made during the passage of the Bill through Parliament (for example, the ordering rules for the split-year cases) and the Bill was enacted on 17 July 2013.

# Statutory developments since Finance Act 2013 and HMRC guidance

**[1.05]** Since the introduction of the SRT, there has only been one statutory change to-date: Finance Act 2014 clarified (and backdated to 6 April 2013) the position for non-domiciled individuals of foreign chargeable gains accruing in the overseas part of a split year (new s 12(1A) TCGA 1992).

HMRC published their first detailed guidance, 'Guidance note: Statutory Residence test, SRT', RDR3, in May 2016. A second edition was released in August 2016 and the main changes to the first edition are noted on page 7 of the new edition. The second edition is reflected in this book.

In addition, there are proposed changes to the taxation of foreign domiciliaries contained in the Finance (No.2) Bill 2017 which are intended to take effect from 6 April 2017. Further changes are anticipated to be included in the Finance Act 2018. The proposed changes as affected by the SRT are outlined in CHAPTER 15.

# Conclusion

**[1.06]** It is perhaps surprising that it was decided to create a test that was broadly similar to the regime that had applied previously. It is a shame that the opportunity was not taken for a radical simplification and the introduction of a test based purely on day counting. The driver appears to have been to achieve cost neutrality, which is not unreasonable, given how difficult it would have been to estimate the difference in tax yield had a different form of test been adopted.

Some elements of the reform, such as the abolition of ordinary residence, and the focus on specific factors in the sufficient ties test, represent a simplification. However, there remain uncertain and complex aspects to the tests and it is questionable whether the SRT has delivered the certainty of treatment that was one of its original objectives. What is certain is that there will in time be further case law challenges to an individual's residence status and these may help taxpayers apply the law. See **CHAPTER 13** for HMRC challenges since 2013.

# Chapter 2

# The Statutory Residence Test: an overview

## Introduction

**[2.01]** This chapter is designed to give an overview of the Statutory Residence Test (SRT): CHAPTERS 4–8 look in detail at particular aspects of the test and the way it is applied.

The number of definitions in the SRT is one reason why the test can be so complex to apply in practice. These definitions are intended to reduce the subjective nature of the test. However, the result is that there are places where quite similar terminology is used, but the definitions may be different. In addition, particular tests can appear to be similar but in fact work slightly differently. This means that great care is required when applying the tests to a client's circumstances.

In using this chapter the reader may find it helpful to cross-refer to CHAPTER 3, which considers in detail the definitions and key concepts of the SRT.

## The shape of the test

**[2.02]** The statutory residence test as enacted in *Finance Act 2013* has three parts or 'tests':

(a)    An automatic residence test
(b)    An automatic overseas test
(c)    A sufficient ties test.

The 'basic rule' in the legislation is that an individual is only resident in the UK if he meets either the 'automatic residence test' or 'the sufficient ties test.'

The automatic residence and overseas tests are actually a number of tests, any of which, if met, will render the individual either resident or non-resident in the UK. The tests are considered in more detail below but broadly focus on days spent in the UK, whether the individual works full time either in the UK or overseas and whether the individual has the use of any UK and overseas homes.

An individual must first consider whether he meets any of the automatic overseas tests. If he does he will not be UK resident. If he does not meet any of these tests, he must next consider the automatic UK tests. If he meets any of these tests he will be resident in the UK. Finally, if he does not meet any of either the automatic overseas tests or the automatic UK tests, he must consider the sufficient ties tests.

The sufficient ties test operates by allowing a specific number of days' presence in the UK before an individual becomes UK resident. The number of days allowed depends on the number of 'ties' (for example, UK resident family, available accommodation) with the UK, and fewer days are allowed the more 'ties' an individual has. The number of days is also fewer for those who have been UK resident in any of the previous three tax years.

All of the tests are considered over a UK tax year, so if an individual is resident under the tests, he will always be resident for the whole UK tax year. However, in certain circumstances 'split year' treatment will be available (*Schedule 45, Part 3, FA 2013*) and in those circumstances, some of the day counts and other tests may be slightly different for the split year (see CHAPTER 8 for details of the split-year test and how it will operate).

Although the automatic residence test comes first chronologically in the legislation, it is the automatic overseas test which must be considered first, since an individual can only meet the automatic residence test if he does not meet any of the automatic overseas tests.

## Automatic overseas tests

**[2.03]** If the individual meets one of the automatic overseas tests, he is not UK tax resident and no more of the SRT needs to be considered. There are five automatic overseas tests. The first two tests are simple day counts, depending on an individual's residence in the UK in recent years; the third deals with individuals who work full-time overseas; and the fourth and fifth deal with those who die during the year. These last two are covered in a separate section below (see para **2.11**).

### The first and second automatic overseas tests

**[2.04]** An individual must consider either the first or the second overseas test depending on whether he has previously been resident in the UK and how recently.

The first and second automatic overseas tests are set out in *paras 12* and *13, Sch 45, FA 2013*:

'12   The first automatic overseas test is that–
  (a)   P was resident in the UK for one or more of the 3 tax years preceding year X,
  (b)   the number of days in year X that P spends in the UK is less than 16, and
  (c)   P does not die in year X.
13   The second automatic overseas test is that–
  (a)   P was resident in the UK for none of the 3 tax years preceding year X, and
  (b)   the number of days that P spends in the UK in year X is less than 46.'

In order to establish residence in any given tax year, therefore, an individual must first know his residence position for the previous three tax years.

An individual who has been resident in the UK in any of the three previous tax years will be automatically non-UK resident if he spends 15 or fewer days in the UK. An individual who has not been resident in the previous three tax years will be automatically non-UK resident if he spends 45 days or fewer in the UK.

See para **2.24** below for transitional rules for determining residence for previous tax years where those years were before the start of the SRT regime.

For the meaning of 'day', the concept of deemed days of residence, and the exclusion for days in transit and days of presence due to exceptional circumstances, see CHAPTER 3.

### The third automatic overseas test

**[2.05]** The third automatic overseas test is concerned with full-time working abroad (or working 'sufficient hours overseas' as the legislation describes it).

Although there was previously only a limited statutory basis for it (*s 830, ITA 2007*, now repealed), there has been a long-standing carve out for full-time working abroad as part of HMRC practice following *Reed v Clark* 58 TC 528, [1985] STC 323. When the idea of a statutory residence test was first proposed, there was extensive lobbying by the CBI amongst others, to ensure that an exemption very much valued by international businesses was retained.

The SRT test is contained in *para 14, Sch 45, FA 2013. Paragraph 14* starts with the conditions that must be met:

'(1)  The third automatic overseas test is that—
    (a)  P works sufficient hours overseas, as assessed over year X,
    (b)  during year X, there are no significant breaks from overseas work,
    (c)  the number of days in year X on which P does more than 3 hours' work in the UK is less than 31, and
    (d)  the number of days in year X falling within sub-paragraph (2) is less than 91.
(2)  A day falls within this sub-paragraph if—
    (a)  it is a day spent by P in the UK, but
    (b)  it is not a day that is treated under paragraph 23(4) as a day spent by P in the UK.'

The test can apply to both employees and the self-employed and, in determining sufficient hours, all employments and self-employments can be combined, thus allowing the test to apply to those who have several part-time jobs. However, the test does not apply to voluntary workers (see para **3.09**) nor to workers with 'a relevant job on board a vehicle, aircraft or ship' (see para **3.15**).

An individual is automatically non-UK resident if he works full-time (or 'sufficient hours') overseas for the tax year, without any significant breaks from that overseas work, provided that he also spends fewer than 91 days in total in the UK and has fewer than 31 workdays in the UK (ie days on which he does more than three hours' work). A significant break for this purpose is defined in *para 29, Sch 45, FA 2013* and is broadly a period of 31 days during which P does not do at least three hours' overseas work on at least one day (there are special rules for annual leave, sick leave and parenting leave). See para **3.14** for more details on the definition of 'significant break' and for other key concepts for this test.

Full-time work abroad is, therefore, tested not just by reference to time spent in the UK, but also by reference to time spent working whilst there. For the 91-day test, the deeming rule (which includes certain days even where the taxpayer was not present at midnight) is specifically disapplied (*para 14(2), Sch 45, FA 2013*). This is a potential advantage of falling within this part of the SRT. The test allows for no more than 90 days per tax year to be spent in the UK, which is similar to the full-time working abroad practice HMRC applied under the previous regime. That allowed for up to 90 days on average to be spent in the UK without impacting on full-time work abroad status. Under the SRT, there is no longer any averaging involved; rather it is a direct count of midnights spent in the UK during the tax year to determine whether or not the 90-day limit is exceeded.

Until the introduction of the SRT there was no prescribed limit on the amount of time that could be spent working in the UK before full-time working abroad status could be brought into question. Instead, the test was whether sufficient work was done in the UK to make a reasonable man question whether the work being undertaken abroad could really be regarded as full-time abroad. Now, under the SRT, the limit is 30 UK workdays. For some taxpayers this is likely to prove a tough limit, not least because of the wide definition of work in this context.

The sufficient hours test is applied over the tax year and *paragraph 14(3)* goes on to set out how it is to be calculated:

'(3) Take the following steps to work out whether P works "sufficient hours overseas" as assessed over year X—

*Step 1*

Identify any days in year X on which P does more than 3 hours' work in the UK, including ones on which P also does work overseas on the same day.

The days so identified are referred to as "disregarded days".

*Step 2*

Add up (for all employments held and trades carried on by P) the total number of hours that P works overseas in year X, but ignoring any hours that P works overseas on disregarded days. The result is referred to as P's "net overseas hours".

*Step 3*

Subtract from 365 (or 366 if year X includes 29 February)—
(a)   the total number of disregarded days, and
(b)   any days that are allowed to be subtracted, in accordance with the rules in paragraph 28 of this Schedule, to take account of periods of leave and gaps between employments.

The result is referred to as the "reference period".

*Step 4*

Divide the reference period by 7. If the answer is more than 1 and is not a whole number, round down to the nearest whole number. If the answer is less than 1, round up to 1.

*Step 5*

Divide P's net overseas hours by the number resulting from step 4.

If the answer is 35 or more, P is considered to work "sufficient hours overseas" as assessed over year X.'

The calculation to determine whether an individual is working 'sufficient hours overseas' is complex and is discussed more fully in para **3.12**, where there is also an example calculation. However, broadly, an individual must be working overseas, on average, 35 hours or more a week. The calculation is, however, quite artificial and requires a calculation of the 'reference period' and the 'net overseas hours' in order to determine whether the 35-hour average is met. For both the reference period and the net overseas hours calculations, days on which an individual works at least three hours in the UK are disregarded and periods of leave and gaps between employments are deducted from the reference period. It should be noted that the reference period is calculated first by days and then divided by 7 (not 5) in order to work out the number of weeks. In order to fulfil the sufficient hours overseas test an individual would usually need to work full-time abroad for the full tax year. However, short gaps (that do not themselves constitute a significant break) at the start or end of the tax year may be possible without jeopardising the calculation. It is also possible to leave the UK for full-time work overseas and be taxed as a non-resident in the UK for part of a tax year as a result of split-year treatment (see **CHAPTER 8**).

**Example 2.1: Jenny**

Jenny took up a full-time role in Singapore in March 2014. She has returned to the UK five times during 2015/16 – once for a full working week lasting five days (on each day she worked more than three hours) and once for a board meeting when she was present in the UK and worked more than 3 hours for two days. On the other three occasions Jenny was visiting family and her total UK presence amounted to four weeks or 28 days.

In May 2016 Jenny's father had a heart attack and Jenny took extended leave and returned to the UK for six weeks to care for him. At the end of the six weeks she returned to her job in Singapore.

Assuming that Jenny's hours in Singapore average 35 per week following the steps in *paragraph 14(3)*, she will meet the third automatic non-residence test for 2015/16 and will be regarded as non-UK resident. However, the six weeks which Jenny spent in the UK during 2016/17 will amount to a 'significant break' and so Jenny will not meet the third automatic residence test for that tax year. She will therefore need to consider the automatic residence test and the sufficient ties test to determine her residence.

# Automatic residence test

**[2.06]** Assuming that an individual is not automatically non-UK resident under one of the automatic overseas tests, he will then need to consider whether he is automatically UK resident. There are four automatic UK tests. Again, the fourth test deals with death during the tax year and is considered separately (at para **2.12**).

### The first automatic UK test

[2.07] As with the first and second automatic overseas tests, the first automatic UK test is simply a day counting test. Under this test an individual is automatically resident in the UK if he spends at least 183 days here: 'This first automatic UK test is that P spends at least 183 days in the UK in year X' (*para 7, Sch 45, FA 2013*).

This test is the most similar to the previous legislation on residence (rather than being a codification of previous case law) and is probably the least controversial part of the SRT.

For the meaning of 'day', the concept of deemed days of residence, and the exclusion for days in transit and days of presence due to exceptional circumstances, see CHAPTER 3.

### The second automatic UK test

[2.08] The second automatic UK test is contained in *para 8, Sch 45, FA 2013* and is concerned with where an individual has their 'home':

'(1)  The second automatic UK test is that—
   (a)  P has a home in the UK during all or part of year X,
   (b)  that home is one where P spends a sufficient amount of time in year X, and
   (c)  there is at least one period of 91 (consecutive) days in respect of which the following conditions are met—
      (i)   the 91-day period in question occurs while P has that home,
      (ii)  at least 30 days of that 91-day period fall within year X, and
      (iii) throughout that 91-day period, condition A or condition B is met or a combination of those conditions is met.
(2)  Condition A is that P has no home overseas.
(3)  Condition B is that—
   (a)  P has one or more homes overseas, but
   (b)  each of those homes is a home where P spends no more than a permitted amount of time in year X'.

'Home' itself is extremely widely defined. For a full discussion of what is meant by home, see para **3.07**. However, for the purpose of this automatic residence test there are three things which must concern us: does the individual, 'P', have a home in the UK and if so, does he spend a 'sufficient amount of time' there and does he have a period of 91 consecutive days during which he both has that UK home and is effectively considered as having no home outside the UK – ie he meets condition A or B. Of that 91-day period, at least 30 days must fall within the tax year in question.

A 'sufficient' amount of time means 30 days as set out in *subparagraph 4*:

'(4)  In relation to a home of P's in the UK, P "spends a sufficient amount of time" there in year X if there are at least 30 days in year X when P is present there on that day for at least some of the time (no matter how short a time).'

Similarly, the 'permitted amount of time' in Condition B is also fewer than 30 days, as set out in *subparagraph (5)*:

'(5)  In relation to a home of P's overseas, P "spends no more than a permitted amount of time" there in year X if there are fewer than 30 days in year X when P is present there on that day for at least some of the time (no matter how short a time).'

In considering both the UK home and the overseas home, the 30 days need not be consecutive (see *subparagraph 6(a)*) nor need they fall within the 91-day period. *Subparagraph 6* also provides that there is no need to be present at midnight to clock up a day of presence but presence only counts if the property is already a home:

'(6)(b)a reference to P being present at the home is to P being present there at a time when it is a home of P's (so presence there on any other occasion, for example to look round the property with a view to buying it, is to be disregarded). An individual is present in the home if they are physically present at sometime during the day; they do no need to be present at midnight.'

Where an individual has more than one UK home, each is considered separately (ie time spent in each is not aggregated for the purpose of the 30-day test) and the second automatic residence test is satisfied provided it is met in relation to one of the homes (see *subparagraph 8*).

**Example 2.2: Thomas**

Thomas comes to the UK and rents a flat 1 May to 31 August 2016. He is present in the flat throughout the period and so has a home in the UK for more than 91 consecutive days, all of which fall within 2016/17. Thomas also meets the two 30-day period tests for his UK home.

Assuming the individual has a UK home for a consecutive 91-day period and 30 of those days fall within the tax year, he must then consider whether he meets either Condition A or B for the 91-day period. Conditions A and B are quoted above. The individual meets Condition A if he has no home overseas.

He meets condition B if, despite having one or more homes overseas, he is not present at any of those homes for at least 30 days during the tax year. If the individual has more than one overseas home he must consider each of them separately for the purpose of the test – so if he has two homes overseas but only spends 28 days at each of them in the tax year under consideration, neither home will meet the test and condition B will be satisfied. The 30 days do not need to fall within the 91-day period (Condition B only requires that the individual has one or more homes overseas during the 91-day period) but the 30 days must all fall within the tax year being considered.

**Example 2.3. More about Thomas**

Thomas was living in rented accommodation in Germany at the time he came to the UK in 2016 and chose to give notice on his flat there. He therefore ceased to occupy it from 30 April 2016. On returning to Germany on 1 September 2016 Thomas moved in with his parents for a fortnight before beginning to rent a new property on 15 September 2016.

Throughout the period 1 May to 31 August 2016, therefore, Thomas will have no home overseas.

Thomas will therefore meet Condition A and so he meets all the conditions of the second automatic UK test and, since he does not satisfy any of the automatic overseas tests, will be considered resident in the UK.

In this example, Thomas does not have a home with his parents as he does not stay there for 30 days. However, in some circumstances a parental home could be a home even where an individual does not spend large amounts of time there. See the discussion in CHAPTER 3.

The fact that the whole of the 91-day period need not fall into one UK tax year means that, potentially, where that period spans two tax years, one 91-day period can result in two years where UK tax residence needs to be considered.

### Example 2.4: Hans

Up to 31 December 2015, Hans has lived in Germany with his family. Then he comes to the UK and he rents a flat in the UK from 1 January 2016 to 30 April 2016. He stays in the flat continuously throughout this period. He then returns to Germany and spends the remainder of 2016/17 there.

Hans had previously been resident in the UK in 2013/14 and, since he does not work full-time, will not meet any of the automatic overseas tests for 2015/16 or 2016/17. He therefore considers whether he meets the second automatic UK test.

Hans will meet part of the second automatic UK test for both 2015/16 and 2016/17 – he has a home in the UK for part of both tax years and he has that home for a consecutive period of at least 91 days (even though this period spans two years). However, in 2016/17, fewer than 30 days of that 91-day period fall within the tax year nor is Hans present in that home for at least 30 days in the tax year (he only has the home and is only present from 6–30 April). He does not meet all the conditions and is not resident in 2016/17 under the second automatic UK test.

However, both the 30 day tests are met for 2015/16 and so Hans would then need to consider whether he meets Conditions A or B for that year.

However, Hans also has a property in Germany – his family home which he left to come to the UK and at which his wife and children remain for the period of his visit.

Although there is a period of 91 days during which Hans does not occupy the German property at all, this will still be considered his home during the 91 days. Therefore Condition A is not met. Moreover since he occupies his German home for a period of at least 30 days during 2015/16, Condition B is not met.

So Hans is not UK resident in 2015/16 under the second automatic UK test.

The fact that the 91 days need not all fall within one tax year will make it a potential trap for the unwary.

Conversely, an individual could have a number of UK homes and no overseas home but not meet the second automatic UK test because they do not spend 30 days in any one home. RDR3 gives the example of 'Fatima' (in RDR3 section 1.35):

'Example 9

Fatima has had four UK homes for several years. In the tax year under consideration, Fatima is present in her home in Swansea on 15 days, 20 days in her home in Loch Lomond, 29 in her London flat and 29 in her Newcastle flat.

Fatima has been present on 91 days in total in those UK homes. However, as she was not present in any individual home on at least 30 days, she will not have spent a sufficient amount of time in any single UK home. She will not meet the second automatic UK test for the tax year under consideration.'

However, it seems likely that there will be more cases where the 91 days gives rise to automatic residence in two tax years than there will be cases of individuals with four UK homes.

RDR3 includes a flowchart (at section 1.31) to help the taxpayer work through the UK home test. It is reproduced below.

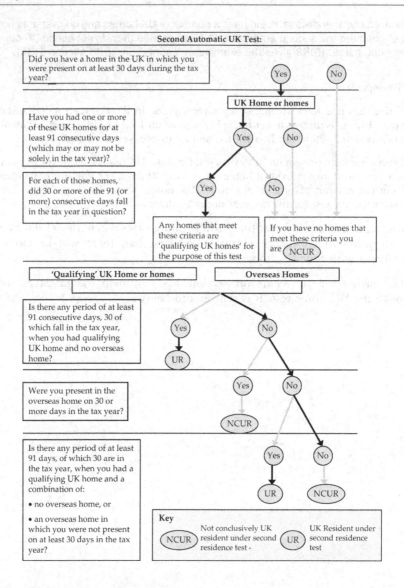

## The third automatic UK test

**[2.09]** The third automatic UK test is the UK equivalent of the third automatic overseas test and is concerned with full-time work in the UK (or working 'sufficient hours in the UK' as the legislation puts it). The test is contained in *para 9, Sch 45, FA 2013*:

'(1)    The third automatic UK test is that—

(a)    P works sufficient hours in the UK, as assessed over a period of 365 days,

(b)    during that period, there are no significant breaks from UK work,

(c)    all or part of that period falls within year X,

(d)    more than 75% of the total number of days in the 365-day period on which P does more than 3 hours' work are days on which P does more than 3 hours' work in the UK, and

(e)    at least one day which falls in both that period and year X is a day on which P does more than 3 hours' work in the UK.

(2)    Take the following steps to work out, for any given period of 365 days, whether P works "sufficient hours in the UK" as assessed over that period—

*Step 1*

Identify any days in the period on which P does more than 3 hours' work overseas, including ones on which P also does work in the UK on the same day.

The days so identified are referred to as "disregarded days".

*Step 2*

Add up (for all employments held and trades carried on by P) the total number of hours that P works in the UK during the period, but ignoring any hours that P works in the UK on disregarded days.

The result is referred to as P's "net UK hours".

*Step 3*

Subtract from 365—

(a)    the total number of disregarded days, and

(b)    any days that are allowed to be subtracted, in accordance with the rules in paragraph 28 of this Schedule, to take account of periods of leave and gaps between employments.

The result is referred to as the "reference period".

*Step 4*

Divide the reference period by 7. If the answer is more than 1 and is not a whole number, round down to the nearest whole number. If the answer is less than 1, round up to 1.

*Step 5*

Divide P's net UK hours by the number resulting from step 4.

If the answer is 35 or more, P is considered to work "sufficient hours in the UK" as assessed over the 365-day period in question.'

Although both the third automatic UK test and the third automatic overseas test are concerned with 'full-time work' (employment or self-employment) and the calculation of 'sufficient hours' is essentially the same for both tests, the test to determine whether an individual is working full time in the UK is quite different from that to determine whether they are working full time overseas. 'Full time' will include several part-time roles where sufficient hours are worked across the different roles.

Whereas to fulfil the automatic overseas test the individual would generally need to work full time abroad throughout the UK tax year, for the automatic UK residence test, it is instead a rolling test and an individual who works full time in the UK for a period of 365 days will be automatically resident in the UK where at least one of the days of the period in which the individual does more than three hours' work in the UK fall within the tax year under consideration. Again in contrast to the automatic overseas test which sets a fixed limit to the permitted days of UK presence and UK work, where an individual is seeking to fall within the automatic UK residence test but does some of their work overseas, the full-time work in the UK test looks at the percentage of days worked in the UK, and not at the absolute number of days worked overseas. The percentage is calculated by reference to the number of days worked in the 365-day period and a day counts as a UK day if it is one on which the individual has worked at least three hours in the UK, even if he has also worked at least three hours overseas on that day.

This means that, unlike with the full-time working abroad test, which only allows an individual to spend a specific numbers of days working in the UK, an individual can do significant amounts of work overseas during the 365-day period and still be regarded as working full time in the UK. The 75% test is applied not over the tax year but over the 365-day period, of which only one day needs to fall within the UK tax year under consideration. This may lead to employees being automatically UK resident when they have worked relatively few days in the UK in a particular tax year.

**Example 2.5: Jean-Pierre**

Jean-Pierre comes to the UK from France to take up a full-time job. He arrives in the UK and begins work on 3 February 2014. He works for the same company for a period of 18 months, returning to France on 1 May 2015.

During this period he makes return trips to France. In the early part of his secondment, he spends more days in France in order to facilitate the handover of his old role and support his replacement. He therefore spends ten working days in France in February 2014, 15 days in March 2014, ten days in April and five further days each in May and June. After that he returns to France just two days per month. On each of the days he works, he works at least three hours either in France or in the UK. There are no days where he works in both France and the UK. On days he travelled to and back from France, his UK travel time is only one hour.

Jean-Pierre has a total of 25 days' holiday plus ten bank holidays in the 14-month period. He takes five days' holiday in March at the end of his three weeks' work in France. He has a further two days' holiday in April, ten days in June, five days in August and three days in December.

Jean-Pierre will need first to look at whether the total period of working in the UK exceeds 365 days, which it does. He must then apply the 75% test to a 365-day period.

Looking at the first possible 365-day period, this begins on 3 February 2014 and ends on 2 February 2015. Assuming that his two French working days for February 2015 fall at the end of February (and therefore outside this period), he will have the following:

| | Total days | Total workdays (allowing for bank holidays) | Holiday/ leave | Total workdays after holiday | French work-days | UK work-days |
|---|---|---|---|---|---|---|
| **Feb** | 26 | 20 | 0 | 20 | 10 | 10 |
| **Mar** | 31 | 21 | 5 | 16 | 15 | 1 |
| **Apr** | 30 | 20 | 2 | 18 | 10 | 8 |
| **May** | 31 | 20 | 0 | 20 | 5 | 15 |
| **Jun** | 30 | 21 | 10 | 11 | 5 | 6 |
| **Jul** | 31 | 23 | 0 | 23 | 2 | 21 |
| **Aug** | 31 | 20 | 5 | 15 | 2 | 13 |
| **Sept** | 30 | 22 | 0 | 22 | 2 | 20 |
| **Oct** | 31 | 23 | 0 | 23 | 2 | 21 |
| **Nov** | 30 | 20 | 0 | 20 | 2 | 18 |
| **Dec** | 31 | 19 | 3 | 16 | 2 | 14 |
| **Jan** | 31 | 20 | 0 | 20 | 2 | 18 |
| **Feb** | 2 | 1 | 0 | 1 | 0 | 1 |
| **Total** | 365 | 250 | 25 | 225 | 59 | 166 |

For the treatment of bank holidays, see para 3.12.

For this 365-day period he would therefore be working 166/225 days or 73% of days in the UK. However, if the 365-day period instead began on 1 March the position would be as follows:

| | Total days | Total workdays (allowing for bank holidays) | Holiday/ leave | Total workdays after holiday | French work-days | UK work-days |
|---|---|---|---|---|---|---|
| **Mar** | 31 | 21 | 5 | 16 | 15 | 1 |
| **Apr** | 30 | 20 | 2 | 18 | 10 | 8 |
| **May** | 31 | 20 | 0 | 20 | 5 | 15 |
| **Jun** | 30 | 21 | 10 | 11 | 5 | 6 |
| **Jul** | 31 | 23 | 0 | 23 | 2 | 21 |
| **Aug** | 31 | 20 | 5 | 15 | 2 | 13 |
| **Sept** | 30 | 22 | 0 | 22 | 2 | 20 |
| **Oct** | 31 | 23 | 0 | 23 | 2 | 21 |
| **Nov** | 30 | 20 | 0 | 20 | 2 | 18 |
| **Dec** | 31 | 19 | 3 | 16 | 2 | 14 |
| **Jan** | 31 | 20 | 0 | 20 | 2 | 18 |
| **Feb** | 28 | 20 | 0 | 20 | 2 | 18 |
| **Total** | 365 | 249 | 25 | 224 | 51 | 173 |

Now he works 173 days out of 224 or 77% of his days in the UK. This is a 365-day period of which at least one UK working day falls within both 2013/14 and

2014/15 so, provided he meets the sufficient hours calculation, he will be automatically resident in the UK for both tax years.

However, he may be able to take advantage of the split-year test for both years (see CHAPTER 8).

As with the full-time working abroad test, this test does not apply to workers with a 'relevant job aboard a vehicle, aircraft or ship' (see para **3.15**).

## Additional tests in the year of death

**[2.10]** Both the automatic UK and automatic overseas tests have tests which only apply to those who die during the tax year. These tests are in addition to the other automatic overseas and UK tests which, with the exception of the first automatic overseas test (fewer than 16 days in the UK), can also apply. Where an individual dies during a tax year, his executors or personal representatives will therefore need to consider these additional tests in order to determine residence. As with the other automatic tests, the automatic overseas tests must be considered first since, if these apply, they take priority.

### Automatic overseas test and death

**[2.11]** The fourth and fifth automatic overseas tests apply to those who die during the tax year. The fourth test will be the one which is relevant to most taxpayers and is contained with *para 15, Sch 45, FA 2013*:

'15(1) The fourth automatic overseas test is that–
    (a)    P dies in year X,
    (b)    P was resident in the UK for neither of the 2 tax years preceding year X or, alternatively, P's case falls within sub-paragraph (2), and
    (c)    the number of days that P spends in the UK in year X is less than 46.
  (2)    P's case falls within this sub-paragraph if–

    (a)    P was not resident in the UK for the tax year preceding year X, and
    (b)    the tax year before that was a split year as respects P because the circumstances of the case fell within Case 1, Case 2 or Case 3 (see Part 3 of this schedule).'

(Cases 1–3 involve departure from the UK.)

The deceased will be automatically non-UK resident under the fourth automatic test if he dies during the tax year and he was either:

- not resident in the UK for the previous two tax years; or
- not resident in the previous tax year and benefitted from split-year treatment in the tax year before that; and
- spends fewer than 46 days in the UK in the tax year of death.

The split-year treatment must be that afforded to those departing from the UK. Specifically: Case 1 (starting full-time work overseas); Case 2 (the partner of someone starting full-time work overseas); Case 3 (ceasing to have a home in the UK).

There is an additional automatic overseas test for employees who work full-time abroad. This test is contained in *para 16, Sch 4, FA 2013*:

'16(1) The fifth automatic overseas test is that—

    (a)    P dies in year X,

    (b)    P was resident in the UK for neither of the 2 tax years preceding year X because P met the third automatic overseas test for each of those years or, alternatively, P's case falls within sub-paragraph (2), and

    (c)    P would meet the third automatic overseas test for year X if paragraph 14 were read with the relevant modifications.

(2)    P's case falls within this sub-paragraph if—

    (a)    P was not resident in the UK for the tax year preceding year X because P met the third automatic overseas test for that year, and

    (b)    the tax year before that was a split year as respects P because the circumstances of the case fell within Case 1 (see Part 3 of this Schedule).

(3)    The relevant modifications of paragraph 14 are—

    (a)    in sub-paragraph (1)(a) and (b) and sub-paragraph (3), for "year X" read "the period from the start of year X up to and including the day before the day of P's death", and

    (b)    in step 3 of sub-paragraph (3), for "365 (or 366 if year X includes 29 February)" read "the number of days in the period from the start of year X up to and including the day before the day of P's death".'

This test will only apply to those who work full-time abroad and have met the third automatic overseas test (ie full-time working abroad) for the previous two tax years, or for the previous tax year and the tax year prior to that was a split year within Case 1 (starting full-time work overseas).

The individual must also work sufficient hours in the year of death. Note this is a modified test which requires the individual to meet the sufficient hours test for the period from the start of the tax year to the day before his death (as opposed to over a 365-day period).

The main difference from the fourth automatic overseas test is that, if the conditions are met, the individual is not limited to spending 45 days in the UK in the tax year.

It is important to note that the fourth and fifth automatic overseas tests are not the only tests under which an individual who dies in the UK could be non-resident. For example, if they have left the UK to work full-time abroad and they die towards the end of the tax year, the third automatic test may apply to treat them as non-resident. The first automatic test, however, where P spends fewer than 16 days in the UK during the tax year, does not apply in the year of death. Although the second automatic test is not specifically disapplied, the fourth automatic test is effectively a more generous version of this test and so the second need not be considered.

## Automatic UK test and death

**[2.12]** If none of the automatic overseas tests are met (for example, because the deceased was resident in the UK during the last two tax years), it is necessary to consider the automatic UK tests. In addition to the three already covered (which must also be considered in the year of death), there is a fourth. This is contained in *para 10, Sch 45, FA 2013*, which is set out in full below:

'(1)    The fourth automatic UK test is that—

(a)    P dies in year X,

(b)    for each of the previous 3 tax years, P was resident in the UK by virtue of meeting the automatic residence test,

(c)    even assuming P were not resident in the UK for year X, the tax year preceding year X would not be a split year as respects P (see Part 3 of this Schedule),

(d)    when P died, either—

    (i)    P's home was in the UK, or

    (ii)    P had more than one home and at least one of them was in the UK, and

(e)    if P had a home overseas during all or part of year X, P did not spend a sufficient amount of time there in year X.

(2)    In relation to a home of P's overseas, P "spent a sufficient amount of time" there in year X if—

(a)    there were at least 30 days in year X when P was present there on that day for at least some of the time (no matter how short a time), or

(b)    P was present there for at least some of the time (no matter how short a time) on each day of year X up to and including the day on which P died.

(3)    In sub-paragraph (2)—

(a)    the reference to 30 days is to 30 days in aggregate, whether the days were consecutive or intermittent, and

(b)    the reference to P being present at the home is to P being present there at a time when it was a home of P's.

(4)    If P had more than one home overseas—

(a)    each of those homes must be looked at separately to see if the requirement of sub-paragraph (1)(e) is met, and

(b)    that requirement is then met so long as it is met in relation to each of them.'

As with the extra automatic overseas tests for the year of death, this automatic UK test is concerned with the deceased's place of residence in previous tax years. The automatic UK test requires P to have been resident for the previous three tax years under the automatic residence test (ie not under the sufficient ties test).

The test also creates a fiction whereby one must assume that P (the deceased) would have been non-resident for the whole of the tax year in question and then consider whether the preceding year would have been a split year. If the preceding year would have qualified as a split year (presumably under the leaving the UK cases – Cases 1 to 3 – although this is not specified) then this test is not met. This is presumably to allow for those who had genuinely left the UK, either for employment or to live abroad but who were unlucky enough to die before they have completed a full UK-tax year of non-residence.

There is an additional factor that must be considered in the year of death and that is the location of P's home. If the individual has an overseas home, then he must not have spent 'sufficient time' there if he is to meet the home part of this test. Sufficient time is defined as 30 days or each day of the tax year up to and including the date of death. In almost all cases, if a taxpayer met this part of the test (ie he had not spent sufficient time in the overseas home), he would also, therefore, meet the second automatic residence test and would not need to consider the fourth automatic test. It should be noted however that this fourth test does not include a 91-day consecutive period of ownership for the UK home or have any requirement as to occupation of the UK home.

The only circumstances in which this test might apply, therefore, is where an individual acquires a home in the UK during the tax year of death or late in the previous tax year such that he has owned the home for too short a period to meet the 91-day part of the second automatic test or did not spend 30 days in his UK home during the year of death. In such cases if the individual has no overseas home or does not spend sufficient time in it, he will meet the fourth automatic test.

If neither the automatic overseas tests nor the automatic UK tests apply, then, as with any individual, it will be necessary to consider the sufficient ties test. The sufficient ties test in the year of death is also subject to special rules and is dealt with in para **2.23** below.

## The sufficient ties test

**[2.13]** Once an individual has decided that they are neither non-resident under the automatic overseas tests nor resident under the automatic UK tests, it becomes necessary to consider the 'sufficient ties' test.

The 'sufficient ties' test, in a nutshell, is a way of combining days spent in the UK with various connection factors to determine whether that combination is sufficient for an individual to be UK resident. The more connection factors an individual has, the fewer days he can spend here before he becomes UK resident.

This test is slightly different depending upon an individual's history of residence. The idea behind this is that residence should be 'sticky' and once it has been acquired it should be difficult to lose. Consequently, when counting days in the UK, those who have been resident in any one of the previous three tax years need to have fewer connection factors for the same number of days spent in the UK before they are considered resident here.

This is set out in *para 17, Sch 45, FA 2013*:

'(1)   The sufficient ties test is met for year X if–
   (a)   P meets none of the automatic UK tests and none of the automatic overseas tests, but
   (b)   P has sufficient UK ties for that year.
(2)   "UK ties" is defined in Part 2 of this Schedule.
(3)   Whether P has "sufficient" UK ties for year X will depend on–
   (a)   whether P was resident in the UK for any of the previous 3 tax years, and
   (b)   the number of days that P spends in the UK in year X.
(4)   The Tables in paragraphs 18 and 19 show how many ties are sufficient in each case.'

In considering an individual's residence position, then, assuming that neither of the automatic tests applies to him, the next step in determining his residence is to consider his residence position for the previous three UK tax years. If he was resident in any one or more of the previous three UK tax years, then it is necessary to consider the table in *para 18, Sch 45, FA 2013*. If he has not been so resident, the table in *para 19, Sch 45, FA 2013* will apply. In determining residence in the UK, there is no requirement to be resident for the complete year and so years of part residence, where split-year treatment applies, will also count (see *para 43(1)(a), Sch 45, FA 2013*).

Having determined which table applies to the individual, it is then necessary to determine the number of days spent in the UK. See **CHAPTER 3** for the definition of a day spent in the UK.

Finally, the individual must consider how many connection factors or 'ties' they have with the UK (see below). He can then apply the appropriate table to determine his residence position. In the year of death there are some modifications to how the tables should be applied, and this is dealt with separately below.

### Sufficient ties for those with UK residence in previous three years

**[2.14]** *Paragraph 18, Sch 45, FA 2013* contains the table for those who have been resident in the UK in any of the previous three tax years (as noted above, it is sufficient for this to be just part of one of the years).

Note that if the individual has the number of ties shown in the second column he *will* be resident in the UK.

| Days spent by P in the UK in year X | Number of ties that are sufficient |
|---|---|
| More than 15 but not more than 45 | At least 4 |
| More than 45 but not more than 90 | At least 3 |
| More than 90 but not more than 120 | At least 2 |
| More than 120 | At least 1 |

### Sufficient ties for those with no UK residence in previous three years

**[2.15]** *Paragraph 19, Sch 45, FA 2013* contains the table showing the combinations of ties and days which determine UK residence in the case of those who have not been resident in the UK in any one of the previous three tax years (they may have been previously resident in the UK before that period).

Again, note that an individual *will* be resident in the UK if he has the number of ties shown in the second column.

| Days spent by P in the UK in year X | Number of ties that are sufficient |
|---|---|
| More than 45 but not more than 90 | All 4 |
| More than 90 but not more than 120 | At least 3 |
| More than 120 | At least 2 |

# Ties for the sufficient ties test

**[2.16]** To apply the tables above to a specific individual it will be necessary to know both the number of days he has spent in the UK and the number of his 'ties'.

The 'ties' which need to be considered also depend on whether the individual has been resident in the UK for any part of any of the previous three tax years.

If the individual has not been resident in any of the three previous tax years, he must consider the following ties:

- a family tie
- an accommodation tie
- a work tie
- a 90-day tie

If he has been resident for any part of the previous three tax years, he must still consider all of these ties, but in addition he must also consider a country tie. Further commentary on this can be found at para **2.21**.

Once an individual's ties have been determined it is simply a case of finding the correct line on the correct table (above) to determine whether or not that individual is UK resident. However, as you might expect, it is not always so straightforward to determine whether an individual has each connection factor.

The definitions of each tie are dealt with more fully in CHAPTER 3. What follows is intended merely as an overview of each factor.

Each tie can only count once – so, for example, if an individual has a family tie by virtue of his spouse's residence and also his daughter's residence, this will only count as one tie for the purpose of the test.

## Family tie

**[2.17]** The 'family tie' is concerned with the residence of one's spouse or civil partner (or equivalent) and one's minor children. So, at its most basic, if an individual is married and his spouse is UK resident, he will have a family tie to the UK. As is now found elsewhere in UK tax legislation (eg 'relevant person' for the remittance basis), family tie also includes partners of the individual where they 'are living together as man and wife' or 'as if they were civil partners.' *(para 32(2), Sch 45, FA 2013)*

There is additional complexity in the test when considering the residence of children who are in full-time education and it is also necessary, in the case of children, to consider how much time the individual spends with the child in the UK. All of these complications are explained in more detail at para **3.17**.

## Accommodation tie

**[2.18]** 'Accommodation tie' is defined in *para 34, Sch 45, FA 2013*. The basic concept is laid out in *para 34(1)–*

'(1)   P has an accommodation tie for year X if.

(a)   P has a place to live in the UK,

(b)   that place is available to P during year X for a continuous period of at least 91 days, and

(c)   P spends at least one night at that place in that year.'

Where the accommodation is the home of a 'close relative' (parent, grand-parent, sibling, adult child or grandchild), P needs to spend at least 16 nights at the home for it to be an accommodation tie. While the definition of a 'place to live' includes home, it may also include more temporary 'available accommodation.' In addition, the legislation includes some quite broad deeming provisions concerning what is meant by 'available accommodation'. See para **3.18** for more detail.

## Work tie

**[2.19]** In broad terms, an individual has a 'work tie' if he works (as employee or self-employed) in the UK for at least 40 days during the tax year. The individual is treated as working in the UK for a day if he does more than three hours' work in the UK on that day. *Paragraph 35(1) and (2), Sch 45, FA 2013* state:

'(1)   P has a work tie for year X if P works in the UK for at least 40 days (whether continuously or intermittently) in year X.

(2)   For these purposes, P works in the UK for a day if P does more than 3 hours' work in the UK on that day.'

There is considerable further definition of what constitutes a 'work day' for a worker with a relevant job on board a vehicle, aircraft or ship (see para **3.15**). In addition, in deciding whether the individual has 'worked' for more than three hours in the UK, it will be necessary to consider the lengthy definition of 'work' for this purpose (see para **3.09**) as well as the definition of 'location of work' (see para **3.11**). For more on the work tie, also see para **3.19**.

## 90-day tie

**[2.20]** This is perhaps the easiest of all the tests to understand since it does not depend on understanding a number of interlinking definitions, but is rather a straight day-counting test.

The individual will have a 90-day tie if he has spent 90 days in the UK in either or both the preceding tax year and the year prior to that (paragraph 37, sch 45, FA 2013). So, in considering 2015/16, an individual will have a 90-day tie if he spent 90 days in the UK in either 2014/15 or in 2013/14 or in both years.

See CHAPTER 3 for the definition of a day in the UK.

There has been some criticism of the 90-day test by practitioners as represent-ing a 'double counting' since an individual who has been resident in the UK in the previous two tax years is likely to have been present in the UK for 90 days. Therefore, in addition to being allowed fewer connection factors for the number of days spent in the UK, the individual will also pick up an additional 'tie' in the form of the 90-day tie.

### Country tie

**[2.21]** The 'country tie' only applies to those who have been resident in the UK in one or more of the previous three tax years. It is essentially a test of where the individual has spent the greatest number of days in the tax year. If the individual has spent more days in the UK than any other country, he will have the country tie. The test is, however, expressed as a counting of 'midnights'. There are also specific rules for circumstances in which an individual has spent the same number of days in more than one country. See para **3.21** for a full definition.

## Applying the sufficient ties test

**[2.22]** The sufficient ties test is straightforward to apply when seeking to determine an individual's residence for the previous tax year; for example, in order to complete his tax return or otherwise assess his liability to UK tax.

Just as commonly, however, those advising clients may well find that they need to advise on the sufficient ties test in advance of a tax year. At first glance this appears to be straightforward, so for example a client who goes to live in Switzerland (perhaps to work part time, therefore not meeting the full-time working abroad test) might have a UK resident spouse who lives in their UK home. In addition, however, assuming this is the individual's first year of non-residence he is likely to meet the 90-day test for the previous tax year.

The individual's advisor knows before the start of the tax year, therefore, that this client will have three UK ties – the family tie, the accommodation tie and the 90-day tie. Assuming that the client has been resident in the previous three tax years, the advisor might consult the table and inform the client that if he wishes to be considered as not resident in the UK, he must spend fewer than 45 days in the UK during the tax year.

However, now consider that the individual spends some of the days he is in the UK working here and that the number of days he works here exceeds 40. Now he has added the work tie to his list of UK ties, which takes him to four UK ties and means he can only spend 15 days in the UK in total – in other words, he has exceeded his days and will be resident in the UK for that tax year.

In addition, there are a number of factors that are likely to give rise to double counting (the 90-day, previous residence test has already been noted above). Another example is that an individual with a UK-resident spouse would be very unlikely not to have available accommodation in the UK so this will mean he has two UK ties.

Great care will therefore need to be taken when giving advice to ensure that all the interrelations of the different factors has been considered.

## The sufficient ties test in the year of death

**[2.23]** As with the automatic overseas and automatic UK tests, the sufficient ties test is applied differently in the year of death.

The specific rules for the year of death are laid out in *para 20, Sch 45, FA 2013*. *Paragraph 20* starts as follows:

'(1)    If P dies in year X, paragraph 18 has effect as if the words "More than 15 but" were omitted from the first column of the Table.'

In effect, the removal of the 'less than 15 days' in the year of death ensures that if, for example, the individual dies in the first two weeks of a tax year, this is not sufficient to make them non-UK resident. This is similar to the disapplication of the first automatic overseas test in the year of death.

Similarly, if an individual does not survive a full tax year they are unlikely to spend as many days in the UK as if they had lived for the full year. To take account of this, the legislation introduces a form of pro-rating for the number of days which can be spent in the UK without being treated as UK resident based on the number of months in the tax year that the individual survives. *Paragraph 20* thus goes on to say:

'(2)    In addition to that modification, if the death occurs before 1 March in year X, paragraphs 18 and 19 have effect as if each number of days mentioned in the first column of the Table were reduced by the appropriate number.

(3)    The appropriate number is found by multiplying the number of days, in each case, by –
A/12
where "A" is the number of whole months in year X after the month in which P dies.

(4)    If, for any number of days, the appropriate number is not a whole number, the appropriate number is to be rounded up or down as follows–
(a)    if the first figure after the decimal point is 5 or more, round the appropriate number up to the nearest whole number,
(b)    otherwise, round it down to the nearest whole number.'

The legislation thus reduces the number of days an individual can be present in the UK in the tax year of death for a given number of ties before being considered UK resident. The pro-rating is performed on the basis of whole months in the tax year after death, rather than days. It will therefore penalise those who die in the first few days of a month by decreasing the number of days of presence in the UK they can have before being treated as UK resident (or rather it will penalise their estate, since it will be for their personal representatives to make the calculation!).

It is assumed that HMRC were aiming to avoid a situation where an individual who died in the early part of a tax year was treated as non-UK resident in spite of having been present here for the majority of that period. However, this will inevitably lead to taxpayers being treated as resident in the UK who would have been non-resident had they survived until the end of the tax year. The majority of individuals would be likely to return to the UK in blocks, having planned their total days over the tax year, rather than, say, coming for one to two days per month evenly throughout the year. After all, outside the world of *The Hitch-Hikers Guide to the Galaxy*, very few people plan their taxes on the basis that they will die during the year!

RDR3 provides some very useful tables to prevent personal representatives and their advisors from having to actually perform the calculation (Tables C and D at 4.11). These are effectively reproductions of the two tables from *paras 18* and *19, Sch 45, FA 2013* of the legislation with the days reduced according to the formula. Note again that an individual who is present for the number of days and has the number of ties shown will be *resident* for that tax year.

*Table C: UK Ties needed by a deceased person who was UK resident for one or more of the three tax years before the tax year under consideration*

| No of ties | | Date of death on or after | | | | | | | | | | | |
|---|---|---|---|---|---|---|---|---|---|---|---|---|---|
| | | 6 Apr to 30 Apr | 1 May to 31 May | 1 Jun to 30 Jun | 1 Jul to 31 Jul | 1 Aug to 31 Aug | 1 Sep to 30 Sep | 1 Oct to 31 Oct | 1 Nov to 30 Nov | 1 Dec to 31 Dec | 1 Jan to 31 Jan | 1 Feb to 29 Feb | 1 Mar to 5 Apr |
| | | Days spent in UK in year of death | | | | | | | | | | | |
| At least 4 ties | Not more than | 4 | 7 | 11 | 15 | 19 | 22 | 26 | 30 | 34 | 37 | 41 | 45 |
| At least 3 ties | | 5-7 | 8-15 | 12-22 | 16-30 | 20-37 | 23-45 | 27-52 | 31-60 | 35-67 | 38-75 | 42-82 | 46-90 |
| At least 2 ties | | 8-10 | 16-20 | 23-30 | 31-40 | 38-50 | 46-60 | 53-70 | 61-80 | 68-90 | 76-100 | 83-110 | 91-120 |
| At least 1 tie | over | 10 | 20 | 30 | 40 | 50 | 60 | 70 | 80 | 90 | 100 | 110 | 120 |

*Table D: UK Ties needed by a deceased person who was UK resident in none of the three tax years before the tax year under consideration*

| No of ties | | Date of death on or after | | | | | | | | | | | |
|---|---|---|---|---|---|---|---|---|---|---|---|---|---|
| | | 6 Apr to 30 Apr | 1 May to 31 May | 1 Jun to 30 Jun | 1 Jul to 31 Jul | 1 Aug to 31 Aug | 1 Sep to 30 Sep | 1 Oct to 31 Oct | 1 Nov to 30 Nov | 1 Dec to 31 Dec | 1 Jan to 31 Jan | 1 Feb to 29 Feb | 1 Mar to 5 Apr |
| | | Days spent in UK in year of death | | | | | | | | | | | |
| All 4 ties | | 4-7 | 8-15 | 11-22 | 15-30 | 19-37 | 23-45 | 27-52 | 31-60 | 34-67 | 38-75 | 42-82 | 46-90 |
| At least 3 ties | | 8-10 | 16-20 | 23-30 | 31-40 | 38-50 | 46-60 | 53-70 | 61-80 | 68-90 | 76-100 | 83-110 | 91-120 |
| At least 2 ties | over | 10 | 20 | 30 | 40 | 50 | 60 | 70 | 80 | 90 | 100 | 110 | 120 |

# Residence in previous tax years

[**2.24**] A central theme running through all of the SRT is the concept that once residence is acquired it should not be easily lost. For this reason, residence in previous tax years is a factor in applying many of the tests.

It is clear that the need to determine residence for previous tax years could lead to continuing uncertainty in many cases. Where there is or could be doubt about an individual's residence position, this would continue that uncertainty indefinitely. For example, an ongoing enquiry into an individual's residence status for 2010/11 could impact on their residence status for 2013/14. An unresolved enquiry would prevent the individual from being able to have certainty about their residence position for 2013/14 since they would not know either which automatic overseas tests to apply or which of the two sufficient ties tables in *paragraphs 18* and *19, Sch 45, FA 2013* should apply to them. This uncertainty would then roll forward to future years until the enquiry was resolved.

To prevent this difficulty, the transitional provisions allow an individual to apply the statutory residence test to the previous three tax years, *only* for the purpose of determining their residence for 2013/14 onwards. This is set out in *para 154, Sch 45, FA 2013*:

'(1)    This paragraph applies if–

    (a)    year X or, in Part 3 of this Schedule, the relevant year is the tax year 2013-14, 2014-15 or 2015-16, 2016-17 or 2017-18 and

    (b)    it is necessary to determine under this Schedule whether an individual was resident or not resident in the UK for a tax year before the tax year 2013-14 (a "pre-commencement tax year").

(2)    The question under this Schedule is to be determined in accordance with the rules in force for determining an individual's residence for that pre-commencement tax year (and not in accordance with the statutory residence test).

(3)    But an individual may by notice in writing to HMRC elect, as respects one or more pre-commencement tax years, for the question under this Schedule to be determined instead in accordance with the statutory residence test.

(4)    A notice under sub-paragraph (3)–

    (a)    must be given no later than the first anniversary of the end of year X or, in a Part 3 case, the relevant year, and

    (b)    is irrevocable.

(5)    Unless, in relation to a pre-commencement tax year, an election is made under sub-paragraph (3) as respects that year—

    (a)    paragraph 10(b) of this Schedule has effect in relation to that year as if the words "by virtue of meeting the automatic residence test" were omitted,

    (b)    paragraph 16 of this Schedule has effect in relation to that year as if—

        (i)    in sub-paragraph (1)(b), the words "because P met the third automatic overseas test for each of those years" were omitted, and

        (ii)    in sub-paragraph (2)(a), the words "because P met the third automatic overseas test for that year" were omitted, and

    (c)    paragraph 49 of this Schedule has effect in relation to that year as if in sub-paragraph (2)(a) for the words from "because" to the end there were substituted "in circumstances where the taxpayer was working overseas full-time for the whole of that year."'

The transitional provisions only apply (and are only needed) from 2013/14 to 2017/18. The default position remains that residence for the pre-SRT three years falls to be determined under the existing law, but the individual may elect to determine residence for these pre-commencement years by applying the SRT. If applying the SRT leads to a different result for that year (for example, an individual who would have been UK resident under the rules in force at the time becomes non-UK resident under the SRT), this will not affect their actual residence position or their tax liability for that tax year, but will only affect years which must be counted as years of residence in applying the SRT.

So, returning to the scenario at the start of this section, the individual would still be subject to enquiry for 2010/11, but would be able to use the SRT to assess their residency position for that year and thus know which tests should be applied to determine their residence position for 2013/14.

RDR3 gives the following information about how to make an election:

'Making an election

8.7.  If you choose to make an election to determine your residence status for a year prior to 2013-14 by reference to the SRT, the election:
  - must be made in writing, either on your Self Assessment return or in a letter sent to HMRC
  - must be made no later than the first anniversary of the end of the relevant year to which it applies or, if the year is a split year, the first anniversary of the end of that year
  - is irrevocable.'

### When to make an election

**[2.25]**  What is perhaps less clear from RDR3 is the attitude that HMRC will take to an election to calculate one's residence position under the SRT rules for previous tax years.

So, for example, it may be clear for an individual whose residence position for one of the previous tax years is under enquiry that electing to apply the SRT for that tax year will give them the necessary certainty in determining their residence position going forward. However, what of the individual whose residence position has not yet been the subject of enquiry and the enquiry window is still open (eg for 2012/13)? Might HMRC view an election to use the SRT test as an indication that the individual has some doubts about their residence position and thus open an enquiry when they otherwise would not have done? This will be a natural concern for many when considering an election.

There is a further (although likely to be small) group of individuals who will wish to consider an election. There may be those who have filed a tax return for an earlier year on the basis that they are resident in the UK, but who would be non-UK resident in applying the SRT. Such individuals may have nothing to lose and everything to gain from an election to apply the SRT for earlier tax years. It must be stressed though that the number of people who would find themselves in this situation is likely be very small.

### The split-year test in previous tax years

**[2.26]**  The rules are slightly different when it comes to considering whether a year prior to 2013/14 is a split year. In these circumstances it is not possible to rely on the new legislation, but instead the extra-statutory concessions which applied before 6 April 2013 must be applied. The transitional provisions (at *para 155, Sch 45, FA 2013*) provide:

'155(1)This paragraph applies if–

    (a)    year X or, for Part 3 of this Schedule, the tax year for which an Individual's liability to tax is being calculated is the tax year 2013-14 or a subsequent tax year, and

    (b)    it is necessary to determine under a provision of this Schedule, or a provision inserted by Part 3 of this Schedule, whether a tax year before the tax year 2013-14 (a "pre-commencement tax year") was a split year as respects the individual.

  (2)    The provision is to have effect as if–

    (a)    the reference to a split year were to a tax year to which the relevant ESC applied, and

    (b)    any reference to the UK part or the overseas part of such a year were to the part corresponding as far as possible, in accordance with the terms of the relevant ESC, to the UK part or the overseas part of a split year.

  (3)    Where the provision also refers to cases involving actual or deemed departure from the UK, the reference is to be read and given effect so far as possible in accordance with the terms of the relevant ESC.

  (4)    "The relevant ESC" means whichever of the extra-statutory concessions to which effect is given by Part 3 of this Schedule is relevant in the individual's case.'

RDR3 summarises the relevant ESCs:

'8.8.  If it is necessary for you to determine whether a year prior to 2013-14 is a split year you must reach your decision by reference to the relevant Extra Statutory Concession (ESC) applicable in that year. The split year rules in the SRT do not apply. The relevant ESCs are:

- A11
- A78 (see part 8.9 of HMRC6)

or, if these do not apply

- D2'

In other words, decisions about whether a particular year is a split year must be made under 'old rules'. In many ways this is sensible as the new, statutory rules governing split years are commonly more restrictive. However, where there is dispute or uncertainty about the position regarding an earlier tax year, this does preserve that uncertainty into the new regime. The number of cases affected in this way are, however, likely to be small.

### Other anomalies in the transitional rules

**[2.27]** There are a couple of places in the legislation where a test is met only if an individual's residence in a previous year (or previous three years) is determined under one of the automatic tests. For example: the fourth automatic UK test, which only applies in the year of death. One of the conditions of this test is that for each of the previous three tax years 'P was resident in the UK by virtue of meeting the automatic test'. This requirement to satisfy an automatic residence test clearly will not function well in the early years of the test, since although an individual may have been resident in the previous year or three years, it will not be by virtue of an automatic test (since these did not apply). In the case of the fourth automatic test, the transitional rules deal with this issue by omitting the requirement for the residence to be by virtue of the automatic test – it is instead enough for the individual to be resident (*para 154(5)(a), Sch 45, FA 2013*). There is a similar adjustment for the fifth automatic overseas test (*para 154(5)(b), Sch 45, FA 2013*). RDR3, para 8.10 explains that non-residence for these pre-SRT years is met if ESCA11 applied to the deceased.

There would be a similar difficulty with Case 6 of the split-year test which requires the individual to have been non-resident in the previous tax year by virtue of meeting the third automatic overseas test. In this case, the transitional provisions amend the legislation in respect of a pre-commencement year to remove this reference to the third automatic test and replace it with wording requiring the individual to have been working full-time overseas (*para 154 (5)(c), Sch 45, FA 2013*).

## Conclusion

**[2.28]** This chapter has provided an overview of the three parts of the SRT. The following chapters go on to look at different aspects of the test in more detail.

# Chapter 3

# Key concepts

## Introduction

**[3.01]** This chapter follows *Part 2* of *Schedule 45, FA 2013* in considering the definitions, or key concepts, that underpin the SRT.

As noted in **CHAPTER 2**, the statutory residence test includes many definitions. This is largely because one of the stated reasons for moving to the SRT was to avoid the subjectivity and uncertainty of the previous regime.

The current version of the test has not achieved certainty in every aspect, as will be seen. In addition, some of the definitions adopted are far from intuitive. Not only are there many definitions in the tests but many of the tests include similar ideas that are defined slightly differently, depending on the test being applied in each case. This is likely to make the test confusing for tax practitioners, and exceptionally so for laymen.

This chapter considers the key concepts in the same order as that in which they appear in the SRT legislation.

## Days of presence in the UK

### Introduction

**[3.02]** Each of the three strands of the SRT requires the taxpayer to count days spent in the UK. The meaning of UK day for this purpose remains substantially the same as under the previous regime and the test applied is whether the taxpayer is or is not present in the UK at 'the end of the day'. The test then goes on to exclude certain days when the taxpayer is in fact present at the end of the day and to include certain days despite the taxpayer not being so present.

### Present at the end of the day

**[3.03]** The taxpayer is present at the end of the day if he is in the UK at midnight UK time, unless he is subject to either of two prescribed exclusions.

### Exclusion 1: days in transit

**[3.04]** The exception for days spent in transit which was introduced as part of the *FA 2008* reforms has been retained.

The law is in *para 22, Sch 45, FA 2013*:

'22(1) If P is present in the UK at the end of a day, that day counts as a day spent by P in the UK.

(2) But it does not do so in the following two cases.

(3) The first case is where –

(a) P only arrives in the UK as a passenger on that day,

(b) P leaves the UK the next day, and

(c) between arrival and departure, P does not engage in activities that are to a substantial extent unrelated to P's passage through the UK.'

There was much debate when the exclusion for days spent in transit was first enacted by *FA 2008* as to whether it was permissible to indulge in activities such as a meal with a friend or a theatre visit en route through the UK or if these would invalidate the transit exclusion. It would appear that a solitary meal could be said to be mere subsistence and so would not be unrelated to the transit, but meals with friends and any pre-planning are likely to be regarded as introducing an unrelated event. Exactly where the line is drawn is explored by HMRC in Examples 17–18(c) of RDR3 as reproduced below:

'Example 17

Holly regularly visits the UK for work and social engagements. She also travels widely. She is planning to visit her Aunt in Philadelphia, and will be flying in from Rome to connect with her continental flight at Heathrow.

Holly's flight lands at 23:05 on Monday evening. Her flight to Philadelphia does not depart Heathrow until 11:05 on Tuesday. Holly decides to stay at an airport hotel to catch some sleep, before returning to board the plane for her onward journey. She merely leaves the airport, catches a taxi to the hotel, sleeps, and snatches a quick breakfast before returning to the airport.

The transit arrival day (Monday) spent in the UK would not count as a day for Holly when she considers how many days she spent in the UK at the end of the tax year. The departure day (Tuesday) may count as a qualifying day under the deeming rule.

Example 18(a)

Holly's brother, Lawrence, has a similarly itinerant lifestyle. He too is visiting their Aunt in Philadelphia, and will be flying in from Toulouse to connect with their continental flight at Heathrow.

Lawrence's flight lands at 17:20 on Monday evening. Their flight to Philadelphia does not depart Heathrow until 11:05 on Tuesday. Lawrence decides to stay at an airport hotel to catch some sleep before returning to board the plane on Tuesday. In this scenario, the midnight spent in the UK will not count as a day spent in the UK for SRT purposes. The departure day (Tuesday) may count as a qualifying day under the deeming rule.

Example 18(b)

The circumstances are as for 18(a) but Lawrence decides that as he has a long transit period in the UK he will meet up with some friends and go to the theatre.

In this scenario Lawrence's meeting friends and visiting the theatre is regarded as being to a substantial extent unrelated to his passage through the UK and therefore the midnight spent in the UK will count as a day spent in the UK for SRT purposes. The following day (Tuesday) may also count as a qualifying day under the deeming rule.

Example 18(c)

The circumstances are as for 18(a) but Lawrence meets his team leader for dinner to discuss work related issues. Their meeting lasted for an hour and a half.

In this scenario the meeting with his team leader is regarded as being to a substantial extent unrelated to his passage through the UK and the midnight spent in the UK will count as a day spent in the UK for SRT purposes. The following day (Tuesday) may also count as a qualifying day under the deeming rule.'

RDR3 also considers two other examples: a chance meeting at the airport and hotel with a colleague during which no work is done and a similar chance meeting which leads to some work being done. The latter is likely to fall outside the transit exemption.

These examples suggest that sleeping is an activity that is not unrelated to transit but that combining subsistence with some social or work-related activity is likely to prevent the day from being regarded as 'in transit'.

## Exclusion 2: exceptional circumstances

**[3.05]** The law then goes on to codify a non-statutory practice from the previous regime by specifying a second set of circumstances, exceptional circumstances, under which days of presence will not count, provided certain conditions are met.

Under the previous regime, HMRC had an exceptional circumstances practice, which derived from SP2/91. This was made at the time of the first Gulf War and was intended to help oil workers forced to flee Kuwait following its invasion by Iraq.

Since that time there had been occasions on which HMRC was invited to comment that a particular event might be regarded as exceptional, although it was not until 2011 that they did so when a combination of civil unrest in various Arabic countries and volcanic dust caused many individuals who had been working outside the UK to return here and disrupted planned travel for others. HMRC at that time allowed exceptional circumstances to apply if the countries the individuals had left were subject to Foreign and Commonwealth Office travel restrictions, and also allowed disruption to travel caused by volcanic dust to be regarded as exceptional. However, what would and would not be regarded as exceptional apart from these specific circumstances continued to be uncertain. For example, there was always some debate with regard to sickness and the degree of ill-health needed to qualify for exceptional circumstances as well as whether the ill-health needed to be one's own or could be extended to cover one's family.

The SRT law, in *para 22(4)* and *(5), Sch 45, FA 2013,* provides the relief for exceptional circumstances:

'(4) The second case is where –
    (a)   P would not be present in the UK at the end of that day but for exceptional circumstances beyond P's control that prevent P from leaving the UK, and
    (b)   P intends to leave the UK as soon as those circumstances permit.
(5)    Examples of circumstances that may be "exceptional" are –

    (a)    national or local emergencies such as war, civil unrest or natural disasters, and

    (b)    a sudden or life-threatening illness or injury.'

HMRC's guidance on exceptional circumstances under the SRT is set out in a separate annex to RDR3, Annex B, which is quite lengthy and shows how difficult it is to determine what the law here is intended to cover. It is disappointing that so much guidance was deemed necessary from the outset to support what was intended to be a clear statutory definition. Further clarification and amendment to the law may be needed in due course.

The SRT law is drafted in terms of events which prevent the individual from leaving the UK, although, as noted above, previously HMRC have accepted as exceptional those events which involved the taxpayer leaving another country and returning to the UK. HMRC's guidance also states that exceptional circumstances will generally apply only where the taxpayer is already in the UK and is prevented from leaving – see paragraph B8 as copied below:

    'B8    Days spent in the UK may be disregarded if the individual's presence in the UK is due to exceptional circumstances beyond their control. This will usually only apply to events that occur while an individual is in the UK and which prevent them from leaving the UK.'

It does, however, go on to soften this and make it clear that exceptional circumstances may also apply to someone returning to the UK, in the right set of circumstances:

    'B9    Exceptional circumstances will normally apply where an individual has no choice concerning the time they spend in the UK or in coming back to the UK. The situation must be beyond the individual's control.'

HMRC has more guidance on when returning to the UK may be regarded as exceptional at paragraphs B16 and B17.

**'Exceptional circumstances and Foreign and Commonwealth Office (FCO) advice**

    B16    Exceptional circumstances will generally not apply in respect of events that bring you back to the UK. However, there may be circumstances such as civil unrest or natural disaster where associated FCO advice is to avoid all travel to the region.

    B17    Individuals who return to and stay in the UK while FCO advice remains at this warning level would normally have days spent in the UK ignored under the SRT, subject to the 60-day limit.'

For the '60-day limit', see below.

Moreover, paragraph B12 indicates that an individual returning to the UK to deal with a sudden illness or injury of a close family member may be able to treat the days as exceptional, but the inference is that this will very much depend on the circumstances:

    'B12    There may also be limited situations where an individual who comes back to the UK to deal with a sudden life threatening illness or injury to a partner or dependent child can have those days spent in the UK ignored under the SRT subject to the 60-day limit.'

This is explored fully in Example B2:

'Example B2 (a)

Henrik is working in the construction industry and lives in Germany. He has business interests in the UK and has spent 68 days working here in the current tax year. He is a lone parent and his children usually live in the family home in Germany with him.

Henrik sends Victoria, his 13 year old daughter, for a two week holiday, at a summer holiday camp, in the UK. Unfortunately, whilst undertaking one of the activities she has an accident and is taken to hospital, unconscious and with a suspected major neck injury. Henrik immediately travels across to the UK, to be with his daughter and arrange for her to be moved back to Germany. This happens three days after the incident. His daughter remains in the hospital in Germany for a further four weeks, and has to wear a neck brace for an extended period of time.

The three days Henrik spends in the UK with his daughter arranging her transfer, after this potentially life threatening accident, would be considered as exceptional circumstances.

'Example B2 (b)

A similar judgement would be applied had Henrik and his daughter been in the UK when the accident had occurred. If Henrik stays with his daughter beyond their planned return date, until she can be transferred back to Germany, the additional days where he is present at midnight would count as exceptional circumstances.

Had he chosen not to arrange for his daughter to be transferred to a German hospital, and elected to stay in the UK until she was released from hospital here, the additional time would not be considered as exceptional circumstances.'

Clearly then, a serious illness or injury to an immediate family member may be exceptional, but only for so long as the taxpayer is unable to plan arrangements to manage it. Once Henrik's daughter was no longer in any danger, but could safely be transferred to another hospital in Germany he was expected to take action to ensure this happened. Had he simply arranged to stay in the UK until his daughter was well enough to return home, any days when she was no longer at risk of her life would apparently not be exceptional. This sort of situation is likely to be very difficult to manage in practice, especially if the medical professionals concerned cannot be definitive about when the relative will be sufficiently recovered to travel.

Concerns were expressed in various meetings during the consultation process that the list of possible exceptional events in *paragraph 22* might be regarded by the Courts as subject to the *'ejusdem generis'* rule so that only similar sets of circumstances might count in law.

HMRC's guidance however states that the list is not meant to be prescriptive but is, rather, intended as examples of the sort of thing that might be regarded as exceptional:

'B10  The type of events which may give rise to exceptional circumstances will be, by their nature, out of the ordinary and it is difficult to be prescriptive about what characteristics such an event would exhibit. However local or national emergencies, such as civil unrest, natural disasters, the outbreak of war or a sudden serious or life threatening illness or injury to an individual are examples of circumstances that are likely to be exceptional.'

The legislation requires that exceptional circumstances must be beyond the taxpayer's control. See also paragraphs B13 and B14:

'B13   In order to be ignored as days spent in the UK, there must be exceptional circumstances beyond the control of the individual. In other words, the event or situation in question must be one over which the individual has no control or influence and which cannot reasonably have been foreseen.

B14   For example, if an individual is a passenger on a commercial aircraft that is forced to make an emergency landing in the UK and there is no available onward flight to their original destination for two days afterwards, the two days that would otherwise count as spent in the UK would be ignored due to exceptional circumstances.'

Thus, whether particular circumstances are exceptional will depend on the facts of the case, the individual taxpayer's circumstances and the choices available to them. The legislation requires that the taxpayer intends to leave the UK as soon as the exceptional circumstances permit. HMRC say that leaving the UK will be taken as evidence of intention (see para B15). However, a change of intention can mean that the situation ceases to be exceptional. This is illustrated by Examples B3 and B4.

'Example B3

Claude is retired and came to the UK for the first time on 1 June for a 5 month extended travelling holiday, intending to leave on 31 October.

On 29 September while travelling to Scotland he is involved in a car crash suffering multiple injuries. He is in hospital for a total of 14 weeks and arranges to travel back to his home in France on the day he is discharged.

Claude has been in the UK for 220 days.

The time Claude spent in hospital is an exceptional circumstance. Claude spent 14 weeks in hospital but because his original intention was to stay in the UK until 31 October, only the days from 1 November up to date of discharge can be ignored due to exceptional circumstances.

The maximum number of days in the tax year that can be ignored is 60. Claude has 160 days counted as spent in the UK.

Example B4

The circumstances are as in Example B3.

However, Claude's nephew who lives in Wales writes to him in hospital and suggests Claude should visit him when he leaves hospital. Claude writes back on 1 December agreeing.

From 1 December, it is no longer Claude's intention to leave the UK as soon as the exceptional circumstance has come to an end and so only the period 29 September to 30 November can be discounted as exceptional circumstances for SRT day counting purposes.'

Events will only qualify if they could not reasonably have been foreseen or predicted. This is particularly relevant in cases of illness or injury.

There have been cases in the past where taxpayers have argued that medical treatment is an exceptional circumstance (Mr Gaines-Cooper for example suggested that days spent in the UK because of heart surgery and the birth of his son should be regarded as exceptional). The guidance is quite clear that the event has to be unexpected for the exception to apply:

'B19 Life events such as birth, marriage, divorce and death are not routinely regarded as exceptional circumstances. Choosing to come to the UK for medical treatment or to receive elective medical services such as dentistry, cosmetic surgery or therapies will not be regarded as exceptional circumstances.'

HMRC's past practice for exceptional circumstances applied only to their 91-day rule and could not be used for the purposes of the 183-day test. Under the SRT, the relief can discount days for any of the specific tests but not for all day counts. Paragraphs B5 and B6 of RDR3 set out the tests where exceptional circumstances can and cannot be taken into account:

'B5 SRT day counting rules where exceptional circumstances can be taken into account when an individual is determining the number of days they spend in the UK

- First automatic UK test – an individual spends 183 days or more in the UK
- First automatic overseas test – an individual spends fewer than 16 days in the UK
- Second automatic overseas test – an individual spends fewer than 46 days in the UK
- Third automatic overseas test – number of days an individual spends in the UK is fewer than 91, excluding qualifying days under the deeming rule
- Fourth automatic overseas test for deceased persons – an individual spent less than 46 days in the UK
- Sufficient ties tables – number of days an individual spends in the UK compared against the number of ties they have
- 90-day tie – an individual spends more than 90 days in the UK in the previous tax year or the one before that
- Split year Cases 1 and 2 – permitted limit of number of days an individual spends in the UK, excluding qualifying days under the deeming rule
- Split year Cases 4 and 8 – an individual spends fewer than 16 days in the UK
- Split year Cases 4 and 5 – proportionately reduced number of days an individual spends in the UK for sufficient ties

B6 SRT day counting tests where exceptional circumstances cannot be taken into account when an individual is determining whether they satisfy the test

Second automatic UK test

- an individual is present in their home on at least (for UK homes) or fewer than (for overseas homes) 30 separate days
- period of 91 consecutive days, at least 30 of which fall within the tax year

Third automatic UK test

- an individual works sufficient hours in the UK, as assessed over a period of 365 days
- 75% of the total number of days
- at least one day in the tax year is a day on which an individual does more than three hours of work in the UK
- significant break – 31 days go by

Third automatic overseas test

- significant break – 31 days go by
- number of days on which an individual does more than three hours of work in the UK is fewer than 31

Full-time work – 15 day gap between employments (and 30 day maximum number of days that may be subtracted for gaps between employments)

Family tie – an individual spends time with their child in person on 60 days or fewer, for all or part of a day

Family tie – an individual's child spends fewer than 21 days in the UK outside term-time

Accommodation tie
–      continuous period of 91 days
–      gap of 15 days or fewer

Work tie – an individual works in the UK for at least 40 days

Country tie – midnight test – greatest number of midnights.

Deeming rule – if an individual has more than 30 qualifying days, the excess are treated as if the individual were in the UK at the end of the day, subject to the conditions set out in paragraph 3.5.'

Under the SRT, only the first 60 days in a tax year can be treated as being exceptional (*para 22(6), Sch 45, FA 2013*). As with all arbitrary cut offs this can lead to individual situations that seem harsh as explored in several of the HMRC examples, one of which, example B1, is reproduced below:

'Example B1

Anna is returning to her home in Denmark having spent her seven week summer holiday working in the UK. This was her first visit to the UK.

On her boat journey home there is an explosion in the engine room. Emergency rescue services attend the vessel and Anna is found unconscious and badly burned. The emergency services make the decision to airlift Anna to a specialist burns unit in the UK where she remains for five months. Anna returns to Denmark as soon as she is discharged from hospital.

Anna has been in the UK for 202 days.

This disaster would be considered to be an exceptional circumstance beyond Anna's control. However, the maximum number of days that can be ignored towards days spent in the UK is 60. So, Anna has 142 days which count as days spent in the UK.'

It is also worth noting that HMRC does not consider travel problems to be exceptional:

'B20   Travel problems, for example a delayed or missed flight due to traffic disruption, train delays or cancellations, or a car breakdown, will not be considered an exceptional circumstance.'

Taxpayers may therefore need to ensure that they keep some UK days 'in reserve' to allow for such events.

### Deemed days of presence

[**3.06**] During the consultation process, HM Treasury expressed concerns about how easy it would be for certain taxpayers to manipulate their midnights spent in the UK (and so UK days for the purposes of the test) while spending much of a day here.

The law now includes an anti-avoidance rule to counter this in *para 23, Sch 45, FA 2013* as set out below:

'23(1) If P is not present in the UK at the end of a day, that day does not count as a day spent by P in the UK.

(2)　This is subject to the deeming rule.

(3)　The deeming rule applies if –

(a)　P has at least 3 UK ties for a tax year,

(b)　the number of days in that tax year when P is present in the UK at some point in the day but not at the end of the day ("qualifying days") is more than 30, and

(c)　P was resident in the UK for at least one of the 3 tax years preceding that tax year.

(4)　The deeming rule is that, once the number of qualifying days in the tax year reaches 30 (counting forward from the start of the tax year), each subsequent qualifying day in the tax year is to be treated as a day spent by P in the UK.

(5)　The deeming rule does not apply for the purposes of sub-paragraph (3)(a) (so, in deciding for those purposes whether P has a 90-day tie, qualifying days in excess of 30 are not to be treated as days spent by P in the UK).'

So, provided the individual meets the three tests of *para 23(3), Sch 45, FA 2013*, any days in excess of 30 on which they were not present at midnight, but were during the day, are counted as days spent in the UK. It should be noted that although *para 23(3)(a)* makes reference to '3 UK ties', the deemed days do not apply only for the purposes of the sufficient ties test, but to most of the day count tests applied under the SRT. One exemption is given by *para 23(5)* for the 90-day tie. In addition, *para 14(1)(d) and (2), Sch 45, FA 2013* exempts those who qualify as non-resident by virtue of full-time work abroad from this deeming rule. However, the deeming rule can work to the disadvantage of the taxpayer, particularly where there is a change of circumstances.

#### Example 3.1: Sophie

Sophie has been working on assignment in France for her UK employer for two years (her year of departure from the UK, which was a 'split' year, was 2013/14). During 2015/16 she was asked to help with a UK-based project, which was expected to involve no more than 25 days of UK working. This suited her quite well because, in May 2015, her husband, who had been in France with her, had to return to the UK through ill-health and reoccupied their home which had previously been let.

In fact, Sophie has additional UK workdays because of travel time and project overruns and, as at 14 February, she has 35 UK workdays. Of these only 20 also counted as days of UK presence, because she left the UK before midnight on the other 15 days. However, all the workdays where she stayed in the UK at midnight were Fridays and she also spent the following Saturdays and Sundays with her husband in the UK, leaving the UK each Sunday evening before midnight.

Sophie will not meet the full-time working abroad test because she has more than 30 UK workdays. She also has three ties to the UK (UK resident spouse, accommodation and more than 90 days in 2013/14). She was resident in at least one of the three preceding UK tax years as noted above. She has 35 days of presence when she is not in the UK at midnight, being 15 workdays and the 20 Sundays noted above. The first 30 of these days will take her up to the permitted limit, so each subsequent day (five in this case) will need to be added to her day count as previously calculated by reference to the midnight test.

This will give her a total of 45 days of presence (being 20 UK workdays, 20 Saturdays and 5 deemed days). Whether this makes her UK resident will depend on the 'sufficient ties' test (see para **3.16** below).

Rather strangely, although there is a general exception for transit when counting days spent in the UK (under the midnight test), this does **not** extend to deemed days. This means that if you have a flight via the UK, so that you have part of a day in the UK, albeit one that is spent wholly in transit, that day can potentially create a day of deemed UK presence. This is made clear in para 3.9 of RDR3; see also Examples 17 and 18(a) and (b), reproduced at para **3.04** above.

The deeming rule is applied after what is a relatively short time in the UK. It is also debatable whether it will catch the people it is intended to catch. The response document to the June 2012 consultation, published in December 2012, referred to a small number of individuals who would manipulate the midnight rule and thereby manage to stay non-resident and, in meetings as part of the consultation, HMRC suggested this might mean 'millionaires with yachts' who could leave the UK overnight. Presumably, if such individuals are already taking steps to avoid being in the UK at midnight, they will be able to adapt their pattern of UK visits so as to keep their qualifying UK days under 30 per UK tax year in the future.

HMRC had previously departed from their normal practice of ignoring days of arrival and departure from the UK in cases where individuals had spent a lot of time in the UK (for example in the case of Gaines-Cooper). It is possible that given the tighter framework of the new test that it was felt some provision needed to be made for these types of cases.

## 'Home'

**[3.07]** Home is a key concept for the second automatic UK test. It is also important for some of the split-year tests. However, the statutory definition is incomplete, concentrating on the structures that can constitute a home and on what is not a home, rather than providing a full definition. Concerns over how home should be defined were raised at each stage of the consultation process, with the tax profession highlighting first the omission and later the inadequacy of the definition. The final version of the test remains extremely wide and therefore difficult to interpret.

The statutory definition is in *para 25, Sch 45, FA 2013*:

'25(1) A person's home could be a building or part of a building or, for example, a vehicle, vessel or structure of any kind.

(2)    Whether, for a given building, vehicle, vessel, structure or the like, there is a sufficient degree of permanence or stability about P's arrangements there for the place to count as P's home (or one of P's homes) will depend on all the circumstances of the case.

(3)    But somewhere that P uses periodically as nothing more than a holiday home or temporary retreat (or something similar) does not count as a home of P's.

(4)    A place may count as a home of P's whether or not P holds any estate or interest in it (and references to "having" a home are to be read accordingly).

(5)    Somewhere that was P's home does not continue to count as such merely because P continues to hold an estate or interest in it after P has moved out (for example, if P is in the process of selling it or has let or sub-let it, having set up home elsewhere).'

From the statute we understand the following:

- the taxpayer need not own the property for it to be a home;
- the property need not be a permanent structure – for example it could be a caravan or a shooting lodge;
- temporary habitation is insufficient; and
- the taxpayer must have access to the property or intend to use it for it to be a home.

We have to turn to HMRC guidance (Annex A of RDR3) to obtain a greater understanding of their interpretation of the concept of 'home' as used in the SRT. It is disappointing that we are already required to rely on HMRC guidance on what is such a fundamental part of the SRT code and this is no doubt likely to be an area of litigation in the future.

Where a taxpayer has only one base, it is unlikely that there will be any dispute that this is their 'home'. Instead the difficulty in applying the concept will arise where a taxpayer uses more than one place on a regular basis. We then need to determine when the place becomes a home rather than a 'temporary retreat' and when there is a sufficient degree of permanence or stability about the taxpayer's arrangements to turn a dwelling place into a home. The legislation tells us to consider all the circumstances of the case, and HMRC guidance states 'for the purpose of the SRT we consider that a person's home is a place that a reasonable onlooker with knowledge of the material facts would regard as that person's home' (RDR3, para A4).

So, let us now see how to apply the 'reasonable onlooker' test to a number of circumstances that may arise in practice:

**Example 3.2: John**

John spends the working week in London where he rents a studio flat, returning to the family home in the country each weekend.

John will have two homes – the family home and the studio flat. He does not have to own the studio flat for it to be considered a home.

What if John worked in London only two days a week and spent his London night in a hotel? Even if he used the same hotel each week, would that be a 'home' for the purpose of the SRT? At first sight, it appears unlikely. As the legislation requires a degree of permanence or stability, a hotel would appear to be unlikely to count unless the same room or suite of rooms was made available to John on a semi-permanent basis.

What if John's parents lived in London and he stayed with them? Would this be a 'home'? The HMRC guidance gives two examples of a taxpayer using their parents' home. The first is example A2:

'Example A2:

Mary comes back to the UK to take up employment after spending three years studying abroad. She has given up the tenancy on the flat she occupied abroad and **moves into** (emphasis added) her parents' house. Her parents' house is her home.'

The second example is example A6.

'Example A6:

Rachel and Tom's kitchen and dining room have suffered flood damage. The estimated clean-up and repair operation will take six weeks, so they **stay with** (emphasis added) Rachel's parents while the work is being done. The property will remain their home even though Rachel and Tom are unable to stay there for the time being.'

This example is used to illustrate the point that the house that is being repaired remains Rachel and Tom's home. Although HMRC do not comment specifically on Rachel's parents' house, there may be a suggestion that the six-week stay, and the fact that the stay has a specific and temporary purpose, is insufficient to make this a home for Rachel and Tom.

So, returning to John, whether his parents' house, used during the working week, becomes a 'home' will depend on the facts. If the arrangement continues for a reasonably long period and John keeps some of his personal effects there, then his parents' house is likely to be a home.

*Paragraph 25(5), Sch 45, FA 2013* states that a place can cease to be a home after the taxpayer has moved out, even if they continue to hold an interest in it. The examples in HMRC guidance Annex A demonstrate that in HMRC's view, the moving out must be absolute. For example, HMRC provide example A10 – Harry puts his home on the market for sale and his furniture and belongings in storage.

'Example A10

Harry's new job requires him to travel extensively around Europe. He spends some time working in the UK but most of his work is carried out in other countries. He decided to sell his UK property. On 3 June, he put his furniture and belongings in storage and two weeks later he handed the keys to his estate agent. He did not return to his UK property after 3 June and stayed in hotels or with friends on the occasions when he came back to the UK. The property is not his home from 3 June, the date he put his furniture and belongings in storage.'

See also example A9 – Ivan lets his flat for two years where the rental agreement gives exclusive use of property to the tenants.

'Example A9

Ivan left the UK to work in Germany. He lets the flat he previously lived in to a tenant on a two-year lease. After 18 months, he was made redundant and returned to the UK. The rental agreement on his flat gave exclusive use of the property to the tenant so Ivan arranged to stay with relatives and friends until the lease expired. For the period, his property was let it is not his home.'

However, regarding Example A9 the guidance goes on to say:

'However, if the rental agreement had allowed Ivan to use the flat and he had stayed there when he visited the UK it would have remained his home throughout.'

Example A5 seems to apply an even harsher test – Asif travels to Sweden to care for his seriously ill father, retaining a property in Liverpool. He does not return to Liverpool but the fact that his apartment remains available for his use is sufficient for HMRC to state that it remains his 'home'.

'Example A5

Asif has lived and worked in the UK for many years, occupying the same apartment in Liverpool since the day he arrived here. Asif's father lives in Sweden and is seriously ill. Ten months ago, Asif decided to take a career break to care for his father and moved to Sweden. He does not know how long he will be out of the UK.

Since moving to Sweden Asif has not returned to Liverpool, but his apartment remains empty and available for him to return to whenever he wants. In this situation Asif will have a home in both Liverpool and Sweden even though he is spending all of his time in Sweden.'

Ceasing to have a home can be critical for obtaining split-year treatment and these examples are discussed in para **5.05**.

When a property may be regarded as a holiday home (and so not a home for the purposes of the test) is also important. It could be key in determining whether someone leaving the UK would qualify for split year treatment.

**Example 3.3: Lucy**

Lucy has decided to emigrate and move to southern France on her retirement. She sells her London home in preparation for this. However, she also has a cottage in the Lake District that she has owned for many years and she has decided that she will retain it for the time being, because she would like to have a 'toe hold' in the UK property market, 'just in case', and might wish to visit it if she becomes nostalgic for rainy weather. She has asked her advisor to confirm that this will not prevent her qualifying for split-year treatment on departure under Case 3 ('Ceasing to have a home in the UK').

In principle Lucy's Lake District cottage should not be a problem, provided that HMRC accept it should be regarded as a holiday home. HMRC guidance provides:

'A20 ...a holiday home where an individual spends time, for occasional short breaks, and which clearly provides a distinct respite from their ordinary day to day life will not be a home...'

However, it is a question of degree; and in Example A11 HMRC discuss Jenny, who starts living in her 'holiday home' for half a year. This then becomes a home for the purpose of the SRT.

'Example A11

Jenny lives in Birmingham and works from home. She also owns an apartment in Spain which she rents out apart from two to three weeks a year when she takes her holiday there. The Spanish property is not her home.

However, Jenny then decides to live in the Spanish apartment throughout the British winter time, from October to March. Her use of the property has changed from being somewhere she used for an occasional short break to somewhere she uses as a home for part of the year. The property is now her home from the point she commences using the property as her home.'

In our example, Lucy's Lake District property has not previously been regarded as anything more than a holiday home. It is not clear what she has to do if she wants it to continue to be regarded as a holiday home, rather than a home, and there is a risk that her usage of the property could increase, given that she is retired and is likely to have more free time as a consequence. In the circumstances, if split-year treatment is important to her in the tax year of departure, the best advice may be that she should not visit the property at all post departure until the new tax year, as HMRC's guidance is specific that you have to visit a property in order for it to be regarded as a home. For a detailed discussion of whether a home can become a holiday home and when this might take place, see para **8.18**.

The condition of a property may also be relevant in determining whether it is or at what point it becomes a home. Merely being unable to occupy a property temporarily because of damage is not enough to prevent it being a home, as is illustrated by HMRC's Rachel and Tom example, quoted above.

It is not clear precisely why in HMRC's view Rachel and Tom's property remains a home in this example, in spite of the fact that the example states that they are 'unable to stay there', but it may be that a combination of the fact that the property has been previously occupied and the period during which they stay elsewhere is relatively short. It may be arguable that if an individual leaves the majority of possessions in a property (furniture, personal effects, etc) then that remains his home even if it is temporarily incapable of being used as a home.

In considering whether a dilapidated home or a home in need of repair continues to be a home, HMRC seem to distinguish between a home which has been previously occupied and one which has never been occupied. Regarding a home which has never previously been occupied, the guidance states:

'A15  Your home starts to be your home as soon as:
 •   it is capable of being used as your home, for example, you have taken ownership of it, even if it is temporarily unavailable because of renovation
 •   you actually use it as your home.
 If the first point above is satisfied, but in fact you never actually use it as your home, then it will not be your home.'

See also A18:

'A18  A place that has never been capable of functioning as a home cannot be a home. For example, a property purchased in such as state of disrepair that it is not capable of being lived in as a home, is not a home until such time as it becomes habitable.'

Presumably A18 needs to be read with A15 so the property needs not only to become habitable but also to be used as a home.

Ultimately these are merely HMRC's interpretations of the meaning of home, and it will be for a court to finally determine the level of occupation needed in the case of a very dilapidated property.

In practice, when determining whether a property starts, continues, or ceases to be a home, it will often be a case of considering where the taxpayer's family resides, and their location is likely to make a place a home.

In Annex A, para A11, HMRC state:

> 'A11 A place can still be a home even if an individual does not stay there continuously. If, for example they move out temporarily but their spouse and children continue to live there, then it is still likely to be their home.'

This is reinforced by the example A4.

So, while the absence of the family does not mean that a property cannot be a home (and see here the comments by HMRC at para A12), their presence, particularly where this is for the majority of a year, is likely to be highly indicative. See the further discussions in Chapter 5 of the significance of the location of a taxpayer's family.

A 2017 High Court case, *Bestolov v Povarenkin* [2017] EWHC 1968, is not a tax case, but includes some considerations of what is needed for a residence to constitute a 'home'. This case arose from a business dispute involving a joint venture to develop mines in Russia. The defendant applied for an order that the Court decline to exercise jurisdiction, claiming that Russia was the most appropriate place for the case to be heard. The Court had to consider whether, within the definitions of the relevant law, the defendant was resident in England and England was his settled and usual place of abode. A key factor in Mr Simon Bryan QC's (sitting as a Deputy High Court Judge) decision was the fact that Mr Povarenkin regularly visited the Belgravia flat in London where his wife and family lived for the majority of the year. Despite spending on average only 80 days in the UK, this was sufficient to make the Belgravia flat his 'home in England'.

Although not sufficient in itself, an intention as to the quality of use, when coupled with actions, may be important in determining whether a property is a home or a temporary retreat. Here another recent case, this time before the First Tier Tribunal, may be of interest. *Stephen Bailey v CIR* [2017] UKFTT 0658 (TC), heard on 18 August 2017, was a private residence case, considering the availability of the CGT exemption. In this case, which emphasised the importance of the quality of occupation in determining the availability of the relief, Mr Bailey's intentions for the property, at which he had in fact spent very little time, were held to be significant to support the relief being given.

To conclude on the meaning of 'home', the concept is important both for the second automatic UK test – does an individual have a home in the UK and elsewhere in the world? – and for some of the split year cases where the emphasis is on ceasing or starting to have a home. The key distinction is between a 'home' and a 'holiday home or temporary retreat', the latter being identified on the grounds of time spent, frequency of use, the activities carried out there and perhaps also intention. Thus, the definition requires a constant monitoring of the circumstances surrounding ownership, the right to use the property and the quality of occupation. In some circumstances, this will be critical for the application of the SRT.

## The definitions for the concept of 'work'

### Introduction

**[3.08]** All three parts to the SRT have a test that involves work:

- the automatic overseas test includes the test of working sufficient hours overseas (commonly referred to as full-time work abroad or FTWA);
- the automatic residence test includes the test of working sufficient hours in the UK (commonly referred to as full-time work in the UK or FTWUK);
- the sufficient ties test includes the tie of 40 days' work in the UK.

This section first considers the definitions that go to make up these tests: 'work', a 'day of work', working 'sufficient hours' overseas or in the UK and where work is carried out. It then goes on to consider the application of the sufficient hours calculation.

### Work

**[3.09]** The basic definition of work is in *para 26(1), Sch 45, FA 2013*:

'P is considered to be "working" (or doing "work") at any time when P is doing something–

(a)   in the performance of duties of an employment held by P, or

(b)   in the course of a trade carried on by P (alone or in partnership).'

The test applied for the performance of the duties of the employment is whether any remuneration received for them by P would be taxed as employment income (*para 26(2)*). The definition for someone undertaking a trade is similar, but rather than looking at how the income is taxed considers whether any expenses incurred in the performance of the duties would be tax deductible (*para 26(3)*). Neither test is determinative, in the sense that the law says only that 'regard must be had' as to the nature of any payment received or the deductibility of expenses incurred, rather than indicating that meeting the test will invariably mean that one is working.

A further aspect to note is that work does not include voluntary work. *Paragraph 26(8)* is specific on this point:

'(8)   A voluntary post for which P has no contract of service does not count as an employment for the purposes of this Schedule.'

The intention here apparently was to exclude instances where individuals decided to travel and then end up taking on charity work abroad, but it could have harsh consequences. For example, if the individual has a UK home prior to departure (possibly with parents rather than independently) and continues to visit the UK, this may be enough to keep him UK tax resident despite a heavy commitment to charity work outside the UK.

Elsewhere the tax code makes a distinction between duties that are incidental and those which are substantive, and duties that are incidental to duties performed outside the UK are deemed (by *s 39, ITEPA 2003*) also to be performed outside the UK. However, in planning the SRT the Government decided that the judgement as to what was and what was not substantive was a subjective one and should be avoided for the purposes of the test. Consequently it is simply a case now of considering the location of work (see para **3.11**). The main impact of this is in relation to training, which was previously regarded as incidental, and now will count as UK work to the extent that it is actually undertaken in the UK.

The law (*para 26(5), Sch 45, FA 2013*) is specific about the circumstances in which training will count as work:

'Time spent undertaking training counts as time spent working if:

(a) In the case of an employment held by P, the training is provided or paid for by the employer and is undertaken to help P in performing duties of the employment, and

(b) In the case of a trade carried on by P, the cost of the training could be deducted in calculating the profits of the trade for income tax purposes.'

For an employee, training that is paid for by the employer and is intended to allow the employee to perform his duties better will count as work. For the self-employed, training time will count as work if the expense would be a tax-deductible expense in calculating profit.

In addition, travel time can now be included as work. The law is in *para 26(4), Sch 45, FA 2013*:

'Time spent travelling counts as time spent working:

(a) If the cost of the journey could, if it were incurred by P, be deducted in calculating P's earnings from that employment under section 337, 338, 340 or 342 of ITEPA 2003 or, as the case may be, in calculating the profits of the trade under ITTOIA 2005, or

(b) To the extent that P does something else during the journey that would itself count as work in accordance with this paragraph.'

Thus, any travel that would be tax deductible for an employee or a business expense for someone who is self-employed will count as work. If the journey would not normally meet this test, it may still count as time spent working if, during the journey, the taxpayer undertakes something else that would count as work. So, catching up on work-related emails while on what might otherwise count as a private journey home will extend the taxpayer's working day. See below (para **3.11**) for the location of work and when travel counts as UK travel or overseas travel. The inclusion of travel in the definition of work is likely to be particularly challenging for those individuals who are seeking to minimise their workdays in the UK. See **CHAPTERS 4** and **6** for a discussion of this.

Whether the meaning of 'work' includes notice periods, periods of garden leave and periods when an employee is required to be on call is far from clear.

All of these things would appear to have the capacity to be work in the context of the test of *para 26(2)*, but such work may not constitute a workday since the law actually requires the employee to be 'working for more than three hours' before work will make a day into a workday, for example, for the purpose of the significant break test. So, days when an employee is on call but is not actually required to do anything and periods spent on garden leave do not appear to qualify as workdays.

In relation to time on call, the guidance (RDR3, para 3.18) goes on to offer two examples that reach different conclusions, depending on whether the individual is employed or self-employed:

'Example 21

Paula works as an engineer and is contractually required to be on-call for four nights a month in addition to her normal full-time attendance. She is paid a retainer for those four nights, in addition to being paid for any work done if she is called out. The four nights are counted as working time.

Example 22

Franek is a self-employed locksmith who keeps his mobile phone switched on 24 hours a day to receive customer calls. For the purposes of calculating working time, Franek should only include the time spent carrying out his jobs and the related travelling time.'

Unfortunately there is no commentary on these examples and so there is no guidance as to why time on call for Paula will be work time (although possibly it is because she is paid a retainer for this) while it does not qualify for Franek (presumably 'carrying out his jobs' would include receiving a call) unless it is considered too easy to manipulate for the self-employed.

With respect to notice periods, HMRC state in RDR3, para 3.13:

'What else is counted as time spent working?

3.13 Your time spent working includes:

– instances where your employer instructs you to stay away from work, for example while serving a period of notice while you remain on the payroll'

This is consistent with the statutory definition of work (at *para 26(2), Sch 45, FA 2013*) but does not specify that a day while on notice counts as a workday. The practical difficulties of this are covered below in para **3.14** and also in **CHAPTERS** 4 and 6. Record-keeping requirements and the difficulties of evidencing when work has been performed are discussed further in **CHAPTER 13**.

## A workday

**[3.10]** A day of work is not directly defined in the final version of the law, but a number of different tests included within the SRT do make reference to a test of more than three hours of work, which will make a day into a workday. For example:

- the 75% UK workdays for full-time work in the UK is measured by reference to days on which more than three hours' work is performed (*para 9(1)(d), Sch 45, FA 2013*);

- the 'less than 31 days in year X' test that a full-time working abroad employee may spend working in the UK uses more than three hours as the test (*para 14(1)(c), Sch 45, FA 2013*);
- significant breaks are defined as periods of at least 31 days and none of these is a day on which 'P does more than three hours' work' (*para 29, Sch 45, FA 2013*); and
- the work tie for the sufficient ties test requires at least 40 days on which P does more than three hours' work in the UK (*para 35, Sch 45, FA 2013*).

The three hours' test does not accord with the hours that might reasonably be expected for a working day. Rather, it is intended as a 'safe harbour', in that someone working for fewer than three hours on any day in theory need not concern himself with that particular day. The problem with this is the practical difficulty of proving that no more than three hours' work was undertaken.

For example, if an employee works for two hours in a morning and a further 30 minutes in the evening, how is he to prove that he has done no additional work in the interim? Will he be expected to produce an account of how he has spent his intervening leisure time? Mobile phone records may establish when telephone calls are made or taken but records for other electronic mobile devices such as Blackberries may be less conclusive. When emails are sent or received is not necessarily any guide as to when documents are drafted, accessed or read in more detail.

It is not clear in law where the burden of proof lies. Past experience of HMRC enquiries, however, suggests that HMRC will expect the individual to produce evidence to support the position claimed and this is consistent with the need to self-assess one's residency status. This is confirmed by paragraph 3.16 of RDR3:

'3.16 You will need to keep records which allow you to identify the number of hours you have worked in a given day.'

See para **13.11** for the first HMRC enquiries under the SRT.

Note also the points made in para **3.09** above to certain days where the individual may be said to be working but which may not count as a day of work.

## Location of work

**[3.11]** For the most part, the law relating to where work is regarded as performed is both logical and entirely reasonable. The provisions are set out in *para 27, Sch 45, FA 2013*:

'27(1) Work is done where it is actually done, regardless of where the employment is held or the trade is carried on by P.

(2)  But work done by way of or in the course of travelling to or from the UK by air or sea or via a tunnel under the sea is assumed to be done overseas even during the part of the journey in or over the UK.

(3)  For these purposes, travelling to or from the UK is taken to –

(a)  begin when P boards the aircraft, ship or train that is bound for a destination in the UK or (as the case may be) overseas, and

(b)  end when P disembarks from that aircraft, ship or train.'

(4)   This paragraph is subject to express provisions in this Schedule about the location of work done by people with relevant jobs on board vehicles, aircraft or ships.'

The inclusion of travel time as work and the definition of UK work is particularly problematic for anyone travelling by air, as all time spent airside, or travelling after that will count. Baggage delays and similar events beyond the individual's control, may therefore give him a UK workday when he does not expect it, perhaps when he travels to the UK in an evening after a full day of work outside the UK. It can be contrasted with the position for someone taking Eurostar into St Pancras who will only be deemed to be embarking on UK travel from the point at which he disembarks on the station.

HMRC's guidance in RDR3 underlines the difference that this might make in practice:

'3.22 Any work you do during your journey to or from the UK is counted as overseas work if you travel by air, sea or through a tunnel under the sea. If you are crossing the land border between Northern Ireland and the Republic of Ireland, work you do in Northern Ireland is work done in the UK, work done in the Republic of Ireland is work done overseas.

3.23 For journeys to the UK, the overseas work period ends when you disembark from that aircraft, ship or train in the UK.

3.24 For journeys from the UK, the overseas work period starts when you get on the aircraft, ship or train taking you out of the UK.

**Example 24**

Shirley flies from Spain to Heathrow Airport where she disembarks her plane and transits to catch a second flight from Heathrow to Glasgow.

Her journey from Spain to Heathrow counts as work done overseas (assuming the cost would have been tax deductible had she met it herself). Once she disembarks the plane, the time she spends in the airport terminal and flying to Glasgow counts as work done in the UK.

**Example 25**

Robert travels to the UK from Paris by Eurostar and leaves the train at London St Pancras to catch connecting trains to Glasgow. The costs of his journey would have been tax deductible had he met them himself.

His train journey from Paris to St Pancras counts as work done overseas. After disembarking at St Pancras, the rest of his journey counts as work done in the UK.'

## Rules for working a 'sufficient number of hours' in a reference period

**[3.12]** The law includes two separate but similar tests that establish whether an employee is working sufficient hours in the UK, or overseas, applying the test to different total periods in each case. The total period may be reduced by certain days and the resulting period is termed the 'reference period'. Provided the employee works 35 hours or more per seven-day period in the reference period, he will work a 'sufficient number of hours'. While this section looks at the various terms introduced into these tests, rather than at the tests itself, it is worth quoting these tests in full in order to set the terms in their context.

For UK work, the test is in *para 9, Sch 45, FA 2013*:

'9(1)  The third automatic UK test is that—
   (a)  P works sufficient hours in the UK, as assessed over a period of 365 days,
   (b)  during that period, there are no significant breaks from UK work,
   (c)  all or part of that period falls within year X,
   (d)  more than 75% of the total number of days in the 365-day period on which P does more than 3 hours' work are days on which P does more than 3 hours' work in the UK, and
   (e)  at least one day which falls in both that period and year X is a day on which P does more than 3 hours' work in the UK.

(2)  Take the following steps to work out, for any given period of 365 days, whether P works "sufficient hours in the UK" as assessed over that period—

*Step 1*

Identify any days in the period on which P does more than 3 hours' work overseas, including ones on which P also does work in the UK on the same day.

The days so identified are referred to as "disregarded days".

*Step 2*

Add up (for all employments held and trades carried on by P) the total number of hours that P works in the UK during the period, but ignoring any hours that P works in the UK on disregarded days.

The result is referred to as P's "net UK hours".

*Step 3*

Subtract from 365—
(a)  the total number of disregarded days, and
(b)  any days that are allowed to be subtracted, in accordance with the rules in paragraph 28 of this Schedule, to take account of periods of leave and gaps between employments.

The result is referred to as the "reference period".

*Step 4*

Divide the reference period by 7. If the answer is more than 1 and is not a whole number, round down to the nearest whole number. If the answer is less than 1, round up to 1.

*Step 5*

Divide P's net UK hours by the number resulting from step 4.

If the answer is 35 or more, P is considered to work "sufficient hours in the UK" as assessed over the 365-day period in question.'

The test for overseas work is very similar, although the law in *para 14, Sch 45, FA 2013* is slightly different, because the hours worked are assessed over a tax year rather than a 365-day period:

'14(1) The third automatic overseas test is that—
   (a)  P works sufficient hours overseas, as assessed over year X,
   (b)  during year X, there are no significant breaks from overseas work,

(c)  the number of days in year X on which P does more than 3 hours' work in the UK is less than 31, and

(d)  the number of days in year X falling within sub-paragraph (2) is less than 91.

(2)  A day falls within this sub-paragraph if—

(a)  it is a day spent by P in the UK, but

(b)  it is not a day that is treated under paragraph 23(4) as a day spent by P in the UK.

(3)  Take the following steps to work out whether P works "sufficient hours overseas" as assessed over year X—

*Step 1*

Identify any days in year X on which P does more than 3 hours' work in the UK, including ones on which P also does work overseas on the same day.

The days so identified are referred to as "disregarded days".

*Step 2*

Add up (for all employments held and trades carried on by P) the total number of hours that P works overseas in year X, but ignoring any hours that P works overseas on disregarded days.

The result is referred to as P's "net overseas hours".

*Step 3*

Subtract from 365 (or 366 if year X includes 29 February)—

(a)  the total number of disregarded days, and

(b)  any days that are allowed to be subtracted, in accordance with the rules in paragraph 28 of this Schedule, to take account of periods of leave and gaps between employments.

The result is referred to as the "reference period".

*Step 4*

Divide the reference period by 7. If the answer is more than 1 and is not a whole number, round down to the nearest whole number. If the answer is less than 1, round up to 1.

*Step 5*

Divide P's net overseas hours by the number resulting from step 4.

If the answer is 35 or more, P is considered to work "sufficient hours overseas" as assessed over year X.'

Both paragraphs specifically exclude holders of relevant jobs on board a vehicle, an aircraft or ship from these parts of the SRT and this is explored further below (see para **3.15**).

In calculating the reference period, disregarded days are subtracted. For the UK test, they are days on which he works more than three hours overseas (regardless of how many UK hours are worked on that day). For the overseas test, they are days on which he works more than three hours in the UK (regardless of how many overseas hours are worked in that day). In addition to subtracting disregarded days, the reference period is also reduced by 'any days that are allowed to be subtracted in accordance with the rules in paragraph 28 of this schedule'. This allows a deduction for 'reasonable amounts' of annual or parenting leave, absence or sick leave where the taxpayer cannot reasonably be expected to work as a result of the illness or injury, and for gaps between employments.

For individuals who normally work particular days of the week, non-working days may only be excluded from the calculation where they are embedded within days of leave, provided that there are at least three consecutive days of leave taken both before and after the non-working day.

In this context, a non-working day is defined as one on which the individual is not expected to work according to his contract of employment or usual pattern of work and does not do so. Whereas one might quite naturally consider the term 'non-working day' in the context of part-time or shift workers, it will also apply to weekends and bank holidays.

What are regarded as reasonable amounts for annual leave or parenting leave is not defined and RDR3 does not offer any kind of numerical guideline as to what might be regarded as reasonable. Rather, it suggests benchmarking the leave taken against what might be expected in the taxpayer's particular line of work:

'1.18   What is a reasonable amount of annual and parenting leave will depend on your situation, including the:
  •      nature of your work
  •      standard number of annual or parenting leave days in the country in which you are working.
1.19   If you are self employed, carrying on a trade, vocation or profession what are reasonable amounts should be assessed against the annual leave or parenting leave an employee doing similar work might reasonably expect to be entitled to.'

As mentioned above, no provision is made to exclude any bank holidays from the calculation (unless they are 'embedded'). In consultation discussions, the view expressed by HM Treasury was that no adjustment was needed in this regard, because the average of 35 hours of work per week required was actually quite low for someone who was in full-time employment and had been set on the assumption that bank holidays would be reducing the average working week overall.

It is possible for a taxpayer to have quite extensive periods of absence from work and still meet the relevant test. This is because there is no prescribed overall limit on the total period of absence allowed (provided that there is no significant break – see para **3.14** below). The calculation for overseas work also allows for more erratic working patterns than may have been accepted in the past as counting as full-time work abroad. For example, in some sectors, such as oil and gas, work will often be done on a days on, days off rota and the averaging calculation will make it possible for employees in this sector to demonstrate an acceptable working pattern whereas in the previous regime it would have been hard to demonstrate that these individuals were working full-time abroad. The position for medical staff, who may also work irregular shifts, is very similar.

**Example 3.4: Roberta**

Roberta is a theatre nurse, specialising in anaesthetics. She is working in Dubai, primarily at one hospital, where she is contracted to work four shifts of eight hours as a regular feature; every other week she also does an extra six-hour shift working in a cosmetic surgery clinic.

Overall her hours will average out to the minimum of 35 hours a week required for her to be regarded as working full-time abroad, assuming that all other conditions are met.

For someone who is working overseas the sufficient hours test is calculated by reference to a particular tax year, with special rules in a split-year of departure (see para **8.09** for more details). So, the reference period applying is never in doubt. However, the law is not specific about when a reference period for UK work is deemed to start and end, so that taxpayers effectively have to calculate 365-day periods on a rolling basis, from the date on which they first start to work in the UK. See para **2.05** for further details.

As soon as such a period is established it will be enough to make the taxpayer UK tax resident in any tax year in which any part of that period falls provided that:

(a)     the 75% test of UK workdays is met; and
(b)     at least one UK workday of that 365-day period falls into the UK tax year concerned.

Arguably, therefore, it is much easier under the SRT to become UK tax resident through working in the UK since the previous regime required an expectation of working in the UK for a minimum period of two years before becoming UK tax resident solely as a result of UK work.

**Gaps between employment**

**[3.13]** There are further complications where there is a change of employment in the reference period. The sufficient hours calculation can be applied across consecutive jobs and not simply across those that are held concurrently. Where there is a gap in working between the two employments, *para 28(8), Sch 45, FA 2013* provides that the reference period is reduced by the number of days in the gap. Assuming that there is no significant break between employments, a gap of up to 15 days between employments may be deducted from the reference period.

If the gap lasts for more than 15 days, only 15 days may be deducted. If there is more than one change of employment, the maximum number of gap days that may be deducted (per tax year or 365-day period as the case may be) is 30 days in total (*para 28(9), Sch 45, FA 2013*).

The legislation refers only to employment and HMRC guidance makes it clear that the provisions about gaps do not apply to the self employed:

'1.13 The provisions about gaps between employments do not apply if you are self-employed; you cannot make deductions from the relevant period for gaps between self-employed work periods.'

For the sufficient hours calculation for overseas work, if the gap spans the end of the tax year, the part of the gap that falls within the tax year may be deducted subject to the normal conditions:

'1.11  . . . If the gap spans the end of the tax year you may subtract from your reference period the part of the gap that falls within the tax year, subject to the other conditions above.'

For the full-time working in the UK test, the reference period is a rolling 365-day period and so gaps between employments will be considered across that 365-day period rather than in relation to tax years.

### Example 3.5: More about Roberta

Roberta originally left the UK on 31 May 2015. After 15 months of working in Dubai she decides to end her contract (with effect from 31 August 2016) and take a four-week break from work. She has decided to tour Australia as an extended holiday and three weeks into this tour she is offered a full-time role at a hospital in Melbourne on an open-ended contract. The job will start at the end of her four weeks off on 28 September 2016. Her contracted hours will be for four long day shifts of ten hours every week, but with the possibility of overtime as well.

Looking at her role in Dubai alone, Roberta will not be regarded as full-time working abroad because her employment abroad has not encompassed a complete UK tax year and so the sufficient hours test could not be met. However, as the break between jobs is not 'significant' (see para **3.14** below), in principle she will be able to treat the employments as continuous.

In addition, in calculating whether she has worked sufficient hours, Roberta may ignore 15 days of her 27-day break. If we consider the whole of the 2016/17 tax year as the reference period, the position breaks down as follows:

6 April – 31 August 2016 11 weeks @ 32 hours and 10 weeks @ 38 hours

28 September 2016 – 5 April 2017: 27 weeks @ 40 hours and 1 day (10 hours).

Roberta took a one-week holiday from her Dubai contract (in one of her 32-hour weeks) and two weeks' holiday after starting work at Melbourne (there are no non-working days embedded within a block of leave).

Therefore, total hours worked in 2015/16 are:

| | |
|---|---:|
| 10 weeks @ 32 hours | 320 |
| 10 weeks @ 38 hours | 380 |
| 25 weeks @ 40 hours | 1000 |
| 1 day @ 10 hours | 10 |
| | 1710 |

The reference period is 338 days (365 days – 15-day gap – 3 weeks' holiday (12 days)).

Divide reference period by 7 = 48 weeks

Sufficient hours test is 1710/48 = 36.625 hours.

Therefore even without taking any overtime into account, Roberta will meet the sufficient hours test and is working full-time abroad in 2016/17.

HMRC's guidance also covers the position where there is a change of employment and in para 1.12 provides a helpful example of the calculation where there is more than one change of employment to be considered in the year.

'Example 1

Jack is calculating his reference period and has two gaps between employments within the 365-day period he is considering.

The first gap was of 21 days and the second one was of five days. Jack does not work at all in either gap. As the first gap exceeded the maximum number of days for a single gap, Jack can only subtract 15 days from his reference period in relation to this gap between employments. He can subtract the full five days of the second gap.

Jack therefore subtracts a total of 20 days for gaps between employments from his 365-day period under Step 3 of the sufficient hours calculation.'

HMRC's guidance (para 1.21) provides an example illustrating the 'embedded leave' and 'gaps between employments' principles:

'Example 3

MayLing is considering whether she meets the third automatic overseas test in respect of her work in Italy in the last tax year. She worked for her first employer there for an average of eight hours a day, five days a week, between 6 April and 23 August (20 weeks). During that period, she took nine days annual leave (there were no embedded non-working days); consequently MayLing had worked for 18 full weeks and for only one day in another week. She ceased that employment and took a break of 30 days to tour around Italy.

She then took up a new employment, again in Italy, between 23 September and 5 April (27 weeks and six days – amounting to 28 working weeks). During that period, she worked for nine hours and 30 minutes from Monday to Thursday and for four hours on a Friday. She took:

- five days of annual leave; for three weeks she only worked three long days and a short day, and for one week she worked two long days and a short day, reducing her number of full working weeks by five weeks
- 10 days of annual leave, with two embedded non-working days (the Saturday and Sunday in the middle of this two-week period), reducing her number of full working weeks by two
- five days, continuous, sick leave (with no embedded non-working days), reducing her number of full working weeks by one.

She therefore worked for only 20 full working weeks in this part of the year. MayLing spends no time in the UK in the tax year.

*Step 1*

MayLing has no disregarded days.

*Step 2*

Net overseas hours:

Employer 1: 18 weeks and one day at (5 days x 8 hours) = 728 hours

Employer 2: 20 weeks at ((4 days x 9.5 hours) + 4 hours) = 840 hours

3 weeks at ((3 days x 9.5 hours) + 4 hours) = 97.5 hours

1 week at ((2 days x 9.5 hours) + 4 hours) = 23 hours

Total net overseas hours: = 728+840+97.5+23 = 1688.5 hours.

*Step 3*

Reference period:

Subtract from 365 days

Disregarded days = 0 days

Other days that can be deducted:

- 9 days leave Employer 1
- 15 days leave Employer 2
- 2 embedded days
- 5 sick days

= 9+15+2+5 = 31 days

Gap between employments = 15 days (total gap 30 days but the amount deducted is limited to 15 days)

Reference period is: 365-31-15 = 319 days.

*Step 4*

Divide reference period by 7 = 319÷7= 45.57 which is rounded down to 45.

*Step 5*

Divide net overseas hours by figure at Step 4 = 1688.5÷45= 37.52.

MayLing meets the sufficient hours test. She will need to consider whether she meets all other parts of the third automatic overseas test, in particular that the number of days spent in the UK in the tax year is less than 91.'

## Significant breaks

**[3.14]** *Paragraph 29, Sch 45, FA 2013* sets out the test for a significant break from either UK or overseas work and although the test is set out separately for each case it is essentially the same test. A significant break is a period of at least 31 days on none of which days the individual does more than three hours' work. If it is a period of UK work that is under consideration, the 'more than three hours' work' must be done in the UK to stop the period becoming a significant break and for a period of overseas work it must be done overseas. There is a specific exclusion from the three-hour test for annual leave, sick leave and parenting leave.

It should be noted that a significant break could occur between two separate employments or as a period in one continuing employment.

Frequently, when employees leave employment, they will do so from a particular date, but take a break between jobs and employers will pay out any accrued holiday. Under the SRT, employees may actually achieve exactly the same result from their personal point of view by deferring the date at which the employment ceases and taking paid holiday to give themselves the desired break. In most sets of circumstances the tax outcome will be identical, but if the employee is trying to establish a pattern of full-time work across two jobs, the second alternative, which minimises the period between the two employments, may be preferable.

**Example 3.6: Michael**

> Michael left the UK on an assignment for his employer on 1 July 2014. After working for that employer in Dubai for a year, Michael was offered and accepted a role with a competitor in Singapore. Originally, he had intended to take a couple of months between roles, but his former employer kept him on contract on garden leave for six months until 28 February 2016. He then decided to take 14 days' holiday and spend two weeks moving and settling in, starting his new job in Singapore on 1 April 2016.

Michael's original employment would not meet the full tax year test on its own for 2015/16, but combined with his new employment it could do so. So the question to be considered is whether the period from the date on which he ceases to work actively until he takes up his new job will be a significant break in the two employments considered together. Of the 31 days in March, 15 days may be deducted as a gap within *para 28(9)(a), Sch 45, FA 2013*, leaving a balance of the 16 days, which would not by itself constitute a significant break. The difficulty is that it is unclear whether he can be said to be 'working' for the six months before that when on garden leave and if so, where he was working. HMRC guidance suggests that garden leave would count as work. See RDR3, para 3.13, quoted above.

However, this is not enough for the significant break test, with its requirement to work more than three hours on a day. Although holiday, sick leave and parenting leave are specifically removed from the reference period calculation, there is no similar removal of periods spent on garden leave. Although garden leave is treated as 'time spent working', there is no concept of deemed duties within the SRT definition of work, nor where any deemed duties might be treated as performed. If deemed duties are in point, presumably HMRC would also accept that if the employee stayed in the country where he had been employed this would also be the location of the deemed duties, but the position is uncertain to say the least.

It would appear therefore that garden leave would be included within the definition of 'work' but, if as is usual, no actual work is done on these days, garden leave of 31 days or more has the potential to count as a significant break and this period will also work to the disadvantage of the taxpayer in the relevant period calculation. It is understood that HMRC's current practice in this regard is to treat days spent on garden leave in the same way as holiday and not regard them as constituting a significant break, but it is unfortunate that HMRC's guidance does not actually state this. Employers in industries where a period of garden leave is the norm may want to revisit their current practice to see if there is any alternative way in which they can actively use employees who have given notice for that notice period.

## Relevant jobs on board vehicles, aircraft and ships

**[3.15]** A taxpayer who has a 'relevant job' (see below) is excluded from the full-time UK and overseas working tests (*para 9(3)* and *para 14(4), Sch 45, FA 2013*). There are also special rules for the way the work tie for the sufficient ties test is applied to such taxpayers (*para 36, Sch 45, FA 2013*). The relevant job rules were introduced into the SRT as a whole at a relatively late stage because of concerns about the distorting effect that the working patterns of such individuals might have in applying tests based around a more typical working pattern. The statutory definition is in *para 30, Sch 45, FA 2013*:

'30(1) P has a "relevant" job on board a vehicle, aircraft or ship if condition A and condition B are met.
(2)  Condition A is that P either—
   (a)  holds an employment, the duties of which consist of duties to be performed on board a vehicle, aircraft or ship while it is travelling, or
   (b)  carries on a trade, the activities of which consist of work to be done or services to be provided on board a vehicle, aircraft or ship while it is travelling.
(3)  Condition B is that substantially all of the trips made in performing those duties or carrying on those activities are ones that involve crossing an international boundary at sea, in the air or on land (referred to as "cross-border trips").
(4)  Sub-paragraph (2)(b) is not satisfied unless, in order to do the work or provide the services, P has to be present (in person) on board the vehicle, aircraft or ship while it is travelling.
(5)  Duties or activities of a purely incidental nature are to be ignored in deciding whether the duties of an employment or the activities of a trade consist of duties or activities of a kind described in sub-paragraph (2)(a) or (b).'

This aspect of the SRT has a clearly defined target group and in most cases individuals will know immediately whether or not they fall into the category. Commonly it will cover aircrew, seafarers (including entertainers on cruise ships) and cross-border lorry drivers.

HMRC guidance explains that 'substantially' for the purpose of *para 30(3)* will typically mean that 80% or more of the individual's total business trips must be cross-border:

'3.26 Examples of relevant jobs may include pilots, airline cabin crew, cross-channel ferry staff, mariners, fishermen and lorry drivers where substantially all of the trips are cross-border trips. Although each case will turn on its own facts, you are likely to be considered to have a relevant job if 80% or more of your trips involve cross-border trips.'

The legislation provides that incidental duties are ignored in determining whether an individual has a relevant job. HMRC's guidance gives an example of incidental duties in para 3.27:

'3.27 In deciding whether or not you fall within one of the categories of relevant job you should ignore duties or activities of a purely incidental nature. For instance, where a pilot whose job consists of making long haul international flights attends a meeting in the UK to hear an announcement about the airline's restructuring, the duties spent at the meeting are incidental to the duties of flying the plane and so can be ignored.'

The guidance also highlights (in para 3.28) that working on a journey will not of itself make you a holder of a relevant job if you are just catching up on emails or some other regular work while travelling.

There is no special requirement in *para 30, Sch 45, FA 2013* that the cross-border travel involves the UK. However, the law in *paragraphs 9(3)(a)* and *14(4)(a)* which excludes people with relevant jobs from the working full time in the UK and overseas tests, only applies if at least six of the cross-border trips in the year end in or begin in the UK or both. Although such individuals cannot apply the full time work tests, they will still use the other automatic tests or the sufficient ties tests to determine their residence status. Holding a relevant job also has implications for how the UK work tie applies under the sufficient ties test. These are considered further in para **3.19** below.

## The ties of the 'sufficient ties' test

**[3.16]** As explained in CHAPTER 2, the 'sufficient ties' test considers a series of ties that the taxpayer may have with the UK and combines those ties with days spent in the UK to determine whether or not he should be UK tax resident for the year. The test itself is not considered in any detail here, but the underlying definitions are explored below.

There are five ties that may potentially apply under the test: a family tie, an accommodation tie, a workday tie, a 90-day tie and a country tie. These are considered below in turn.

### Family tie

**[3.17]** The definition of a 'family tie' is in *paras 32* and *33, Sch 45, FA 2013*:

'32

(1)    P has a family tie for year X if –

    (a)    in year X, a relevant relationship exists at any time between P and another person, and

    (b)    that other person is someone who is resident in the UK for year X.

(2)    A relevant relationship exists at any time between P and another person if at the time –

    (a)    P and the other person are husband and wife or civil partners and, in either case, are not separated,

    (b)    P and the other person are living together as husband and wife or, if they are of the same sex, as if they were civil partners, or

    (c)    the other person is a child of P's and is under the age of 18

(3)    P does not have a family tie for year X by virtue of sub-paragraph (2)(c) if P sees the child in the UK on fewer than 61 days (in total) in –

(a)    year X, or

(b)    if the child turns 18 during year X, the part of year X before the day on which the child turns 18.

(4)    A day counts as a day on which P sees the child if P sees the child in person for all or part of the day.

(5)    "Separated" means separated –

(a)    under an order of a court of competent jurisdiction,

(b)    by deed of separation, or

(c)    in circumstances where the separation is likely to be permanent.

33

(1)    This paragraph applies in deciding for the purposes (only) of paragraph 32(1)(b) whether a person with whom P has a relevant relationship (a "family member") is someone who is resident in the UK for year X.

(2)    A family tie based on the fact that a family member has, by the same token, a relevant relationship with P is to be disregarded in deciding whether that family member is someone who is resident in the UK for year X.

(3)    A family member falling within sub-paragraph (4) is to be treated as being not resident in the UK for year X if the number of days that he or she spends in the UK in the part of year X outside term-time is less than 21.

(4)    A family member falls within this sub-paragraph if he or she –

(a)    is a child of P's who is under the age of 18,

(b)    is in full-time education in the UK at any time in year X, and

(c)    is resident in the UK for year X but would not be so resident if the time spent in full-time education in the UK in that year were disregarded.

(5)    In sub-paragraph (4) –

(a)    references to full-time education in the UK are to full-time education at a university, college, school or other educational establishment in the UK, and

(b)    the reference to the time spent in full-time education in the UK is to the time spent there during term-time.

(6)    For the purposes of this paragraph, half-term breaks and other breaks when teaching is not provided during a term are considered to form part of "term-time".'

It is worth noting that a person can have more than one relevant relationship (eg spouse and children) but will still only have one family tie and so one tie for the purposes of the sufficient ties test.

The basic definition of a spouse or civil partner and/or a minor child constituting a family tie is straightforward enough, but as usual the devil is in the detail. For example, it may be difficult in these circumstances to determine what is meant by 'living together'. RDR3 refers the user to guidance set out in the Tax Credits Manual (TCTM). Although lengthy, this guidance gives no hard and fast rule on when you might be regarded as living together if you are living in separate households. The TCTM considers a number of 'sign-posts' at TCTM09341 which should be considered in determining whether a couple are 'living together':

'These "signposts" are the only indicators to help form a sustainable view of whether two people are living together as husband and wife or as civil partners for the purposes of a tax credits claim. The weight and worth of each indicator will vary from relationship to relationship and an officer of HMRC should conclude their decision on the balance of evidence, based on all the facts.

The signposts include:

- living in the same household TCTM09342
- stability of the relationship TCTM09343
- financial support TCTM09344
- sexual relationship TCTM09345
- dependent children TCTM09346
- public acknowledgement TCTM09347

For information regarding absences from the home and temporary absences from the UK see TCTM09360.'

This is especially difficult to consider where, by definition, individuals are often living in a different country from their partner. This is also touched on in the TCTM (at TCTM09360):

'Short-term absences from the home, whether occasional or regular, do not necessarily mean that two people should not be regarded as living together as a married couple (LTAMC) or as civil partners (LTACP). Absences could be due to:

- work (for example an oil rig worker or long distance lorry driver)
- being a hospital in-patient
- a holiday
- a visit to relatives
- training or education
- a custodial sentence of less than 52 weeks
- a forces posting

This list is not exhaustive.

The common feature of the reasons for the absence from the home listed above is their temporary nature (for temporary absences from the UK – see below; for claims from couples where only one partner is in the UK – see TCTM09370).

There is no specific period of time after which a couple's absence from one another ceases to be temporary, factors to be considered include:

- the length of the absence
- how much longer the absence is expected to last
- to what extent the partners have maintained contact
- the couple's future intentions

An absence from the UK can only be regarded as temporary if, at its start, it is expected to last for no more than 52 weeks.'

The additional difficulties in cases where a couple are living in separate countries is perhaps best illustrated by considering an example:

### Example 3.7: Jeremy

Jeremy is unmarried, but does have a significant other, whom he describes as his partner, and he generally spends his weekends with her at her home in Leicestershire. During the week he works in London and lives at his own flat there. His employer asks him to take up a temporary role in their Paris office that will last for at least two years. Jeremy is not expected to meet the tests for full-time working abroad as he will retain responsibility for a project in London that will require him to return frequently. So he needs to consider the sufficient ties test.

Will his partner be a family tie for him? It would appear so despite Jeremy's role in Paris and if advising him for the purpose of not being UK tax resident under the sufficient ties test this would certainly be the safer assumption. However, the position is not certain, because there are no parameters set on how much time you have to live with someone to be 'living together'. It may also be very difficult to identify circumstances in which couples are living together if they also maintain separate households and do not regard themselves as living together as spouses or civil partners.

When the family tie was first devised, there was a potentially circular element to the test. For example, if you are looking at a married couple and trying to determine whether either of them counts as a UK tie for the other you have to know whether the other spouse is or is not UK tax resident, which may in itself depend on the first spouse being UK resident and a family tie.

In this scenario, *para 33(2), Sch 45, FA 2013* provides that any such relationship can be ignored so that the residence position of the two spouses can be considered entirely independently.

HMRC's example C1 in Annex C illustrates the point:

'George and his wife Mary both spend 140 days in the UK (a fewer number of days than the 183 day threshold in the automatic residence test). Neither of them was resident in any of the three previous tax years. Under the sufficient UK ties test of the SRT they will each be resident if they have two or more UK ties.

Both George and Mary have an *accommodation tie*. They also have a relevant relationship to each other because they are man and wife. Therefore, if they have a family tie they will both be regarded as resident in the UK. However, because the family tie only exists because of their relevant relationship, the tie can be ignored.

As each of them now only has one UK tie neither of them is UK resident.'

Where children are concerned we return to the need to count days both in terms of determining whether they are resident in the UK for the purpose of the family tie, and in terms of determining whether the time spent with them creates a family tie. There is a helpful exclusion for a child who is in the UK solely for full-time education. If the child spends fewer than 21 days in the UK outside term time he will be treated as non-resident for this element of the test and so will not create a family tie for his parents. Even if the child does spend sufficient time during school holidays to be regarded as UK tax resident, the parent may still avoid having a family tie by limiting the time that they spend with the child in the UK to a maximum of 60 days per UK tax year (although in this context any part of a day will count as a day).

#### Example 3.8: Sarah

Sarah has recently married her second husband, Jonathan, who has lived in France for a number of years and she has decided to move there to join him. Her daughter,

Hannah, is 16 years old and remains at boarding school in the UK, dividing her holiday time between her friends in the UK and her mother in France. Provided Sarah is careful to limit her time spent in the UK with Hannah, she should not represent a family tie for Sarah.

In an early draft of the law, term time excluded all holidays, so that children who stayed in the UK for half-term breaks could easily exceed the 21-day limit. The definition of term time was revised to include this type of short interim break during the consultation process (now in *para 33(6), Sch 45, FA 2013*) and there is a specific example in HMRC's guidance covering this aspect:

'2.8 . . . You should treat half-term breaks, and other breaks when teaching is not provided (for example inset days) during a term, as part of term-time.

**Example 13**

Yok Lin attends a boarding school in the UK. Term dates are:

Saturday 6 April to Friday 5 July

Sunday 3 September to Friday 15 December

Sunday 7 January to Friday 23 March

Sunday 15 April to Friday 6 July

She remains in the UK for the half terms, staying with various friends and relatives but returns to the family home in Thailand during the Christmas and Easter holidays. She spends two weeks of the summer break with her friends but travels home to Thailand on 21 July.

As Yok Lin is only in the UK for 14 days outside of term time, her parents will not have a family tie with Yok Lin for the purposes of SRT.'

Finally, when considering who is a child for the purposes of this test, HMRC guidance (Annex C, paragraph C15) provides that a child means a natural child or adopted child. The term does not include a stepchild unless adopted.

## Accommodation tie

**[3.18]** The accommodation tie is intended as a test that may be satisfied more easily than the 'home' test and consequently the definition is wider and the accommodation tie itself may be met more easily. The law is in *para 34, Sch 45, FA 2013*:

'34(1)P has an accommodation tie for year X if –

    (a)    P has a place to live in the UK,

    (b)    that place is available to P during year X for a continuous period of at least 91 days, and

    (c)    P spends at least one night at that place in that year.

(2)    If there is a gap of fewer than 16 days between periods in year X when a particular place is available to P, that place is to be treated as continuing to be available to P during the gap.

(3)    P is considered to have a "place to live" in the UK if –

    (a)    P's home or at least one of P's homes (if P has more than one) is in the UK, or

(b)    P has a holiday home or temporary retreat (or something similar) in the UK, or

(c)    accommodation is otherwise available to P where P can live when P is in the UK.

(4)    Accommodation may be "available" to P even if P holds no estate or interest in it and even if P has no legal right to occupy it.

(5)    If the accommodation is the home of a close relative of P's, sub-paragraph (1)(c) has effect as if for "at least one night" there were substituted "a total of at least 16 nights".

(6)    A "close relative" is –

(a)    a parent or grandparent,

(b)    a brother or sister,

(c)    a child aged 18 or over, or

(d)    a grandchild aged 18 or over,

in each case, including by blood or half-blood or by marriage or civil partnership.'

This section considers both the meaning of the term 'accommodation' and the application of the test; namely, the availability and use of accommodation. HMRC comment extensively on both of these in their guidance RDR3 in Annex A.

As noted above, the term 'accommodation' is intended to have a wider meaning than the term 'home'. HMRC comment in Annex A:

'A27    The main difference between the term "home" for SRT purposes and available accommodation is that accommodation can be transient and does not require the degree of stability or permanence that a home does.'

The term thus includes a holiday home, a temporary retreat or similar. There is no requirement for the individual to have any legal right to occupy the accommodation. The home of an individual's parents or friends can therefore be accommodation, as can a hotel room. These are all considered below.

It is not enough for there to be accommodation available; it must be available for a continuous period of 91 days and the individual must actually use it if the accommodation is to be a tie for the purposes of the sufficient ties test.

The legislation refers to a continuous period of 91 days and HMRC guidance is that the taxpayer must be able to use it or it must be at their disposal at all times throughout the period (RDR3, para A33). This is subject to a gap of fewer than 16 days. If there is such a gap in availability, it is ignored. This will be particularly relevant for property owned by relatives and friends. Para A33 goes on to say:

'A33    . . . If a relative were to make their home available to you casually, for a social visit, say, it will not mean that the accommodation would be regarded as being available to you. However, if it is available to you for a continuous period of 91 days and you use it casually, it will be a tie.

A34    Similarly, a casual offer from a friend to "stay in my spare room any time" will not constitute an accommodation tie unless your friend really is prepared to put you up for 91 days at a time (whether he actually does so or not).'

Some taxpayers with very close friends who have spare rooms may therefore need to be careful.

A taxpayer may also have an accommodation tie from employer-provided accommodation or by staying in a hotel on a reasonably regular basis. It is very common, for example, for an employer to have a preferred hotel, chosen because of its proximity to the workplace and because it offers a discounted rate to the employer's staff. An employee who visits head office frequently, if irregularly, may have an accommodation tie on this basis.

**Example 3.9: Pierre**

Pierre is asked to work on a temporary project in London, where he will be required to visit site for approximately two days every fortnight over the course of the 2016/17 UK tax year. He is expecting to have two days in London on each visit, travelling by Eurostar and will spend the middle night at the same hotel in London each time. He has decided that he will always be in London Wednesday into Thursday as this will make it easier to juggle his family commitments in France.

Assuming that he carries out his plans, Pierre may not expect that he would have an accommodation tie. However, on a strict reading of the legislation, the hotel is likely to be an accommodation tie for Pierre. This is because gaps of fewer than 16 days are ignored in deciding whether accommodation is available continuously throughout a 91-day period. Pierre may wish to make some modification to his plans to avoid dispute.

HMRC's guidance here offers little comfort, because it does not consider very short, regular visits of this nature:

'A42. Short stays at hotels and guesthouses will not usually be considered to be an accommodation tie. However, if an individual books a room in the same hotel or guesthouse (and does not cancel those bookings) for at least 91 days continuously in a tax year, bearing in mind that short gaps may be discounted, it will be an accommodation tie. (See example A17)'

Example A17 actually considers a rather different situation, where an individual is staying at a hotel over a more extended period:

'Example A17

Hyo lives and works in Poland. He is his company's European sales manager. This year he will be responsible for launching a new product in the UK and will need to spend time here. His sales force are on the road the last week of every month so he books a room in the same hotel for the first three weeks of June, July, August, and September.

Hyo has an accommodation tie this year.'

On a practical level anyone coming to the UK from a Treaty country in a situation like either Pierre or Hyo, would be likely to remain Treaty resident in the other country and so unlikely to care whether he establishes an accommodation tie in the UK. However, these examples illustrate the potential consequence of even relatively short-term and minor working commitments in the UK. In respect of any property which the taxpayer owns, rents or leases, the requirement to spend at least one night in it during the tax year is a welcome condition. It means for example that the taxpayer need not sell the property, give up the lease etc, on leaving the UK in order for him to avoid an accommodation tie for the year, but simply not use it during the tax year. One might expect that a taxpayer who is renting out their property while overseas would be unlikely to have available accommodation although presumably they would need to be careful if there were periods of 91 days or more between lets. It is therefore perhaps surprising that HMRC actually comment in their guidance:

> 'A40  Accommodation owned by an individual but which they have wholly let out commercially would not be considered as available to live in unless they retained the right to use the property or part of the property.'

Indeed the guidance provides the example of Simone (Example A15) who has a holiday home in the UK, usually let out but kept free for her use for three months in the summer.

> 'Example A15
>
> Simone has lived and worked in France all her life. She and her brother purchased a cottage in the UK several years ago as a holiday home. The cottage is let for most of the year but June, July and August are always kept free so that Simone or her brother can stay there. There is sufficient accommodation in the cottage to ensure that Simone is able to stay there, even when her brother and his family are there also.
>
> Simone spent two weeks in the cottage last year and three weeks this year. Simone has an accommodation tie both last year and this year.'

Many non-domiciled individuals have typically used UK properties owned through non-UK structures (eg trusts and companies). It is likely that such a property would be treated as 'available' unless steps were taken such as excluding the individual from benefit from the trust. To avoid an accommodation tie, such individuals are likely to have to avoid spending a night at the property.

The legislation makes it clear that the taxpayer does not have to own or have any legal entitlement to occupy the property (*para 34(4), Sch 45, FA 2013*). In this context, it is clear that the legislators particularly have in mind that property owned by a close relative (eg parent) may be available accommodation, presumably on the basis that close relatives are likely to be willing to put up the taxpayer whenever he requests and so the 91 continuous day period will be met. However, the requirement to spend at least 16 nights in the home of a close relative (*para 34(5), Sch 45, FA 2013*) is relatively helpful. Consider, for example, HMRC example A18, Ravi:

> 'Example A18
>
> Ravi can stay with his grandparents whenever he is in the UK. They will put him up for more than 91 days if he wishes. He usually comes from India every year to visit them and stays with them for the whole summer.
>
> Last year Ravi spent only the first two weeks with his grandparents then went on a one-off visit to his uncle (who would not be regarded as a close relative for the purposes of the SRT) for two months before returning home. So although accommodation at his grandparents, who are regarded as close relatives, was available for more than 91 days, Ravi stayed with his grandparents for only 14 days and therefore had no accommodation tie.
>
> This year Ravi spent the whole summer with his grandparents.
>
> This year Ravi has an accommodation tie.'

One year Ravi stays two weeks – no accommodation tie; the following year he stays 'the whole summer' and has an accommodation tie.

However, the definition of 'close relative' for the 16 night test is fairly limited. The one night test applies to other relatives (eg uncles) and also to friends. Presumably it was felt that the period of 91 continuous days was less likely to be met in these circumstances.

The definition of accommodation is very broad and individuals and advisers will need to scrutinise arrangements very carefully to ensure that taxpayers do not inadvertently acquire an accommodation tie.

## Work tie

**[3.19]** The work tie is relatively straightforward as, for most people, it will be a question of whether at least three hours' work has been performed in the UK on at least 40 days in the tax year. The position is, however, more complex for holders of 'relevant jobs'. The law is set out in *paras 35–36, Sch 45, FA 2013*:

'35(1)P has a work tie for year X if P works in the UK for at least 40 days (whether continuously or intermittently) in year X.

(2) For these purposes, P works in the UK for a day if P does more than 3 hours' work in the UK on that day.'

Unlike the tests that apply for full-time working abroad and full-time working in the UK, it is the total of UK workdays in a tax year rather than the overall working pattern that is determinative.

The meaning of 'work', the test to determine when work is done 'in the UK', and the challenge of demonstrating how many hours of work have been done, have all been considered earlier (see para **3.09**). For many taxpayers in employment or self-employment it may be a case of accepting that each day spent in the UK is a workday unless they can clearly demonstrate that no or little work has been done.

There are special rules for holders of 'relevant jobs' on board a vehicle, aircraft or ship, and these are set out in *para 36, Sch 45, FA 2013*.

'36(1)This paragraph applies for the purposes of paragraph 35.

(2) It applies in cases where P has a relevant job on board a vehicle, aircraft or ship.

(3) When making a cross-border trip as part of that job–

    (a) if the trip begins in the UK, P is assumed to do more than 3 hours' work in the UK on the day on which it begins,

    (b) if the trip ends in the UK, P is assumed to do fewer than 3 hours' work in the UK on the day on which it ends.

(4) Those assumptions apply regardless of how late in the day the trip begins or ends (even if it begins or ends just before midnight).

(5) For the purposes of sub-paragraph (3)(a), it does not matter whether the trip ends on that same day.

(6) A day that falls within both paragraph (a) and paragraph (b) of subparagraph (3) is to be treated as if it fell only within paragraph (a).

(7) In the case of a cross-border trip to or from the UK that is undertaken in stages–

    (a) the day on which the trip begins or, as the case may be, ends is the day on which the stage of the trip that involves crossing the UK border begins or ends, and

    (b) accordingly, any day on which a stage is undertaken by P solely within the UK must (if it lasts for more than 3 hours) be counted separately as a day on which P does more than 3 hours' work in the UK.'

The test applied for holders of relevant jobs is not an unreasonable one in that days of departure are deemed UK workdays, but days of return are not. So each out and back journey should count as one UK workday only, but the day of return will still count as a UK workday if the taxpayer makes another cross-border trip, leaving the UK, on the same day.

Any day which does not involve a cross-border trip for these taxpayers will be treated as a UK workday if more than three hours' work is done in the UK.

Where a journey involves several days of transit, each must be considered separately in order to determine whether or not it counts as a UK workday. HMRC's guidance has a number of examples, the fullest of which is reproduced below:

'3.36. If you undertake a cross-border trip in a series of stages over a number of days, each day will be treated separately for the purposes of determining which days you spent working in the UK.

**Example 30**

Sally is employed by a haulage company to transport fresh produce to Spain. On day one she travels from Birmingham to Dover (taking more than three hours), on day two she travels from Dover to Toulouse, and on day three she completes her journey in Barcelona.

On day one Sally does not make a cross-border trip, but as she works in the UK for more than three hours she has a UK work day for the purposes of the work tie.

On day two she made a cross-border trip starting in the UK. Sally will have another UK work day for the purposes of the work tie.

On day three, Sally has not crossed the UK border and nor is it a day on which she has worked for more than three hours in the UK, so it will not be a UK work day for the purposes of the work tie.'

The concerns noted above about the burden of proof and how the taxpayer can prove he has worked no more than three hours remain true here, although the deeming provisions mean that days of departure and arrival for holders of relevant jobs will typically be outside the three hours test.

## 90-day tie

[**3.20**] The 90-day tie tests days spent in the UK in either or both of the preceding two tax years. The relevant law is in *para 37, Sch 45, FA 2013*:

'37    P has a 90-day tie for year X if P has spent more than 90 days in the UK in–
    (a)    the tax year preceding year X,
    (b)    the tax year preceding that tax year, or
    (c)    each of those tax years separately.'

As noted in **CHAPTER 2** above, this does feel like double counting to some degree as anyone who has been tax resident in the previous two UK tax years is also at risk of meeting this tie, which makes the sufficient ties test especially adhesive for someone who has previously been UK tax resident.

## *Country tie*

**[3.21]** The country tie only applies to someone who was tax resident in the UK for one or more of the three preceding UK tax years (*para 31(2), Sch 45, FA 2013*).

The law covering the country tie itself is in *para 38, Sch 45, FA 2013*:

'38(1) P has a country tie for year X if the country in which P meets the midnight test for the greatest number of days in year X is the UK.

(2)    If –

    (a)    P meets the midnight test for the same number of days in year X in two or more countries, and

    (b)    that number is the greatest number of days for which P meets the midnight test in any country in year X,
        P has a country tie for year X if one of those countries is the UK.

(3)    P meets the "midnight test" in a country for a day if P is present in that country at the end of that day.'

For this test, it is not enough for the taxpayer simply to divide his year into UK days and non-UK days; instead he needs to keep a record of which country he is in at midnight on each day. It may be very difficult for some individuals to do this, especially if they travel frequently and across different time zones. Added complications may occur if they need to count days for the purpose of another country's residency rules and the measure of 'days' is different. They are then required to keep several different versions of the same data.

HMRC guidance adds little, except to say (at para 2.18):

'For the purpose of this SRT test presence at midnight in any state, territory or canton into which a country is subdivided is regarded as presence at midnight in that country.'

### Example 3.10: more about Sophie

Consider Sophie (Example 3.1 above) again in the light of the various ties tests that we have now considered. As noted above, Sophie has been living and working in France, but will not be regarded as working full-time abroad because of her UK workdays (35 in the tax year). She has had 40 actual UK days (20 Saturdays and 20 workdays) plus five extra deemed days under the deeming rules.

If we consider how the 'sufficient ties' test relates to her, it is not good news. Her husband will be a family tie, their home is likely to be an accommodation tie if she has stayed there at all and she is also likely to meet the 90-day test having been resident in the UK in the previous three tax years. So, she can have at most 45 days in the UK in the tax year without becoming UK tax resident and we know that even as at 14 February she was already at that limit.

We do not know enough about her days in France and elsewhere to estimate whether or not she may also have a country tie to the UK and five extra UK workdays before the end of the tax year would also give her a UK work tie. Either of these additional ties would make her UK resident on the number of days she has already spent here. The way the different ties are interconnected could make it very difficult for her to avoid UK tax residence.

## Conclusion

**[3.22]** The chapter has looked at the definitions used in the SRT in detail and highlighted some of the complications that are likely to arise in practice. The chapters that follow consider the practical application of the test to taxpayers coming to and leaving the UK.

# Chapter 4

# Leaving the UK: employees, the self-employed and their partners

## Introduction

**[4.01]** CHAPTERS **4** and **5** consider the residence position of individuals leaving the UK. This chapter considers those individuals who leave the UK to take up full-time employment or self-employment abroad. It also covers the practice for accompanying spouses and partners. CHAPTER **5** considers all other departing taxpayers, including those leaving for full-time voluntary work abroad.

This chapter considers the full cycle; year of departure, intervening years of non-residence and year of return and compares and contrasts the SRT position with that of the previous regime. It should be noted that although earlier drafts of the SRT legislation referred to full-time working abroad, the law is phrased in terms of a taxpayer working sufficient hours overseas over a tax year. The term 'full-time working abroad' has been retained as a familiar, convenient shorthand used by practitioners and HMRC alike.

Brief notes on the previous regime are included, even though we are now several years into the SRT, as this sets the scene for the detail of the SRT.

## Year of departure

**[4.02]** The first step is to consider how and when the individual becomes non-UK resident for tax purposes.

Under the previous regime, by concession and HMRC practice, it was possible to split the tax year of departure (at least for income tax purposes) into resident and non-resident periods when an individual left the UK for full-time work overseas. In order to qualify for this treatment, both the employment contract and the full-time work normally had to last beyond the end of the following tax year and the individual had to restrict his days in the UK in the year of departure and subsequent years. In some cases, HMRC would accept that separate employments with a short break in between could be regarded as continuous for the full-time work test. In addition, it was possible for an individual to leave the UK for full-time employment abroad and have a change in circumstance because the employment ceased earlier than was expected, but to remain non-resident for other reasons, because, for example, he had no on-going links with the UK having no UK accommodation, no UK job and no close family here.

The practice applied in a very similar way for the self-employed, in that it was possible to qualify for split-year and then non-resident treatment if the taxpayer worked outside the UK on a full-time basis, for a period encompassing at least one complete tax year.

Split-year treatment for those leaving for full-time work abroad is also available under the SRT and the relief is now set out in statute, but it works rather differently, typically being revoked if the full-time work does not continue at least until the end of the first full tax year post departure.

### When does non-UK residence begin?

**[4.03]** UK residence has always been assessed on a whole tax year basis and that remains the case under the SRT. In certain circumstances, where an individual is UK resident and meets the criteria of the split-year provisions, he can be taxed largely as though he is non-UK resident for part of the year.

Under the SRT, the legislation providing split-year treatment for those leaving the UK for full-time work overseas (Case 1 of the eight split-year cases) is set out in *para 44, Sch 45, FA 2013*. See also **CHAPTER 8** for a full explanation of the split-year legislation.

In order to obtain split-year treatment under Case 1, the taxpayer must:

- have been resident in the UK for all or part of the previous UK tax year;
- have at least one period in the year for which the overseas work criteria are met and which begins with a day on which more than three hours' work is done overseas and runs to the end of the tax year;
- stay within particular limits in terms of the workdays and total days he spends in the UK in the period from the day on which his overseas work starts through until the end of the UK tax year concerned (this is explained below); and
- be not resident in the UK for the following UK tax year by virtue of meeting the third automatic overseas test (ie full time working abroad test) for that tax year. This test is considered more fully below as well as in **CHAPTERS 2** and **3**, but in broad terms the individual must be working for at least 35 hours a week on average and must stay within particular limits (30 days and 90 days respectively for UK workdays and days spent in the UK in total).

The law (*para 44(6), Sch 45, FA 2013*) also states that in considering days in the UK for the overseas part of the year, the rule that deems days of UK presence will not apply. This is a welcome relaxation in the law, which is considered in more detail in **CHAPTER 3**.

Case 1 is thus very similar to the previous concessionary treatment but with the SRT's rigidity of the prescribed limits for hours worked and days in the UK.

The key concepts relevant for the full-time work abroad test, which are also relevant for Case 1 of the split-year tests, are considered in detail in **CHAPTER 3**. As noted above, the taxpayer needs to meet the third automatic overseas test for the tax year following the year of departure. Therefore the taxpayer will not know for certain that he will obtain Case 1 treatment in the year of departure until the end of the next tax year. The taxpayer may find because of a late change in circumstances, such as losing his job in the March of the tax year following that in which he left the UK and not taking up alternative employment, that the relevant conditions for the third automatic overseas test are not met, even if he does not return to the UK. This may mean he has to amend his tax return for the year of departure on the assumption that this was previously filed on a split-year basis.

### Example 4.1: Jerry (and Margot)

Jerry is an HR director of a UK company which is the subject of a takeover by an Italian company in a related field. Jerry is asked to take on the group HR role and agrees to move to Italy. As his children are all now adults and living independently, his wife Margot agrees to go with him. They leave the UK in July 2015, anticipating being in Italy at least until Jerry retires, which is expected to be in five years' time.

In fact, after 18 months, Jerry feels he has given the role as much as he can and decides to retire early since he has a defined benefit pension scheme. He stops work at the end of December 2016. However, he and Margot prefer the climate in Tuscany and decide to make their home there rather than returning to the UK. Margot is happy with this too as over the previous year she has been able to return to the UK regularly to see her children and grandchildren.

Under the SRT, Jerry is not able to claim split-year status under Case 1 for 2015/16, because although he is non-resident for 2016/17 he will not meet the third automatic overseas test as he does not work full-time throughout the tax year. Therefore unless he meets the conditions of Case 3, he will need to amend his 2015/16 tax return. In practice, under the previous regime HMRC did not typically require any amendment to a prior year tax return in these circumstances.

Whether the split year would similarly have been lost under the previous regime was a matter of some debate. Most practitioners assumed that a taxpayer who had genuinely left the UK would have to do something more than simply stop working to become UK resident again or lose split-year status. There was, for example, no maximum gap between separate employments, after which full-time employment would be treated as interrupted. Similarly, if at the time the employment ceased the taxpayer had divested himself of all UK links, it was often supposed that he would be accepted as being non-resident by other means. However, this was not a view shared by HMRC/HMT during consultation meetings on the SRT (despite the prevailing practice noted above), which may explain why, under the SRT, the split-year condition for full-time working abroad may only be applied where the taxpayer is non-resident for the following UK tax year by virtue of the full-time working abroad test.

While Case 1 follows the third automatic overseas test in setting limits for the days and workdays that may be spent in the UK, the full year limits are pro-rated for the overseas part of the split year. The normal 90 and 30-day limits are reduced by reference to the number of whole UK tax months that have elapsed prior to the date on which the overseas work started. HMRC's guidance (RDR3, para 5.13) has a helpful table (reproduced below) that sets out the number of UK days and UK workdays that would be permitted in a tax year, depending on when the individual starts his overseas work.

*Table E*

| | Overseas part of tax year starts on or after | | | | | | | | | | | | |
|---|---|---|---|---|---|---|---|---|---|---|---|---|---|
| | 6 Apr to 30 Apr | 1 May to 31 May | 1 Jun to 30 Jun | 1 Jul to 31 Jul | 1 Aug to 31 Aug | 1 Sep to 30 Sep | 1 Oct to 31 Oct | 1 Nov to 30 Nov | 1 Dec to 31 Dec | 1 Jan to 31 Jan | 1 Feb to 29 Feb | 1 Mar to 31 Mar | 1 Apr to 5 Apr |
| X – permitted limit on days where you can work more than three hours and maximum number of days that can be subtracted for gaps between employments | 30 | 27 | 25 | 22 | 20 | 17 | 15 | 12 | 10 | 7 | 5 | 2 | 0 |
| Y – permitted limit on days spent in the UK | 90 | 82 | 75 | 67 | 60 | 52 | 45 | 37 | 30 | 22 | 15 | 7 | 0 |

It may be particularly challenging to stay within permitted limits for return visits when starting work abroad late in the tax year, because the pro-rated day limits are so low. This is considered further in **CHAPTER 8**.

There is also a significant record-keeping and administrative burden for the individual because he will need to keep records of his UK days and his UK workdays, and these will not necessarily be the same days. A day on which the individual is working in the UK all day and remains in the UK at midnight is likely to count both as a UK workday and a day of presence; but a day on which the individual does no more than three hours' work in the UK will not count as a UK workday, although it will be a day of UK presence if he remains in the UK at midnight.

The bigger challenge may be in tracking UK workdays where the taxpayer does not think of himself as working in the UK at all. For example, if he catches a late flight into the UK for a business meeting the following day, but has more than three hours of UK travel on the day that he flies into the UK he will have a UK workday on that day. Similarly, on a day of departure, travel to an airport and time spent airside before getting on a plane could easily create a UK workday on a day of departure, even though the day of departure will not generally be a day of UK presence.

Where the day limits and the full-time working abroad criteria are met, other personal circumstances of the individual are wholly irrelevant in determining his UK tax residence. Thus there is no need to consider whether or not the taxpayer's family will accompany him, or whether he sells or rents out the family home. From 1993/94 this was broadly the same under the previous regime for those working full-time abroad.

Although there was a risk to an individual's non-residence status under the previous regime if the taxpayer undertook any UK duties and if the family remained in the UK, in practice it was fairly common for the taxpayer to return to the UK frequently and to undertake some duties from home for his own convenience. Given that there was no definition of full-time working abroad under the previous regime, it was impossible to judge what level of UK duties could safely be undertaken in the UK without the taxpayer's full-time work abroad, and therefore his non-resident status, being called into question. The key advantage of the SRT in this circumstance therefore is certainty of treatment, provided the taxpayer is able to meet the constraints of the UK day and workday limits.

Where the conditions are met, the overseas part of the year begins on the day on which the taxpayer does more than three hours' work overseas. This is subtly different from the position under ESC A11, which allowed non-resident treatment from the day after the day on which the taxpayer left the UK. However, HMRC 6 specifically indicated that concession ESC A11 only applied if the taxpayer was taking up full-time work abroad and not if he was leaving the UK for some other reason, such as a holiday.

The operation of Case 1 where the taxpayer does not start work overseas immediately is illustrated by the example below.

### Example 4.2: Jonathan

Jonathan is a university lecturer specialising in information technology. His wife Akiko is Japanese and they have two young children. Jonathan is offered an opportunity to work in Japan for two years as part of a university exchange programme and they agree that it would be sensible to take full advantage of this before the children are settled in UK schools.

The family leaves the UK at the end of June 2015 because Jonathan's sabbatical includes the summer holidays. However, he is not required to start work in Tokyo until September in preparation for the new term which will begin in October. They spend July and August settling in and introducing the children to Akiko's friends and relations.

Jonathan is likely to remain UK tax resident until he starts work in September at least under UK domestic law. The analysis under the UK/Japan Double Tax Treaty may be different.

If split-year treatment is not available under UK domestic law, it may be possible to take a split-year position under a Double Tax Treaty and have a very similar outcome in tax terms. If the individual is tax resident in both countries but tie-breaks to the host country location under the Double Tax

Treaty, he may be treated as UK Treaty non-resident, which will generally limit the UK's ability to tax him (see **CHAPTER 12**).

However, Treaties will not necessarily solve every situation and there are various reasons for this. For example, sometimes the employee is going to a non-Treaty country such as Brazil or the UAE, so this possible solution is not available.

Where the employee is going to a Treaty country, a Treaty tie-breaker position will generally be decided by reference to where the family is; even where an employee is accompanied on his overseas assignment, the family will not necessarily leave on the same day. It is quite common for the spouse and children to follow later in order to work around schooling and accommodation. In this situation the employee may be Treaty non-resident but it may be from a later date than the day on which he starts working overseas. Moreover, in practice, especially where the employee's family goes with him on business trips or return visits to the UK, an individual's centre of vital interests may move several times during a tax year which can make application of the Treaty and determination of Treaty residence very difficult. As this in turn determines which country has primary taxing rights it is easy to reach a complete impasse in this situation, to which the only possible solution is a competent authority claim.

Split-year treatment is important because, without it, the UK may, at least under domestic law, be entitled to tax all earnings of the entire tax year. This can easily lead to double taxation if the employee happens to be going to a country where no Treaty applies, because the unilateral provisions for credit will not solve every situation.

### Self-employed (sole practitioners and partners)

**[4.04]** The split-year treatment described above is available for self-employed individuals including partners. The challenge for self-employed sole traders or practitioners lies in demonstrating full-time work abroad, and the commencement of this, in the absence of a contract of employment or partnership structure. Record-keeping will be critical and it may be sensible to defer the first return to the UK until after the start of the next UK tax year and until the business is clearly established overseas. The practice for partners, particularly those who are members of a relatively large, formal partnership, is probably more straightforward.

Another practical problem for the self-employed may be demonstrating that a day spent in the UK is not a UK workday. This is the age-old problem of trying to prove a negative. Unless the individual can show with documentation that they have spent the whole day engaged in non-work activities (eg attending a family wedding), they may find HMRC seek to argue that every day in the UK is a workday. While this may have been a problem under the previous regime, there is arguably more certainty under the SRT if the self-employed person takes the approach of assuming any UK day will be treated as a UK workday. He can then limit his days to accommodate the relevant limit.

## Accompanying spouses etc

[4.05] The previous regime had a concession to allow split-year treatment and non-residence for an accompanying spouse (ESC A78). The SRT also has a special case within the split-year rules for such individuals (Case 2). The legislation is found in *para 45, Sch 45, FA 2013*. The following conditions are required:

- the individual must have been UK tax resident for part or the whole of the previous UK tax year and must have a spouse or partner who falls within Case 1 for the relevant year or the previous tax year;
- on a day in the tax year concerned he or she must leave the UK in order to live with the working spouse;
- he or she must stay within permitted limits for return visits to the UK during this tax year (see below);
- from the deemed departure date (see below), he or she must either have no UK home, or must spend more time living in the overseas home than in the UK home;
- the individual must be non-UK resident for the following year.

In this context, 'spouse or partner' includes husband, wife or civil partner and any person with whom an employee lives as if they were spouses or civil partners. Provided the conditions are met, the individual is treated as non-resident from the later of the day on which the employee becomes non-resident (usually when the employee starts to work overseas), and the day on which the non-working spouse joins the working spouse abroad (*para 45(7) and (8), Sch 45, FA 2013*). This allows the trailing spouse to remain in the UK to arrange personal matters and join the working spouse at a later date, and still qualify for split-year treatment.

There are circumstances in which it may be difficult to meet this test and, as discussed in **CHAPTER 8**. the element of the test relating to the home, in particular, may be a trap for the unwary. In addition to the points made in **CHAPTER 8**, there can be specific problems with employer-provided accommodation. For example, assume that the couple moves first to temporary accommodation, such as a hotel, in the host location. It will not matter for the working spouse whether or not they have a home outside the UK. However, for the non-working spouse, if there is no overseas home, split-year treatment cannot be in point if the UK home is retained and kept available for use. If instead they move to more permanent employer-provided accommodation, the issue will be whether the quality of occupation will be sufficient to make this a home for the trailing spouse. This is a far from easy question. See the discussion at para **3.16**.

The additional consideration regarding the home is new under the SRT and makes this test more exacting than ESC A78, which simply set limits for the length of time that the trailing spouse could spend in the UK before their resident status was affected.

Where families choose to retain full access to the UK home whilst abroad, this may make it harder to meet the split-year test. Even in this case, though, it may be possible for the spouse to tie-break to the host location under a Double Tax Treaty and so effectively have a Treaty-based split-year treatment.

In the year of departure the day limit for return visits is a pro-rated limit based on no more than 90 UK days for a full tax year in the same way as for the working spouse (refer to Table E above, which illustrates how the day limits apply pro rata). This is subtly different from the previous concession, which was based on a 'no more than 90 days on average' test.

Concession A78 also covered the on-going non-residence position for the trailing spouse, which is not preserved in similar legislation under the SRT. Rather, the trailing spouse will have to consider the automatic overseas tests or keep within the day limits of the sufficient ties test rather than having a special test for accompanying someone who is full-time working abroad. This is explored further in para **4.06** below.

### Example 4.3: Akiko

Akiko has agreed with Jonathan that they should not sublet their UK property under a formal arrangement as she may want to return to the UK in the interim with or without the children. As luck would have it, her cousin, Man Yee, is currently studying at the university where Jonathan usually works and is looking for accommodation for the next academic year, so they agree that she will occupy the property. As the family may still want to use the property they have agreed that Man Yee will pay only a peppercorn rent. Under these arrangements, Akiko will be treated as retaining a home in the UK.

Although Akiko is unlikely to be returning to the UK very regularly she will need to consider how time spent in her Japanese home and UK home compares and limit return visits to her UK home as necessary to ensure that she has more days of presence in the Japanese home.

It is also worth noting that where an accompanying spouse has determined their residence position on the basis of that of their working spouse, both are very vulnerable to any change in circumstances of the working spouse. It has already been noted that split-year treatment can be jeopardised for the working spouse where the employment abroad does not extend at least until the end of the tax year following the tax year of departure. The position is no better for a non-working spouse because the accompanying spouse treatment will be lost if the working spouse ultimately fails to qualify for Case 1 split-year treatment.

### Example 4.4: Margot (and Jerry) continued

Example 4.1 considered the case of Jerry and his wife Margot. Jerry lost his Case 1 position. due to a change in his circumstances. He and Margot left the UK for Italy in July 2015, originally anticipating working there for at least five years but, in fact, Jerry chose to take early retirement after 18 months. Although he gives up his employment, the couple remain in Tuscany to make their home there.

This has implications for Margot.

Since Jerry is not within Case 1, Margot will not qualify under Case 2. She will then need to consider Case 3 (see paras 5.03 and 8.11 for a detailed discussion of this case). However, Case 3 imposes a strict limit of 16 UK days during the overseas part of the year and Margot may well have exceeded this.

Margot may still qualify for split-year treatment under the UK/Italy Double Tax Treaty, but is likely to have to revisit her tax return to include an appropriate claim.

# Maintaining non-residence

**[4.06]** As this chapter is concerned only with those individuals who leave the UK for full-time work abroad (and spouses), we assume that in the intervening years spent overseas the individual will meet the third automatic overseas test (ie the test for those working full-time abroad). This test is covered in CHAPTER 2, with a detailed discussion of the key concepts in CHAPTER 3, and the record-keeping requirements in CHAPTER 13 and so only a brief discussion is required here.

The third automatic overseas test is found in *para 14, Sch 45, FA 2013*.

'14(1)	The third automatic overseas test is that—
  (a)	P works sufficient hours overseas, as assessed over year X,
  (b)	during year X, there are no significant breaks from overseas work,
  (c)	the number of days in year X on which P does more than 3 hours' work in the UK is less than 31, and
  (d)	the number of days in year X falling within sub-paragraph (2) is less than 91.
(2)	A day falls within this sub-paragraph if—
  (a)	it is a day spent by P in the UK, but
  (b)	it is not a day that is treated under *paragraph 23(4)* as a day spent by P in the UK.'

*Sub-paragraph (2)* is a particularly helpful aspect of this law, in that it excludes any days that might otherwise count as days of UK presence under the 'deeming days' rule (see CHAPTER 3 for more details) from counting for the purpose of the 91-day test.

The main challenge for taxpayers aiming to meet this test will be staying within the permitted number of UK workdays (30 in a full UK tax year). This sounds relatively innocuous as a test but, due to the wide definition of 'work' is more exacting than it first appears. All UK-based work, including business travel and training, is included and any day on which more than three hours' work is done will count as a workday. The definition of business travel includes any travel that would normally be deductible under the 'wholly, exclusively and necessarily in the performance of the duties' test, but also includes journeys that are deductible under 'detached duty provisions.' Private travel or travel claimed under the home leave provisions will not normally count in this context, but as many employees will combine business travel with a trip home, the distinction may not limit the time spent on work-related travel to any extent.

This is particularly harsh because for air travel, as noted in CHAPTER 3, UK travel time starts as soon as the passenger disembarks from the aircraft. Any delay in baggage collection, immigration control or Customs, or a slow journey from the airport due to bad weather or traffic delay can easily cause an individual to have a UK workday when he was not engaged in activities that he perceived as work on the day in question.

Although there is another hurdle to be met in the sense of needing to keep to fewer than 91 days for return visits in a full tax year, this is more likely to be manageable. The 90-day limit is tested by reference to where the taxpayer is at midnight, which is generally something that can be predicted, in a way that the amount of time expended on a business journey, especially for someone who happens not to live or work next to a UK airport, sometimes cannot be.

If the individual does not meet the full-time working abroad test, they will need to determine their residence position by reference to the other tests. See treatment in CHAPTER 5 (and elsewhere). If the individual is neither full-time working abroad nor able to establish that he has left the UK to live abroad such that Case 3 applies, he may not qualify for split-year treatment.

**Example 4.5: Simon**

Simon has a full-time role as a senior marketing manager with a multinational advertising company and is asked to take up a role in Amsterdam for the next three years to support the strategy for the group's expansion into northern Europe.

He is also a director of various family companies and will not be able to give up his responsibilities here despite his overseas assignment. He will come back to attend board meetings and to attend to related business in the UK. He will not be selling or letting out his UK home as he will wish to stay there on his return visits. His wife and young children will go with him to the Netherlands.

Prior to the introduction of the SRT, it would have been extremely difficult to determine whether or not Simon remained resident under UK domestic law, as it would depend on whether or not he was accepted as full-time working abroad despite also having on-going UK directorships.

Under the SRT, it will be clear what he needs to do if he wishes to become non-resident under the third automatic overseas test. He will need to ensure that:

- his work overseas averages at least 35 hours a week over the course of the tax year;
- he is not in the UK at midnight on more than 90 days in the UK tax year; and
- he has no more than 30 UK workdays in the UK tax year.

As noted above, it is the last of these three conditions that is likely to be the most challenging, but there are some guidelines Simon could take into account that will help him to manage this:

- If he works (or undertakes work-related travel) for more than three hours in the UK on any day it will be a UK workday, so once the 'more than three hours' threshold has been broken Simon should spend as much of that day as possible working as that will maximise the UK work time available within the maximum 30 UK workdays.
- For the same reason, travelling into and out of the UK on the same day may minimise the extent to which UK travel will add to his UK workday count.

- He may wish to consider alternative means of travel that will reduce his UK travel time, and so his UK work. If he takes Eurostar to London his travel will not count as UK work (even if he is in fact doing work for the UK directorships) right up to the time that he disembarks from the train.
- He should avoid reporting back to the advertising company he is working for while in the UK because, while this might be regarded as incidental to his role in the Netherlands, the SRT makes no distinction between incidental and substantive duties for the UK workday test. Such reporting will therefore count as UK work. If such work is necessary he should try to combine it with duties for his family companies on the same day, or to keep the time spent in this way to three hours or less and do no other work on that day.

If, despite this, Simon is unable to stay within the workday limit and remains UK tax resident under UK domestic law, he may still be able to use the UK/Netherlands Tax Treaty to mitigate the tax impact of that. Although he has a permanent home available to him in both the UK and the Netherlands, his family and main job are in the Netherlands and his centre of vital interests is also likely to be there. Again, this is explored further in **CHAPTER 12** on Treaties.

### Accompanying spouses

**[4.07]** As mentioned above, there are no special rules for an accompanying spouse for these years. They will need to determine their residence status in years after the year of departure from the UK by reference to the normal statutory rules. In order to be automatically non-resident this means that for the first three tax years following the year of departure the accompanying spouse will need to restrict their days in the UK to a maximum of 15 (see *para 12, Sch 45, FA 2013*) assuming they themselves will not be undertaking full-time work abroad. Alternatively, they may need to consider the sufficient ties test.

It will be quite easy, therefore, for an accompanying spouse to be resident in the UK under UK domestic law in a full UK tax year, even where otherwise they may have qualified for split-year treatment in the UK tax year of departure. This would cause the spouse to lose split-year treatment and so they would be treated as UK resident in both years. Where the host location is a country with which the UK has a Treaty, an alternative approach in these circumstances may be for the accompanying spouse to make a claim to be Treaty non-resident in the UK. This should help to mitigate the tax consequences of remaining tax resident domestically.

# Year of return

## Overview

**[4.08]** As this chapter is concerned with those leaving the UK to work full-time abroad, we next consider the situation where the individual comes back to the UK and resumes full-time work in the UK. Under the previous regime, extra-statutory concession A11 covered both the year of departure and the year of return for those working full-time abroad and gave split-year treatment for both years, provided all the necessary conditions were fulfilled.

The situation is a little different under the SRT as there is no working abroad 'package'. This means that the year of return needs to be considered separately when determining residence status. In the absence of any special rules, it is likely that such an individual would become automatically UK resident throughout the year of return. This may be because they satisfy the third automatic UK test (full-time work in the UK). Alternatively, they may satisfy the second automatic UK test (home in the UK) particularly if, on leaving their last country, they give up the accommodation which they used there. Refer to **CHAPTER 2** for these tests. However, returnees will want to consider whether they can avail themselves of split-year treatment in the year of return and it is to this that we now turn.

**CHAPTER 8** considers the split-year cases in detail and so, once again, here we focus on some of the practical points for returning employees. Determining the availability of split year is more time-consuming under the SRT because it is necessary to consider each of the five cases for individuals coming to the UK and to determine the priority between the cases. In most circumstances, the earliest possible date for the commencement of UK residence is likely to apply.

In summary, the five cases are:

Case 4 – meets the 'only home in the UK' test

Case 5 – starts to work full time in the UK

Case 6 – ceases to work full time overseas

Case 7 – has a partner who falls within Case 6

Case 8 – starts to have a home in the UK

The priority of the cases and the related law are considered in detail in **CHAPTER 8**. However, in summary, priority is given to Case 6, where applicable, unless Case 5 can also apply in which case the earlier date of the two is taken as the date on which UK residence commences. Where the employee does not meet the conditions of Case 6 (perhaps because they have been non-UK resident for too long), and on the basis that they do not have a full-time working spouse, they will need to consider Cases 4, 5 and 8 and priority will be given to the case which results in the earliest start date.

For the trailing spouse it is necessary first to consider whether the conditions of Case 6 are met by them personally (with the same conditions as above). If Case 6 does not apply, Cases 7 and 5 must be considered and if both apply, again, the case which gives the earliest date of UK residence will take priority. If neither Case 6 nor Case 7 apply consider Cases 4, 5 and 8 and again priority is given to the case which results in the earliest start date.

In all circumstances, split-year treatment on returning to the UK can only apply to someone who was not UK tax resident throughout the previous tax year. The split-year cases on departure all require the taxpayer to be non-resident for the following tax year. It is not, therefore, possible to have split-year status in consecutive tax years when departing from and returning to the UK.

## Case 5

**[4.09]** In order to qualify for Case 5 treatment the taxpayer must:

- be non-UK resident for the previous tax year;
- be UK tax resident for the current tax year;
- have at least one 365-day period beginning in the year with a day on which more than three hours' work is done in the UK and for that period he must have:
  - sufficient hours working in the UK;
  - no significant breaks from working; and
  - at least 75% of the days on which he works for more than three hours, working in the UK; and
- in the part of the tax year before that 365-day period begins, not meet the sufficient ties test.

When applying the sufficient ties test to the overseas part of the year, the day count limits are pro-rated by reference to the number of whole months in the overseas part. The formula is set out in *para 48(6), Sch 45, FA 2013* and the RDR3 provides a helpful table, with the calculations already done (Table F in para 5.26, reproduced in **Chapter 8** at para **8.19**).

Although Table F refers to a UK home, it is intended also to apply here as 5.30 of RDR3 confirms this explicitly. The heading should be interpreted as 'Overseas part of year ends on or before' rather than being applied only to the Case 4 and 8 tests.

It should also be noted that in applying the sufficient ties test the day limits within the ties themselves are not pro-rated; so a work tie still requires 40 days of UK work, regardless of how early in the year the overseas part of the year may be ending. Similarly, accommodation still has to be available for 91 days before it can represent a tie, even if the taxpayer returns to the UK before 91 days of the tax year have elapsed.

If all the conditions are met the tax year is treated as split from the date on which full-time work in the UK begins.

## Case 6

**[4.10]** In order to qualify for Case 6 treatment the taxpayer must:

- be non-UK resident for the previous tax year by reason of the third automatic overseas test;
- have been resident in the UK in one or more of the four tax years immediately preceding that year;
- be resident in the UK for the following tax year; and
- have a period starting with the first day of the relevant tax year ending with a day on which more than three hours' work is done overseas, during which he must have:
  - sufficient hours working overseas;
  - no significant breaks from overseas work;
  - no more than the permitted number of UK days and UK workdays.

Again, RDR3 (Table G, para 5.37) has a convenient table that summarises the maximum number of days and workdays the taxpayer can have in the UK, depending on the date on which full-time working abroad ceases. See para **8.22** below.

If all the conditions are met, the tax year is treated as split from the date on which full-time work overseas ceases.

### Case 7

**[4.11]** In order to qualify for Case 7 treatment the taxpayer must:

- be non-UK resident for the previous tax year;
- have a partner who falls within Case 6 for the relevant year or the previous tax year;
- move to the UK so as to continue to live with that partner on his relocation to the UK;
- be tax resident for the following tax year; and
- in the overseas part of the year either:
    - have no UK home, or have a UK home and overseas home and spend more time in the overseas home; and
    - not exceed the permitted number of days in the UK. Again, these are the permitted UK days as set out in Table G (noted above).

If all conditions are met, the trailing spouse is deemed to return to the UK on the later of the first day of the UK part of the tax year for the working spouse or the date on which the trailing spouse actually moves to the UK.

Cases 4 and 8 may be of relevance, for example to trailing spouses or to those who work overseas long enough to be outside the conditions of Case 6. A full discussion of these cases is set out in **CHAPTER 8** and some practical considerations in **CHAPTER 5** so they are not considered in any detail here.

In all cases, if the conditions are met the taxpayer is still regarded as tax resident for the whole year but is largely taxed as though he were non-resident for the overseas part of the tax year. See **CHAPTER 8** for full details.

### Which Case applies?

### The returning employee

**[4.12]** The starting point for the returning employee will be to consider Cases 6 and 5. In practice, Case 6 is likely to apply most widely, because its effect is to make the taxpayer tax resident from the date that he ceases to meet the full-time working abroad criteria. Whilst it is theoretically possible to start full-time work in the UK before ceasing full-time work abroad, the number of hours required in both places will make it relatively rare that Case 5 applies instead. Case 6 does require the taxpayer to have been UK tax resident relatively recently (see above) and so will not apply where the taxpayer has been non-resident for at least five full UK tax years.

It will be more typical for a taxpayer within Case 6 to 'miss' the day on which he became UK tax resident, because it will not generally have anything to do with his return to the UK. So if, for example, he decides to take a holiday at the end of his assignment and return to the UK after that, he will nevertheless be tax resident from the date that he ceases to satisfy the overseas work criteria (either altogether or to meet the necessary criteria, whichever is the earlier date).

In circumstances where Case 6 does not apply to an employee (and assuming that they do not have a spouse to whom Case 6 applies), they will need to consider Cases 4, 5 and 8 (see discussion of ordering rules above and at para **8.03**).

Which case applies will very much depend on the individual's circumstances; for example, have they retained a UK home while working overseas or have they sold their property or let it out? Do they have family who move to the UK ahead of their starting employment here? Do they move to temporary accommodation when they move back to the UK? With all these factors to consider, individuals will need to take great care to ensure that they do not begin to be resident in the UK on an earlier date than expected. Often there will be some uncertainty as to which case applies and individuals may wish to plan their affairs as though they become resident in the UK on the earliest possible day.

We might expect someone returning to work in the UK to begin to have a home here before beginning work so that Case 4 or 8 might be expected to take priority. However, if the accommodation first occupied by the employee on his return to the UK is temporary and his occupation of it does not have the quality to make it a home, Case 5 may take priority. We have already seen that the distinction between home and accommodation is a fine one and unless a taxpayer can decide with certainty whether or not the place in which he lives on his return to the UK is a home, he will struggle to determine which of the cases applies and in turn to establish his 'arrival' date.

It still remains to be seen whether in practice it is more difficult to achieve split-year status on returning to the UK from a period of working full time abroad under the SRT, but the new cases are far more prescriptive in the conditions that need to be fulfilled. In addition, the year of departure and year of return are looked at in isolation, rather than the entire period of absence being considered as a whole. Under the SRT, entitlement to split-year treatment in the year of return in several of the new cases is calculated by reference to absolute day counts tied to 'the date of return', rather than a test of staying within 91 days on average over a period including the stub period of the tax year of return up to the return date.

Where the taxpayer returns to the UK to work full time, it is worth noting that the tests for full-time working abroad and full-time working in the UK may both require a minimum 35-hour working week on average but the calculations are undertaken entirely separately, even where employment is all within the same group of companies and effectively continuous. Holidays between the two are unlikely to constitute a significant break, but, as noted above, may make a difference to the date on which UK tax residence is resumed.

In practice, there may be a period of handover while the individual works partly in the UK and partly overseas. Careful consideration of which case is relevant will be necessary where the UK working is so extensive that it brings the hours spent working abroad below the average 35 hours per week level. Where the particular case requires the individual not to meet the sufficient ties test for the overseas part of the year, further care may then be needed. For example, someone returning to the UK who has a month of split overseas and UK working prior to moving back could easily meet the 40 UK workdays needed for a UK work tie, and would then have to make sure he limits his UK days prior to his return in order to qualify for split-year treatment.

It should be noted that however complex the split-year domestic law test may become, it should still be possible to consider a Treaty split-year position if the employee's spouse and family remain with him in the host location and the whole family returns to the UK at the same time. This is not always the case, however, as it is reasonably common for a non-working spouse and children to move to the UK at an earlier or later date to accommodate better any on-going education commitments.

### Example 4.6: Adrian

Adrian is a production engineer, working for a major confectionary brand, which has moved one of its manufacturing plants from the UK to Poland. Since June 2015 he has been working full time in Poland, helping to set up the new operation and making sure it is all running smoothly. His wife Sally and their twin daughters Mary and Martha who are now seven have accompanied him on his assignment overseas.

At the end of June 2017, Adrian is reaching the end of the project and will be returning to the UK in three months' time. There are three different UK plants where his services may be needed and during June he visits each of them in turn for a couple of days at a time to help to make up his mind about what will be most suitable. With travel days in and out of the UK each time (he does not want to leave the plant in Poland for a full week while his involvement there is running down), he has 12 workdays as a result of these visits. He also has five days at head office, reporting back on progress in Poland and scoping out his new UK role. During this time he stays in the family home, which has remained available for the family to use during their time in Poland.

It is decided that Adrian will start his new full-time role in the UK on 2 October, but Sally is keen to return home before that and particularly to settle the girls into their home and a new school before the new academic year starts in September. So she moves back to their house with the girls in mid July, as soon as they have taken their annual holiday as a family. Sally will not be working full time in the UK on her return. Adrian retains his employer-provided home in Poland after the rest of the family have returned to the UK.

If we consider first Adrian's position, he will start by considering whether Case 6 can apply to him and, if it can, whether Case 5 can also apply.

Whether Case 6 applies will depend on his working pattern and in particular the number of UK workdays he has in the overseas part of the year.

With the 12 days spent on site visits and the five days that Adrian has spent at head office he already has 17 UK workdays for the current tax year. This is the maximum number of UK workdays he would be permitted if he is to qualify for Case 6 assuming he returned on 2 October as planned (see Table G noted above). So he will need to refrain from having any more UK workdays until that point. He will also need to ensure that he has met the sufficient hours test for the overseas part of the year, despite having some UK workdays.

Turning to Case 5, although Adrian has had some UK workdays, he is unlikely to have started a period of full-time work in the UK as required by Case 5 before 2 October 2015. Most of his earlier UK workdays are in June and so, prior to October, he is unlikely to have attained the 35-hour average UK working week required or have had 75% of his workdays in the UK. He may also have had a significant break from UK work if 31 days have gone by without him performing more than three hours' work on any day. By 2 October, Adrian may have two UK ties (accommodation and UK resident family) but he has had only 17 days in the UK so far and so is still well within the sufficient ties limit of Table F. So there is a reasonable chance that he will fall within Case 5.

If Adrian falls within both Cases 6 and 5, the UK part of his split year is likely to start on 2 October 2015. However, if Case 6 does not apply (because he has further UK workdays while still based in Poland), it will be necessary to consider Cases 4 and 8 as well as 5.

As the family has retained a UK home throughout his time in Poland, Adrian cannot be within Case 8. However, he could fall within Case 4 once he gives up the Polish property and returns to the UK at the end of his assignment. The earlier date of Cases 4 and 5 will then give the date on which the UK part of the year starts.

## Accompanying partner

[**4.13**] In the same way that ESC A11 covered both the years of departure and return for an individual going overseas for full-time work, so too ESC A78 covered the year of departure and return for an accompanying spouse. However, once again, under the SRT, accompanying spouses need to consider the year of return separately.

Accompanying spouses will start by considering whether they fall within Case 7 and, if so, the only other case which they need to consider will be Case 5. However, a comparison of the two will only be necessary where the spouse also begins full-time work in the UK. Where the spouse is not within Case 7 they will need to consider Cases 4, 5, and 8 (see above).

If we continue the example above but consider Sally's position rather than that of her husband, it quickly becomes apparent that her situation is not clear cut. Whether or not she will have the potential to be within Case 7 will depend on whether Adrian is within Case 6 and as noted above that is far from certain at this stage. However, even if Adrian is within Case 6, Case 7 is unlikely to apply to Sally. With Adrian within Case 6 for 2017/18, the same UK tax year in which Sally returns to the UK, this would give her a date for the start of the UK part of the split year around 2 October. Under Case 7, Sally would then be allowed 52 days in the UK in the overseas part of the tax year (see Table G – the Y figures). Since Sally arrived back in the UK mid July, she is likely to have exceeded this figure. Alternatively, Sally may find she has spent more days in her UK home than the overseas home in the overseas part of the year and thus fail a different part of Case 7. This illustrates the difficulty of applying Case 7 where the non-working spouse returns to the UK in advance of the working spouse.

Since Sally will not be working in the UK full time, Case 5 is not relevant to her and it therefore remains for her to consider Cases 4 and 8.

Once again, as the family has retained the use of their UK home throughout their stay in Poland, Sally cannot be within Case 8. However, Case 4 may be in point if she is able to meet the conditions. So in broad terms she will need to start to have an only home in the UK and not meet the sufficient ties for the part of the year before her 'arrival date'.

Since the home in Poland was retained until Adrian's return, the date that Sally needs to consider for Case 4 is 2 October rather than the date of her physical return to the UK in mid July. By this point she would have a family tie (her children) and an accommodation tie. However, Sally is again restricted to 52 days in the UK if she is to meet the sufficient ties condition of Case 4. She is thus unlikely to qualify for split treatment under domestic law in these circumstances, but may qualify for Treaty split-year treatment under the UK/Poland Treaty.

The SRT prescribes a more rigid framework than the extra-statutory concession A78 that previously applied for 'trailing spouses'. If the date of becoming UK resident under domestic law is likely to be significant, for example because it will determine whether or not the temporary non-resident regime applies, great care must be taken in monitoring return visits to the UK and the permitted number of days for such visits.

### Return in the tax year immediately following the year of departure

**[4.14]** Where the taxpayer leaves in one year for full-time work overseas and returns to the UK in the next (so that he is not working full-time overseas for a full UK tax year), in the majority of cases none of the split-year cases will apply in either year. Split-year treatment may however be possible in the year of departure where the taxpayer returns to the UK very late in the second year, in circumstances such that they can satisfy one of the automatic overseas tests for that year. In many cases, however, taxpayers will therefore need to consider their residence status for the years of departure and return according to the general SRT rules. This is similar to the previous regime where the benefit of ESC A11 would only be obtained if the individual's contract of employment, period of absence abroad and actual overseas work lasted for a complete UK tax year. If non-resident status under the SRT is preferred, subject to any possible Tax Treaty position, the individual may need to restrict their days in the UK or connections with the UK in order to achieve this.

#### Example 4.7: Malcolm

Malcolm has lived in the UK all his life and works for a brewing company here. He is asked to take on an 18-month assignment in Koblenz to see if he can pick up any new ideas from a sister company based there. As he is leaving the UK on 15 May 2016, he will not be non-resident under the third automatic test (full-time work abroad) treatment. He would be automatically non-resident in either 2016/17 or 2017/18 if his UK days in the tax year were fewer than 16, but this will not apply for 2016/17 and is unlikely to apply to 2017/18 based on current plans.

On the basis that Malcolm returns to full-time work within the same UK brewing company at the end of his 18-month secondment, he is likely to remain UK tax resident in both years under the third automatic UK test (full-time work in the UK). In these circumstances, none of the split-year cases for the year of departure 2016/17 will apply to him as all three cases require him to be non-resident throughout the following tax year. Similarly, none of the split-year cases for the year of arrival (return) – 2017/18 – can apply as they all require him to be non-resident throughout the previous tax year.

## Self-employed returnees

**[4.15]** In practice, the considerations for self-employed practitioners are likely to be very similar to those discussed already for employees. However, individuals who are self-employed will need to know the date on which their UK residence begins with some certainty because that will determine the date on which their overseas business ceases and their UK business commences. This may not always be straightforward for the self-employed who may 'drift' into UK residence and may therefore not qualify for split-year treatment.

### Example 4.8: Peter

Peter is an independent property consultant who has been based in Stuttgart for the past five UK tax years. Over that time he has worked with some major entities helping them to develop properties to meet their office space requirements. He has also started a side-line in residential property for individuals.

One of Peter's existing clients in Germany is keen to have a new home built for him in rural South Wales and so in 2016 Peter begins investigating opportunities for his client along the Pembrokeshire coast. Although Peter comes from Cardiff originally it is some years since he has visited the area. He has to revive a lot of local contacts and also build up expertise locally to help his client to secure a site and appropriate planning permission. While he is doing this he is surprised by the interest he is generating both with his existing client base in Germany and in the UK.

After a couple of months during which Peter has spent no more than two weeks in the UK in total he decides to make a bigger commitment to potential UK business and agrees with a local hotel that he will host an event there for two days at a time once a month over the next three months just to see how things go.

Business takes off but Peter continues to be based in Germany with business trips to the UK. Peter stays with his parents when he visits the UK for sufficient nights to give him an accommodation tie and this together with his UK workdays gives him two UK ties, With the increase in UK business his UK days exceed 120 days and he will be resident in the UK for 2016/17.

At what point will UK tax residence start? Peter will not meet Case 6 because he has been outside the UK for too long. Peter's working pattern does not seem likely to meet the 'full-time working in the UK' test for Case 5, but if, for example, he chooses to acquire a UK home to facilitate his travel while doing business in the UK, he may qualify for split-year treatment under Case 4.

For the self-employed it can be even more critical to monitor UK workdays carefully because their working pattern will not be governed by a contract as many employees would be. The complications for deciding the start of UK residence mean that the self-employed may wish to have a definite break between their overseas business finishing and their UK business beginning. Where this is not possible they will need to plan as though they are UK resident from the beginning of the tax year.

### The five-year trap

**[4.16]** Individuals who return to the UK having had a period of non-residence of less than five years might find that anti-avoidance legislation brings into charge in the year of return certain income or gains that arose during their non-resident period. See para **5.24** for a brief description of this and also CHAPTER 11.

# Death of the taxpayer overseas

**[4.17]** The detailed application of the SRT in the event of the death of the taxpayer is set out fully at paras **2.10–2.12** and **2.23**. This section is concerned purely with the death of a taxpayer who dies while working full time overseas.

### Death in the year of departure from the UK

**[4.18]** There are two automatic overseas tests that can apply on the death of the taxpayer (see para **2.11**). If the taxpayer dies in the UK tax year of departure from the UK, he will not fall within either, since both require the years preceding the year of death to be years of non-residence.

There are circumstances in which a taxpayer could die in the year of departure and be non-resident under the automatic overseas tests, but they will be very limited. For example, he could qualify under the full-time working abroad provisions if he were to leave the UK on 6 April and die so close to the end of the tax year that his absence from employment could not constitute a significant break from employment within that tax year, which is strictly what the law appears to allow. It is difficult to imagine, however, that this will allow many taxpayers to die and cease to be UK tax resident (other than in the sense of being resident nowhere after death) in the same tax year, but the possibility should not be ruled out.

Where none of the automatic overseas tests applies, the employee's residence position for the tax year of death must, as usual, be determined by reference to the automatic UK tests or the sufficient ties tests. See paras **2.12** and **2.23**. How likely these are to apply will depend on when the individual left for full-time work overseas and their connections to and time spent in the UK.

It should be noted that when the employee dies in the tax year of departure, and they are resident in the UK, it is not possible to qualify for split-year treatment in the year of departure, because each of Cases 1, 2 and 3 requires the taxpayer to be non-resident for the following tax year. This will also prevent any accompanying spouse from qualifying under Case 2, since the working spouse will not meet the conditions for Case 1, as originally expected.

### Death in the year following the year of departure

[4.19] Once again, the special automatic overseas tests for the year of death cannot apply and so it is simply a case of considering the usual overseas tests. If none of these tests apply, the executors need to consider the automatic residence tests. It is worth noting that the fourth of these (death of taxpayer in the year) cannot apply if, assuming the year of death were one of non-residence, the year of departure would be a split year. Note also the pro-rated days that apply for the sufficient ties test. See para **2.23**.

Depending on the final position, it is possible that the split-year treatment in the year of departure will be lost if the deceased is UK resident in the year of death. Once again, the accompanying spouse is also likely to be affected.

### Death in second or subsequent year after departure

[4.20] If the taxpayer dies in what was expected to be the second full year of non-residence, or in a later UK tax year, when he remains full-time working abroad up to the date of death he may be non-resident for that year under the fourth automatic test if he meets the following conditions (*para 15, Sch 45, FA 2013*):

(1)   he was non-resident throughout the previous tax year; and
(2)   he was either non-resident throughout the year before that or he was split-year non-resident under one of the cases related to leaving the UK;
(3)   he spends fewer than 46 days in the UK.

Alternatively, the fifth automatic overseas test is designed specifically for taxpayers who die while working full-time overseas. This has two possible legs (*para 16, Sch 45, FA 2013*):

(1)   the taxpayer was non-resident throughout the two UK tax years immediately before the year of death by reason of full-time work abroad and in that year would meet a slightly modified test for calculating the sufficient hours test of a minimum of 35 hours a week on average (see below); or
(2)   the taxpayer was non-resident for the previous tax year by reason of full-time working abroad (the third automatic overseas test) and the tax year before that he was split-year non-resident under Case 1 (leaving the UK for full-time employment abroad). In this case he must also meet a modified sufficient hours test as explained below.

The 35-hour average working week requirement is calculated by reference to the year up to the day before the taxpayer dies. This reduced period may have no implications where the taxpayer dies in an accident, but there may be some implications where death follows a period of illness during which the taxpayer may have been working reduced hours, for example.

Whether or not *para 15* or *16* apply, death after a full UK tax year of non-residence will not require any review of the split-year provisions applying to the UK tax year of departure, since there will be the required full year of non-residence intervening.

If *para 15* or *16* do not apply, the remaining automatic and sufficient ties tests must be considered (see CHAPTER 2).

### Death in planned year of return to the UK

**[4.21]** If the taxpayer dies in the year of return to the UK, he may stay non-resident, or may become UK tax resident, possibly from the start of the tax year rather than from a planned return date.

In principle, the process for determining the taxpayer's residence position is identical to the situations described above for the year of departure and intervening years. However, the added complication where someone has planned to return to the UK is that he may have expected to be resident but eligible for split-year treatment, which may no longer apply as anticipated because of death.

**Example 4.9: Steve**

Steve left the UK to take a full-time employment assignment in China on 7 September 2013 and qualified for split-year treatment from 9 September, the day on which he started work in China.

After five years' working in China Steve plans to return to the UK permanently from Christmas 2018. Although he was initially non-resident by virtue of full-time working abroad, from the start of 2017 he wanted to spend some time experiencing more of China while he had the opportunity, and so took a three-month sabbatical for the summers of both 2017 and 2018. He remained non-resident for 2017/18 because he only spent two weeks back in the UK during that tax year.

He had let out his UK flat while abroad, but he sold it in November 2018, prior to his return to the UK. He also liquidated his investment portfolio, having decided to make a fresh start while back in the UK.

Steve finishes work in China on 20 December 2018 and travels home, before spending the festive season with his parents. He had negotiated the purchase of a new UK property while still in China and moves into it, occupying it as his home on 2 January 2019. He starts work for a new employer at the start of the following week.

Unfortunately, he is killed in a car crash on 4 April 2019. He does not meet any of the automatic residence or non-residence tests that may apply on death. Nevertheless, he is likely to be resident for the whole UK tax year 2018/19 under the second automatic UK test because he has his only home in the UK for a period of at least 91 days and occupies the home for at least 30 days. He might have expected to qualify for split-year treatment under Case 8, but will not do so because he will not have a UK home for the whole of the following tax year as this test requires. He might also have expected to qualify for split-year treatment under Case 4, but arguably will not, because dying on 4 April will mean that he does not meet the only home condition for the whole of 2018/19.

The disposal of his investment portfolio will therefore fall into the charge to CGT since split-year treatment will no longer be in point.

### Conclusions on death

**[4.22]** Death in the near future is not generally anticipated by those who are internationally mobile for work, as the majority are relatively young. The SRT rules may work to the disadvantage of those unfortunate enough to die while on secondment or in either the year of their departure from or return to the UK. It is difficult to escape the conclusion that many will remain UK tax resident and quite possibly will also be tax resident in the host country where they had been working, leaving their personal representatives with an unenviable task, negotiating with two different tax systems and possibly also with their Competent Authorities.

## Conclusions

**[4.23]** One of the aims of the SRT regime was to replicate the existing system and put it on a statutory footing. In the case of individuals working full-time abroad, it might therefore be assumed that there would be no real difference between the regimes.

There are, however, marked differences in the way that the SRT operates compared with the practices that applied previously. The SRT looks at each tax year in isolation rather than considering the period of overseas work as a whole. In doing so, it imposes a framework of statutory UK day and workday limits per tax year, which is more rigid than the previous averaging practice. The UK workday tests of more than three hours' work and work-related travel are likely to be especially challenging and impose new record-keeping requirements. Calendars will need to be sufficiently detailed to indicate not just whether the taxpayer was working and where but also for how long and the time taken to travel there. The split-year cases may require a consideration of circumstances beyond the overseas working hours and the employment contract return date.

The one advantage the SRT brings is clarity. If a taxpayer can meet the rigid demands of the various tests, he has certainty of non-residence status.

# Chapter 5

# Leaving the UK: high net worth individuals

## Introduction

**[5.01]** This chapter forms the companion to CHAPTER 4 in so far as they both consider the residence position for individuals leaving the UK. While CHAPTER 4 covers those individuals who fall within the SRT definition of full-time work abroad, this chapter considers all other individuals.

Since there is more to leaving the UK than the year of departure, and indeed the position for that year is likely to depend upon the position in subsequent years, this chapter considers the full cycle: the year of departure; the period of non-residence and the year of return.

When compared to the former regime based on case law the SRT gives greater certainty for those leaving the UK and seeking to become non-UK resident. However, it is still complex and in many ways it is now harder for those who are already resident here to break UK residence, certainly for the initial year.

## Year of departure

**[5.02]** Having decided to leave the UK an individual must then consider what steps are necessary in order for him to cease to be UK resident for tax purposes. Prior to the introduction of the SRT it was necessary to look at case law for the answer to this question and an individual would have been well advised to make a 'distinct break' in the pattern of their life. The degree of change necessary to effect this (eg selling of UK home, moving of family) was then the subject of much debate.

Following the introduction of the SRT, the individual can at least be clear that, whilst he may choose to retain some or all of his ties to the UK, he will have to do so in exchange for fewer days spent here. In theory, at least, this is intended to reflect a position similar to that which would have been arrived at under the old case law, although there are bound to be some differences.

It is worth noting that UK connections other than those appropriate for the sufficient ties test (eg credit cards, cars, investments etc) no longer have any relevance for determining the residence status of individuals.

### When does non-UK residence begin?

**[5.03]** UK residence has always been assessed on a whole tax year basis, and that remains the case under the SRT. However, as with the previous regime in certain circumstances, where an individual is UK resident, he can be taxed *as though he is* non-UK resident for part of the year, where he meets the criteria of the split-year provisions. The RDR3 sets this out at para 5.1:

'5.1 Under the SRT, you are either UK resident or non-UK resident for a full tax year and at all times in that tax year. However, if during a year you either start to live or work abroad or come from abroad to live or work in the UK the tax year will be split into two parts if your circumstances meet specific criteria:

• a UK part for which you are charged to UK tax as a UK resident;
• an overseas part for which, for most purposes, you are charged to UK tax as a non-UK resident.'

Split-year treatment and the tax consequences are set out in the SRT statute *(part 3, Sch 45, FA 2013)*. See **CHAPTER 8**.

Assuming that an individual leaves the UK part way through a tax year, although he will not technically begin to be non-UK resident until the following tax year, in determining his tax position for the year of departure he will nevertheless need to know whether the split-year treatment will apply to his circumstances. A detailed exploration of the split-year provisions is included in **CHAPTER 8**. However, an overview of the provisions as they relate to those leaving for reasons other than full-time employment or self-employment is provided here.

The new split-year test is divided into a number of different sets of circumstances, or 'cases,' the conditions of which an individual must fulfil in order for the split-year provisions to apply.

Those leaving the UK for a reason other than full-time work abroad (either their own or their partner's) can only qualify for split-year treatment under 'Case 3', which is in *para 46, Sch 45, FA 2013*. Case 3 provides as follows:

'Case 3: ceasing to have a home in the UK

46(1) The circumstances of a case fall within Case 3 if they are as described in subparagraphs (2) to (6).

(2) The taxpayer was resident in the UK for the previous tax year (whether or not it was a split year).

(3) At the start of the relevant year the taxpayer had one or more homes in the UK but—

(a) there comes a day in the relevant year when P ceases to have any home in the UK, and

(b) from then on, P has no home in the UK for the rest of that year.

(4) In the part of the relevant year beginning with the day mentioned in subparagraph (3)(a), the taxpayer spends fewer than 16 days in the UK.

(5) The taxpayer is not resident in the UK for the next tax year.

(6) At the end of the period of 6 months beginning with the day mentioned in sub-paragraph (3)(a), the taxpayer has a sufficient link with a country overseas.

(7) The taxpayer has a "sufficient link" with a country overseas if and only if—

(a) the taxpayer is considered for tax purposes to be a resident of that country in accordance with its domestic laws, or

(b) the taxpayer has been present in that country (in person) at the end of each day of the 6-month period mentioned in sub-paragraph (6), or

(c) the taxpayer's only home is in that country or, if the taxpayer has more than one home, they are all in that country.'

Thus in order for Case 3 split-year treatment to apply, an individual must:

• have been UK resident in the previous tax year (although this can be a split year);

• have a UK home which they give up (so that they then have no UK home);

• be non-UK resident for the following tax year (in this case the non-residence must apply for the whole of the tax year).

In addition, the individual must then spend fewer than 16 days in the UK in the part of the tax year during which they are treated as non-resident and must establish a 'sufficient link' with a new country (this latter requirement is explored further in para **5.07**).

The 16-day test is a very strict limit and contrasts with the position in the split-year test for coming to the UK which applies a version of the sufficient ties test with a reduced day count. Here it is instead a straight day-count test (other ties with the UK during this period of the year of departure are irrelevant). For those leaving the UK towards the end of a tax year (after say, January), the 16-day test may be easy to meet, but for those leaving in the early part it may prove too onerous.

## Increased importance of UK home

**[5.04]** Prior to the introduction of the SRT, an individual was dependent upon an extra-statutory concession (ESC A11) in order to obtain split year treatment for income tax in the year of departure (an extra-statutory concession, D2, could also apply for CGT but in much more restricted circumstances). If the individual was not leaving the UK for full-time employment or self-employment abroad, then he was only eligible for split-year treatment if he was leaving the UK 'for permanent residence abroad.' As with achieving non-UK resident status, what precisely was involved in permanent residence abroad was a matter of some debate. However, it was generally agreed to be dependent upon a number of factors and involved the breaking of existing ties with the UK. This normally included, but was not limited to, losing the tie of one's UK home either through sale or renting it out.

By contrast, the new test concentrates solely on the whereabouts of the individual's home. CHAPTER 3 explores in detail the definition of 'home' for the purpose of the SRT, so far as there is one, but it is worth reminding ourselves here that this definition can be extremely broad and there is no requirement for an individual to have any legal interest in the property for it to be considered his home. Indeed it may even be someone else's home, for example that of his parents. How one would cease to have a home in the UK in these circumstances would be an interesting question – but perhaps statements of intent together with removing one's belongings would be indicative.

Assuming the tests are satisfied, then the day that the individual gives up their home will be key, since the overseas part of the year starts from that date and so they will be taxed as though they are not UK-resident from that day, regardless of the day on which they actually leave the UK (*para 53(4), Sch 45, FA 2013*).

## When does a home cease to be a home?

**[5.05]** What is not clear is precisely when an individual can be said to have given up their UK home – for example, do they need to have moved all of their possessions out of the property, or is it merely enough to have put the property up for sale and not to return there? It would certainly be common practice to leave one's furniture in a property until it is sold, but then, by extension, it might be normal practice to use the UK property as overnight accommodation on return visits to the UK until such time as any sale has been completed and HMRC guidance suggests that this, at least, may be sufficient to ensure a property remains a home. See, for example, HMRC comments in paras A10, A13, A17 and A19 of Annex A of RDR3 (also covered in **CHAPTER 3**). Indeed, example A5 in Annex A of the guidance deals with a situation in which a property is not occupied at all but simply kept empty and available for use:

'Example A5

Asif has lived and worked in the UK for many years, occupying the same apartment in Liverpool since the day he arrived here. Asif's father lives in Sweden and is seriously ill. Ten months ago Asif decided to take a career break to care for his father and moved to Sweden. He does not know how long he will be out of the UK.

Since moving to Sweden Asif has not returned to Liverpool, but his apartment remains empty and available for him to return to whenever he wants. In this situation Asif will have a home in both Liverpool and Sweden even though he is spending all of his time in Sweden.'

It is interesting that HMRC consider the property remains a home even though Asif does not visit it, even for one night for a ten-month period. This seems to set the bar for a home very low (possibly lower than a court would do). This example, like many in the HMRC guidance, deals with a case that is much more clear cut than would often arise in real life. It would have been more interesting to know HMRC's view, for example, if Asif had put the flat up for let but failed to find a tenant, although some further information on this is provided at A17 (see below). It would also be interesting to know whether the property would still be considered by HMRC to be his home if he did not return to it for a full tax year and, if not, on what date it ceases to be his home.

The HMRC guidance, RDR3 para 5.25, gives one example of home in the context of the application of Case 3:

'Example 36

Maureen has been based in the UK for most of her working life, and has been resident here for tax purposes. On holiday in Bali in the summer of 2013 she meets Maurice, who lives and works in the United Arab Emirates.

Some twelve months later, they marry. Maureen resigns from her job and moves out of her home on 24 September 2014. She spends the nights of 24 and 25 September in a hotel and flies out to the UAE to live with Maurice on 26 September 2014. She has no close family in the UK and does not return to the UK in the remainder of the tax year. She does not take up any employment in the UAE. Maurice and Maureen plan to live in the UAE for at least another five years.

Maureen will receive split year treatment for 2014-15 as she meets the Case 3 conditions.

- She was UK resident for 2013-14
- She is non-UK resident for 2015-16
- From 24 September 2014 until 5 April 2015 she has no home in the UK and spends fewer than 16 days in the UK.'
- She had established her only home is in UAE within six months.

For Maureen, the overseas part of the tax year will start on 24 September 2014, the day she no longer had a home in the UK."

In this example, Maureen 'moves out of her home' and moves into a hotel. It must be assumed that the home is either sold or let out (although this is not stated in the example) particularly given the comments above regarding Example A5.

HMRC suggest at A17 that a property will cease to be an individual's home if he moves out of it completely and 'makes it available to let commercially on a permanent basis.' It is not clear how long 'a permanent basis' is in this context – however, in Example A9 (Ivan – reproduced in para **8.17**) Ivan lets out his property on a two-year lease and this is sufficient for HMRC to state that it is not his home.

The safest course of action for those looking to qualify for split-year treatment under Case 3 would be to sell their home or arrange for it to be let out commercially for a period of two years or more. This is in line with HMRC guidance at A19 and Example A10:

'A19 If an individual completely moves out of a dwelling and makes no further use of it whatsoever it will no longer be their home.

**Example A10**

Harry's new job requires him to travel extensively around Europe. He spends some time working in the UK but most of his work is carried out in other countries. He decided to sell his UK property. On 3 June he put his furniture and belongings in storage and two weeks later he handed the keys to his estate agent. He did not return to his UK property after 3 June and stayed in hotels or with friends on the occasions when he came back to the UK. The property is not his home from 3 June, the date he put his furniture and belongings in storage.'

In this example, the individual has not sold his property at the time it ceases to be his home but he has removed all his personal belongings and put all of his furniture into storage. An individual wishing to be sure that he ceases to have a home in the UK on a particular day might follow the same course, but in the ordinary course of events, where a property is on the market, larger items of furniture at least will remain there until it is sold. Where property is let out, often it will be let out on a furnished basis. It is suggested that provided the individual does not spend time at the property the removal of furniture should not always be necessary to show that a property has ceased to be his home.

In spite of suggestions to the contrary in RDR3, it does not seem necessary that the property is sold or even let; simply that it ceases to be an individual's home. However, it is considered that where the property is not at least advertised for sale or letting, the circumstances in which it would cease to be an individual's home for this purpose must be very limited. To strengthen the argument an individual should consider removing all their furniture and belongings and make no further use of the property.

An individual who leaves the UK without taking their spouse or family is extremely unlikely to qualify for split-year treatment under Case 3, since a property in the UK in which they have lived and which their family continue to occupy is unlikely to cease to be their home for this purpose, even if they do not return to it for the rest of the tax year. See also HMRC comments in para A11 of Annex A:

> 'A11 A place can still be a home even if an individual does not stay there continuously. If, for example they move out temporarily but their spouse and children continue to live there, then it is still likely to be their home.'

### Holiday homes

**[5.06]** Where an individual has more than one home in the UK, they will need to consider letting or selling all of those homes to qualify for split-year treatment. However, the exclusion of holiday homes from the definition of home (at *para 25, Sch 45, FA 2013*) should be noted:

> '(3)    But somewhere that P uses periodically as nothing more than a holiday home or temporary retreat (or something similar) does not count as a home of P's.'

So, if the individual has, say, a family home in Birmingham in which he lives on a day-to-day basis and also a cottage in the Lake District that he uses, say, one weekend a month, then arguably he need not dispose of the cottage. Precisely where the line falls between what is a 'home' and what is a 'holiday home' will be an interesting question for this purpose. The position may for example be different if the individual moved his treasured possessions to the Lake District property if they planned to rent out the Birmingham home.

There may, for example, be an argument that when an individual goes to live overseas, his main home in the UK then becomes a temporary retreat that is used only for short holidays to the UK. If that argument holds, the home would cease to be a home and there would be no need for the individual to sell or let the property. However, it seems unlikely that HMRC would accept this argument.

For more details on 'holiday homes', see paras **3.07** and **7.05**.

### Establishing a 'sufficient link'

**[5.07]** Assuming that an individual has ceased to have a home in the UK, they must then fulfil the next part of the test. In addition to spending fewer than 16 days in the UK during the 'overseas part' of the year and remaining non-UK resident for the whole of the next tax year, the individual must, at the end of a six-month period, establish a 'sufficient link' with a country overseas (*para 46(7), Sch 45, FA 2013*). The HMRC guidance, RDR3, gives very little assistance here, effectively only repeating the legislation:

> '5.23 From the point you cease to have a home in the UK you must:
> - spend fewer than 16 days in the UK
> - in relation to a particular country, either:
>   - become resident for tax purposes in that country within six months
>   - be present in that country at the end of each day for six months, or

–   have your only home, or all your homes if you have more than
one, in that country within six months.'

The concept of a sufficient link is dealt with more fully at para **8.13**. However, this need to establish a sufficient link with another country is likely to have a significant bearing on the timing of an individual's departure so a brief exploration is included here.

Taking the last part of the test first – since we have already been considering an individual's home – in order to qualify for split-year treatment, an individual must, by definition, have given up their UK home so having all his homes in other countries is unlikely to prove a problem. However, the individual must have all his homes in the same other country which, for some taxpayers, may prove more difficult. Here the line between a 'holiday home' and a 'home' may prove crucial since any home which is only a 'holiday home' can be ignored for this purpose and this may be an area in which we see developing case law as time goes by. If the individual is able to meet this test, then there will be no need to consider either of the two more difficult parts of the sufficient link test.

Assuming that the individual retains homes in more than one country, then he is left having to meet one of the other two parts of the test. The first alternative is that he must be 'considered for tax purposes to be a resident of that country in accordance with its domestic laws.' This is where the timing of departure may prove crucial, since with the UK having such an unusual tax year, an individual might have left the UK, say in October 2016, be present in the other country for the following six months, but not yet be tax resident there: since he has effectively spent three months there in each of the calendar years 2016 and 2017. It is assumed that it is not necessary to take a snapshot at the six-month point.

So in the example of the individual leaving in October 2016, it is assumed that if the individual proves to be resident for the whole of 2017 for the purpose of that country's domestic law this will be sufficient, and it will be possible to look back to April 2017 with hindsight with no need to take the test as at April 2017, when the individual may not yet have done enough to make himself resident in his destination country. From a self-assessment perspective, in most cases this should not give rise to problems since the individual would usually know the position by the time of submitting his return for the split year. However, in cases of uncertainty he would presumably have to self-assess based on the most likely outcome and then revise his return if necessary.

Finally, if neither the only home nor the residence condition is fulfilled, an individual must be present in his destination country on every single midnight between his date of the departure from the UK and the end of the six-month period. This may prove difficult for many – it allows for no return visits to the UK whatsoever during this six-month period, but also it allows for no overnight visits to any other country, whether on business or as part of a holiday. Note also that there is no 'exceptional circumstances' concept for this rule.

## Timing is everything

**[5.08]** In view of the above factors, particularly the 'sufficient link' test, individuals will need to give careful consideration to the timing of their departure. If there is any doubt about their being able to meet the 'only home in the new country' test, then in most cases, they may wish to ensure that they will meet the requirements to be considered resident in their destination country since the alternative, that of spending every single midnight for six months in that country, is likely to prove too onerous for most.

In making their decision about the timing of their departure, however, individuals will also need to consider, for example, whether they will be able to restrict their return visits to the UK to just 16 days for the remainder of the tax year and, also, whether they are likely to be able to sell their UK property, or at least cease to occupy it in such a way that it could no longer be regarded as a home.

A further alternative, of course, is to take the old-fashioned route of leaving the UK towards the end of March and so not needing to rely on the split year and, in view of the restrictive nature of the split-year provisions, this is likely to be the approach taken by many. Such individuals will remain subject to UK tax on income and gains arising during the final few weeks of the tax year when they are no longer in the UK, but may well either be in a position to take advantage of a Double Tax Treaty (see below and CHAPTER 12) or may not yet be subject to tax in their destination country. Those individuals will need to think quite carefully about possibly planning to defer income and gains until the following tax year (but see the five-year trap at para **5.24** below).

## Double Tax Treaties

**[5.09]** Individuals leaving the UK to take up residence in another country should always give consideration to any double tax agreement between the UK and their destination country, particularly in the year of departure. An individual may not meet the stringent tests under the split-year provisions, but may still benefit from a favourable form of taxation due to being treaty resident in another jurisdiction.

Assuming that the individual is resident in both the UK and the destination country under the two countries' respective domestic laws, then it will be necessary to consider the tie-break provision of the relevant Treaty to determine in which country the individual is Treaty resident. For more detailed commentary on double taxation agreements in this context, see CHAPTER 12.

# Maintaining non-residence

**[5.10]** Whatever timing the individual decides on with regard to leaving the UK, they will then need to ensure that they maintain their non-residence status throughout the period overseas. The most straightforward way to do this would be to ensure that they pass one of the automatic non-residence tests. Failing this, they will then need to consider what ties they have retained with the UK and then limit the days they spend in the UK accordingly.

## Automatic non-residence

**[5.11]** Since this chapter deals with those who have gone overseas for a purpose other than full-time working abroad, we can assume that the third automatic test (full-time working abroad) will not be relevant. We can also assume that the individual does not die in the year and so the fourth test equally need not be considered.

We are then left with the first and second automatic tests. Assuming that the individual was resident in the UK in the previous tax year (ie we are looking at the tax year after departure) then the first and not the second automatic overseas test will apply. This test is in *para 12, Sch 45, FA 2013*:

'12   The first automatic overseas test is that –
   (a)   P was resident in the UK for one or more of the 3 tax years preceding year X,
   (b)   the number of days in year X that P spends in the UK is less than 16, and
   (c)   P does not die in year X.'

So the most straightforward way for an individual who is seeking to remain non-UK resident to achieve this would be for them to limit their days spent in the UK to 15 or fewer. Broadly, a day is a day of UK presence if the individual is here at midnight, but see paras **3.02–3.06** for a fuller definition. In particular, if an individual spends a number of days in the UK, but is not present at midnight the deemed days rule (see para **3.06**) may apply.

Many will find spending only 15 days in the UK too restrictive, especially if they have maintained business interests in the UK or have family here.

## Avoiding automatic UK residence

**[5.12]** Clearly the individual will need to avoid being resident in the UK under any of the automatic residence tests. For this purpose, it is assumed that the individuals who are the subject of this chapter will not work sufficient hours in the UK to meet the third automatic test (although see para **5.16** below) and it should be a fairly straightforward matter to ensure that the number of days spent in the UK will be less than 183.

The individual will nevertheless need to take care that they do not meet the 'UK home' test at any point – see para **2.08**. This would be on the basis that they have not given up their UK home and qualified for split year treatment on departure under Case 3. The difficulty here is that the definition of home is very broad (see para **3.07**). The definition for the purpose of this test is narrowed such that the home must be the individual's home for a period of more than 91 days (not necessarily in the same tax year) and they must be present there for a total of at least 30 days within the tax year. However, where an individual's family remain in the UK, this test could easily be met. If this should coincide with a period of at least 91 days when they have no home outside the UK, they will be automatically UK resident.

**Example 5.1: Bob**

Bob is self-employed and decides to expand his business into Europe. He decides to base himself in Germany for this purpose and spends six months there in a rented flat getting settled. Bob has young children who are in school in the UK and he and his wife do not wish to disturb their education so his wife decides to remain in the UK in the family home. Bob employs a manager to look after his existing UK business.

Bob leaves the UK on 30 March 2016 and rents a flat in Hamburg on a six-month lease (from 1 April 2016 to 30 September). During that time, Bob does not return to the UK. At the end of the six months, Bob's business in Germany is well established and he decides to spend some time in the UK with his family (from 6 November). He then returns to Germany for the rest of November spending time in a hotel before spending the following two months (December and January) travelling in France, Italy and Spain to further expand the business. He returns to Germany during this time, but in view of the amount of time spent travelling he chooses to stay in a number of different hotels. He also spends a further five nights with his family over Christmas.

Since Bob's family remain in the UK, he will have a home in the UK. As he chooses to spend five weeks in October and November with his family, the UK family home will pass the 30-day test and the family home will count as his home throughout the tax year 2016/17 for the purpose of the second automatic test. Note that although in this example the 30 days are consecutive there is no need for them to be so.

Since Bob gives up his German flat and does not establish another home for a period of four months, there will be a period of at least 91 days when his only home is in the UK. Bob would therefore be resident in the UK during 2016/17 under the second automatic residence test, despite only spending 40 nights in the UK.

The 'UK home' test is a rolling one and the 91 days need not all fall within one tax year, so careful monitoring here will be essential. In addition, although the individual must spend 30 days in a property for it to be considered his home for the purposes of the test, these days could fall outside the 91-day period during which he has no home outside the UK. So in the above example if Bob had spent 25 days in the family home during the period when he was also renting the Hamburg flat, this together with the five days at Christmas would also have been sufficient for him to meet the 'UK home' test and be automatically UK resident.

## Sufficient ties test

**[5.13]** Assuming that the individual spends more than 15 days in the UK and has successfully negotiated the automatic residence test, he will then need to consider the sufficient ties test. As with the automatic overseas test, it is assumed that initially the individual will have been UK resident in the previous three tax years, so it is the table of ties and days in *para 18, Sch 45, FA 2013* which needs to be considered. More detail on this test is included in CHAPTER 2 and for more detail on the definitions of the ties see CHAPTERS 2 and 3.

Note that if the individual has the number of ties shown in the second column he *will* be resident in the UK.

| Days spent by P in the UK in year X | Number of ties that are sufficient |
|---|---|
| More than 15 but not more than 45 | At least 4 |
| More than 45 but not more than 90 | At least 3 |
| More than 90 but not more than 120 | At least 2 |
| More than 120 | At least 1 |

For an individual seeking to establish himself as non-UK resident it will be a matter of balancing those ties which he cannot or does not wish to give up with the number of days which he needs or wishes to spend in the UK. In many ways this does not differ from the advice which an individual would have been given under the old regime using limited statute and HMRC practice derived from case law – effectively: minimise your connections with the UK and minimise the number of days spent here. However, under the SRT this basic principle now assumes some hard edges.

For an individual who has been previously UK resident, now seeking to become non-resident, it is exceedingly likely that he will have the 90-day tie – ie he will have been present in the UK for 90 days in one, if not both, of the preceding two tax years. This is not a tie which he will be able to give up, so for the first two years of his non-residence at least he will have at least one tie (he is therefore immediately limited to spending fewer than 120 days in the UK if he wishes to be non-UK resident).

The individual will then need to consider whether there are any other ties which he has or is likely to have with the UK and which he cannot or does not wish to give up and then manage the time he spends in the UK accordingly.

### Maintaining a UK property

[**5.14**] Those who wish to maintain their property in the UK may wish to consider whether it will be possible to do this without that property being treated as an accommodation tie. The criteria for the accommodation tie are in *para 34, Sch 45, FA 2013* and a detailed discussion of this tie is included at para **3.18**.

Many individuals seeking to become non-UK resident do not wish to surrender their UK property permanently and for them it will be important to decide whether they are happy for the property to remain their 'home' – in which case it will be a further tie as an accommodation tie. Assuming that the property is available for a period of 91 days continuously during the tax year then the individual need only spend one night in that place for it to be 'available' and therefore give the individual the accommodation tie. If a property is occupied by their immediate family, then it will be assumed to be available. The HMRC guidance RDR3 gives the following example in Annex A:

'Example A19

Peter and his civil partner Andrew share an apartment in London. Last year Andrew moved to the USA to take up a university place to study marine biology.

This year Andrew came back to the UK for a three-week holiday which he and Peter spent in Scotland. Andrew spent the first night and last night of his holiday in their London apartment.

This year Andrew has an accommodation tie.'

It is not clear from this example whether Peter and Andrew own or are renting their apartment. However, the key point here is that, although Peter is only in the UK for three weeks, the apartment is considered available to him continuously and his spending two nights there is enough to give him an accommodation tie.

Thus, if an individual wishes to maintain their UK property, they must either ensure that it is unavailable to them for the majority of the year or they must spend no time in that property at all during the tax year in question.

The simplest way to ensure that a UK property is not available is to let it out. The HMRC guidance confirms that this will be sufficient, as well as the treatment outlined above – ie when the individual does not occupy the property at all:

'**When accommodation is not considered to be a connection factor**

A40   Accommodation owned by an individual but which they have wholly let out commercially would not be considered as available to live in unless they retained the right to use the property or part of the property.

A41   Accommodation that is available to an individual but in which they have not spent at least one night in the tax year will not be an accommodation tie.'

What the HMRC guidance does not deal with is when an individual has made a property available for letting but has failed to actually let it. Presumably such accommodation would still be available to him, and he would therefore need to avoid spending any nights in the property if he did not wish to have an accommodation tie.

If the individual's family lives in the property, he must either accept that he has an accommodation tie or ensure that he does not spend even one night there in the tax year.

### Example 5.2: Matthew

At the end of 2014/15 Matthew moves to Spain for work and remains there throughout 2015/16 and 2016/17. As he will be spending more than 30 days working in the UK he will not meet the third automatic overseas test with regard to full-time working abroad.

Matthew's wife and 14-year-old daughter remain in the UK in the family home because his daughter is at school here and the family do not want to disrupt her education.

In 2015/16, he returns to the family home for two nights over the Christmas period. He therefore has available accommodation for 2015/16 and will have an accommodation tie for that year.

In 2016/17, he and his family decide to spend Christmas with his parents and they stay there for seven nights. Even though his parents would be happy for Matthew to stay with them whenever he wishes, because the period he in fact spends in their home is less than 16 days and they meet the definition of a close relative (*para 34(6), Sch 45, FA 2013*), this accommodation will not be available to him.

Although Matthew's wife and daughter remain in the family home throughout 2016/17 and Matthew could return to it whenever he wishes, because he does not spend even one night in the property it will not be available accommodation for 2016/17 and Matthew will not have an accommodation tie for that year.

It is important to note that visiting the property (without spending the night there) will not make it an accommodation tie, nor will keeping furniture and other personal belongings in the property. An individual who wished to maintain his UK property, therefore, and did not wish to let it out, could choose to leave the property furnished and empty and could even visit the property to pick up post and perform maintenance tasks, provided he spent the night elsewhere. Indeed, an individual whose family lives in the UK could even, in theory, spend time with his family in the family home during the day time provided he spent the night elsewhere. If an individual did wish to take this approach it would be important to document carefully the arrangement to ensure that there is clear evidence that the individual had spent the night elsewhere.

### Accommodation traps

**[5.15]** The way in which the available accommodation tie works can give some odd results and there are some traps into which the unwary can fall. The biggest trap probably comes as a result of the deeming rule which comes into play when there is a gap of fewer than 16 days between periods of occupation of the same property. As the HMRC guidance RDR3 identifies, this can even give rise to a hotel room being treated as available and therefore an accommodation tie (see para **3.18**). There is a hotel example in the guidance (reproduced in **CHAPTER 3**) which considers an individual who comes to the UK over an extended period with short breaks but, as identified in **CHAPTER 3**, even a fortnightly return to the same hotel can be enough to give an individual available accommodation if there are enough return visits.

There seems to be at least a theoretical trap where an individual stays the night with a good friend, if that friend is sufficiently close that they would always make their home available should the individual need it. This is because, although there is an exception for close family that requires an individual to spend 16 nights there, as opposed to just the one night needed for most properties, there is no such exception for close friends. Although a theoretical problem, provided the friend does not put the sentiment into writing and there are not regular return visits, it is difficult to see how HMRC would prove that the accommodation is available and the fact there is no 16-day additional rule for close friends suggests there is no presumption of accommodation being available in such cases as there might be with family. The same would apply to relatives who do not meet the definition of a 'close relative.'

However, RDR3 gives an example in Annex A of an uncle (who would not meet the definition of a close relative):

'Example A14

Mary has lived and worked in the USA for many years. Her uncle has a holiday houseboat in the UK where he has agreed Mary can stay any time she wishes, for as long as she wishes, when she comes here. Mary's uncle does not allow other people to stay in the houseboat.

Last year Mary came to the UK twice. She made arrangements to stay for three weeks with a friend and for four weeks with her brother. Although the houseboat was available for a continuous period of at least 91 days, Mary did not use it at all. Therefore, she had no accommodation tie in respect of the houseboat last year.

This year Mary again visited the UK twice, spending her five-week summer holiday on her uncle's houseboat. This year Mary has an accommodation tie as the houseboat is available for a continuous period of at least 91 days and she has stayed on it for at least one night.'

In this example, Mary spends five weeks on the boat, but in fact if the boat is available for a period of 91 days, she need only have stayed on the boat for one night for it to be 'available'.

RDR3 does make clear, however, that accommodation being available involves more than a casual offer of accommodation or an open invite for a social visit:

'A33  Accommodation is regarded as available to you for a continuous period of 91 days if you are able to use it, or it is at your disposal, at all times throughout that period (subject to the 16 day gap rule covered below). If a relative were to make their home available to you casually, for a social visit, say, it will not mean that the accommodation would be regarded as being available to you. However, if it is available to you for a continuous period of 91 days and you use it casually, it will be a tie.

A34  Similarly, a casual offer from a friend to "stay in my spare room any time" will not constitute an accommodation tie unless your friend really is prepared to put you up for 91 days at a time (whether he actually does so or not).

**Example A16**

Sacha visits the UK on business and usually stays in different hotels. On one of these visits he takes an opportunity to attend the Wimbledon Tennis Championships. A business associate who lives in Wimbledon invites Sacha to stay at his flat for three nights rather than use a hotel. The arrangement is a one-off invitation and the accommodation is not available to Sacha for 91 days. It is not an accommodation tie.'

The example given here is not very illuminating (especially as the Wimbledon Championships only last two weeks!). The comments do nevertheless suggest that there would need to be a high level of use of a friend's property (or perhaps some formal agreement or other arrangement) before it was assumed by HMRC to be 'available' for 91 days.

Although the 16-day limit for staying with close family may seem generous, there will be times, for example a family illness, when the 16-day limit could become quite restrictive. If an individual remains in the UK to care for a suddenly and seriously ill parent or other close relative, or is taken ill himself while visiting a relative, he might expect those days in the UK not to count as days of presence due to the exceptional circumstances provisions in *para 22(4)–(6), Sch 45, FA 2013* (see para **3.06**). However, the exceptional circumstances provisions *only* relate to days of presence in the UK and not to determining whether any of the sufficient ties tests applies. So, if the individual were to stay in their sick parent's home for more than 16 days then they may be treated as having available accommodation and so have an accommodation tie for that tax year.

### Example 5.3: Mary

Mary took early retirement from her job and moved to Spain with her husband in March 2015/16, where they have a property on the Costa del Sol. She has sold her UK property and therefore does not have available accommodation in the UK. Her children are all over 18 so she has no family tie.

When she retired from her job she was asked if she would be able to work on a consultancy basis for her old employer from time to time, which she agreed to do. During 2016/17 she returns to the UK eight times, each for a period of one week (seven days) and she spends five days of each week working for more than three hours. In total, therefore, Mary works 40 days in the UK and has the work tie. She also has the 90-day tie from her days in the UK in 2015/16.

Mary also returns to the UK in December 2016 for seven days when she stays with her parents over the Christmas period. Unfortunately on the day when Mary intended to fly back to Spain, she develops appendicitis. After a brief (three-day) stay in hospital, Mary returns to her parents' house to recuperate for 14 days before returning to Spain.

At the beginning of the tax year Mary expects to have two ties under the sufficient ties test – the 90-day tie and the work tie. She therefore expects to be able to return to the UK for up to 90 days without being treated as UK resident. Before her illness, Mary had spent 63 days in the UK – well under the 90 days.

The exceptional circumstances provisions should apply to the additional 17 days which Mary spends in the UK as a result of her illness. In any case, in the absence of a further tie, the days would only take Mary's total day count to 80 – still well under the 90 days permitted for someone with two ties. However, Mary has now spent a total of 21 days staying in her parents' house during the tax year. This is sufficient to give Mary an accommodation tie to the UK. Mary now has three UK ties and will therefore be UK resident for 2016/17.

In the above example, if Mary were to have stayed elsewhere during the period of recuperation – eg with a sibling – because this was for fewer than 16 days, she could have avoided having an accommodation tie and would not, therefore, have been UK resident. Similarly, she could have stayed with a close friend, potentially for more than 16 days, provided that the friend was not prepared to offer her accommodation for a period of at least 91 days.

It is worth reiterating that it is not sufficient simply to spend more than 16 days in the property in order for an individual to have available accommodation – the property must also be available to the individual for a continuous period of at least 91 days. However, it is likely that in respect of the home of a close relative the onus will be on the individual to prove that the accommodation was not available.

## Working in the UK

[5.16] When a HNWI is considering maintaining his non-residence position he will often need to factor in the need to work in the UK. In these circumstances, there are two tests which must be considered. First, the third automatic UK residence test of full-time working in the UK and, assuming that is not met, the work tie in the sufficient ties test. The rules for workers with a 'relevant job' are different, and are considered in para **3.15**.

It is not uncommon for a HNWI seeking to become non-UK resident to have a business interest in the UK, or to be a director of a UK company. Prior to the introduction of the SRT, many advisors would have been concerned that maintaining a position as director of a UK company would have had a negative impact on the individual's residence position, when balancing all the relevant factors, and common advice would have been to surrender that position if at all possible.

Following the introduction of the SRT, retaining the position as director of a UK company, or maintaining UK business interests, in itself, will have no impact on an individual's residence position. However, the duties which the individual must perform as a result of, for example, holding the office of director, and where those duties must be performed will need to be considered in order to ascertain whether that will be sufficient to meet the two work-related tests.

### Full-time working in the UK

[5.17] Assuming the individual wishes to remain non-UK resident, he will obviously need to ensure that he does not pass the third automatic UK test by working full time or 'sufficient hours' (as defined) in the UK. A detailed explanation of working sufficient hours in the UK is included at para **2.09**.

However, due to the fact that the bar for full-time working is set quite high (at an average of 35 hours per week over the period), it should usually be relatively easy for an individual to avoid working sufficient hours in the UK to be treated as working full time here. Care may be needed in the initial period, however, if the individual has been working full time in the UK before the date of their departure. The full-time working in the UK test considers a 365-day period and not a tax year, so an individual who has been working long hours in the UK prior to leaving could continue to be working full time in the UK on an averaging test.

### Example 5.4: Stephanie

Stephanie left the UK to live in France at the end of March 2016. She has worked in the UK all her life and built several successful businesses and decides to retire overseas. She sells her UK property (the sale completes in March 2016) and buys a property in France.

Stephanie owns a software development company in the UK and has worked full time for that company for 12 years as CEO. However, over the last two years she has been working in the business with her eldest daughter and now decides it is time to pass the baton to her daughter and step down herself from her active role. She is to remain as President of the company for the foreseeable future.

Stephanie has to-date taken a very hands-on attitude to management and commonly works a 45 to 60-hour week. For the tax year 2015/16 her average weekly hours were 48. Following her departure in March, there is a funding crisis in the company and despite her retirement Stephanie returns to the UK two days a week for four weeks in April 2016 to help manage the crisis and works for ten hours on each of those days.

Stephanie's circumstances are such that she is not non-resident in 2015/16 and so 2016/17 is the first year for which she would expect to be non-resident. Assuming that she will spend more than 16 days in the UK in 2016/17, Stephanie will not be automatically non-resident. She will therefore next need to consider the automatic residence tests.

In order to be resident in the UK under the third automatic test, Stephanie only needs a 365-day period, one day of which falls into the 2016/17 tax year, during which she meets the conditions. Broadly these conditions require that she averages 35 hours per week under the complex averaging calculation and 75% of her workdays in the period are UK workdays. The day which falls within 2016/17 must be a day on which she does more than three hours' work in the UK.

The first week of April 2016 falls within the 2015/16 tax year. However, Stephanie also does more than three hours' work on 11 April 2016. If we take a 365-day period from 12 April 2015 to 11 April 2016, Stephanie will almost certainly work more than an average of 35 hours per week in the UK – since this will include the period during which she worked long hours.

Stephanie must then consider whether any of the split-year Cases will apply to her. As she has not gone abroad for full-time work, the only case which could apply would be Case 3 which, as considered in para 5.03 above, will only apply in the year the individual ceases to have a home in the UK. Stephanie ceased to have a home in the UK in 2015/16 so the split-year test cannot apply to her for 2016/17. Stephanie is therefore likely to be resident in the UK under UK domestic law for the whole of 2016/17.

For a more detailed explanation of the sufficient hours calculation, together with worked examples, see CHAPTER 2.

Wherever possible, when the individual intends to continue to work in the UK after moving abroad, he should aim to have a break of at least 31 days when he does no work (or less than three hours' work per day) in the UK. In Stephanie's case, if the crisis at her company had happened in, say, May, and she had been able to have a break of 31 days she could then have returned to the UK in exactly the same manner and avoided being treated as working full time here.

## Work tie

**[5.18]** Difficulties with the third automatic residence test in the first year of non-residence aside, an individual who remains a director of a UK company or maintains a business interest in the UK is much more likely to need to consider whether he has a work tie with the UK. So, in Example 5.4 above, Stephanie will need to consider whether her activities as President of her company create a work tie.

The definition of 'work tie' is at *para 35, Sch 45, FA 2013* (for those who do not have a 'relevant' international transport job):

'(1)  P has a work tie for year X if P works in the UK for at least 40 days (whether continuously or intermittently) in year X.

(2)  For these purposes, P works in the UK for a day if P does more than 3 hours' work in the UK on that day.'

*Paragraph 36, Sch 45, FA 2013*, concerned with those with a 'relevant job', is not explored in this chapter.

So, on first glance, avoiding having a UK work tie should be fairly straight-forward – it is simply a matter of ensuring that fewer than 40 days of work are done in the UK – this amounts to approximately eight working weeks. There are nonetheless a couple of areas worthy of consideration in the context of an individual remaining a UK director: the three-hour rule and the location of work.

### The three-hour rule

**[5.19]** As noted in CHAPTER 3 (see para **3.08**), the term 'work' is interpreted quite broadly. In summary, 'work' will include time spent in training and travel time. The most pertinent of these to a HNWI continuing a UK directorship or maintaining a UK business interest would almost certainly be travel.

Travel time counts as time spent working where the cost of the travel would be a deductible expense had the individual incurred it himself. In these circum-stances, the whole of the journey will count as work, even where no actual work is done. Otherwise, travel time only counts as time spent working to the extent that the individual actually is working.

Time spent working on a flight, ferry or train journey to the UK from overseas will count as overseas work (see location of work, below). Once an individual has disembarked from the plane, boat or train, any further time spent travelling – including negotiating passport control and baggage handling – will count as time spent travelling in the UK.

In view of the fact that only three hours' work is needed to count as a day of working in the UK, an individual may wish to think quite carefully about the timing of his travel to the UK and also, possibly, the method of travel since, for example, travelling by Eurostar would not involve a need to collect baggage and in some circumstances may allow for a shorter amount of time spent travelling in the UK. This will only be relevant where the cost of the journey would be tax deductible, so is most likely to be of relevance to those who are employed abroad and need to return to carry out some duties in the UK but who do not (for whatever reason) meet the full-time working abroad test.

### Example 5.5: George

George has left the UK to set up a new branch of his business in Germany. He has to report back to the board of the UK company. He returns to the UK for monthly board meetings throughout 2016/17. In addition, he returns to the UK for a two-week (ten working day) period in June to train his successor in the UK.

The board meetings tend to last for a full afternoon – between three and four hours. However, George likes to make a trip of it and flies to the UK the day before, staying in a hotel close to the office and spending time with friends or family (checking emails whilst he is here). He then stays overnight to have dinner with his work colleagues and flies home the following day. The UK company meets all of his travel costs for attending the board meeting. George's office is a two-and-a-half hour journey from the nearest airport and clearing passport control and collecting his luggage usually takes approximately one hour.

George will have three days of UK working for every board meeting in the UK – since he will have three hours of work on each of his days of travel (assuming that on the day of his return flight he arrives at the airport at least half an hour before his journey). He will therefore have 36 UK workdays in respect of the board meetings. This, taken together with his ten days in June, will amount to 46 UK workdays and will be sufficient for George to have a work tie.

The above example illustrates how easily an individual can accumulate UK workdays – especially if their office is a long way from the nearest airport. Individuals wishing to continue working in the UK, but not wishing to have a UK work tie, will need to consider how they can do this efficiently. For example, in the case of George, if he had flown into the UK on the morning of the board meeting and left the same evening, he would only have a total of 22 workdays and would not have a UK work tie.

Patterns of working will also be important – so, once an individual passes the three-hour threshold, he has nothing to lose by working the rest of that day in the UK. Similarly, if an individual can keep his working hours below this threshold on a given date, he might avoid a UK workday altogether – for example if he limits his work on a given day to one two-hour meeting. As discussed at para at **3.10**, there will be a practical point in these circumstances about keeping records to prove that the individual is not working. HMRC published guidance gives only very limited assistance as to the kind of records which would be acceptable (see **CHAPTER 13**). See also **CHAPTER 13** on enquiries.

It is important to remember that journey time only counts as work where the cost of travel would be tax deductible or where the individual actually works during the journey.

If, for example, George had simply retired overseas from his main 'occupation' and was returning to the UK for director's duties then, assuming he does not work on the journey, these days will not count as UK workdays. For many HNWIs retaining UK directorships, therefore, travel time may not be a concern. George will, of course, still need to watch his days of presence in the UK.

Thus, where travel costs are not tax deductible, the individual will still need to consider whether they have actually worked during the journey as this will bring the travel time back into the definition of work. So if, for example, Stephanie of Example 5.4 reads company papers or emails while travelling back to the UK in her role as President, this will count as time spent working, with the relevant portion treated as time spent working in the UK. Conversely, if the journey time is counted as travel because of the tax deductibility rule, an individual has nothing to lose by working during the journey.

Those who have their travel costs met by their employers may wish to try to keep a few UK workdays 'in hand' – ie limit their UK workdays to, say, 35 days to allow for problems with baggage handling or other delays at airports which may result in their having unexpected, additional UK workdays.

*Location of work*

**[5.20]** Another practical issue for those continuing with UK employments or UK business interests will be the location of the work they carry out. See para **3.04** for a more detailed explanation of the location of work.

Location of work is defined in *para 27, Sch 45, FA 2013* which states helpfully that 'work is done where it is actually done.' In other words, it does not matter in which country an individual is employed or the residence of the company that pays their wages – it is where they are physically located when carrying out the work which is significant when it comes to counting UK workdays.

RDR3 gives an example to illustrate this:

'3.21 In most cases work is considered to be done at the location where it is actually done rather than where an employment is held or a trade, profession or vocation is carried on.

**Example 23**

Robert is an employee of a French clothing manufacturer and he is based in Paris. He spends two days each month working in Glasgow to meet company clients. For those two days Robert is working in the UK, regardless of where he is usually based.'

This may present an opportunity for those wishing to continue to have a hand in running UK businesses, either as an employee or in a self-employed capacity. Where it is possible for an individual to carry out any part of their work overseas, this will allow them to minimise both their UK workdays and also their days of presence in the UK.

Looking at the example of George again, if he had been able to attend half of the UK board meetings by phone, only attending in person every other month, for example, this would have allowed him to almost halve his UK workdays. In some circumstances it may also be possible and desirable to hold board meetings overseas to assist a non-resident director seeking to avoid a UK work tie, although this may give other tax considerations that would need to be taken into account.

As noted above, there is a specific rule regarding work done as part of international travel – by air, sea or 'via a tunnel under the sea' (in other words Eurostar). Any work carried out until the individual disembarks in the UK or from the time of boarding when travelling to or from the UK in this way is treated as being done overseas.

Paragraph **3.04** contains a detailed discussion regarding the effect that this may have on an individual's travel choices. However, there may be other considerations – for example, an individual who has a certain amount of preparation to do for a UK meeting might choose to do that preparation on the plane as opposed to on the train journey from the airport to the meeting (assuming that the travel from the airport will not otherwise count as work time).

Today's technology means it is often possible to do the same work from anywhere in the world and this will present an opportunity to minimise workdays in the UK, but may also present a problem with record-keeping to prove one's location when the work was completed. For example, if an individual writes a report on the plane and it takes him six hours, but does not email that report until he gets into the office in the UK (after a further two-hour train journey), how does he prove that he did not, in fact, continue to write the report while on the train in the UK?

## *Family*

**[5.21]** The definition of a family tie is in *paras 32* and *33, Sch 45, FA 2013* of the SRT and is explored in more detail at para **3.17**. However, RDR3 contains a fairly good summary of the rules, in Chapter 2:

'2.2    You have a family tie for the tax year under consideration if any of the following people are UK resident for tax purposes for that year:
- your husband, wife or civil partner (unless you are separated)
- your partner, if you are living together as husband and wife or as civil partners
- your child, if under 18-years-old.

2.3    For the purpose of the SRT, HMRC will use the same principles applied to tax credits to determine if people are living together as husband and wife or civil partners. You will find further guidance on this point in our manual TCTM09330.

2.4    You will not have a family tie with a child who is under the age of 18 if you spend time with the child in person in the UK on fewer than 61 days (in total) in the tax year concerned. If your child turns 18 during that tax year you will not have a family tie in respect of that child if you see that child in the UK on fewer than 61 days in the part of the tax year before their eighteenth birthday.

2.5    Any day or part of a day that you see your child in person in the UK counts as a day on which you see your child in the UK.

2.6    Partners can be living together either in the UK or overseas, or both, and still meet this test.

2.7    Separated means separated:
- under an order of a court of competent jurisdiction
- by deed of separation, or
- in circumstances where the separation is likely to be permanent.'

The position with regard to children is slightly more complicated as they will not be treated as UK resident for this purpose if they are in the UK for full-time education and they spend fewer than 21 days in the UK outside term time.

If the individual seeking to become non-UK resident does not take his family with him when he leaves the UK, then this will obviously result in him having the family tie and will mean he can spend fewer days in the UK before being treated as UK resident.

As far as the traditional UK nuclear family is concerned, there may be nothing that can be done in the way of planning from a tax perspective. However, where the individual has children from a previous marriage, for example, so that he has children who are UK resident but no UK resident spouse, he may consider limiting the amount of time he spends with that child in the UK. There is no limit to the amount of time he can spend with the child in his destination country or in another location (eg on holiday). It is worth noting that there is no midnight test with regard to time spent with children – so, for example, if the individual and his daughter both sleep over at grandma's house for one night he will very likely see the child in the evening of the first day and the following morning, so this will count as two days.

There will also be interesting questions about when a partner who is neither a spouse nor civil partner should be treated as such in view of the fact that the individuals are living in separate locations, and this is explored at para **3.17**.

Where an individual has UK resident family it may be difficult for them to avoid also having available accommodation (see para **5.14** above). An individual whose family remains in the UK is therefore likely to have at least three ties in the first two years of residence – the family tie, the accommodation tie and the 90-day tie. Such an individual will be restricted to just 45 days in the UK if they do not wish to become UK resident and must avoid acquiring a work tie.

### Country tie

**[5.22]** It is important not to overlook the country tie.

An individual will have the country tie where he 'meets the midnight test' for the greatest number of days in the UK; in other words, if the individual is present in the UK (at midnight) for more days than he is present in any other country. Theoretically, this could be a very low number if the individual spends a lot of the year travelling and visits many different countries, but in practice is more likely to mean that the individual spends the majority or at least a significant proportion of his time in the UK.

Where the individual spends the same number of days in more than one country and one of those countries is the UK, if that is also the greatest number of days the individual spends in any country then he will have the country tie for that year.

# Year of return

**[5.23]** Assuming that the individual has not left the UK permanently (which some will have done), there will come a time when they need to consider their return. Many of the considerations for those returning to the UK will be exactly the same as for those coming to the UK for the first time, and these are dealt with in **CHAPTER 7**. However, there will be some additional concerns specific to those who have had a period outside the UK and are returning and these are considered in this chapter.

## The five-year trap

**[5.24]** HMRC were concerned that the increased certainty of a statutory residence test might give rise to additional avoidance activity, and specific anti-avoidance legislation was therefore introduced to combat this. Anti-avoidance along the lines of that which has applied to capital gains since *Finance Act 1998* (in the shape of *s 10A, TCGA 1992*) has now been introduced for certain forms of income, which it is assumed HMRC consider would be easy for an individual to manipulate. In addition, *s 10A* itself has been rewritten. A detailed consideration of the anti-avoidance legislation is contained in CHAPTER 11.

In summary, the rules will apply where an individual is temporarily non-resident and the period of their non-residence is five years or less. A period of non-residence for this purpose can include a period where the individual is resident in the UK, but also resident in another country. Like the previous CGT anti-avoidance, the rules will only apply to individuals who have been resident in the UK for four out of the seven tax years immediately preceding the year of their departure. The period of non-residence is calculated by reference to actual years and not tax years. There are, however, some complications where either or both of the individual's year of arrival or departure do not qualify for split-year treatment (see para **11.02**).

The following types of income (or amounts treated as income) will be affected in addition to capital gains:

- Pensions (withdrawals, lump sums and certain other charges)
- Relevant foreign income which is remitted to the UK during the period of temporary non-residence
- Certain amounts taxable under the disguised remuneration provisions
- Dividends or other distributions from close companies (or companies which would be close if they were UK resident)
- Chargeable event gains
- Offshore income gains

There are different specific rules in relation to each of the different types of income, but, broadly, each of these treats income which arose during the period of non-residence as arising in the period after the individual returns to the UK (or ceases to also be resident in another country). This will be the case even if the income has been subject to tax in another country and if it would otherwise be protected by a Double Tax Treaty. An individual returning to the UK who is close to the five-year limit will therefore wish to give careful consideration to the timing of his return, as far as possible, to prevent triggering these anti-avoidance provisions. This may affect certain decisions regarding particular actions – for example, the purchase of a property in the UK – which would result in the split-year provisions applying and may affect the date from which the individual is treated as becoming UK resident.

## When does UK residence begin?

**[5.25]** As with the period of non-UK residence, the time at which UK residence begins will depend on whether the split-year provisions apply in the year of return to the UK; although, again, it is worth saying that if the individual is resident at all in the year of return, then he will be resident for the whole tax year. If he also qualifies for split-year treatment, then he will be *taxed* broadly as though he is non-resident for the overseas part of the year.

Assuming that the individual has not worked full time abroad and is not coming to the UK for reasons connected with his own or his spouse's employment, the relevant cases for the split-year test will be Cases 4 and 8. In both cases the crucial question is concerned with the individual's home, and individuals who have previously been UK resident, but had a period of non-residence, may have some particular concerns here.

Under Case 4 (*para 47, Sch 45, FA 2013*), the individual will qualify for split-year treatment if he does not meet the 'only home' test at the beginning of the tax year, and at some point during the tax year he begins to meet this test and he does so for the remainder of the tax year. It is worth noting that this is a different test to the test under the automatic UK tests and there is no minimum availability or minimum occupation required for property to be a home. To qualify under this test, the individual must also be not resident under the sufficient ties test for the period of the year before he met the only home test. More details on this element of the test are given at para **8.19**.

Case 8 is also concerned with a home, but here the taxpayer must begin the year with no home in the UK and then end the year with such a home. He will also need to have a home for the remainder of that tax year and the whole of the following tax year. Again, it will be necessary for the taxpayer not to have been resident in the UK under the sufficient ties test for the period of the year before he acquires a home.

The returning taxpayer who has retained property in the UK must therefore make a qualitative judgement about the nature of that property – is it a 'home' or is it merely 'available accommodation' (it could in fact be one, both or neither). The significance of the question is that, if the property that the individual maintained while he was overseas remained his home then any accommodation which he has overseas will need to cease to be his home in order for split-year treatment under Case 4 to apply. If, on the other hand, he maintained a property which was not his home, he need only begin to live there again as though it were his home in order to qualify for split-year treatment under Case 8 (assuming, of course, that he meets the other conditions).

#### Example 5.6: Marianne

Marianne is French, but has lived and worked in the UK since she came here to attend university and married her husband, Steve. In March 2016 her mother became ill and Marianne chose to leave the UK and move back to Nice to care for her. Her mother's condition deteriorated and, after 18 months, Marianne decided that she would need to arrange for her mother to go into a nursing home in the UK. Marianne therefore returned to the UK in September 2017. During the period of her non-residence, Marianne returned to the UK for a number of weekend visits, always staying with Steve in their home.

Given that the property that Marianne occupied with Steve was her home before she left to go overseas, it is likely that the property continues to be her home (rather than merely 'available accommodation') during the period of her non-residence, particularly since she returns to the home at weekends. In addition, it is likely that while Marianne lives with her mother in France, that property is also her home.

Since Marianne has maintained a home in the UK, she will therefore need to cease to have the home in France in order to qualify for split-year treatment. See para 5.05 for a detailed discussion of when a home ceases to be a home. The timing of her UK residence for split-year purposes will be dependent on the timing of her French home ceasing to be her home, rather than on her return to the UK.

Where an individual's immediate family continue to live in the UK in what was previously the family home and that individual spends some nights in the home during their period of non-residence, it seems reasonable to conclude that the property remains their home throughout that period and this is certainly HMRC's interpretation, borne out by numerous examples in RDR3. In order to qualify for split-year treatment, therefore, the individual will need to have had a home overseas (which is likely if they have been non-UK resident) and will need to cease to have that home (ie they will need to seek to fall within Case 4).

By contrast, if the individual had rented out their UK property while they were non-UK resident, it is clear that they had no home in the UK during their period of non-residence and they need only either re-occupy that property or occupy another UK property as their home in order to qualify for split-year treatment under Case 8 (provided the other conditions, including the sufficient ties test, are also met).

What is less clear is a case where an individual leaves family in the UK in what was previously their home but either does not return to the UK at all during his period of non-UK residence or does return, but does not sleep at the property (perhaps to avoid having an accommodation tie). It is tentatively suggested that if an individual does not sleep at a property for a prolonged period it cannot be his home, but in a case where his family remain there and he keeps property there, it is far from clear cut. Indeed, Example A5 in RDR3 suggests that HMRC would not agree with this view (see para **5.05** above for a detailed discussion of ceasing to have a home in the UK).

### Example 5.7: James

James leaves the UK in March 2014 to spend two years writing a novel on a small Greek Island. James does not spend enough hours per week working on the novel to meet the full-time working abroad test. He rents a villa on a long lease for the time he is in Greece.

James has a UK resident son from a previous relationship and returns to the UK for several weekends and during school holidays to spend time with him. James spends sufficient time with his son to have a family tie. As he had lived in the UK for a number of years before his departure he also has the 90-day tie.

In order to be able to spend as much time as possible in the UK with his son, James decides that he will aim to avoid having the accommodation tie. However, James does not want to give up his UK property and does not like the idea of renting it out.

He therefore maintains the property, but does not sleep there when he returns to the UK (although he does visit the property to mow the lawn, pick up post and carry out small maintenance tasks).

The novel takes slightly longer than expected and James returns to the UK in June 2017. James re-occupies his UK property on 3 June 2017, but decides to keep his Greek property for a further six months in order to have a couple of holidays with his son, as well as spend some time there making final revisions to the book. He finally gives up the lease on the property on 30 November 2017.

James will certainly be resident in the UK for 2017/18. However, how the split-year provisions will apply will depend on whether he falls within Case 4 or Case 8. In order to fall within Case 8, James must not have a home in the UK at the beginning of the tax year and must start to have one during the tax year. In this case, that means the UK property must not be his home on 2 June and must begin to be his home on 3 June. It certainly seems possible to argue that a property that James maintains and keeps his belongings in but in which he does not sleep for a period of over two years has ceased to be his home (in spite of Example A5 in RDR3). If this is correct, and assuming the other part of the test regarding sufficient ties is met, James will begin to have a home in the UK on 3 June and will qualify for split-year treatment.

However, HMRC might well wish to argue that keeping furniture and personal belongings in a property that has been your home is sufficient for it to remain so (especially in view of James's visits to the property). On this basis, James would need to consider the test in Case 4, and would begin to have an only home on 1 December. If this is the case, he may have difficulty meeting the sufficient ties test (see para 5.26 below) and may be treated as resident throughout the tax year.

If James wants certainty about his residence position for 2017/18, he will need to give up his Greek property when he returns to the UK, so that he can meet the test either way. However, in the real world it is unlikely that he will be able to arrange for this to happen on the precise day that he begins to reoccupy his UK property.

An individual returning to the UK and his advisor will need to give careful consideration to the quality of any accommodation which that individual has, both in the UK and overseas, and may wish to adjust his plans depending upon how sure they can be about the status of his UK property.

## Timing

**[5.26]** A decision about when to return to the UK will be dependent on a number of factors. From a tax perspective, a large part of this decision is likely to be based upon the operation of the split-year tests. As identified above, many of the issues with regard to the split-year test will be the same for those returning to the UK as for those coming here for the first time, and these are dealt with in detail in **CHAPTERS 7** and **8**. The two additional complications for those returning to the UK will be whether they have retained a UK property (and the issues relating to this as outlined above) and the five-year trap.

Assuming that the five-year trap is not a consideration (either because an individual needs to return well within the limit or because he is, in any case, outside of it) then the main driver from a tax perspective is likely to be the application of the split-year test (with the possible complications regarding UK property). As well as understanding whether he needs to consider Case 4 or Case 8 of the split-year test (see para **5.25** above), an individual will need to consider whether he is likely to be resident under the sufficient ties test for the 'overseas period' of the split year. Again, this is likely to be more of an issue for those returning to the UK than for those coming for the first time, as they are more likely to have maintained some UK ties and may well have more days of presence in the UK.

The sufficient ties test is applied to the overseas part of the tax year by reducing the days of presence allowed in the UK on a pro-rata basis, based on the number of whole months in the UK part of the year. These are whole calendar months (eg June) as opposed to whole months counting from the day of non-residence (eg 28 May – 28 June). The calculation works by calculating the days which would apply to the UK part of the year and reducing the total days for the year by this amount. The actual calculation is likely to be academic, however, since there is a useful table (Table F) at paragraph 5.26 of RDR3 (reproduced at para **8.19**) which shows the number of days which an individual can have in the UK under the sufficient ties test for each of the relevant numbers of ties – it is set out as a substitution (eg an individual whose overseas part of the year ends on or before 30 April, must substitute one day for 15 days, four days for 45 days and so on). The date on which the overseas part of the year comes to an end will depend on which of the two tests (Case 4 or Case 8) is relevant.

In considering returning to the UK then, as well as considering his UK property and whether it could be considered a home, an individual must consider the sufficient ties test for the period before his return. In a sense, therefore, an individual must begin planning for his return to the UK in the tax year before that in which he wishes to return, if he wishes to ensure that the sufficient ties test is not breached and the split-year test will apply.

An individual returning to the UK in the early part of the year can have a very limited number of days of presence in the UK without being treated as UK resident (and thus failing the test and not qualifying for split-year treatment). For example, an individual with three UK ties returning to the UK on 28 June after two years overseas, would only be able to have 11 days in the UK before failing to meet the test.

The fact that the sufficient ties test applies on a whole-month basis means that the exact day on which the UK home is acquired (or the overseas home is given up) can be quite crucial. For example, if the individual with three UK ties had returned three days later on 1 July, he would have been able to have 15 days in the UK and still meet the sufficient ties test for the overseas portion of the year.

It is also worth remembering that if an individual meets the 'only home' test in Case 4 he is likely to be automatically resident in the UK. So, if the split-year treatment does not apply, the individual will be taxed as a UK resident for the whole tax year – even if he does not meet the 'only home' test until March. Therefore, if the individual is unlikely to be non-UK resident under the sufficient ties test for the overseas period, but would be so for the full tax year, as far as possible they should avoid meeting the only home test at all during the year – perhaps by delaying their return; by maintaining an overseas property; or by staying with friends or relatives for short periods before acquiring a UK home.

In conclusion, the timing of an individual's return will be crucial for their residence position for the year of return to the UK – even down to the exact day of their return. This will be an area which an individual will need to explore very carefully with his advisor, and as early as possible before return. In cases of uncertainty, and where it is possible in view of other considerations, the safest course may be to avoid returning to UK residence until early April (ie after April 6) thus removing the danger of being considered resident in the UK throughout the immediately preceding tax year as a result of meeting the only home test, despite only having spent a small number of days in the UK.

## Conclusion

**[5.27]** For those individuals leaving the UK other than for full-time work abroad, the circumstances surrounding their ownership or use of any UK property are likely to be key, especially in the years of departure and return. For the intervening years, where the individual wishes to spend more time in the UK than is permitted under the first or second automatic overseas tests, it is likely that it will be important to monitor very carefully the application of the sufficient ties test.

# Chapter 6

# Coming to the UK: employees and the self-employed

## Introduction

**[6.01]** CHAPTERS **6** and **7** consider practical aspects for taxpayers coming to the UK. They take the same approach as the 'leaving the UK' chapters, and consider separately two categories of taxpayer: those who come to the UK as part of their full-time work (and their partners), and everyone else. This chapter concentrates on the former category, whether the individual is working as an employee or in a self-employed capacity. Individuals coming to the UK for other reasons, whether on a short-term or long-term basis, are considered in CHAPTER **7**.

The chapter is broadly divided into two parts and considers two types of individuals (although it is entirely possible for one individual to fall under either head at different stages):

- those who visit and spend time in the UK, but who wish to do so without establishing UK residence (paras **6.02–6.05**)
- those who come to the UK for longer periods, who accept that UK residence will apply to them (paras **6.06–6.19**).

The individual will only become UK tax resident if he fails to meet all of the automatic overseas tests and meets at least one of the UK residence tests, either under the automatic residence tests or under the sufficient ties test. Each of these possibilities is considered below in more detail.

## Working in the UK without establishing UK residence

### *Automatic non-residence – limiting days in the UK*

**[6.02]** It remains common for individuals to come to the UK for employment for a number of different reasons without any intention of becoming resident here. Equally, the self-employed may come to the UK for particular projects with no intention of establishing UK tax residence. Examples falling within this category include those coming to the UK for very short-term assignments to gain experience or share their expertise, and non-residents with a specific reason to visit the UK regularly, such as non-resident directors of UK companies. The amount of time spent in the UK can vary considerably, but should be always less than the 183 days in a UK tax year that would make such individuals resident automatically under the first automatic UK test.

Under the previous regime, the point at which individuals in this group might become UK tax resident was based on expectations combined with actual visits to the UK, so that typically an individual would become UK tax resident after averaging at least 91 days in the UK over a number of tax years, or when it was clear that he intended to and would attain this average over the requisite number of years. So an element of anticipation was involved and, where the taxpayer later changed his plans, the point at which he became UK tax resident could also change.

Under SRT anyone in this category, who has not previously been UK tax resident, can spend 45 days in the UK in any tax year without ever having to question whether he would become UK tax resident. This number is reduced to 15 for any taxpayer who has been tax resident in the UK in the previous three UK tax years. The law is in *paras 12–13, Sch 45, FA 2013* (reproduced at para **2.04**, and also para **7.01**).

Certain days (days spent in transit and UK days due to exceptional circumstances) can be excluded. There is also an additional deeming days rule that can come into play, although it can only do so if the individual has been UK tax resident in at least one of the three preceding tax years. See paras **3.04–3.06**.

Where the day limits of the automatic overseas test are met, the SRT brings certainty on a year-by-year basis in contrast to the previous regime. For those who have never been UK tax resident, the limit of up to 45 days appears quite generous and indeed this is more likely to be relevant for short-term visitors to the UK than the limit of up to 15 days. However, if circumstances were such that the individual tripped into UK residence, he would then only have 15 days a year for the next three years, which might not be enough. Moreover, where an individual spends more than 45 days in the UK, he may lose the protection of automatic non-residence status and so need to consider his position more carefully.

Prior to SRT it was relatively unusual for a short-term business visitor to the UK to become UK tax resident, and many employees coming to the UK from a Treaty country as short-term business visitors would rely on remaining a Treaty resident of their home country whilst in the UK and expect to claim a Treaty exemption under the employment income article of that Treaty. So generally the domestic UK residence position would have little impact on the tax position overall. In some circumstances under the SRT, individuals visiting the UK for 46 days or more may become UK tax resident under domestic law and also potentially under a Double Tax Treaty, and so individuals need to review their position carefully.

The Treaty position has always been rather different for directors, as the Treaty taxing rights tend to be dependent not just on the individual's residence position, but also on the corporate tax residence of the company concerned. For the self-employed, the Treaty position often depended on whether they had a fixed base in the UK.

## Automatic non-residence – full-time working abroad

**[6.03]** Assuming that the individual is in the UK for more than 45 or 15 days, they may wish to see if they can satisfy the other automatic overseas test, that of working full time abroad. An individual who comes to the UK occasionally for work may be able to meet the conditions to be regarded as non-resident because he is full-time working abroad (although this will be unusual). This assumes that he does not have a 'relevant job' on board a vehicle, vessel or aircraft engaged in cross-border traffic, as such workers are excluded from this test – please see para **3.15** for more details. The law for working full time abroad is detailed in *para 14, Sch 45, FA 2013*, and although this is considered in more detail in para **4.06**, *para 14(1)* is reproduced below as a summary of the conditions that have to be met:

'14(1) The third automatic overseas test is that—
- (a)  P works sufficient hours overseas, as assessed over year X,
- (b)  during year X, there are no significant breaks from overseas work,
- (c)  the number of days in year X on which P does more than 3 hours' work in the UK is less than 31, and
- (d)  the number of days in year X falling within sub-paragraph (2) is less than 91.'

So, provided all other conditions are fulfilled, an individual who has no more than 30 workdays in the UK, may meet the conditions for this test. However, as noted elsewhere in this work, it is very easy for an individual to have UK workdays on any business visit to the UK, not least because any UK travel that would be eligible for a deduction as a business expense will count as work performed in the UK and anyone flying into the UK will start this UK travel from the moment that he disembarks from the aircraft onto the tarmac. Similarly, any day of departure from the UK risks being a UK workday if travel to the airport and time allowed for check-in leave the traveller at risk of exceeding the 'more than three hours' work' in the UK limit, regardless of whether any duties are undertaken on that day. So days of departure from and arrival in the UK can all too easily count as UK workdays.

Once the 'more than three hours' work' limit is exceeded, the taxpayer can work until midnight if he so desires without creating an extra UK workday; so those coming to the UK for specific business with travel on the same day may find it relatively easy to keep within this limit. However, a frequent traveller to the UK may find the 'working while travelling' rules take up too many of his permitted UK working days and so prevent him from being regarded as full-time working abroad although he may be non-resident under some other part of the SRT.

### Example 6.1: Frank

Frank is a Dutch national and long-term resident of the Netherlands where he works for the Rijksmuseum. He has helped to negotiate the borrowing of certain fine art objects from the British Museum for a six-month period from January to June 2016.

Frank is invited to come to the UK in December 2015 to collect the exhibits and to do a similar journey in reverse in July 2016 to escort the exhibits home at the end of the exhibition. Each of these visits is expected to require him to spend two weeks in the UK.

This is ideal timing for him, because his girlfriend Joanna is currently also spending a lot of time in the UK having been assigned here by her employer for 18 months from 1 February 2015. In 2015/16, because of his visits to Joanna, Frank anticipates exceeding the 45 days of presence he could have in the UK if he is to be not UK tax resident under the second automatic overseas test. However, he is quite confident that he can stay within the 30 UK workdays per tax year limit, especially as each of his two visits to the British Museum is likely to fall into a different UK tax year.

Obviously, Frank's circumstances are a little contrived, but as a general guide the fewer work-related trips that can be made per tax year, the easier it will be to stay comfortably within the workdays' limit. Had the exhibition spanned the six months from 1 July to 31 December 2016, both visits would have fallen in the same tax year and without knowing details of hours worked we could not be confident that the conditions for full-time working abroad would be met. The frequency of Frank's UK trips could also easily affect the outcome.

### Example 6.2: More about Frank

The original exhibition and Frank's visits to the UK proceed as planned. In fact, it proved so successful that Frank is asked to oversee a similar exhibition at the British Museum starting in September 2016. He is asked to spend three days in London helping to set everything up and then to spend a day each week at the exhibition, giving lectures and guided tours, over the next 25 weeks.

Frank has a travel-related workday on his first visit of three days, and on the first of his 'day a week' visits, giving him anticipated workdays of 30 in total in 2016/17. If he is not able to manage each of his subsequent visits so as to travel on his workday, he will risk exceeding the maximum number of UK workdays he could have and still be regarded as working full-time abroad.

This would not necessarily mean that Frank was UK tax resident in 2016/17, but would prevent him from being automatically non-resident by virtue of full-time working abroad. This can be significant, because an individual who meets this automatic overseas test is outside the deeming days rule which can otherwise apply. *Para 14(2), Sch 45, FA 2013* states that days spent in the UK for the purpose of the 90 days limit ignore the deeming days rule:

'(2)  A day falls within this sub-paragraph if—
    (a)   it is a day spent by P in the UK, but
    (b)   it is not a day that is treated under *paragraph 23(4)* as a day spent by P in the UK.'

For detail of the deeming days rule, see para **3.06**.

## Remaining non-resident: avoiding the automatic residence tests

**[6.04]** Assuming that the individual does not satisfy any of the automatic overseas tests, he will need to ensure that he does not fall within any of the automatic residence tests. These are covered in detail elsewhere in this work but, for ease of reference here, the tests he will need to avoid are spending 183 days in the UK, meeting the UK home test and finally, working 'full-time' in the UK. It is assumed for the purposes of this section that the individual's work is such that he does not meet the third test (works full-time in the UK) and that he can avoid spending 183 days or more in the UK. So the key test becomes the UK home test.

For a detailed consideration of this test, see para **2.08** and for a discussion on the meaning of 'home', see para **3.07**. Many of the considerations here will be similar to those for HNWIs and the reader is referred to the discussion at para **7.05**.

Readers may recall that there are effectively two parts to this test: does the taxpayer have property that meets the SRT definition of a home; and is the availability and use of this property (and any overseas homes) such that the UK home test is met.

Since most of these individuals will have a home overseas in which they spend at least 30 days in a given tax year, it will be unusual for an individual doing limited work in the UK to need be concerned with meeting the UK home test. On the rare occasion that the availability and use part of the test is met, it will be necessary to consider whether the UK property in question meets the definition of a home. In addition to the discussion at para **7.05**, one further point needs consideration here: can employer-provided accommodation ever be a home?

Certainly, in principle, employer-provided accommodation could be a home, since, as RDR3 makes clear at para A22 of Annex A, ownership or legal tenancy makes no difference to the analysis. Whether or not a property constitutes an individual's home is a question of the quality of his occupation. There must be a risk that accommodation that is kept available for one employee's exclusive use could be considered a home, especially if the employee keeps personal belongings (clothes, toiletries) there for use between business trips. However, even this could arguably fall short of being a 'home' if it is only used by the individual as accommodation when working in the UK. Each case will, of course, be dependent on its own facts, but where employer-provided accommodation is used sufficiently that the UK home test may prove a concern, the individual and his employer may want to minimise the risk of its being considered a home, for example by making the accommodation available to more than one employee, ensuring the accommodation must be booked for a specific trip and that keys must be returned at the end of each trip.

An individual might be tempted to consider that a property that was only used occasionally while visiting the UK for business (employment or self-employment) could be a 'temporary retreat' and therefore outside the definition of home. However, a temporary retreat is included in a list in the legislation along with 'holiday home' which suggests that the property would need to be used for some form of leisure as opposed to business. This is confirmed in RDR3 at para A20 of Annex A.

### Remaining non-resident under the sufficient ties test.

[6.05] On the basis that the individual's circumstances are such that they do not meet any of the automatic overseas tests or the automatic resident tests, they will need to consider the sufficient ties test.

The sufficient ties test is considered in detail in **CHAPTER 2**, with the definitions considered in detail in **CHAPTER 3**. For the individuals we are considering in this section of the chapter (those who work full time but with limited visits to the UK for work), the two most relevant ties are likely to be the work tie and the accommodation tie, although clearly all the ties will need to be considered.

An individual will have a work tie if he has 40 days or more of work in the UK. It should be remembered that a workday for these purposes is a day on which more than three hours of work is undertaken in the UK. The inclusion of travel within the definition of work will make it all too easy to meet this three-hour threshold. With the onerous record-keeping required to demonstrate that no more than three hours' work is undertaken, from a pragmatic perspective some individuals may therefore find it easiest to accept that each day they spend in the UK is a day of work for the purposes of this test.

For the accommodation tie, see the discussion at para **7.06**. An additional consideration for some individuals coming to the UK for workdays will be whether accommodation provided by their employer can create an accommodation tie. This will depend on their employer's arrangements but if they are such that this accommodation is available for the employee's use whenever he visits the UK, this may be enough to give him an accommodation tie once he has spent one night in the accommodation. Going forward, it may be necessary for employers to review their arrangements to ensure that the accommodation is not continuously available if it is important for the individual not to have this UK tie.

Where the individual has a maximum of two ties, they will be able to spend 90 or 120 days in the UK (depending on whether they were UK tax resident in any of the previous three years). See the sufficient ties tables reproduced at paras **2.04** and **2.05**.

## Coming to the UK for work in such a way as to become UK tax resident

### Introduction

[6.06] There are a number of different circumstances in which employees who come to the UK to work for the longer term will become UK tax resident. Employees may be overseas nationals seconded to the UK to work, remaining employed by their overseas employer or they may independently have come to the UK with an offer of employment. Alternatively, they may be UK expats returning to the UK after a period of employment abroad or to take up a new employment in the UK. In the latter case, it is assumed that such expats will continue to work once they come to the UK (for those who return to the UK in other circumstances, see **CHAPTER 7**).

The full-time working in the UK and abroad provisions encompass both self-employment and those with two or more roles that, taken together, would add up to a full-time role. References to employment, therefore, could equally be references to self-employment.

In most instances, this section is concerned with individuals who are working full-time and who establish UK tax residence as a consequence of this. Many who come to the UK to work part time will not meet the criteria to fulfil the third automatic UK test, unless they have several part-time jobs that combine to be equivalent to a full-time role, but may still be UK tax resident under other parts of the SRT. They may, for example, be UK tax resident under the first automatic test because they are in the UK for at least 183 days in the tax year

There are also specific and different rules for individuals who hold a 'relevant job' and these are outside the scope of this chapter. For such individuals, see para **3.15**.

## *Year of arrival*

### Establishing residence

**[6.07]** On the basis that the individual satisfies the third automatic UK test (by working 'full time' in the UK), they will be resident throughout the year of arrival, even if they arrive midway through the UK tax year.

In order to satisfy this test, the individual needs to meet:

* the 'sufficient hours' test for a 365-day qualifying period with no significant breaks from UK work in that period; and
* the 75% test – ie of the total days in the 365-day period on which the individual does more than three hours' work, more than 75% are days on which he does more than three hours' work in the UK.

If at least one day of that 365-day qualifying period falls within the UK tax year and this is a day on which the taxpayer does more than three hours' work in the UK, this is sufficient to make the taxpayer UK tax resident for that entire year.

For the important 'key concepts' within this test and a worked example of the sufficient hours calculation, see **CHAPTER 3** and **CHAPTER 8** (Guido). Here we are simply concerned with the application of the test for the year of arrival.

As the 365-day period need not be co-terminus with the UK tax year, it is possible for an individual to come to the UK during the tax year and satisfy this test. This is made clear by the HMRC example in RDR 3, example 10, Henri:

'Example 10

Henri travels to the UK on 1 July 2013 to start a new job on the following day. His posting finishes on 1 July 2014 and he leaves the UK on 6 August 2014, 400 days after he arrived in the UK. Over the 365-day period to 30 June 2014 Henri calculates that he worked full-time in the UK and has not taken a significant break from his UK work during this period. Part of the period of 365 days falls within the tax year 2013-14 and part falls within the tax year 2014-15.

Over the period of 365 days ending 30 June 2014 Henri works for over three hours on 240 days, 196 (80%) of which are days when Henri worked for more than three hours in the UK. At least one day when Henri does more than three hours work in the UK falls within the tax year 2013-14 therefore Henri is resident in the UK under the third automatic UK test for tax year 2013-14.

There is also at least one day when Henri does more than three hours work in the UK within the tax year 2014-15, so Henri also meets the third automatic UK test for that year.'

It is also not necessary to apply the test over the first possible 365-day period. Thus in the Henri example, if Henri worked in the UK for a longer period than 365 days in total, it would not be necessary for Henri to apply the calculation over the 365-day period starting on 2 July 2013. The legislation simply refers to 'a period of 365 days' and HMRC confirm this point at paragraph 1.37 of RDR3:

> '1.37 If you identify a period of 365 days when you have worked full-time in the UK, but you do not then meet the 75% test relating to that 365-day period, you must consider whether there is another 365-day period when you do meet the 75% test. If there is no such period, you do not meet the third automatic UK test.'

It is therefore likely that many employees will become UK resident in the year of arrival under the third automatic residence test. Anyone who comes to the UK for full-time work only has to have one day of his qualifying reference period falling in a tax year for that to have the potential to make him tax resident for the whole of the tax year concerned. So becoming UK tax resident in a year of arrival will be very common. This was also the case under the previous regime, but only if the taxpayer intended to be in the UK for at least a two-year period on arrival.

The sufficient hours test, which is based on a 35-hour working week on average, requires more consideration than might at first be supposed. The mechanics of the test – for example, the fact that one must include bank holidays – mean that employees who work a 37-hour or 40-hour week in total, including all travel time, may struggle to meet the sufficient hours target. In practice, the vast majority of employees working in the UK will work significantly longer hours and will have no difficulty in reaching the required hours. Evidencing this may be more of a challenge but as it will generally be in HMRC's interests for this type of taxpayer to be UK tax resident, HMRC may be prepared in such circumstances to accept a taxpayer has worked the hours he says that he has, especially if his employment contract indicates that he will work overtime as required. There will, however, be exceptions to the above and taxpayers who will not become UK tax resident in this way include anyone who:

- arrives late in a tax year and has fewer than 46 days of UK presence in the tax year, never having been UK tax resident previously;

- arrives late in a tax year and has fewer than 16 days of UK presence in the tax year, having been UK tax resident in one of the previous three UK tax years;
- spends at least 25% of the days on which he works for more than three hours working outside the UK;
- has a significant break in UK working or an irregular or part-time working pattern; and
- arrives in the UK very late in the tax year and takes a holiday, so having no day on which they do three hours' work in the UK in the tax year of arrival.

It is important to remember that, with the exception of the first two categories of taxpayer who will be automatically non-resident, the categories mentioned above only take the employee outside the third automatic test and he may still very easily be UK tax resident, under one of the other tests, possibly through spending 183 days in the tax year, or meeting the UK home test, or meeting the sufficient ties test. So, for example, an employee who takes on a regional sales role for his employer that encompasses the whole of Europe, may not have 75% of his workdays in the UK, but could easily nevertheless have 183 days in the UK and therefore be UK tax resident. Similarly, someone in a part-time or casual employment is unlikely to have sufficient hours to meet the third automatic test, but may be UK tax resident under the UK home or under the sufficient ties test, especially if they are the spouse or partner of someone who does meet the third automatic UK test and who therefore becomes a UK family tie.

To conclude, most individuals coming to the UK to work under a full-time contract of employment will become UK resident in the year of arrival under the third automatic test, although for those with international roles, an irregular working pattern, insufficient hours or who arrive late in the tax year concerned, all the facts and circumstances will usually need to be scrutinised before the residence position can be determined.

## Split-year treatment

**[6.08]** Assuming that the taxpayer is UK tax resident in the year of arrival, it will then be necessary to determine whether they will be entitled to split-year treatment. For an individual coming to the UK for full-time employment, potentially all five split-year cases for coming to the UK could be relevant. In summary these cases are:

- Case 4 – starting to have a home in the UK only (*para 47, Sch 45, FA 2013*)
- Case 5 – starting full-time work in the UK (*para 48, Sch 45, FA 2013*)
- Case 6 – ceasing full-time work overseas (*para 49, Sch 45, FA 2013*)
- Case 7 – the partner of someone ceasing full-time work overseas (*para 50, Sch 45, FA 2013*)
- Case 8 – starting to have a home in the UK (*para 51, Sch 45, FA 2013*)

Under the law as initially proposed, it would have been necessary to consider each of the cases for all individuals, determine how many of them applied, and take the earliest possible date as the date on which the UK part of the year commenced. This would have made advising such individuals unnecessarily onerous. Fortunately, before the Finance Bill was enacted, an ordering rule was established for these cases, but the law, as enacted, still requires the taxpayer to consider two or three alternatives in most circumstances. The ordering rules are in *para 55, Sch 45, FA 2013* and are as follows:

- If Case 6 applies, it is only necessary also to consider Case 5. If both cases apply, the earlier date of these two cases applies. Otherwise, Case 6 applies.
- If Case 7 applies and Case 6 does not, it is only necessary also to consider Case 5. If both cases apply, the earlier date of these two cases applies. Otherwise Case 7 applies.
- If Cases 6 and 7 do not apply, and more than one of Cases 4, 5 and 8 apply, take the earliest date from those three cases.

See **CHAPTER 8** for a detailed consideration of the five cases. However, there are some particular points to note in relation to the subject matter of this chapter. Although Case 5 (starting full-time work in the UK) is likely to be particularly relevant, under the ordering rules it is necessary first to consider Case 6.

If Case 6 applies, only Case 5 can take priority, and will only do so if this gives an earlier arrival date than Case 6.

Case 6 is set out and discussed at para **8.22**. In summary, it requires that the individual:

- was non-resident in the previous tax year by virtue of full time working abroad;
- had been UK tax resident at in at least one of the four tax years immediately preceding that year;
- is UK tax resident in the following tax year; and
- has at least one period in the tax year, starting at the beginning of the year and ending with a day on which more than three hours' work is done overseas, which satisfies the overseas criteria.

Case 6 will therefore apply to individuals returning to the UK after a period of employment overseas, and will not apply to someone coming to the UK for the first time. It should be noted that Case 6 is concerned with ceasing 'full time' work overseas but there is no requirement on arrival other than UK tax residence. The individual may or may not therefore be working in the UK.

Where Case 6 applies, the overseas part of the split year ends on the last day of the period throughout which the individual satisfies the overseas work criteria, this being a day on which the individual does more than three hours of work overseas. Broadly, an individual satisfies the overseas work criteria if he works sufficient hours, with no significant breaks and has no more than the permitted number of days of presence and work in the UK. If there is more than one such period, the overseas part of the year ends on the latest possible date *(para 53(7), Sch 45. FA 2013)*, which normally works to the advantage of the taxpayer.

However, the day in question may not coincide with the employee's final day overseas or with the actual day of their arrival in the UK and care will be needed when the employee's overseas work is terminated with a period of garden leave or where the employee takes a break between the end of his overseas employment and coming to the UK to take up employment. See paras **3.13** and **3.14** for more details

Where the exact date at which an individual resumes residence is likely to be important, the employee may need to plan holidays at the end of the assignment with care. For example, rather than taking a holiday at the very end of an overseas assignment, an employee might wish to take a holiday and then resume overseas work, even if only for a day or two, because reasonable amounts of holiday would normally not be regarded as constituting a significant break. Alternatively, if the employment has definitely ended, and a Double Tax Treaty may be in point, the taxpayer may wish to keep his home in the host location and return there after the holiday with his family, in the hope of remaining Treaty resident in that country until the date of his actual return to the UK.

If Case 6 applies, it is only necessary to consider Case 5 of the other cases. It is therefore possible to ignore the date on which a home is acquired in the UK. This removes the need to consider whether property used by the employee is 'accommodation' or a 'home' for SRT purposes. Case 5 is concerned with full-time work in the UK and so an individual within Case 6 will only need to consider his position further if he is returning to the UK for full-time work in the UK.

Where Case 5 applies, the overseas part of the year ends on the day before the start of the qualifying 365-day period of full-time work in the UK. Where both Cases 5 and 6 apply, the overseas part of the year ends on the earlier of the two dates *(para 55(3), Sch 45, FA 2013)*. In many cases this will be the Case 6 date, unless there is an overlap between UK and overseas duties. This may come as a surprise to an individual who, say, ceases employment overseas in the July and takes a month off before coming to the UK to take up a new role. He may find he has already been resident in the UK for a month before he arrives!

Case 5 requires the individual to:

- be non-UK resident for the previous tax year;
- have at least one 365-day period beginning with a day on which more than three hours' work is done in the UK and for that period he must:
  - have sufficient hours working in the UK;
  - have no significant breaks from working; and
  - have at least 75% of the days on which he works for more than three hours, as days on which he does more than three hours' work in the UK; and
  - in the part of the tax year before that 365-day period begins, not meet the sufficient ties test.

Rather bizarrely, the test of having at least 75% of workdays in the UK is subtly different from the one in the third automatic UK test, which requires the taxpayer to have more than 75% of his workdays in the UK. It is therefore mathematically possible for an employee to meet the Case 5 conditions without automatically being UK tax resident by means of full-time UK work.

**Example 6.3: Janette**

> Janette is a US national assigned to the UK to take on a Europe-wide sales role for her US employer. She has never previously been UK tax resident so Case 6 cannot apply to her. She comes to the UK in June 2017, with the expectation of working full time in the UK from that date, but with some overseas duties.
>
> If her overseas duties amount to exactly 25% of her 'more than three hours' workdays she will not meet the requirements of the third automatic UK test. She may, however, be UK tax resident under the first automatic 183 days UK test and fall within Case 5 by meeting the 'at least 75%' UK workday requirement.

While it might seem that such a working pattern would be unusual, there may be circumstances when it would apply. For example, if Janette's working week comprised four long workdays, one of which was always spent outside the UK, it would fit the required pattern.

As noted above, Case 5 also requires the individual to have been non-resident in the previous tax year and to have not met the sufficient ties test for the earlier, overseas, part of the tax year concerned. However, there are no requirements as to the year following the year of arrival and this will be helpful for short periods of working in the UK which fall into two tax years, beginning in one year and ending in the next such that the individual's UK connections end part way through the second year.

If Case 5 applies, the UK part of the year begins at the start of the 365-day period. That is, it begins on the first day of the period, being a day on which more than three hours' work is done in the UK. This may not be the date of arrival in the UK, but a later date, if the individual first comes to settle in. This will be relevant when considering the application of the sufficient ties test to the earlier part of the year as it may require the individual to take into account additional days spent in the UK.

In looking for the 365-day period for the purposes of Case 5, the legislation allows for the possibility that there may be more than one such period, and *para 53(6), Sch 45, FA 2013*, provides that, where there is more than one such period, the overseas part of the year ends before the first of those periods. The practical effect of this is minimising the overseas and maximising the UK parts of the tax year concerned. Individuals who have several workdays in the UK in preparation for the formal start of their UK contract may need to be particularly careful here. They may find that the UK part of the split year starts at an earlier date than they were expecting. This may particularly be the case given that the three hours of work can include travel time (see para **3.09**).

If Case 6 does not apply, the ordering rules then require the taxpayer to consider Case 7. As noted above, Case 7 applies to the partners of taxpayers within Case 6 and requires that the individual:

- was non-resident in the UK for the previous tax year;
- will be UK tax resident for the following UK tax year;
- has a partner who meets the Case 6 requirements for the UK tax year concerned or the previous UK tax year; and
- at some point in the tax year he or she moves to the UK to live with the working spouse when they return or relocate to the UK.

The individual must also stay within pro-rated limits for days of UK presence before the deemed arrival date and, if a UK home is retained during the non-resident period, spend more time in the overseas home than the UK one in the overseas part of the year. Again, this is explained more fully in para **8.23**.

Under the ordering rules noted above, an individual to which Case 7 applies need only also consider Case 5, and the earlier date for the end of the overseas part applies. Which case will give the earlier date will depend on whether the spouses return to the UK together and when the trailing spouse starts work – see **CHAPTERS 4** and **8** for more on this.

In the modern age, both partners in a couple may very well relocate and take up full-time work. In these circumstances, Case 7 can apply to individuals who are themselves coming to work in the UK and so should not be seen as simply applicable to non-working partners. For example it may be relevant for an individual who has never previously been UK resident (and so Case 6 cannot apply to them), but who is coming to work in the UK and accompanying a partner who does fall within Case 6.

### Example 6.4: Maria

Maria is a Russian national, married to John who is British. John met Maria when he was working overseas and is returning to the UK after three years of working in Kazakhstan, during which time they only visited the UK for short holidays to see John's parents. Both Maria and John have been working in Kazakhstan and will continue to work in the UK on their return.

Case 6 will not be applicable for Maria because she has never previously been UK tax resident. However, both Case 7 and Case 5 have the potential to apply to her depending on the circumstances. If Maria's work is part time, or if it is full-time but with on-going overseas duties that will account for more than 25% of her workdays, she is unlikely to meet the requirements for Case 5. She may, however, be able to apply Case 7 to split the tax year, provided that John meets the Case 6 requirements for the year that she becomes UK tax resident, or for the previous UK tax year.

If neither of Cases 6 and 7 is applicable, the individual must consider together Cases 5 (full-time work in the UK) and 4 and 8 (home in the UK).

It is highly likely that someone coming to the UK to work full time will acquire a home (as defined – see para **3.07**) in the UK and so may need to consider the application of Cases 4 and 8. Whether both of these cases are relevant will depend on the circumstances. However, it should be noted that Case 8 simply requires the acquisition of a home in the UK and the retention of it throughout the next year; there are no requirements regarding homes in any other country. Case 4, on the other hand, requires the acquisition of an 'only home' in the UK. Case 4 may be relevant for returning employees who may have had a temporary home while working overseas but give it up on returning to the UK. For those individuals coming perhaps for the first time to work in the UK from their home country, Case 4 will only be relevant where the individual does not retain a home in their home country for personal use (eg they sell their home or rent it out in circumstances such that it is unavailable for their use). For

Case 8, the UK part of the year will start on the day on which the individual acquires their UK home. With Case 4 the UK part of the year starts on the day the individual acquires an only home in the UK. Depending on the arrangements for selling or letting their overseas home, this may in fact be a later day than the day on which they first acquire a UK home and, if so, the ordering rules mean that Case 8 is likely to take precedence. In many circumstances therefore, when the two home cases are considered, the relevant date will be the day on which the individual acquires the UK home. See also **CHAPTERS 3, 7** and **8** for further consideration of Cases 4 and 8 and for more detail on when a property becomes a home.

There could be circumstances where the individual on first coming to the UK has accommodation available for use but this accommodation is not within the definition of a home for the purposes of the SRT. If this continues throughout the year of arrival, Cases 4 and 8 will not be relevant. For example, the individual may stay in a hotel while making longer-term arrangements or the individual may take a very short let of temporary accommodation (say a month) or stay with friends.

There will be instances where a taxpayer clearly acquires a UK home before starting work in the UK. For example, if a trailing spouse and children come to the UK to settle into a home before the start of an academic year, a working spouse may find that he too has acquired a home before formally coming to the UK to work, if he visits the property ahead of that point. For any taxpayer particularly sensitive to the date on which UK residence is likely to be established, care is needed in deciding which of the possible tests might bite first and taking action to defer that point as appropriate.

**Example 6.5: Emilio**

Emilio has been asked by his employer in Brazil to take up a three-year assignment in the UK with effect from June 2017. Emilio is married with two young children and he and his wife have concluded that this would be an ideal opportunity to move the family to the UK and enrol them in English-speaking schools. His son, who will be five in July, will start school in September, but Emilio has been advised that he should move the family during the Easter holidays, with a view to getting them properly settled in a home within the catchment area for a suitable nursery before the summer term starts.

The family, including Emilio, come over and acquire a home in March 2017 and Emilio then returns to Brazil for two more months before returning to the UK to start his assignment in June 2017 (his family stayed in the UK in this period). The question will be whether Emilio is entitled to split-year treatment for 2017/18.

On the basis that Emilio has never previously been UK resident and his wife was not working in Brazil, Cases 6 and 7 are not relevant. Emilio will therefore need to consider Cases 4, 5 and 8.

Emilio may fall within Case 4 (assuming any home in Brazil is let or sold when he returns to the UK in June 2017) or Case 5 if he has the right work pattern, or possibly both (in which circumstance the earlier date of the two possible arrival dates will apply). He is unlikely to fall within Case 8 if the UK home was acquired in March 2017 as it would have been held throughout 2017/18.

In this example, there is no Treaty to consider and so the domestic position under the SRT is likely to be particularly important. Even if a Treaty were relevant, if an employee has a young family, any Treaty analysis is likely to give considerable weight to where that family is, and the country in which the family is situated is likely to be regarded as the centre of his vital interests.

### Accompanying partner

**[6.09]** For ease of reference, in this section we will refer to the couple as the employee and the accompanying partner and we assume that the partner will not be themselves working full time in the UK.

If the employee's family accompany him to the UK, it will be necessary to consider their residence position independently. If we assume that the accompanying partner will not be working full time in the UK, it will be necessary to consider whether they are resident under the first or second automatic residence tests (183 days or more in the UK or UK home). Alternatively, it may be necessary to consider the sufficient ties test. These tests are considered in **CHAPTER 2** and elsewhere. For the UK home test, it will be necessary to take into account the arrangements for the family's overseas home and the time the non-working partner spends there and in the UK home. For the sufficient ties test, the partner is likely to have at least two ties – accommodation and family – and so will be resident if they spend more than 90 days in the UK (if resident in any of the three previous tax years) or more than 120 days (if not so resident).

In applying the split-year cases to the partner, again, assuming that they are outside the Case 6 conditions, the starting point will be to consider Case 7. If Case 7 applies, it is only necessary to also consider Case 5. So, Case 7 should always be considered first for partners coming to the UK with an employee where Case 6 cannot apply to them personally either because they have not had the necessary earlier period of UK residence or because they did not meet the full-time working abroad criteria whilst outside the UK.

Case 7 does not apply to partners accompanying employees to the UK unless the employee falls within Case 6, and is clearly aimed primarily at the partners of returning employees to the UK. As noted at para **8.23**, Case 7 allows the partner to come to the UK either in the same tax year as the returning employee or the following tax year. It therefore allows the partner to stay behind in the other country and finalise the arrangements for the departure. However, it does not cater for a partner coming to the UK in a tax year before the employee, eg to make arrangements for the UK period.

As noted in **CHAPTER 8**, Case 7 can apply to a partner where the employee falls within the circumstances of Case 6 (*para 50(3), Sch 45, FA 2013*). Therefore it is enough that Case 6 could apply to the employee and the partner is not precluded from considering Case 7 because the employee falls within Cases 5 and 6 and, under the ordering rules, Case 5 takes precedence.

Where Case 7 applies, the UK part of the year starts on the deemed arrival date. Where Case 6 applied to the employee in the previous tax year, the deemed arrival date is the date on which the partner moves to the UK. If Case 6 applies to the employee in the same tax year, the deemed arrival date is the later of two dates: the date on which the partner moves to the UK and the Case 6 date (ie the last day on which the employee completed more than three hours of work overseas).

Where the partner moves to the UK before the employee, this initially seems to work to the advantage of the taxpayer by giving a later start to the UK part of the year. However, there are conditions that must be met by the partner for the overseas part of the year: their UK days must be within the 'permitted limit' (90 days as reduced by reference to the whole months in the overseas part of the year) and they must either have no UK home in the overseas part of the year or have both an overseas and UK home and spend the greater part of their time in the overseas home. Both these conditions are such that they could be difficult to meet for a taxpayer who returns to the UK but has as their deemed date of arrival a later date. Individuals may therefore need to time their arrival in the UK carefully in order to meet the conditions of Case 7, or accept that Case 7 cannot apply and instead seek to fall within Cases 4 or 8.

If Case 7 does not apply, and for partners of employees coming to the UK for the first time, it will not, the partner's split year will be determined by reference to Cases 4 and 8 only. See **CHAPTER 8** and **CHAPTER 7** for a discussion of these cases.

Where none of the spit-year cases apply, or where a split year is available but at an earlier than expected date, the position under any relevant tax Treaty should be considered. See **CHAPTER 12** for a discussion of how this could apply and the consequences.

## Years of residence

**[6.10]** Having established UK tax residence, the taxpayer may either continue to be tax resident for a few years, or may cease to be UK tax resident in the tax year after the one in which they become UK tax resident. In the latter case, it is possible for someone coming to the UK to qualify for split-year treatment in consecutive years, first on arrival in and then on departure from the UK. This is in contrast to a UK outbound employee, who has to be non-resident for an entire UK tax year before he can qualify for split-year treatment in any year of return to the UK.

Here we look in more detail at the position for those who maintain UK tax residence for one or more tax years. For further commentary on ceasing UK tax residence, see paras **6.14–6.18** below.

It would seem natural that the starting point in determining residence for individuals working full time in the UK would be to seek to apply the third automatic test (working sufficient hours in the UK). However, the detailed calculations required may in many cases mean that an easier test to apply might be the first (at least 183 days in the UK) or even the second (UK home). Nevertheless, if the third automatic test is to be considered, whether an employee continues to meet the test will obviously depend on all the facts and circumstances. For example, they might decide to work part time rather than full time, or find that ongoing duties outside the UK mean that they no longer meet the more than 75% UK workday test. In this case the point at which the 365-day rolling period ceases is critical as the tax year in which it falls will be the last tax year for which the individual is automatically UK tax resident under this part of the SRT.

**Example 6.6: Astrid**

Astrid first came to the UK from her native Sweden to train to be a vet. She marries Joe who is also in training as a vet and, as soon as they both qualify, they set up in practice together, both working full time in the practice.

Astrid became pregnant in January 2014. She continues to work full time, averaging 45 hours a week until a month before her expected due date, which is 15 September 2014, so she stops work on 15 August 2014. In the event, her daughter is born only two weeks later on 30 August 2014.

Astrid decides she no longer wants to work other than to provide emergency cover for Joe. This works out to an average of ten hours per week from the date that she resumes work on 1 December 2014, and is maintained at that level at least until the week ending on Friday 3 April 2015.

Over the period from 4 April 2014 through until 3 April 2015 Astrid has working hours of 1,045 (9 hours on 4 April itself, plus 19 weeks x 45 hours, plus 18 weeks of 10 hours). Her total number of days in the period are 204 (4 April plus (29 weeks x 7 days)). This equates to 29.14 weeks, which is rounded down to 29 weeks. Dividing her 1,045 hours by 29 gives an average working week of 36 hours, so for 2014/15 Astrid is UK tax resident under the full-time working in the UK test.

In order to consider the position for 2015/16, let us now move Astrid's 365-day reference period forward by a week, so it runs from 11 April 2014 to 10 April 2015. Her total working hours will be 1010 (1045 – 45 + 10) but the number of days in the calculation (and therefore the 'weeks' as calculated) will remain the same. Astrid's new average working week is only 34.82 hours, which is not enough to give a qualifying reference period, but further calculations may be needed, depending on exactly when Astrid works during the first week of April. If she manages to do all 10 hours on 5 and 6 April, her reference period could run from 7 April 2014 to 6 April 2015 and her total hours would be 1046 (1045 – 9 (the 4 April hours) + 10). This would give her an average working week of 36 hours, so that she would have a qualifying period ending in 2015/16. Her reduced working hours from December 2014 would not therefore prevent her from meeting the third automatic UK test until 2016/17.

As the Astrid example shows, the point at which the (rolling) 365-day period ends is not dependent on when working hours reduce but will instead be triggered by the point at which the averaging drops below the required 35 hours a week. This could produce some very odd results, as one could be considered full year UK tax resident by virtue of full-time working when in fact working on a part-time basis for the entire UK tax year concerned.

## Other employees

[6.11] Except where part-time work is preceded by a period of full-time work, it is unlikely that the working pattern of part time workers will make them UK tax resident under the third automatic UK test (full-time working in the UK) of the SRT. However, they are likely to be resident under the first automatic UK test (183 days) or second (UK home) automatic UK tests if they have become based in the UK. If they do not meet these, they will still need to consider the sufficient ties test.

As has been noted elsewhere in this work, voluntary work does not count as work for the purposes of the SRT. Therefore an individual who comes to the UK to undertake voluntary work, even if this is a full-time activity, will not be able to satisfy the third automatic UK test and will also have to consider the other tests as summarised above. See CHAPTER 7 for a fuller discussion of how these tests may apply where the taxpayer involved is not working full time in the UK.

## Accompanying spouses

[6.12] While there are special split-year cases for partners of employees who either come to or leave the UK for full-time work, there are no special rules for the intervening years. Partners will therefore assess their residence status independently of the employee and according to the normal three-part test.

## The self-employed

[6.13] While the third automatic UK test can apply to those taxpayers who are self-employed, in the same way as it does to employees, the challenge may be in demonstrating hours worked. Detailed diary notes will probably be required and a distinction may be made between working eg on projects and being between projects. This is suggested by HMRC's contrast between an employee and a self-employed contractor being 'on call' as already discussed in detail at para 3.09.

### Example 6.7: Claude

Claude is a famous French artist who comes to the UK for a period of five years while his daughter attends school here. He establishes a studio in the UK and continues to receive commissions for which he undertakes some of the work in the UK. He also spends time planning new speculative works and makes a number of trips to soak up the UK atmosphere and seek inspiration.

The time Claude spends in his studio may – probably uncontroversially – be treated as work time but could Claude also include the time he spends outside the studio in less structured activities, which are more preparatory in nature?

## Year of departure and subsequent years

### Introduction

**[6.14]** This section assumes that the employee's period of working in the UK has come to an end and they leave the UK, either returning to their home country or moving on elsewhere. Following the tax year of departure it is likely that the employee will no longer satisfy any of the automatic UK tests. The key considerations are first whether the split-year provisions will apply for the tax year of departure, and second whether, in subsequent years, they will be automatically non-resident or will need to monitor their UK days under the sufficient ties test in order to be non-resident in the UK.

### Year of departure – the split-year cases

**[6.15]** There are three split-year cases for individuals leaving the UK. All of these may be relevant for departing employees. They are:

Case 1 – starting full-time work overseas (*para 44, Sch 45, FA 2013*)

Case 2 – the partner of someone starting full-time work overseas (*para 45, Sch 45, FA 2013*)

Case 3 – ceasing to have a home in the UK (*para 46, Sch 45, FA 2013*)

It should be noted that there is no specific case for a taxpayer ceasing to work full time in the UK (see **CHAPTER 8** for a more detailed discussion of the split-year rules).

The ordering rules mean that it is necessary to consider the cases in the order in which they appear in the legislation. Hence, if a taxpayer satisfies Case 1; there is no need to consider Cases 2 and 3 and if a taxpayer satisfies Case 2, there is no need to consider Case 3 (see *para 54, Sch 45, FA 2013*).

*Case 1*

**[6.16]** Case 1 is reproduced at para **8.09**. In summary, the taxpayer must:

• be non-resident for the following tax year by virtue of the third automatic overseas test (full-time working abroad) and this must not be a split year;
• be resident (either full or part year) in the previous UK tax year; and
• have at least one period of work beginning with a day on which more than three hours' work is done overseas and ending with the last day of the tax year, for which the relevant criteria are met.

The relevant criteria are that:

• an average working week of at least 35 hours per week is attained following the prescribed methodology set out in the law (see para **2.05** and para **3.12** for details);
• there are no significant breaks from overseas work (again see para **3.14** for definition); and

- the taxpayer stays within the pro-rated UK workdays and UK days of presence, arrived at again by following a formula in the law applied to the full year 30 UK workday and 90 days of UK presence limits. For an easy point of reference on how the limits apply based on different departure dates, refer to table E of RDR3, reproduced in para **8.09**.

Where Case 1 applies, the overseas part of the year starts on the first day of the period for which the relevant criteria are met.

Case 1 focuses on the individual's work overseas; it requires a period that starts in the year of departure and goes on to the end of that year and the period must be one for which the taxpayer 'satisfies the overseas work criteria'. Case 1 also requires the individual to be non-UK resident in the next tax year under the third automatic overseas test (ie works sufficient hours overseas). It should be noted that Case 1 is not concerned with ceasing to work full time in the UK and indeed under both the 'overseas work criteria' and the third automatic overseas test, some UK work is permitted.

Case 1 may therefore apply when an employee leaves the UK at the end of their period of UK working and immediately starts working full time overseas. In addition, Case 1 may apply where the individual takes a break at the end of their UK contract, spending free time either in the UK or overseas, before starting work overseas (although in these circumstances the date on which residence ceases will obviously be later).

### Example 6.8: Jonas

Jonas has been on assignment in the UK for his non-UK employer for a period of three years. This comes to an end on 30 June 2017 and, although the same group of companies has offered Jonas a job in his native Sweden, which he can start as soon as he wishes, he decides that he would like to take a two-month break to catch up with friends and family in Sweden and does so. He starts his new full-time contract in Sweden on 1 September 2017.

Assuming he meets all the other relevant conditions, Jonas may qualify for split-year treatment under Case 1 although it would be from the date he started work in Sweden and not from the date on which he left the UK. A more favourable position might be achieved by using the Double Tax Treaty between the UK and Sweden – see comments below and CHAPTER 12 for further analysis.

The permitted number of days of UK presence and/or work for the overseas part of the year of departure can be tight and may need to be very carefully monitored (see para **8.09** for more detail).

There is no requirement for the individual to give up their UK accommodation or for their family to leave the UK with them in order to satisfy Case 1. This should allow some flexibility for the taxpayer.

### Example 6.9: more about Jonas

Jonas has met and become engaged to Maggie while he has been working in the UK. Ultimately, they plan to marry and settle in Sweden, but they have lived together in Maggie's flat. So Jonas has ongoing UK accommodation for the time being and arguably a family tie if Maggie and Jonas are regarded as living together as if they were husband and wife.

None of this will prevent Case 1 from applying to Jonas if he meets all the relevant conditions for it. Under previous law it was also possible to have a home and family in the UK and still qualify as full-time working abroad,

Case 1 will not apply where an individual simply stops full-time UK working, without starting work again elsewhere. So someone retiring abroad will not qualify for split-year treatment under Case 1, but may do under Case 2 or Case 3.

As a practical matter, the vast majority of expatriates who have come to the UK on assignment, and who return to their home country at the end of the assignment, are likely to qualify for a form of split-year treatment, whether or not they meet the conditions for one of Cases 1 or 3. This is because if they return to a country with which the UK has a Double Tax Treaty and they have ongoing links with that country, they are likely to be split-year Treaty non-resident in the UK, regardless of whether or not the restrictive tests of these cases are met – see CHAPTER 12 for more details.

However, because there is no working full time in the UK 'package', it cannot be assumed that split-year treatment will always apply on departure. Although perhaps slightly unusual circumstances, the following example illustrates this.

**Example 6.10: Nathan**

Nathan has come to the UK for full-time work here and starts what becomes a 365-day period of full-time work on 13 April 2016. He is advised on 13 April 2017 that he has won £30 million on the Euro millions lottery, and he decides he would prefer to live a life of leisure, and stops work with effect from 21 April 2017. He decides to travel as soon as possible and books himself on a round the world cruise which departs on Sunday 23 April. He moves all his belongings into storage and hands over the keys of his UK home to an estate agent on Saturday 22 April and spends his last evening in the UK with friends, before leaving on his cruise which he expects to last for a full year.

Nathan will have too many UK days to be automatically non-resident in 2017/18 because he is a prior year tax resident and he will not have fewer than 16 UK days prior to his departure. So it is necessary to consider the automatic residence tests. He will not have a UK home (his property is available to him for only 17 days and so cannot be a UK home). His period of absence means he is also unlikely to meet the 183 days of UK presence test. However, since he has a 365-day period that falls partly within 2017/18, he will remain UK tax resident for the full year.

Nathan will not qualify for any of the split-year cases for 2017/18. In addition, the transient nature of his travels may also mean that he never becomes tax resident in any other territory, but the UK's Treaty network may help prevent him from establishing tax liabilities in the countries he visits on the cruise. See CHAPTER 12 for further commentary on Treaties.

The example of Nathan shows that anyone who is UK tax resident by reason of full-time work in the UK is likely to be tax resident for at least two years, unless his first day of UK work as defined falls on 6 April. If the start of his qualifying period is later than 6 April, any qualifying 365-day period is likely to spill into a second UK tax year of residence. It is rare for expatriates who are inbound to the UK to fix their UK start date to the beginning of the UK tax year. It is quite possible, therefore, for a period of 365 days, or a little more, to make someone tax resident for at least two UK tax years.

*Case 2*

**[6.17]** Case 2 is relevant for accompanying spouses etc. It is reproduced at para **8.10** but may be summarised as follows.

The taxpayer must:

- be non-resident for the following tax year;
- be tax resident in the previous UK tax year whether or not that is a spilt year;
- have a partner whose circumstances fall within Case 1 for the tax year or the previous tax year;
- from the deemed departure date either have no UK home or have both an overseas and UK home and spend more time in the overseas home than the UK one; and
- stay within permitted limits for days spent in the UK post the 'deemed departure day' (see para **8.10** for full analysis).

Case 2 allows the partner of the employee to leave the UK either in the same UK tax year or in the following UK tax year, thus allowing some flexibility for family arrangements. On the basis that this chapter is concerned with employees and their families on short-term assignments to the UK, it is likely that the Case 2 requirement as to a UK home will be met. However, it is worth noting that Case 2 will only apply to a taxpayer who is the partner of an employee leaving the UK to work full time overseas, and so will not apply in the case of all partners of employees leaving the UK at the end of their period of full-time work in the UK. There will no doubt be some situations where Case 2 is not available.

**Example 6.11: more about Maggie**

Although Jonas expected to meet the conditions for Case 1 to apply to him after his holiday, his Swedish employer has asked him to return to the UK on business trips that mean he is likely to have too many UK workdays to make this possible. He may still be able to qualify for split-year treatment under a Treaty, as may Maggie, but she will not be able to apply Case 2 because he is not within Case 1.

*Case 3*

**[6.18]** Those taxpayers, who do not return to full-time work overseas (eg retirees and part-time workers) and those who cannot fall within Case 2, will need to consider Case 3.

Case 3 is reproduced at para **8.11** but may be summarised as follows.

The taxpayer must:

- be non-resident in the following UK tax year;
- be resident in the previous UK tax year whether or not it was a split year;
- have one or more homes in the UK at the start of the tax year, but cease to have any UK homes at some point during the tax year;
- in the part of the year after that date have fewer than 16 days in the UK; and
- have a 'sufficient link' with an overseas country at the end of a period of six months beginning with the date on which the UK home is given up.

See para **8.11** for further details

Case 3 requires the individual to cease to have a home in the UK. For an employee leaving the UK at the end of a period working here and either giving up a lease or selling their property, this part of the test may be met. Where the employee retains the property for personal use, the considerations will be similar to that of HNWIs leaving the UK. See the discussion at paras **5.05–5.06**.

See also the comments in para **5.07** on the 16-day requirement and the need to establish a sufficient link with a country overseas. On the basis that the employee returns to their home country, it may be relatively easy for them to establish a sufficient link, but there may be exceptions to this, for example where their home country has no concept of tax residence.

### Maintaining non-residence in subsequent years

**[6.19]** One important consideration for employees and their families after they have left the UK is ensuring that any return visits they make to the UK in subsequent years do not make them UK tax resident, perhaps under the sufficient ties test. If the employee retains accommodation in the UK for their use and has some UK workdays, in the first two years after departure, they may have three ties (UK work, accommodation and the 90-day tie) and possibly four if their family remain in the UK for a period that takes them into the following tax year (eg to complete a period of study). This would mean that they would have to spend no more than 45, or possibly 15, days in the UK before becoming UK resident. It should also be noted that, with at least three ties, and an earlier period of UK residence, they will be subject to the deemed day rule which could potentially increase their day count (see para **3.06**).

Even if the employee trips into UK residence in this way, they may also be tax resident in their home country and so need to apply the tax Treaty tie-breaker test where available. In circumstances where the employee has homes in both countries, and family in one with economic ties in the other, the application of the tie-breaker test may not be straightforward. See para **12.02** for more on this topic.

## Conclusion

**[6.20]** Under the previous regime, an individual coming to the UK to work for a period of at least two years would, in most circumstances, become UK resident from the day after arrival and remain so resident until the day of their departure. Under the SRT, each tax year needs to be considered separately, with particularly detailed considerations required for the years of arrival and departure. For some taxpayers this is likely to provide more onerous than the previous regime.

# Chapter 7

# Coming to the UK: high net worth individuals

## Introduction

**[7.01]** This chapter considers the position of all individuals who come to the UK whether on a short-term or long-term basis, other than as part of their full-time work. Issues concerned with full-time employment in the UK, whether or not the employment meets the full-time working test in the automatic UK test, are dealt with in CHAPTER 6.

The chapter is broadly divided into two parts and considers two types of individuals (although over the course of his life, one individual might fall into both camps):

- those who visit and spend time in the UK, but who wish to do so without establishing UK residence (para **7.02–7.10**);
- those who come to the UK for the longer term or for a larger part of the tax year, who accept that UK residence will apply to them (paras **7.11–7.21**).

## Spending time in the UK without establishing residence

**[7.02]** There will always be people who need or want to spend time in the UK, perhaps for business reasons or for personal reasons, and who would like to do so without becoming UK tax resident. Under the previous regime, for those who had not previously been UK resident, any advice would probably have focused on the need to keep visits to the UK below 90 days on average (among other considerations). However, in recent years it had become clear that the approach of the courts in such cases was to look at a number of other circumstances and it had become increasingly difficult to advise the regular visitor to the UK about when the UK residence line had been crossed.

The 90-days test continues to play a role under the sufficient ties test (see para **7.06** below) both in terms of being one of the day thresholds and as a UK tie in itself. Nevertheless, under the SRT the 90 days is a much less significant part of the test and a temporary visitor to the UK or a serial short-term visitor will commonly have many more elements to consider in the now more complex test. For the most part, however, it should be possible with care for the serial visitor to be certain that he has remained non-UK resident.

The statutory residence test has the advantage of setting out precisely what factors need to be taken into account and the weight which should be given to them, thus giving increased certainty to those visiting the UK. In addition, for the casual visitor to the UK, with few connecting factors, it is often possible to spend more than the 90 days in the UK without becoming UK resident.

### Automatic non-residence – limiting days in the UK

**[7.03]** It goes without saying that an individual wishing to avoid UK residence will need to avoid being resident under the 'Automatic UK tests' in *paras 6–10, Sch 45, FA 2013*. However, before considering these tests, one must consider *para 5, Sch 45, FA 2013*:

'5     The automatic residence test is met for year X if P meets–
    (a)     at least one of the automatic UK tests, and
    (b)     none of the automatic overseas tests.'

In other words, if an individual can fall within one of the automatic overseas tests, he can avoid having to consider any of the automatic UK tests, or indeed, the sufficient ties tests. Falling within the automatic overseas tests would allow the individual to remain non-UK resident with certainty – regardless of whether they have a UK home, for example (see para **7.04**).

For an individual who does not die in the tax year, there are three automatic overseas tests to consider. The first two tests are concerned with days in the UK and the third with full-time working abroad. It is assumed for the purpose of this chapter that the individual will not be working full time abroad, although it may be possible for someone employed abroad to continue in that employment and visit the UK in a manner that allows them to continue to pass the third test and this is explored in more detail in **CHAPTER 6**.

Those who are not working abroad must consider a days test. The number of days which can be spent in the UK while remaining non-resident under the automatic overseas test is dependent on an individual's previous UK residence as set out in *paras 12 and 13 of Sch 45, FA 2013*:

'12    The first automatic overseas test is that–
    (a)     P was resident in the UK for one or more of the 3 tax years preceding year X,
    (b)     the number of days in year X that P spends in the UK is less than 16, and
    (c)     P does not die in year X.
13    The second automatic overseas test is that–
    (a)     P was resident in the UK for none of the 3 tax years preceding year X, and
    (b)     the number of days that P spends in the UK in year X is less than 46.'

For individuals coming to the UK who have been UK resident at any time in the previous three years, the number of days which can be spent in the UK is extremely low – just 15 or fewer. This strict day count limit will apply if the individual was UK resident for any time in the previous three tax years, including short periods under a split year of residence.

The day count for those who have not previously been UK resident is more generous, however, and may enable regular short-term visitors to the UK to remain non-UK resident. An individual who has not been resident in the UK at any point in the previous three tax years who spends 45 or fewer days in the UK will be automatically non-UK resident and will not need to consider any further tests.

An individual is resident in the UK for a day if he is present in UK at the end of that day, ie midnight (*para 22(1), Sch 45, FA 2013*). However, a day will not count if an individual is present in the UK at midnight purely as part of his travel through the UK or if he is here due to exceptional circumstances (see paras **3.04** and **3.05** for more details of these exceptions).

The 45-day limit provides a very useful safe harbour for those who wish to visit the UK without becoming UK resident and, provided the day limit is never exceeded, the individual can continue to visit the UK for as many years as he likes without having to consider the more complex parts of the SRT.

## Automatic UK residence

**[7.04]** Assuming that an individual has exceeded the day limit in the automatic overseas test (and does not meet the third automatic overseas test in respect of an overseas employment – see **CHAPTER 2**), he will next need to ensure that he does not meet any of the automatic UK residence tests. As with the automatic overseas test, assuming that the individual does not die during the tax year, there are three tests which he will need to consider:

• spends 183 days or more in the UK;
• meets the home test;
• works 'full-time' in the UK.

It should be a relatively straightforward matter for the individual to ensure that he does not fall within the first automatic residence test – that of spending 183 days or more in the UK.

It is assumed for the purpose of this chapter that the individual will not meet the third automatic test (full time working in the UK) – this test is considered in more detail in **CHAPTER 6**. However, the second automatic test or 'UK home' test is more complex and needs to be considered in detail.

## The importance of the UK home

**[7.05]** **CHAPTER 5** highlighted the increased significance the SRT gives to the home from the perspective of those leaving the UK and seeking to become non-UK resident. The home is no less significant for those seeking to maintain an existing position of non-UK residence, although some of the specific considerations are likely to be different in this context.

As an example of how a non resident can have a UK home, note the 2017 High Court case, *Bestolov v Povarenkin* [2017] EWHC 1968. This case, also discussed in **CHAPTER 3**, **3.07** is not a tax case, but includes some considerations of what is needed for a residence to constitute a 'home'. The case arose from a business dispute involving a joint venture to develop mines in Russia. The defendant applied for an order that the Court decline to exercise jurisdiction, claiming that Russia was the most appropriate place for the case to be heard. The Court had to consider whether, within the definitions of the relevant law, the defendant was resident in England and England was his settled and usual place of abode. A key factor in Mr Simon Bryan QC's (sitting as a Deputy High Court Judge) decision was the fact that Mr Povarenkin regularly visited the Belgravia flat in London where his wife and family lived for the majority of the year. Despite spending on average only 80 days in the UK, this was sufficient to make the Belgravia flat his 'home in England'.

The second automatic test is contained in *para 8, Sch 45, FA 2013* and is reproduced at para **2.08**. Of all the automatic UK residence tests, this test – the 'UK home' test – is perhaps the most difficult to avoid with certainty. This is so hard partly because of the subjectivity of the term 'home,' and partly because of the rolling 91-day test. There is much discussion on the difficulties of defining 'home' in **CHAPTER 3**. However, the problem for an individual wishing to spend time in the UK will be to ensure that they either do not acquire a home in the UK or that, if they do so, there is no 91-day period during which they have no home outside the UK. They must also spend sufficient time each tax year in one of their overseas homes.

In order to be considered resident in the UK for an entire tax year (or possibly even two entire tax years), an individual need only have one 91-day period during which they have a home in the UK but no home overseas (or no home at which they are present for at least 30 days during the tax year under consideration). This 91-day period need not all fall within the same tax year, but at least 30 days of it must fall within the tax year under consideration.

In addition, the individual must be present at that 'home' for 30 days during the tax year, although any part of a day will count for this purpose (ie it is not a midnight test). These 30 days need not be consecutive and need not fall within the 91 days during which the individual has no home outside the UK (or no home which they occupy for at least 30 days during the tax year).

In view of the broad definition of 'home', there is always a risk that an individual who spends a significant amount of time in the UK will acquire a 'home' here. However, there may be an argument in some cases that the property in the UK is a 'holiday home' *(para 25(3), Sch 45, FA 2013)*. See para **3.07** for further discussion of this point.

### Example 7.1: Clara

Clara lives in New York but has a keen interest in Shakespeare as well as other UK theatre. After many years of visiting the UK she has a wide social network and decides to acquire a flat in Kensington where she spends a few weeks each year attending performances, shopping and seeing friends. Clara nevertheless retains her New York apartment, where she spends the majority of her time.

Clara's UK property is kept fully furnished and she never lets it out. She never comes to the UK for more than one month at a time and most of her visits last no more than a few days. Clara keeps personal belongings in the property, for example toiletries and some clothing, but she usually brings a suitcase when she spends time there.

It is likely that this property would be a holiday home within the meaning of *para 25(3), Sch 45, FA 2013*.

However, in the absence of case law and with only limited HMRC guidance (in the form of paragraph A20 and Example A11 in Annex A of RDR3), it is not precisely clear where the line between a 'holiday home' and any other kind of home lies. An interesting question, for example, would be whether a holiday home like this might become more than a holiday home in circumstances where the individual ceased to have a home overseas for any reason.

### Example 7.2: Clara again

In January 2017, Clara sells her New York apartment and acquires a new property in New York. However, the new apartment is in a state of considerable disrepair and needs extensive building work and refurbishment before Clara can move in. Clara therefore puts her New York furniture and other belongings into storage and decides to spend an extended period of time in her UK property interspersed with some short stays in a New York hotel. The building work and refurbishment takes longer than expected and Clara does not move into her new property until June 2017.

HMRC guidance tells us that in circumstances where a property is purchased in such a state of disrepair that it is incapable of being lived in as a home, it is not a home until it becomes habitable (Annex A, at A18), so we can assume the new property is not Clara's home until she moves into it.

An interesting question in these circumstances would be whether the UK property acquired a more permanent quality by Clara's longer occupation. It is certainly arguable that the UK residence does not change its nature and that Clara simply occupies it for a longer period in that tax year – she still effectively lives in New York; she simply chooses to have a long holiday in very particular circumstances.

However, there must remain a risk that when Clara ceases to have any other property that could be called her home and chooses to occupy the UK property for an extended period of time, it becomes more than a 'holiday home' and is no longer ignored for the purpose of the second automatic test. If this is correct, then the property is her home for a period longer than 90 days, so assuming that she spends at least 30 days in the property in both 2016/17 and 2017/18 she will be automatically resident in the UK for both of those tax years.

In view of the difficulty with the definition of 'home' and 'holiday home', therefore, the safest approach for an individual wishing to fall outside the second automatic UK test will be to ensure that they do not cease to have a home overseas. Again, this should usually be fairly straightforward for someone who is only a visitor to the UK since they are likely to maintain a property in their own country. Individuals should nevertheless beware of the 91-day trap illustrated in Clara's case above should there be a delay as part of moving property overseas. Clara, perhaps, could have occupied the property for one night before the building work was carried out and thus fall within the terms of A15 and Example A7 in Annex A of the HMRC guidance (RDR3) such that the property met the definition of a home throughout. Individuals should also take steps to ensure that they spend at least 30 days in an overseas home during any given tax year (remembering that they do not need to spend the night there).

### Example 7.3: Tom

Tom has lived in Singapore for all of his working life. When he retires in 2013/14 he decides to divide his time between Singapore, Australia and a property in the UK. He is lucky enough to have acquired considerable wealth while he was working and therefore keeps a property in each of the three locations.

In a typical year, Tom spends between two and three months in the UK during the summer (always less than 90 days), three to four months in Singapore and six months in Australia. Tom continues this pattern for a number of years. Tom does not have any further connections or ties with the UK and therefore remains non-UK resident.

After a few years, Tom decides that he would like to spend some time travelling more widely and books a 'round the world trip' which departs from Heathrow on 1 July 2017. In view of his impending trip he leaves Australia towards the end of April, spends a couple of weeks in May sorting out his property in Singapore and then comes to the UK for the remaining time until he leaves on 1 July. Tom does not return to the UK until July 2018 but he also does not return to any of his other properties.

Tom has spent fewer than 30 days in 2017/18 in both of his properties in Australia and in Singapore. Therefore, if his UK property is a home and not a 'holiday home' he will pass both conditions of the second automatic test and will therefore be UK resident for the whole of 2017/18.

Tom may wish to argue that his UK home is a 'holiday home' but this will depend on the quality and quantity of time which he spends there and HMRC may not agree with his interpretation.

If Tom had been able to spend slightly fewer days in the UK, such that he met the second automatic overseas test, he would be non-UK resident, even if he would meet the second automatic UK test that tax year, since the automatic overseas tests take priority.

## Sufficient ties

**[7.06]** For those who need to spend more than 45 days in the UK and who have successfully negotiated the automatic UK tests (and so are spending fewer than 183 days in the UK), the sufficient ties test will need to be considered. Paragraph **2.13** looks in detail at the sufficient ties test.

For those who have not been resident in the UK in the previous three tax years, the sufficient ties table is in *para 19, Sch 45, FA 2013*:

| Days spent by P in the UK in year X | Number of ties that are sufficient |
|---|---|
| More than 45 but not more than 90 | All 4 |
| More than 90 but not more than 120 | At least 3 |
| More than 120 | At least 2 |

It should be remembered that an individual whose days fall within one of the three categories and who has the number of ties shown *will* be UK resident. Therefore, an individual wishing to spend time in the UK without becoming tax resident will need one less tie than those shown in the table.

The relevant ties in these circumstances are in *para 31(3), Sch 45, FA 2013*:

'(3)    . . . each of the following types of tie counts as a UK tie–
(a)    a family tie,
(b)    an accommodation tie,
(c)    a work tie, and
(d)    a 90-day tie.'

For the short-term visitor to the UK, in the first year in which they start to visit the UK, the first three ties are likely to be the most significant. Commentary on the detailed definitions of these ties can be found at para **3.16**ff.

The practical considerations under the 'work tie', for an individual seeking to visit the UK while remaining non-UK resident, are likely to be very similar to those for an individual leaving the UK and are explored in more detail at para **5.18**.

The family tie may be relevant if, for example, the individual's spouse and children have come to the UK (for example for schooling) and the detailed conditions of that tie will need to be considered (see para **3.17** for a detailed definition of this tie).

A short-term visitor can in fact spend up to 182 days in the UK provided he does not have more than one UK tie, although more than 90 days will give him a second UK tie for the following two years. See para **7.08** below.

## Accommodation tie

**[7.07]** Those who visit the UK who wish to avoid acquiring an accommodation tie will need to be very careful if they stay anywhere other than a hotel (and in extreme circumstances, even a hotel room may constitute an accommodation tie – see HMRC guidance Annex A, para A42 and example A17).

In considering the accommodation tie an individual should remember that it is the availability of that accommodation which is the crucial test, not the degree to which the individual makes use of it. Provided that an individual spends at least one night in particular accommodation, then if it is available for them to occupy it for a continuous period of 91 days in the tax year, that accommodation will give rise to an accommodation tie. This may have an impact on the timing of an individual's acquisition of property in the UK (or entering into leases or other agreements regarding property).

**Example 7.4: Rory**

> Rory has his own business, based in France, but has been spending an increasing amount of time in the UK in the last three years to build business links here. For the first two years, 2015/16 and 2016/17 he was able to keep his day counts below 45 days and so remain automatically non-UK resident. In 2017/18 he spent much more time here and expects to exceed 120 days. His total days for the year, however, should still be well below the 183 which would make him automatically resident.
>
> As a result of his business activities, Rory has the work tie, but he has always stayed in different hotels in the UK, so does not currently have the accommodation tie.
>
> Since Rory's business in the UK has taken off and he is obliged to spend more time here, he decides it would be useful to rent a flat. He begins looking for a flat in December 2017 and finds one quickly, signing a six-month lease on 15 December. He is then able to use the flat for the rest of the tax year when he comes to the UK to stay.
>
> The combination of the flat being available for a period exceeding 91 days and the fact that Rory spent at least one night there in 2017/18 will be sufficient for him to have an accommodation tie for 2017/18. Rory will therefore have two UK ties and, as he has spent more than 120 days in the UK, he will be UK resident.
>
> If the flat has sufficient permanence to be considered a home, Rory may be able to claim split-year treatment for 2017/18 under Case 8, but he will need to consider whether he would be non-resident in the UK under the sufficient ties test up to 15 December. Alternatively, had Rory acquired the accommodation later in the tax year, he might have avoided having an accommodation tie for that year.

For the visitor to the UK hoping to avoid an accommodation tie, there are a couple of traps. The first is the fact that if an individual returns to the same accommodation within 16 days then it will be treated as being available throughout that time. This appears to be the case even for hotel rooms or bed and breakfast accommodation and even if the accommodation is, in fact, occupied by others during the gap. As highlighted in CHAPTER 3, this means that a return to the same hotel on a fortnightly basis could lead to a hotel room being treated as available accommodation. Where individuals are returning to the UK regularly with short periods between visits, they should therefore consider booking into different hotels, for example.

The other trap for the unwary might be staying with family, or to a lesser extent, friends, in the UK. There is a presumption in this part of the SRT that family (eg children, parents) will always 'put you up' – in other words, having family in the UK is akin to having available accommodation here. As a result of this presumption, the number of nights which can be spent with family before their home is treated as available accommodation is increased from the one night for other types of accommodation to 16 nights. This is still a relatively short period of time, and can easily be breached. Family in this context excludes immediate family (ie spouse/civil partner and minor children) but includes siblings, adult children and grandchildren and parents and grandparents. The 16 nights is a separate limit which applies to each household and an individual could, say, spend 15 nights in his parents' home and a further 15 nights with a sibling without acquiring an accommodation tie.

An individual wishing to avoid acquiring an accommodation tie would ideally limit his visits to close family to fewer than 16 days. Where this is not possible, he should take whatever steps possible to ensure the accommodation is not available – he should not, for example, leave any personal belongings in the relatives' property. The accommodation tie is discussed further at para **3.18**.

In theory it would be possible for an individual to acquire available accommodation by spending only one night with a friend or a more distant relative – eg an aunt. However, given the presumption in the law regarding close family, it would seem that the onus would be on HMRC in these circumstances to prove that the accommodation was as a matter of fact available to the individual throughout the period of 91 days and the problem therefore seems less likely to arise in practice.

Guidance on staying with friends and relatives in RDR3 is very limited and is discussed at para **3.18**.

## The 91-day trap

**[7.08]** For an individual who has never previously visited the UK who then wishes to spend time here, the day counts and ties can appear quite generous. It is possible to have two ties – say, an accommodation tie and a work tie – and spend up to 120 days here in the first year without becoming UK resident.

However, once an individual has spent more than 90 days in the UK in one tax year, it then becomes more difficult to remain non-resident in the following two tax years. The act of spending more than 90 days in the UK in any one tax year will result in an additional tie for the following two tax years (*para 37, Sch 45, FA 2013*). So an individual who has spent 120 days in the UK with two ties in one tax year, will then have three ties for the following two tax years and will therefore be limited to just 90 days or fewer if he wishes to remain non-UK resident for those years.

This could potentially lead to some odd patterns of visits.

### Example 7.5: Andre

Andre is self-employed and wishes to spend some time in the UK to build his business. He rents a flat in London (while maintaining his home in France). He spends more than 40 days working in the UK during 2014/15 and is present in the UK for a total of 118 days.

Andre is not resident in the UK for 2014/15. However, for 2015/16 and 2016/17 he now has an additional tie – the 90-day tie. This gives him a total of three ties to the UK for those years (as he maintains his flat and his working pattern). He therefore limits his days in 2015/16 and 2016/17 to just 88 days and so remains non-resident.

In 2017/18, therefore, Andre has lost the 90-day tie and can once more spend up to 120 days in the UK without becoming UK resident.

In this way, the 90-day tie is quite similar to the old 91-day averaging test from IR20. However, when compared to that test, the new test does appear more generous – under the old averaging test, having spent 120 days in the UK in one year, Andre would have needed to spend a much smaller number of days in the UK for 2015/16 and 2016/17 in order to keep his average days for the period below the 91. The other main difference with this new test is that it is a cliff-edge – once 90 days is exceeded, the individual will have an additional tie for the next two years. The result would have been the same if Andre had only been in the UK for 91 days in 2014/15.

### The impact of the deemed day rule

**[7.09]** On the face of it, to remain non-UK resident under the sufficient ties test, an individual need only keep track of the number of midnights he spends in the UK and ensure that the total is less than the permitted amount for the number of UK ties which he has. There is a further complication, however, in *para 23, Sch 45, FA 2013* (reproduced in para **3.06**), which can result in additional days being deemed to be days of presence in the UK.

As a result of this paragraph, if an individual meets the necessary conditions and has more than 30 days in the tax year during which he is present in the UK at some point during the day, but absent at midnight, then every one of these days after that initial 30 days will be counted towards the total number of days. This is a potential trap for anyone, but serial short-term visitors to the UK, with a previous year of residence in the UK, will be particularly vulnerable.

### Example 7.6: Stephanie

Stephanie is currently living in Sweden researching a book but her husband, Matthew, lives and is resident in the UK. Stephanie visits Matthew most weekends during 2016/17. In order to stay within the 45-day limit, she flies in on a Saturday and flies out on a Sunday evening. She was resident in the UK in 2015/16. Stephanie therefore has three UK ties – the family tie, the accommodation tie and the 90-day tie.

Stephanie wants to spend the maximum amount of time she can with her husband, but wishes to remain non-UK resident to avoid complicating her tax affairs. With three ties she can, therefore, have up to 45 days of presence in the UK before becoming UK resident. She therefore comes to the UK for 45 weekends, thinking that she will be within the 45-day limit.

However, although Stephanie will only have 45 days on which she is present in the UK at the end of the day, there will also be 45 days during which she is present at some point during the day, without being here at midnight. The first 30 of these days can be ignored, but the remaining days must be counted and added to Stephanie's total days. Stephanie now has 60 days in the UK and will therefore be UK resident under the sufficient ties test.

The deemed days rule is likely to have a particular impact for those who visit the UK for a number of short visits. If, alternatively, Stephanie had come to the UK for 22 visits but stayed for two nights (flying in on a Friday and out on a

Sunday) she would have had 44 days in the UK during which she was present at the end of the day, but would only have had 22 days which would need to be considered under the deemed days rule. Since this is below the 30-day threshold after which such days have to have counted, her day count would not be increased and she would have remained non-UK resident.

### Double Tax Treaties

**[7.10]** Individuals who find themselves spending sufficient time in the UK to be considered UK resident under the sufficient ties test may nevertheless remain resident in another country (perhaps their country of origin). In these circumstances, they may wish to give consideration to any double tax agreement between the UK and that other country. An individual may benefit from a favourable form of taxation due to being Treaty resident in another jurisdiction, in spite of being resident in the UK under domestic law. The same may be true for those who find themselves resident under one of the automatic tests, although this will be more unusual. For more detailed commentary on double taxation agreements in this context, see CHAPTER 12.

# Establishing UK residence

**[7.11]** The remainder of the chapter considers those individuals who come to the UK in circumstances such that they become UK tax resident and looks at the full cycle: the year of arrival in the UK; the period of UK residence; and the year of departure.

### Year of arrival

**[7.12]** Where an individual's visit to the UK has a higher degree of permanence, or where an individual has accepted that the number of days which he wishes to spend in the UK will be too high for him to remain non-resident, he will wish to be sure of the date on which his UK tax residence will begin. He may also wish to take planning steps to ensure that his residence does not begin earlier than necessary.

#### When does UK-residence begin (the split-year test)

**[7.13]** As has been highlighted in previous chapters, UK residence is assessed on an annual basis and so, strictly, where an individual is resident in the UK, they will be resident for the whole tax year. Nevertheless, the split-year tests enable an individual to be treated for most tax purposes as though they were non-UK resident for part of the tax year and as though their residence began on a particular day during the year.

For this chapter, the relevant split-year tests for an individual coming to the UK will be Cases 4 and 8, in *paras 47* and *51, Sch 45, FA 2013* (reproduced in paras **8.15** and **8.24**). It is assumed for the purpose of this chapter that an individual will not be affected by the cases concerned with full-time work in the UK or abroad (such individuals are the subject of CHAPTER 6). Both Cases

4 and 8 are concerned with an individual's home. Case 4 will apply when an individual begins to meet the 'only home' test during a tax year and Case 8 will apply when an individual begins to have a home in the UK and continues to have one for the whole of the next tax year. Many individuals are likely to retain a home overseas and so Case 8 is therefore most likely to be of relevance. However, if an individual has been a previous visitor to the UK but remained non-resident, they may already have acquired a UK home. If this is the case, they can only become eligible for split-year treatment by ceasing to have a home elsewhere (at least for the purpose of the only home test).

### Starting to have a 'home' in the UK

**[7.14]** Assuming that an individual who is coming to take up residence in the UK has no home here already and is relying on Case 8 of split treatment, the date on which he acquires his home could be critical to the date that his residence begins. This is not just because the Case 8 split-year test treats residence as beginning on the day that the individual acquires a home, but also because in order for that treatment to apply, they must be non-resident under the 'sufficient ties' test for the period ending the day before the home is acquired (*para 51(4), Sch 45, FA 2013*).

For the purpose of applying the sufficient ties test, the number of days must be reduced by the 'appropriate number' which is found by pro-rating the number of days allowed for a full tax year by the number of whole months (not tax months) remaining in the tax year from the date on which the taxpayer acquires a home in the UK. HMRC guidance includes a useful table which shows the allowable days depending on the month of arrival (Table F – reproduced at para **8.19**).

In applying the sufficient ties test to the part of the year before the home is acquired, there appears to be no requirement to consider any ties which the individual may have later in the tax year. So, for example, if an individual comes to the UK with their family and acquires a property in October, he will have both the accommodation tie and the family tie for the second half of the tax year, but neither of these ties will be considered for the purpose of *para 51(4), Sch 45, FA 2013*.

This is borne out by the example of Olan in the HMRC guidance (Example 37, reproduced at para **8.19**).

An interesting question for these split-year cases will be where the line is between something being regarded as 'available accommodation' and being a home. This is particularly relevant where the individual already had access to accommodation before coming to the UK. It is suggested that for a property to be a 'home' it needs to have some degree of permanence that would not be found in 'accommodation'. However, the fact that the UK home test (the second automatic UK test) only requires a home to be available for a period of 91 days, suggests that the degree of permanence needed will not be high.

This could be critical in the case of those coming to the UK.

**Example 7.7: Maria**

Maria, who is French, met Michael (a UK resident) three years ago when they were both students and he was studying in France. Their relationship continued after they both left full-time education with weekend and holiday visits between the two countries. As a result of their relationship, Maria has spent increasing amounts of time in the UK, but never sufficient to be resident here. Maria does not work while in the UK, so does not have the work tie. Maria spent 92 days in the UK in 2016/17.

Maria and Michael plan to get married on 26 August 2017 and so Maria comes to the UK on 1 July to organise the wedding and moves in with Michael. Until this time, Maria was living with her parents in France, but has spent every weekend in the UK (a total of 26 days). The couple live together in Michael's rented flat until the wedding (at the point where Maria moves in with Michael, it is likely that she begins to have a family tie). They spend a fortnight honeymooning in Thailand and return on 16 September. At the beginning of October they move into a new rented flat which they have chosen together and on which they have signed a 12-month lease. The lease on Michael's flat ends on 30 September.

It will be critical in this case to decide when Maria acquires a home in the UK. If she acquires a home on the day she moves in with Michael, then the table for sufficient ties for the period prior to 1 July will look like this:

| Days spent by P in the UK in period | Number of ties that are sufficient |
|---|---|
| More than 15 but not more than 30 | All 4 |
| More than 30 but not more than 40 | At least 3 |
| More than 40 | At least 2 |

Maria will have only two ties prior to 1 July (the 90-day tie and the accommodation tie) and will therefore be non-UK resident under the sufficient ties test and her residence will begin on 1 July.

However, it is arguable that, given she is already planning to move into other accommodation and the flat she moves into belongs to Michael, this does not have the necessary permanence to be a home. In that case, Maria acquires a home on 1 October, and the table would look like this:

| Days spent by P in the UK in period | Number of ties that are sufficient |
|---|---|
| More than 26 but not more than 52 | All 4 |
| More than 52 but not more than 70 | At least 3 |
| More than 70 | At least 2 |

Prior to 1 October, Maria will have spent 97 days in the UK and she will also have three ties for this period (the family tie, the accommodation tie and the 90-day tie). In this case, at the point Maria acquires a UK home, she would have been resident in the UK under the sufficient ties test for the 'overseas part' of the year and she will therefore not qualify for split-year treatment and will be taxed as resident throughout the tax year.

In a case like this, Maria might well file her tax return on the basis that Michael's flat was her 'home' for however short a period and hope that HMRC are prepared to take a pragmatic view. However, there may well be cases where HMRC would dispute this.

A similar difficulty might arise in a situation where an individual comes to the UK and moves in with friends. It will be clear that such an individual has an accommodation tie (assuming he stays there over a long enough period that the accommodation can be said to have been available for 91 days in the tax year). What is less clear is whether staying with friends could ever have the degree of permanence needed to constitute a home. It does seem that this might be possible, for example, where an individual has his own room in a friend's property, pays rent for that room and makes use of communal areas, eg kitchen, living room on a long-term basis.

However, the position will depend on the precise facts in each case and much is likely to turn on the intention of the parties – for example whether staying in the property is seen by both parties as a stop-gap measure while the individual searches for a more permanent UK home or whether both parties see the arrangement as continuing for the medium to long term. The length of occupation is also likely to be of relevance – so if the individual stays for under three months it is much less likely to be a home than if he stays for a year, for example.

Whether or not a friend's property is an individual's home could be crucial, since an individual who has been living with a friend for four months, say, from June to September, before acquiring his own home is unlikely to be non-resident under the revised sufficient ties test for the early part of the tax year. He may therefore not qualify for the split year basis at all, unless his friend's property could be counted as a home. An individual who finds himself in these circumstances may well wish to argue that his friend's property is a home and he therefore acquires a UK home when he moves in in June.

Where an individual has been visiting the UK for a number of years and has UK property, he may not be able to take advantage of the split-year treatment under Case 8 – 'starting to have a home in the UK.' This would be the case if the property has been occupied in such a way as to give the character of a home. He may not have considered this point previously, for example because he has been automatically non-resident. Once again, there must be some question about the line between 'home' and 'accommodation' and whether the same property could change from being one to being the other (this, for example, might be a situation in which a friend's property to which an individual returns year after year but for relatively short periods is accommodation but not a home).

RDR3 paraphrases the legislation by suggesting that a home 'can be a building (or part of a building), a vehicle, vessel or structure of any kind which is used as a home by an individual. It will be somewhere which an individual uses with a sufficient degree of permanence or stability to count as a home' (Annex A, A9). This is not very elucidating, but the suggestion from this is that although there is no need for a 'home' to be a building or even a permanent structure, there must be some degree of permanence to one's occupation of it – not everywhere a person spends time living, in other words, will necessarily be a 'home'. This is echoed later in Annex A:

'A27 The main difference between the term "home" for SRT purposes and available accommodation is that accommodation can be transient and does not require the degree of stability or permanence that a home does.'

However, could something that is only available accommodation later become a home? Could there be an argument, perhaps, that a furnished flat in Central London that you use sporadically on visits to the UK does not have the permanence required to be a home, but that when you move in for six months and bring most of your personal belongings it becomes a home? Where an individual finds themselves in these or similar circumstances and would otherwise be resident for a full tax year, it may be worth mounting an argument that this is the case. In the absence of case law or clear guidance on this point, it is not clear what position HMRC would take. In view of the above difficulties regarding 'home' and 'available accommodation', those who plan to become resident in the UK will want, wherever possible, to arrange their accommodation and limit their days in the UK prior to moving into that accommodation to prevent any dispute regarding the application and timing of the split-year test.

In addition to acquiring a home in the UK, in order to qualify for split-year treatment under Case 8 the individual must continue to have a home in the UK for the rest of that tax year and the whole of the next tax year. However, there is only a requirement that the individual has 'a' home for that period – not that it is the same home, nor necessarily that it is occupied throughout the period (provided it does not cease to be a home – see comments above). Note that for Case 4 there is no requirement that the individual has their only or indeed any home in the UK throughout the next tax year.

### Ceasing to have a home outside the UK (Case 4)

**[7.15]** Where an individual has accommodation in the UK with sufficient permanence to be considered a home in a year before they move to the UK, they will not be able to take advantage of the split-year provisions in Case 8.

In order to qualify for split-year treatment, such individuals would need to qualify under Case 4 and begin to meet the 'only home' test under automatic residence. In practice, this will mean giving up their home in their country of origin (or at least the country they are moving from) as well as any other homes they may have. This is unlikely to be attractive in many cases, but for comments on beginning to have an only home in the UK, see para **5.25**.

### Timing

**[7.16]** The way in which the sufficient ties test is applied to the overseas part of the year (only by looking at those ties that exist before the individual acquires a home in the UK) is helpful for those who acquire a UK home in the year of arrival. In most cases, the generous day-count tests, coupled with the fact that most individuals will not acquire many ties before coming, mean that it should be possible to be taxed in the UK broadly as though beginning residence on the day the home is acquired – whether that be at the beginning, in the middle or at the end of the tax year.

However, for those who already have a home in the UK, in many cases the split-year treatment is unlikely to be available. Some individuals may, for example, purchase or let a property which would meet the home test (and also the accommodation test) but not initially spend sufficient days in the UK to be resident. For these individuals, it will be best to plan their affairs so as to become UK resident from the beginning of a tax year and, even where they do not physically move to the UK, any pre-arrival tax planning will need to be carried out before the tax year begins.

## Years of presence in the UK

**[7.17]** If an individual develops a settled presence in the UK, such that he spends 183 days or more in the UK, he will be automatically resident in the UK under the first automatic UK test. Similarly, if an individual has a UK home and either no overseas home or spends very little time in any of his overseas homes, he will be automatically resident in the UK.

However, for many internationally mobile, high net worth individuals who spend time in a number of different countries (and less than 183 days in the UK) and who have more than one property which could be considered a home, it is likely that they will still need to consider the sufficient ties test to determine residence.

Once an individual has been resident in the UK for one tax year, it should be remembered that the sufficient ties test will be stricter for the following *three* years.

In the second year of residence, an individual will need to apply the sufficient ties test in *para 18, Sch 45, FA 2013* (for individuals who have been resident in any of the previous three tax years).

| Days spent by P in the UK in year X | Number of ties that are sufficient |
|---|---|
| More than 15 but not more than 45 | At least 4 |
| More than 45 but not more than 90 | At least 3 |
| More than 90 but not more than 120 | At least 2 |
| More than 120 | At least 1 |

Effectively, this means that once an individual has had one year of UK residence, they will be resident in the UK with one less UK tie for the same number of days than would be the case for someone who has never been resident (or has not been resident in the previous three years). In addition, there is a fifth tie, the country tie, to consider (see para **3.21** for this tie). This may not be particularly significant once an individual has accepted that he is and will remain UK resident for a period, but is likely to assume greater significance once an individual wishes to leave the UK or end his period of UK residence. In addition, the 90-day trap (identified at para **7.08** above) means that an individual may have an additional tie for the second year of residence.

### Example 7.8: Pierre

Pierre is a French national with business interests in the UK, although he has remained non-UK resident. In October 2016, Pierre acquires a home in the UK and therefore has available accommodation. He maintains his property in France where he stays when he is not in the UK and he considers this also to be his home. As a result of his business interests in the UK, Pierre has the work tie. Pierre is currently single and has no children, so does not have the family tie.

In 2016/17, Pierre spends 130 days in the UK. He does not meet any of the automatic UK or overseas tests and is resident under the sufficient ties test. However, since he acquires a home in the UK during the tax year and he meets the other conditions of Case 8, he qualifies for split-year treatment in 2016/17.

In 2017/18 Pierre spends just 70 days in the UK. However, he now has three UK ties – the accommodation tie, the work tie and the 90-day tie – and will be resident for 2017/18.

An individual who is resident in the UK under the SRT may nevertheless be in a position to benefit from a Double Tax Treaty if he has remained resident in his country of origin. The tie-breaker for residence should always be examined to determine where the individual will be treated as resident for the purpose of the Treaty. In the example above, Pierre may wish to consider his position under the UK/France Double Tax Agreement to determine whether he will be Treaty resident in France and whether this may give him some tax relief.

For commentary on Double Tax Treaties, see CHAPTER 12.

## Long-term consequences of UK residence

**[7.18]** As noted above, once an individual has spent even a single year resident in the UK, the sufficient ties test and day counts become less generous for determining residence for the next three tax years. This is so even if the individual returns to their country of origin or is tax resident elsewhere for the two intervening years, and so under ordinary circumstances might consider themselves to be an 'arriver' in that fourth tax year. Those advising individuals coming to the UK will need care to ensure that a full history of UK visits is taken, since a previous brief period in the UK may have been sufficient to trigger residence. An individual might not expect or recognise the period of earlier residence as such and this may then have an impact on the sufficient ties test for any subsequent visit to the UK.

For non-domiciled individuals, any year of residence will count towards the '7 out of 9' or '12 out of 14' years of residence test for the remittance basis charge (in *s 809C, ITA 2007*) and towards the '15 out of 20' year test to be deemed domiciled in the UK (new *s 835BA ITA 2007* as inserted by Finance Act (No 2) 2017). Or for years up to 6 April 2017, for the '17 out of 20' year test for IHT deemed domicile (*s 267, IHTA 1984*). For all of these tests, years of residence will include split years, even where an individual has only been present in the UK for a relatively short period.

Again, all years of residence including split years will count for the '4 out of 7' years needed to trigger the anti-avoidance rules for temporary non-residence discussed below at para **7.19** and in more detail in CHAPTER 13.

## *Years of non-residence and the limitation of the anti-avoidance rules*

**[7.19]** A detailed discussion of the anti-avoidance rule is included at CHAPTER 13. However, a limited opportunity for planning remains for those who have only been resident in the UK for a short period.

The opportunity arises as a result of the definition of 'temporarily non-resident' at *para 110, Sch 45, FA 2013* which, from 2013/14, applies both for the purpose of *s 10A, TCGA 1992* and the new income tax anti-avoidance rules. For a period of non-residence to be a period of temporary non-residence in respect of the individual, he must have had sole UK residence for four of the seven tax years preceding the year of departure (a split year where an individual had sole residence for part of the tax year counts as a year of residence for this purpose). So for those who have been resident only for a relatively short time, or have maintained their residence in their country of origin, the anti-avoidance rules will not apply.

A similar opportunity arises in relation to the remittance of an individual's relevant foreign income (*s 832A, ITTOIA 2005*), since the rules which treat income remitted during a period of temporary non-residence as remitted in the year of return also only apply to an individual who has been UK resident and not treaty non-resident for four of the previous seven tax years.

This means that for the first few years of residence, an individual could become non-resident for a single tax year and so receive or remit certain income and gains without exposure to UK tax and without these anti-avoidance rules applying.

## *Leaving the UK*

**[7.20]** For high net worth individuals who have come to the UK for a fixed period, the timing of their departure will be important to their UK tax position in the final year of residence and is likely to be dependent on whether they expect to qualify for split-year treatment in this final year.

The relevant cases for split-year treatment for those leaving the UK are Cases 1 to 3. For those who are not leaving the UK for reasons connected with their own or their partner's full-time employment, the relevant case is Case 3. A detailed discussion of the principles of Case 3 and the considerations for an individual leaving the UK are included at paras **5.02** and **8.11–8.14**.

Provided all the conditions are met, it is possible to fall within Case 3 of the split-year test, even if you were only resident in the UK for part of the previous tax year (ie the previous tax year was also a split year). So, for example, an individual who has only been resident in the UK for a total of nine months, say, might qualify for split-year treatment in the year of arrival and the year of departure.

#### Example 7.9: Natalia

Natalia is a Russian student who decides to spend some time in the UK in order to improve her English. With this in mind she rents a flat in London on a six-month lease, beginning on 15 January 2017 and ending on 15 July 2017. Prior to coming to the UK Natalia lived in rented accommodation in Moscow. She gives notice on the Moscow property and moves out on 15 January. She has not previously visited the UK. When the lease is up on the flat on 15 July, Natalia returns to Russia and moves in with her parents.

Considering only the UK rules for both 2016/17 and 2017/18 Natalia therefore meets the second automatic UK test, as her only home is in the UK (the flat is available for more than a 91-day period of which at least 30 days falls within each tax year and during that period Natalia does not have another home).

For 2016/17 Natalia will meet the split-year test (under Case 4), since Natalia begins to meet the only home test during the tax year – on 15 January 2017. She will also meet the split-year test for 2017/18 (under Case 3) because she will cease to have any home in the UK and has no home for the rest of the year. It is assumed for this purpose that Natalia will be resident in Russia under its domestic law six months after 15 July, that she spends fewer than 16 days in the UK between 16 July 2017 and 5 April 2018, and is not UK resident in 2018/19.

## Timing of departure

**[7.21]** As noted above, the split-year test can be difficult for high net worth individuals – essentially, it is entirely dependent on the individual giving up a 'home' in the UK. For individuals who have properties in a number of different jurisdictions, this may prove difficult and the tax planning requirements may not fit with their other requirements – for example, maintaining a UK property for investment purposes or to facilitate short-term visits to the UK.

For those whose circumstances do not fit within the limited split-year conditions, there remains the old-fashioned approach of leaving the UK at the end of the tax year or availing themselves of a favourable tax Treaty and so not needing to rely on any split-year treatment. For many HNWIs this is likely to remain the best option.

# Conclusion

**[7.22]** For the individual visiting the UK, the SRT provides some certainty around the conditions which must be met for them to be considered resident. However, once an individual has met the conditions for residence for even one tax year, it can become more difficult to return to a position of non-residence.

# Chapter 8

# Split-year treatment

## Introduction and overview

**[8.01]** Under UK law an individual has always been resident or non-resident for a complete UK tax year. However, in recognition that this might lead to unfair taxation, under the former regime by concession it was possible in some circumstances for individuals coming to or leaving the UK to be taxed as though they were resident for only part of a tax year.

### Background and the old concessionary treatment

**[8.02]** The former regime had separate concessions for income tax and for capital gains tax and their application was slightly different.

For income tax the main concession was ESC A11, which allowed an individual to be taxed as though non-resident for part of the year in the following circumstances:

- he had come to the UK to take up permanent residence or to stay for at least two years; or
- he had left the UK for permanent residence abroad; or
- he had left the UK for full-time service under a contract of employment or returned from such an employment during the tax year concerned and certain conditions were met. The conditions were that both the employment and the period abroad encompassed at least an entire UK tax year and that any interim visits to the UK in the period totalled fewer than 183 days in any tax year or 91 days on average per tax year.

Individuals who worked full-time overseas in a self-employed capacity were also eligible for split-year income tax treatment.

A further extra-statutory concession ESC A78, often referred to as the 'trailing spouse' concession, extended split-year treatment for years of departure and return to the spouses of those who had left the UK to work full time abroad. The spouse had to meet the same conditions with regard to visits to the UK – ie no more than 183 days in any one tax year and an average of 91 days or less per year – but otherwise there were no conditions that had to be met other than that they went out with, or later joined, the working spouse.

Assuming that either of the concessions applied, the individual would be subject to income tax as though they were not UK resident for the part of the year before their arrival or after their departure. There was no legislative basis for this; it was simply a case of applying all the relevant legislation as though the individual were not resident for part of the tax year.

Capital gains tax had its own concession, concession D2, which was more limited in its application. For those coming to the UK, the concessionary treatment only applied to those 'treated as resident here for any year from the date of arrival' (in other words, the categories to which ESC A11 or ESC A78 applied) who had not been resident or ordinarily resident during the previous five tax years.

For those leaving the UK, the concession only applied to those who had been not resident and not ordinarily resident for the whole of at least four out of seven tax years preceding the year of departure. This part of the concession therefore did not apply to individuals who were longer-term residents in the UK.

Assuming the concession applied, gains before arrival or after departure were not subject to UK tax, although there were exceptions to this rule (for example, gains on UK trading assets and gains of settlements treated as arising to the settlor).

One of the difficulties of the split-year treatment prior to *Finance Act 2013* was that it was purely 'concessionary'. HMRC had made clear in guidance that, as with all extra-statutory concessions, the treatment would not be available to those who sought to rely on it for tax avoidance. Indeed, the capital gains tax manuals gave guidance as to the circumstances in which HMRC might withhold the benefit of the concession (see CG25793 Arrival in and departure from the UK: withholding benefit of ESCD2: HMRC approach). This left individuals and their advisors having to make judgements about the line between 'tax avoidance' which would prevent the application of the concession and 'tax planning' (for example, a straightforward delay to the date of contract) which would not.

In the light of the findings in *R (on the application of Wilkinson) v Inland Revenue Commissioners* [2005] UKHL 30, [2006] 1 All ER 529, [2005] 1 WLR 1718, and given the codification of residence, this split-year treatment has now been included in legislation for the first time. However, the split-year treatment, as enacted, has some significant differences from the concessionary treatment.

### The statutory treatment

**[8.03]** The statutory split-year treatment is contained in *Part 3 of Schedule 45, Finance Act 2013* and consists of a number of cases. In order to qualify for split-year treatment in the year of arrival or departure, a taxpayer's circumstances must fit within one of these cases. When draft clauses for the Finance Bill were published in December 2012, the split-year tests consisted of five cases. By the time the SRT was enacted, this had been expanded into eight separate cases.

There are three cases which apply to those leaving the UK:

Case 1 (*para 44*) – Starting full time work abroad (see para **8.09**)

Case 2 (*para 45*) – Partners of those who meet the conditions of Case 1 (see para **8.10**)

Case 3 *(para 46)* – Ceasing to have a home in the UK (see para **8.11**)

There are then a further five cases which apply to those arriving in the UK:

Case 4 *(para 47)* – Starting to have an 'only home' in the UK (see para **8.15**)

Case 5 *(para 48)* – Starting full-time work in the UK (see para **8.21**)

Case 6 *(para 49)* – Returning to the UK after full-time working abroad (see para **8.22**)

Case 7 *(para 50)* – Partners of those who meet the conditions of Case 6 (see para **8.23**)

Case 8 *(para 51)* – Starting to have a home in the UK (see para **8.24**)

This chapter is intended to provide an overview of each of the tests, the circumstances in which they will apply and the result of their application. More detailed examples on the application of the split-year tests for those coming to or leaving the UK are contained in CHAPTERS 4–7.

It is only necessary to consider the application of the split year if the individual would otherwise be resident throughout the year, either under the automatic residence test or under the significant ties test. This means that an individual who leaves the UK very early in the tax year, or arrives very late in the year, and who is automatically non-resident, will not need to consider the split-year cases.

It is worth noting that the split-year treatment does not require a claim or election. If an individual meets the conditions of one of the cases, then the split-year treatment will apply to them. The test applies to individuals (it does not apply to personal representatives) but there are special rules where an individual who is a trustee falls within one of the cases (see para **8.31** below).

An individual who is arriving in or departing from the UK may need to consider a number of different cases to decide whether they apply in his circumstances and thus to determine the date from or until which he will be taxed as though resident in the UK.

It is possible to fall within the circumstances of more than one case – for example, an individual may begin to have a home in the UK during a tax year (Case 8) and that home may be their 'only home' (Case 4). The law gives two different ordering rules for the eight cases, one for those arriving in the UK and a separate one for those leaving. The rule for those leaving is fairly straightforward and gives a simple ordering.

'Priority between Cases 1 to 3

54(1) This paragraph applies to determine which Case has priority where the taxpayer's circumstances for the relevant year fall within two or all of the following–
Case 1 (starting full-time work overseas);
Case 2 (the partner of someone starting full-time work overseas);
Case 3 (ceasing to have a home in the UK).
(2)     Case 1 has priority over Case 2 and Case 3.
(3)     Case 2 has priority over Case 3.'

So a taxpayer who meets Case 1 need not consider any further cases. Likewise if Case 2 is met, he need not consider Case 3.

However, for those arriving in the UK, the position is far more complex:

'Priority between Cases 4 to 8

55(1) This paragraph applies to determine which Case has priority where the taxpayer's circumstances for the relevant year fall within two or more of the following–
Case 4 (starting to have a home in the UK only);
Case 5 (starting full-time work in the UK);
Case 6 (ceasing full-time work overseas);
Case 7 (the partner of someone ceasing full-time work overseas);
Case 8 (starting to have a home in the UK).

(2)  In this paragraph "the split year date" in relation to a Case means the final day of the part of the relevant year defined in paragraph 53(5) to (9) for that Case.

(3)  If Case 6 applies–
  (a)  if Case 5 also applies and the split year date in relation to Case 5 is earlier than the split year date in relation to Case 6, Case 5 has priority;
  (b)  otherwise, Case 6 has priority.

(4)  If Case 7 (but not Case 6) applies–
  (a)  if Case 5 also applies and the split year date in relation to Case 5 is earlier than the split year date in relation to Case 7, Case 5 has priority;
  (b)  otherwise, Case 7 has priority

(5)  If two or all of Cases 4, 5 and 8 apply (but neither Case 6 nor Case 7), the Case which has priority is the one with the earliest split year date.

(6)  But if, in a case to which sub-paragraph (5) applies, two or all of the Cases which apply share the same split year date and that date is the only, or earlier, split year date of the Cases which apply, the Cases with that split year date are to be treated as having priority.'

So for a taxpayer who meets the conditions of Case 6 (ceasing full-time work overseas), this case will take priority unless he also starts full-time work in the UK and meets the conditions of Case 5. In these circumstances, the year will be split at the earlier date of the two Cases (to give the maximum period of UK residence). However, a taxpayer who meets Case 6 need not consider any of the further cases.

Assuming Case 6 does not apply, Case 7 (the partner of someone ceasing full-time work overseas) will have priority. However, again, if Case 5 also applies it will be necessary to look at both cases and consider which gives the earlier date on which the individual will be treated as UK resident. Again, a taxpayer who meets Case 7 need not consider any further cases.

If neither Case 6 nor Case 7 applies, but at least two of Cases 4, 5 and 8 apply it will be necessary to consider which of the three cases gives the earliest date of effective UK residence and that case will have priority. This may mean that a taxpayer who acquires a home in the UK may be treated as UK resident under the split-year test from a date before he arrives here and begins full-time work, for example.

The decision trees on the following page may assist with the analysis required.

## The split year ordering rules - leaving the UK

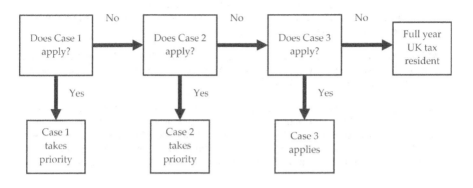

## The split year ordering rules - coming to the UK

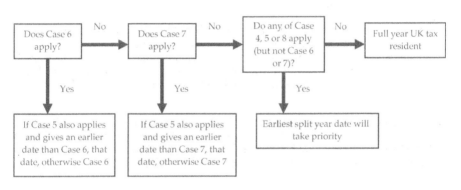

If an individual qualifies for split-year treatment under one or more of these cases, he will qualify for a special tax treatment for what is termed 'the overseas part' of the year (this 'overseas part' is specifically defined and is different depending on the case – see para **8.08** below). This special tax treatment is broadly similar to the individual being taxed as though he were not resident in the UK. However, it is not identical and there are some important distinctions (see para **8.33** below). It should also be noted that the day on which the 'overseas part' starts or ends may not be the same as the day on which the individual leaves or comes to the UK. It may also be different from any date on which he might qualify for split-year treatment under a Double Tax Treaty – please see CHAPTER 12.

**Example 8.1: Andrew**

Andrew has been living and working in Russia for the past three years and is now returning to the UK to live. His work overseas has been sufficient to be considered full-time working abroad and so he meets the conditions of Case 6. He ceases work for his Russian employer on 30 June 2017.

Although Andrew will do some work while he is in the UK for a UK employer, it will not be sufficient for him to be considered to be full-time working in the UK, so he will not meet the conditions of Case 5.

Andrew decides not to buy a property in the UK straight away but to rent a furnished property. He and his wife visit the UK in June and find a property that would be suitable. They enter into a rental agreement beginning on 15 June 2017 and spend two nights there before returning to Russia. The property is occupied sufficiently to be considered a home in the UK, and so Andrew will meet the conditions of Case 8.

Andrew puts his Russian property on the market on 25 July and on 1 August he and his wife move to the UK. The property is finally sold on 30 August. It is an interesting question precisely when the property in Russia ceases to be a home (which in this case does not matter) but at some point in the year Andrew would meet the conditions of Case 4.

Andrew, therefore, meets three cases of the possible five split-year cases – Cases 4, 6 and 8 and must consider which takes priority. *Para 55, Sch 45, FA 2013* tells us that where Case 6 applies it takes priority unless Case 5 also applies. Case 5 does not apply in Andrew's case and the UK part of his split year will therefore begin on 1 July. This means that Andrew will be taxed as resident in the UK before he moves here.

If Andrew were working sufficient hours in the UK to meet the conditions of Case 5, he would need to consider which of Cases 6 and 5 gives the earlier date. This is likely to give the same result in this case, even though there is a month between his ceasing employment in Russia and commencing employment in the UK.

# General concepts and terminology

**[8.04]** The SRT split-year legislation has some specific terminology which is defined in *paragraphs 43, 52–53 and 56, Sch 45, FA 2013*. It is necessary to understand the terminology both in determining whether a particular year is a split year in relation to an individual and in understanding the effect of a year being split, especially the date on which the special tax treatment accorded by meeting the split-year criteria begins or ends.

## Tax years

**[8.05]** The legislation of the eight cases refers to specific tax years as follows:

(a) 'the relevant year' – means the tax year that will be split: ie the year of arrival or departure.

(b) 'the previous tax year' – means the tax year preceding the relevant year.

(c)     'the next tax year' – means the tax year following the relevant year.

See *paras 43* and *52, Sch 45, FA 2013*.

A number of the cases place certain conditions not just on the year under consideration but also on the previous or the next tax year or both. For example, it is a requirement of Case 8 that the taxpayer was not resident for the *previous* tax year, that he acquires a home during the *relevant year* and that he continues to have a home for the whole of the *next* tax year.

## Partner

**[8.06]** 'Partner' is defined as a husband, wife or civil partner or someone who is living with the taxpayer in the same way as someone who is a spouse or civil partner *(para 52(4), Sch 45, FA 2013)*. An added complication for partners who are not in a formal relationship may be how and when they might be judged to be living together if they leave the UK at different times.

The commentary in HMRC's RDR3 guidance cross-refers to the *Tax Credits Technical Manual*, which contains some limited guidance on dealing with this situation. See para **3.17** for more discussion on the meaning of partner.

## Overseas and UK parts of the year

**[8.07]** The overseas part of the tax year is defined differently for each of the cases *(para 53, Sch 45, FA 2013)* and the particular split applying in each case is considered in more detail below. The UK part of the tax year is defined as the part of that tax year which is not an overseas part *(para 56, Sch 45, FA 2013)* and will not necessarily start at a point where the taxpayer has gained or lost any obvious UK connection.

## Self-assessment

**[8.08]** Each of Cases 1–3 include a requirement that the taxpayer is non-UK resident for the next tax year. This may give rise to complications for some taxpayers, where the tax return must be completed before the next UK tax year has ended. The individual will have to complete the tax return based on their best estimate and intentions of remaining non-UK resident, but inevitably some taxpayers will find that their circumstances change between 31 January and 5 April and so may need to amend their previous year's return.

There may be further complications for Case 3 where domestic law in the destination country means that an individual may not be able to assess whether or not he has established a 'sufficient link' with that country in time to complete his tax return.

There may be similar complications for some of the arrival cases – eg Case 8 (where a taxpayer must have a home for the whole of the following tax year).

# Case 1: Leaving the UK and starting full-time work overseas

**[8.09]** This case broadly applies to a taxpayer leaving the UK for full-time work overseas. This case is set out in *para 44, Sch 45, FA 2013*:

'(1)    The circumstances of a case fall within Case 1 if they are as described in subparagraphs (2) to (4).

(2)    The taxpayer was resident in the UK for the previous tax year (whether or not it was a split year).

(3)    There is at least one period (consisting of one or more days) that—
    (a)    begins with a day that—
        (i)    falls within the relevant year, and
        (ii)    is a day on which the taxpayer does more than 3 hours' work overseas,
    (b)    ends with the last day of the relevant year, and
    (c)    satisfies the overseas work criteria.

(4)    The taxpayer is not resident in the UK for the next tax year because the taxpayer meets the third automatic overseas test for that year (see paragraph 14).

(5)    A period "satisfies the overseas work criteria" if—
    (a)    the taxpayer works sufficient hours overseas, as assessed over that period,
    (b)    during that period, there are no significant breaks from overseas work,
    (c)    the number of days in that period on which the taxpayer does more than 3 hours' work in the UK does not exceed the permitted limit, and
    (d)    the number of days in that period falling within sub-paragraph (6) does not exceed the permitted limit.

(6)    A day falls within this sub-paragraph if—
    (a)    it is a day spent by the taxpayer in the UK, but
    (b)    it is not a day that is treated under paragraph 23(4) as a day spent by the taxpayer in the UK.

(7)    To work out whether the taxpayer works "sufficient hours overseas" as assessed over a given period, apply paragraph 14(3) but with the following modifications—
    (a)    for "P" read "the taxpayer",
    (b)    for "year X" read "the period under consideration",
    (c)    for "365 (or 366 if year X includes 29 February)" read "the number of days in the period under consideration", and
    (d)    in paragraph 28(9)(b), as it applies for the purposes of step 3, for "30" read "the permitted limit".'

Thus, a taxpayer falls within Case 1 if they meet the following conditions:

(a)    they were resident in the UK for the previous tax year, whether or not it was a split year;

(b)    they satisfy the 'overseas work criteria' for at least one period that starts in the relevant tax year and continues to the end of that year (see below and **CHAPTER 4** for more details);

(c)    they are not resident in the UK for the next tax year because they satisfy the third automatic overseas test (work sufficient hours overseas). This automatically excludes taxpayers with a 'relevant job' from this case as they can never qualify as non-resident under that particular test.

If these conditions are met, the overseas part of the year starts on the first day of the period in (b).

It should be noted that the period in (b) must start with a day of work on which the taxpayer does more than three hours of work overseas. If there is more than one period in the tax year which fulfils all the relevant criteria, the taxpayer is treated as non-resident under Case 1 from the first day of the longest of those periods (*para 53(2), Sch 45, FA 2013*). The application of this is explored further below. The taxpayer's overseas period starts at the beginning of this period and this may not be the day on which the taxpayer leaves the UK (eg if he first takes some time to settle in).

The period in (b) always ends on the last day of the relevant year concerned. This is important as it defines the end of the period over which the overseas work criteria must be satisfied. In order to determine whether the taxpayer satisfies the overseas work criteria for the period, it is necessary to consider:

- whether the taxpayer works 'sufficient hours overseas' for the period (at least 35 hours a week on average over the relevant period). Any days on which the taxpayer also works more than three hours in the UK are disregarded in the calculation, which may mean that days on which the taxpayer leaves the UK and has to travel to and check in at an airport will be disregarded;
- whether there are any significant breaks from overseas work. This is a period of more than 30 days on which the taxpayer does not perform more than three hours' work overseas and the absence from work is not attributable to sick leave, parenting leave or reasonable amounts of holiday;
- how many days (again calculated as a day on which the taxpayer does more than three hours' work) the taxpayer spends working in the UK in the period (these must not exceed the 'permitted limit'). Again, this is explored further below;
- how many days the taxpayer spends in the UK in the period (these must not exceed the 'permitted limit'). For this purpose the deeming rule (refer to para **3.06** for more detail) does not apply;
- whether there are any gaps between employment. In calculating whether an individual has worked sufficient hours, a gap between employments may be deducted from the period. However, where the gap exceeds 15 days, the deduction is limited to 15 days. Where there is more than one gap between employments, the maximum number of days that can be deducted must not exceed the 'permitted limit'.

The critical issue for most taxpayers leaving the UK for full-time working abroad will be controlling any return visits, and especially any return visits for UK duties. If either of the statutory permitted limits is breached it will prevent Case 1 split-year treatment from applying. It has already been noted in CHAPTER 4 that the day and workday limits which have to be met in order for an employee to qualify for Case 1 split-year treatment in the year of departure are pro-rated for that tax year using an A x B/12 formula. This pro-rating can make it particularly difficult to qualify, especially if the employee leaves the UK late in a tax year and has to return unexpectedly.

Table E, at para 5.13 of HMRC's RDR3, details the number of UK days and UK workdays permitted, depending on the date of departure from the UK and is a good point of reference.

*Table E*

| | Overseas part of tax year starts on or after | | | | | | | | | | | | |
|---|---|---|---|---|---|---|---|---|---|---|---|---|---|
| | 6 Apr to 30 Apr | 1 May to 31 May | 1 Jun to 30 Jun | 1 Jul to 31 Jul | 1 Aug to 31 Aug | 1 Sep to 30 Sep | 1 Oct to 31 Oct | 1 Nov to 30 Nov | 1 Dec to 31 Dec | 1 Jan to 31 Jan | 1 Feb to 29 Feb | 1 Mar to 31 Mar | 1 Apr to 5 Apr |
| X – permitted limit on days where you can work more than three hours and maximum number of days that can be subtracted for gaps between employments | 30 | 27 | 25 | 22 | 20 | 17 | 15 | 12 | 10 | 7 | 5 | 2 | 0 |
| Y – permitted limit on days spent in the UK | 90 | 82 | 75 | 67 | 60 | 52 | 45 | 37 | 30 | 22 | 15 | 7 | 0 |

**Example 8.2: Edith**

Edith leaves the UK on 18 January 2016 to take up a two-year assignment in France and does more than three hours' work in France on that day. One week after her departure, her great aunt Matilda dies leaving her entire estate to Edith who has always been her favourite niece.

The main asset is a country house in Suffolk, which the estate agent has warned may deteriorate if it is not sold quickly. Edith therefore agrees that she will come back every weekend through till the end of March, spending two nights in the UK on each trip and will also go to the house for a final clearance and check, at the start of April, spending the whole of the first week of the month back in the UK.

If Edith sticks with her plans, they will prevent her from qualifying for split-year treatment under Case 1 from 18 January. This is because she will have 9 x two-day weekend visits plus five days in the UK at the start of April, giving her a total of 23 days when the maximum number of days she could spend in the UK post-departure and qualify would be 22 days. If instead she were to defer the start date of her week in the UK in April to 5 April 2014, she would only have 19 UK days post-departure and could continue to qualify for split-year treatment.

An employee may find it difficult to satisfy the Case 1 conditions where they are required to return to the UK to undertake duties that were not anticipated on departure. It is then a question of considering which date to take as the start of the period for which they will seek to satisfy the overseas work criteria. If the UK workdays were sufficient to prevent Case 1 applying from the original start date, it would be advisable to consider whether applying the tests from a later overseas workday might allow Case 1 to apply. The same approach might be considered where an employee would exceed the number of UK days (Y days) in Table E if split-year treatment is claimed from the first date on which he does three hours' work overseas.

So, for example, Edith of Example 8.2, who failed to qualify for split-year treatment from 18 January, may wish to consider whether a later starting date (on which she also does three hours' work) might allow her to claim Case 1 split-year treatment as her UK days would be within the specified limit. However, with her regular visits back to the UK, this consideration may be fruitless in her case.

If there are a number of possible start dates for the necessary period of overseas working, the law applies to the longest of the periods, for which all conditions are met.

### Example 8.3: Florence

Florence and her colleague Joanne operate the office support for the sales function for their employer, Nordig Cruises, which specialises in arranging leisure cruises to Scandinavia and the Arctic Circle. It has recently established a new venture in Norway, arranging cruises through the Fjords. This is proving very successful, but they have been unable to recruit anyone to provide appropriate sales support locally in Norway and have asked Florence if she will move to Oslo for two years to set up operations there and recruit a local team.

It is agreed that Florence will leave the UK in July 2016, after someone has been recruited to work with Joanne while she is away, and to provide maternity cover for Joanne who is due to go on maternity leave from Christmas 2016. Rebecca joins their team at the end of May and Florence leaves the UK as planned but in the event, Joanne is unwell and has to start her maternity leave at the end of August. Florence agrees to return to the UK as an emergency measure from August 25 through the month of September, at the end of which time it is anticipated Rebecca will be able to provide the support needed in the UK, with Florence working remotely from Norway to offer back-up as needed.

Florence will have 27 UK workdays in August and September, assuming that she works Monday to Friday each week, which is more than the 22 she could have and still qualify as full-time working abroad from her departure date in July.

As noted above she should look for a later date in the tax year from which the split-year tests would be met. An obvious candidate might be 1 October depending on her return visits in the remainder of the tax year.

Alternatively, if Florence had been able to limit her days of physical working in the UK and perform some of the same duties from overseas she may have been able to prevent this need to move the split-year date to a later point in the tax year.

Under Case 1, the working sufficient hours test is calculated over a period that starts with a day on which more than three hours' work overseas is undertaken and which continues to the end of the tax year. HMRC guidance uses the term 'relevant period' for this period, although it is not found in the law. The term has been adopted here as a helpful shorthand. Were it not for a specific provision, each time an individual had an overseas workday, he could potentially restart the relevant period. However, as noted above, *para 53(2), Sch 45, FA 2013* provides that the overseas part of the year starts at the earliest possible date.

**Example 8.4: Rachel**

> Rachel starts a full-time employment in Brussels on 30 June 2016, working more than three hours in Belgium on that day. She takes two weeks' holiday at the start of August 2016, returning to work on Monday 15 August. This is also a day on which she works for more than three hours outside the UK and is the start of a period of such working. Fortunately, *para 53(2)(b), Sch 45, FA 2013* puts it beyond doubt that in these circumstances, provided Rachel meets all the necessary conditions, the relevant period starts on 30 June as that would give her a longer relevant period.

The requirement to be non-resident for the whole of the following tax year by virtue of full-time working abroad is also worthy of mention. This means that a taxpayer who leaves for full-time work abroad, but has a change of circumstances after departure, may have to amend his tax return some time after the event. For example, if an employee leaves the UK for full-time employment abroad with his current employer, but decides in year 2 to pursue a lifestyle change, perhaps involving a change of employment and a move to part-time working, this will prevent split-year treatment under Case 1 for the prior UK tax year. This is far less flexible than the previous concessionary basis. There, the requirement was simply that the individual anticipated on departure that his full-time employment abroad would encompass at least one complete UK tax year. In circumstances where full-time employment ceased he could have continued to qualify for the concession provided he remained non-resident for the complete UK tax year, since there was no direct link to full-time employment for the following tax year as is now required.

## Case 2: Leaving the UK – the partner of a taxpayer starting full-time work overseas

**[8.10]** This case applies to the partner (as defined – see para **8.06**) of a taxpayer who falls within Case 1 (ie who leaves for full-time work overseas). It allows the partner either to leave the UK in the same year as the working taxpayer or to go out to join them in the next tax year. The case looks at the days spent in the UK by the partner and whether the partner has a home in the UK and, if so, the extent to which they use it. Case 2 is found in *para 45, Sch 45, FA 2013* and is as follows:

'(1)    The circumstances of a case fall within Case 2 if they are as described in subparagraphs (2) to (6).

(2)    The taxpayer was resident in the UK for the previous tax year (whether or not it was a split year).

(3)    The taxpayer has a partner whose circumstances fall within Case 1 for–

    (a)    the relevant year, or

    (b)    the previous tax year.

(4)  On a day in the relevant year, the taxpayer moves overseas so the taxpayer and the partner can continue to live together while the partner is working overseas.

(5)  In the part of the relevant year beginning with the deemed departure day–

(a)  the taxpayer has no home in the UK at any time, or has homes in both the UK and overseas but spends the greater part of the time living in the overseas home, and

(b)  the number of days that the taxpayer spends in the UK does not exceed the permitted limit.

(6)  The taxpayer is not resident in the UK for the next tax year.

(7)  If sub-paragraph (3)(a) applies, the "deemed departure day" is the later of–

(a)  the day mentioned in sub-paragraph (4), and

(b)  the first day of what is, for the partner, the overseas part of the relevant year as defined for Case 1 (see paragraph 53).

(8)  If sub-paragraph (3)(b) applies, the "deemed departure day" is the day mentioned in sub-paragraph (4).'

So, a taxpayer falls within Case 2 if they meet the following conditions:

• they were resident in the UK for the previous tax year, whether or not that year was a split year;

• they have a partner who meets the requirements for Case 1 for the relevant year or the previous tax year;

• they move abroad on a day in the tax year concerned to join the partner who is full-time working abroad;

• they are not resident in the UK in the following tax year (there is no requirement in this case for them to be non-resident under any particular part of the SRT);

• in the part of the year beginning with the deemed departure date, they either have no UK home or if they have homes both in the UK and overseas, they spend the greater part of the time living in the overseas home; and

• they do not exceed the number of days they are permitted to spend back in the UK. In the same way as for the working spouse, this is a pro-rata limit of the full year 90-day figure depending on the deemed departure date. The pro-rata limits are available as the 'Y' figures in Table E in HMRC's guidance (see para **8.09** above).

The deemed departure date is either the actual date on which the taxpayer leaves the UK to join their partner or the date which is the start of the overseas part of the year for the partner (under Case 1), whichever is the later. In relation to the first of these dates, HMRC guidance (RDR3, para 5.18) suggests that the key date is the date on which the individual joins their partner overseas, rather than the date on which they leave the UK.

Where a taxpayer has homes both in the UK and overseas the requirement of the test is not entirely clear, as the statutory test is that they spend 'the greater part of the time living in the overseas home'. It is not, for example, clear whether or not this is a midnight test or whether total hours of presence should be compared. The best advice must be to spend as little time as possible in any UK home that is retained so as to put the matter beyond doubt. However, days spent elsewhere can also affect the comparison.

**Example 8.5: Michelle**

Michelle's husband Ron left the UK to take up full-time work in Switzerland and departed on 12 May 2016. Michelle had been working as a teacher, but did not wish to remain in the UK by herself any longer than was necessary and so left to join Ron as soon as her academic year was completed on 15 July 2016. Her flight to Geneva was on the morning of 16 July.

They had already decided not to let their home, so that it was available to them on any return visits to the UK whether for Ron's work or for leisure. Michelle found life in Switzerland lonely as Ron was working long hours and she missed her friends and family in the UK. She decided initially that she would spend a week back in the UK most months, although having regard to the need to keep her visits to no more than 67 days (ie the pro rata 90 days limit as per Table E). In July and August she has 14 days back in her UK home in total. She also spent a week visiting friends in France while they were on holiday there.

Michelle and Ron take a trip to the Far East for the whole of September, in Ron's case combining business with leisure. They spend October in Geneva, but Michelle's younger sister has an opportunity to work in Canada for six months starting in November 2016 and Michelle joins her for the first six weeks to help her settle in and see some of the sights. Michelle then returns to the UK on 15 December and remains there until 3 January to make the most of the Christmas festivities.

Michelle returns to Switzerland for a week but then as one of Ron's colleagues has been asked to work at UK HQ for a couple of months she travels to the UK with him and his wife and spends another three weeks at home. She then joins Ron skiing in France for a week, returning to Switzerland at the beginning of March. Michelle has calculated that she can spend a further 13 days in the UK during 2016/17, so she returns to her UK home on 13 March, leaving on 25 March to return to Switzerland.

Unfortunately, almost as soon as she has left her mother has a serious fall and after surgery is admitted to ICU. Michelle returns to the UK on 1 April, visiting her mother each day, but spending her nights in her home. Michelle has thus spent 71 days in the UK since her departure.

Michelle may be able to argue that the five days she spends with her mother are exceptional and should not prevent split-year treatment from applying (exceptional circumstances can exclude days in these circumstances – see para B5 of RDR3). Even if she does so, however, she has spent 71 days in the UK and 70 in her home in Geneva since her departure from the UK in July 2016, and so does not meet the necessary conditions, because she has spent more time in the UK home than in her Swiss one. The fact that five days were due to exceptional circumstances will not help her, as relief for this will only apply in respect of the day count for the 67 limit.

Another particular difficulty for a taxpayer with a travel pattern such as Michelle's is that if they have not kept exceptionally detailed records of where they have been on each day, they may have some difficulty establishing whether or not they have spent the greater part of their time in the current spousal home. Even with records, proving where they have been may be difficult. For more details on record-keeping see CHAPTER 13.

As noted earlier, the majority of time must be spent in the overseas home with the partner who is engaged in full-time work outside the UK. The pattern may therefore be distorted as it is in Michelle's case by extensive trips to any other location.

The law is a little ambiguous in its drafting and it is not clear whether in considering the 'greater part of the time' this should be a straight comparison between the time in the UK home and the overseas home or whether the individual needs to spend the greater part of the whole period in the overseas home. Consider an example where a taxpayer goes overseas late in the tax year and spends ten days in an overseas home, followed by five days in their UK home before taking a two-week holiday overseas which takes them to the end of the tax year. They cannot say the greater part of the period is spent in their overseas home, but may wish to argue that they have spent more time in their overseas home than their UK home and have therefore spent 'the greater part of the time living in the overseas home' and so meet the split-year conditions.

Overall, taxpayers may find it more difficult to meet the Case 2 conditions than to satisfy ESC A78, because the averaging in the 91 days' test of ESC A78 allowed a little more flexibility between years and from 1993/94 onwards it made no difference whether or not access to a home was retained or how it was used.

# Case 3: Leaving the UK and ceasing to have a home in the UK

**[8.11]** Case 3 is the only split-year test available to individuals leaving the UK who are not either leaving to take up full-time employment themselves or the partner of someone leaving to take up full-time employment. This is therefore the case most likely to be of relevance for HNWIs.

Under the old concessionary treatment, an individual going overseas for some purpose other than employment would only qualify for split-year treatment if he had left 'for permanent residence abroad'. In practice, this did not generally mean that the individual could never return, but rather that his period of non-UK residence must have had some settled purpose and he must have broken many of his existing ties with the UK. The precise degree of break from the UK and the required length of and purpose for the visit overseas necessary in order to qualify for split-year treatment remained open to debate and the fact that the treatment was concessionary meant any decision on the part of HMRC was difficult for an individual to challenge.

The new legislative treatment promises to bring certainty to this area, and in one sense it does: if an individual meets the criteria of the case he will qualify for split-year treatment – HMRC has no discretion. However, given the difficulties with defining 'home' for the purpose of the legislation (see para **3.07**), an individual is left with a degree of uncertainty regarding precisely what is meant by a 'home' in this context and whether he may have ceased to have a UK home.

Case 3 itself is found within *para 46, Sch 45, FA 2013*. To fall within Case 3, an individual must meet conditions for each of three tax years: the tax year under consideration (for which split-year treatment will apply), the previous tax year and the following tax year.

'46(1) The circumstances of a case fall within Case 3 if they are as described in subparagraphs (2) to (6).

(2) The taxpayer was resident in the UK for the previous tax year (whether or not it was a split year).

(3) At the start of the relevant year the taxpayer had one or more homes in the UK but—

    (a) there comes a day in the relevant year when P ceases to have any home in the UK, and

    (b) from then on, P has no home in the UK for the rest of that year.

(4) In the part of the relevant year beginning with the day mentioned in subparagraph (3)(a), the taxpayer spends fewer than 16 days in the UK.

(5) The taxpayer is not resident in the UK for the next tax year.

(6) At the end of the period of 6 months beginning with the day mentioned in sub-paragraph (3)(a), the taxpayer has a sufficient link with a country overseas.

(7) The taxpayer has a "sufficient link" with a country overseas if and only if–

    (a) the taxpayer is considered for tax purposes to be a resident of that country in accordance with its domestic laws, or

    (b) the taxpayer has been present in that country (in person) at the end of each day of the 6-month period mentioned in sub-paragraph (6), or

    (c) the taxpayer's only home is in that country or, if the taxpayer has more than one home, they are all in that country.'

As a first condition, therefore, the individual must be resident in the UK for the preceding tax year. However, there is no requirement that this year should be a full tax year, and the individual may qualify even if he also qualified for split-year treatment in the previous tax year.

The individual must then meet two conditions with regard to the tax year under consideration:

(1) The individual must have a home in the UK, which he must give up during the tax year.

(2) Having given up his home, from that date the individual must spend fewer than 16 days in the UK.

It is not clear why, in contrast to later cases, where an individual comes to live in the UK, it was decided that an individual could spend only a fixed number of days in the UK as opposed to applying a version of the sufficient ties test. That decision having been made, however, 16 is an obvious number since this fits with the automatic overseas test, which allows an individual who has been previously resident in the UK to spend up to 15 days here while remaining automatically non-UK resident (and not having to consider the sufficient ties test). This day count test does at least have the merit of being easy to understand, but may prove challenging for some individuals who leave the UK early in the tax year – since one fortnight-long visit to the UK and an additional weekend would be sufficient to see it breached.

## Ceasing to have a home in the UK

**[8.12]** The main part of the test, of course, relates to the individual 'ceasing' to have a home in the UK. In deciding whether this test is met, an individual must ask himself three questions: 'did my accommodation in the UK have the character of a home?' and, if so, 'can it be said to have ceased to be my home?' and finally 'from what date?'

The definition of 'home' is in *para 25, Sch 45, FA 2013* and is not particularly instructive. See para **3.07** for a consideration of the definition of home in this context. A detailed consideration of what is meant by 'ceasing to have a home' is included in para **5.03**. In some circumstances, it may be very far from clear-cut exactly what would constitute a home and at precisely what point such a property might cease to be a person's home. It is likely that the definition of home will be the subject of much case law in the near future.

## The following tax year and establishing a sufficient link

**[8.13]** If an individual has met the conditions in relation to the previous year and to the tax year under consideration, he must also meet certain conditions in relation to the following tax year and the next six months (*para 46(5)–(7), Sch 45, FA 2013*):

First, the taxpayer must not be resident in the UK for the subsequent tax year (he may be non-resident under any test).

Second, the taxpayer must also have established a 'sufficient link' with a country overseas at the end of the period of six months from the date he ceases to have a home in the UK. In fact, depending on the date of departure, this six-month cut-off may fall either in the tax year for which split-year treatment applies or in the following tax year. It is a snapshot test, which is applied 'at the end of the period' so need not necessarily consider the period in between (with the exception of point (b) below).

There are three ways that the taxpayer could establish a sufficient link (*para 46(7), Sch 45, FA 2013*):

(a)  he is considered a tax resident of the other country in accordance with its domestic laws;

(b)  he is present in that country at the end of each day of the six-month period;

(c)  his only home(s) is/are in that country

For HNWIs, part (c) of the test may be difficult to fulfil. Although they may have ceased to have a home in the UK, they may have a number of homes in more than one country outside the UK. Here the distinction between a 'holiday home' and a 'home' will have particular significance, since an individual with more than one property may wish to argue that those in other countries are merely 'holiday homes' or 'temporary retreats'. HMRC gives very little guidance on this subject, but does suggest that a single property could move between the two definitions:

'A20  A property which is used as nothing more than a holiday home, temporary retreat or something similar is not a home. So a holiday home where an individual spends time for occasional short breaks, and which clearly provides a distinct respite from their ordinary day to day life will not be a home. However if there comes a time when an individual's use of a holiday home or temporary retreat changes so that it is used as a home it will become a home from the time of the change. It will then continue to be a home until such time as circumstances change again and it ceases to be used as a home.'

The guidance also gives an example (Example A11) where a property which is used as a holiday home becomes a 'home' when the individual begins to use it for longer periods. It seems clear from the guidance that HMRC consider that both the quality and quantity of the occupation of the property must be taken into account in deciding whether a property is a 'holiday home.'

A court may take the approach that a property used for an extended period each year for a settled purpose will not be a holiday home following the approach taken in the case of *Cooper v Cadwalader* (1904) 5 TC 101, 42 SLR 117. The case was an ordinary residence case where an individual who lived in New York took on the lease of a furnished shooting lodge in Scotland and visited for two months of each year for the purpose of hunting. The lodge was available for his use throughout the year. The court found in this case that he did not fall into the then exemption of a person in the UK for some temporary purpose only. It seems likely that a lodge occupied in a similar way today would be a 'home' for the purpose of the SRT and not a holiday home or temporary retreat. However, the fact that the property was not used for business, but instead for a hobby, may be sufficient to tip the balance the other way.

Certainly it seems likely that a property which is occupied in part as a base for an individual's work is likely to fail this test, even if only occupied occasionally.

### Example 8.6: Henry

Henry left the UK during 2016/17 to live and work in France. He has a number of business interests both in France and elsewhere, but does not meet the conditions for full-time working abroad. On 1 July 2016, Henry sold his only UK property, which he considered to be his home, and purchased a property in France.

Henry also has a small property in Tuscany, which is mainly used for family holidays, but which he also uses from time to time when doing business in Italy.

The fact that Henry uses the property in Tuscany when he is on business trips as well as for holidays may mean that the property is more than a 'temporary retreat' and therefore not be a holiday home. If this is correct and the occupation of the property was sufficient for it to be a home, therefore, Henry would not meet the test in *para 46(7)(c), Sch 45, FA 2013*.

If a taxpayer has more than one home, and cannot meet the only home test, he can still qualify as having established a sufficient link if he has established tax residence in his destination country at the end of the six-month period. This may prove impossible in some cases as, although many countries share the UK rule that a person is resident for tax purposes if they spend 183 days out of a year in that country, this is not the case for all countries. Hong Kong, for example, does not really have the concept of 'residence' for tax purposes, but instead observes a territorial basis of taxation and Singapore bases residence on presence in the country during the previous tax year. Where the destination country does not have a concept of 'tax residence' the individual will be left to rely on either the only home test or the 'present for six months' test – both of which may present difficulties for HNWIs.

There is a further potential difficulty where a taxpayer leaves the UK part-way through a UK tax year to go to a country which has a significantly different tax year from the UK (eg a calendar year). In such cases an individual may not have had sufficient time in the destination country by the end of the six-month period to have established residence there. It is assumed that it will be possible to look at the tax year of the destination country as a whole (rather than simply apply the host country's residence test at the end of the six-month period). So if the end of the six-month period falls halfway through a tax year in the destination country, it may be necessary to wait until the end of that year to establish whether the individual is resident there. This may give rise to difficulties for those completing self-assessment tax returns for the year of departure and such individuals will have to complete their returns based upon their best estimate and then amend their tax return if necessary.

An individual will need to consider carefully the tax rules of his destination country in ascertaining whether he is likely to qualify as having acquired a 'sufficient link' in that country at the end of the six-month period. This adds a further, and arguably unnecessary level of complication for those leaving the UK.

The final option open to those who have more than one home and who are unable to fulfil the requirement with regard to tax residence (perhaps because their destination country has no such concept) is to fulfil the conditions of *para 46(7)(b), Sch 45, FA 2013* and be present in their destination country at the end of every day for six months. It is not sufficient that the individual does not spend time in the UK for that six months; he cannot even spend one night in a third country. Meeting this condition makes it impossible for such individuals to go on holiday or on business trips, or to return to the UK to visit relatives for even one night during the first six months after leaving the UK.

This condition also raises the question of the level of record-keeping needed to prove that an individual was present in the destination country at the end of every day for a six-month period. There is no specific help in HMRC guidance with regard to the proof which will be expected but, as a minimum, an individual seeking to rely on this test to prove a sufficient link should keep a diary note of his presence in the destination country and if he leaves the country during a day for any reason, he should keep records of both the journey out and back (eg train/plane tickets, receipts, etc).

It is this need to establish a sufficient link with the destination country which is likely to prove the biggest sticking point with the Case 3 split-year test and may result in many choosing to take the more traditional path of leaving the UK towards the end of a tax year.

### The overseas part of the year

[8.14] Assuming that the individual meets all the conditions of Case 3 (and no other case) the 'overseas part of the year' (see para 8.07 above) will begin on the day that he 'ceases' to have a home in the UK (which may not be the same as the day on which he leaves the UK). In many cases it will be clear on which day this takes place. However, there will be plenty of cases where there is room for disagreement as to the relevant date on which an individual's home ceased to be his home. See para 5.05 for a detailed discussion of when a place of residence ceases to be an individual's home.

## Case 4: Coming to the UK and starting to have a home in the UK only

[8.15] Case 4 is the first of the cases to be concerned with those who are arriving in the UK, as opposed to those who are leaving. It is one of two cases (the other being Case 8) available to those who are coming to the UK with no connection with full-time employment either in the UK or overseas. It may also be of relevance to those coming to the UK for employment purposes who do not meet the conditions of Cases 6 or 7, while those who meet the conditions of Case 5 will need to consider Case 4 as well as Case 8 and, if they meet more than one of the sets of circumstances, consider the ordering rules in *para 54, Sch 45, FA 2013* to determine which case will take priority.

The old concessionary treatment under ESC A11 (for those who were not returning after a period of full-time overseas employment) required that an individual be coming to the UK 'to take up permanent residence or to stay for at least two years' in order for split-year treatment to be available. The test was based around the intentions of the individual when he arrived in the UK and was therefore subjective. In addition, the fact that the treatment was concessionary meant that HMRC had some discretion as to its application (see the comments above under Case 3).

The legislative test in Case 4, by contrast, does not require any intention as to a minimum period of residence, but simply that the 'only home' test (see below) is met for the whole of the rest of the year. The test is designed to bring certainty – if the individual meets the 'only home' test and fulfils the other conditions he will qualify for split-year treatment. However, the lack of clear definition of 'home' means that considerable uncertainty will remain with regard to this test.

Case 4 is found in *para 47, Sch 45, FA 2013*. The case requires that the individual meet certain conditions for two tax years – the 'relevant year,' or year to be split, and the previous year. There are however no requirements for the year following the split year.

An individual will only qualify for split-year treatment if he was not resident in the previous tax year (*para 47(2), Sch 45, FA 2013*). This means that an individual cannot qualify for split-year treatment under Case 4 if the previous year was a split year.

Assuming that this condition is fulfilled, then in the year under consideration the taxpayer must meet a number of conditions:

'(3) At the start of the relevant year, the taxpayer did not meet the only home test, but there comes a day in the relevant year when that ceases to be the case and the taxpayer then continues to meet the only home test for the rest of that year.

(4) For the part of the relevant year before that day, the taxpayer does not have sufficient UK ties.

(5) The "only home test" is met if—
   (a) the taxpayer has only one home and that home is in the UK, or
   (b) the taxpayer has more than one home and all of them are in the UK.

(6) Paragraphs 17 to 20 (and Part 2 of this Schedule so far as it relates to those paragraphs) apply for the purposes of sub-paragraph (4) with the following adjustments—
   (a) references in those paragraphs and that Part to year X are to be read as references to the part of the relevant year mentioned in subparagraph (4), and
   (b) each number of days mentioned in the first column of the Table in paragraphs 18 and 19 is to be reduced by the appropriate number.

(7) The appropriate number is found by multiplying the number of days, in each case, by—
   A/12
   where "A" is the number of whole months in the part of the relevant year beginning with the day mentioned in sub-paragraph (3).

(8) Sub-paragraph (6)(a) does not apply to the references to year X in paragraphs 32(1)(b) and 33 of this Schedule (which relate to the residence status of family members) so those references must continue to be read as references to year X.'

In summary then, the individual must meet the following conditions:

• he must not have an 'only home' in the UK at the beginning of the tax year;

• he must begin to meet the 'only home' test at some point during the year and must continue to do so for the remainder of that tax year; and

• he must be 'not resident' under the sufficient ties test for the period of the year before meeting the only home test (according to an adapted sufficient ties test – see below).

Assuming that the individual meets all the conditions, the overseas part of the year will end on the day before the individual starts to have an 'only home' and the UK part will begin on that day (*para 53(5), Sch 45, FA 2013*). In many cases the day on which the individual begins to have an 'only home' will be obvious, but in some cases, there may be a number of possible options and the individual will have to decide in filing his tax return which is the right one.

## Beginning to have an 'only home' in the UK

**[8.16]** The definition of an 'only home' for this purpose is not quite the same as the UK home test for automatic UK residence. While it has been felt necessary to add a number of conditions to the homes which should be considered for the purpose of the automatic residence test (based on periods of availability and occupation), there have been no such additional conditions added for the purpose of Case 4 of the split-year test.

In theory, therefore, an individual might have an only home in the UK for the purpose of the split year Case 4 but not for the automatic residence test.

However, the requirement that the home remain the individual's only home for the remainder of the tax year means that this is only likely to be of practical concern in a very few cases, and only where an individual acquires a home within 30 days of the end of the tax year.

There are two ways in which an individual could begin to have an 'only home' during the tax year. One might be the acquisition of a property in the UK (not necessarily as a purchase) when the individual previously had no such property and has no overseas home, and the second might be the giving up of a property overseas (when the individual may have had a UK home for a number of years). Since there is another split-year case for those who acquire a home in the UK (Case 8), Case 4 is perhaps most likely to be applicable to those who are moving to the position of having an 'only home' in the UK during the tax year, by ceasing to have a home overseas. However, it may still be of application in some other cases where a home is acquired since, unlike Case 8 which requires the home to be owned for the whole of the subsequent tax year, Case 4 only imposes conditions on the tax year in question and the previous year.

The test may be of limited relevance to those taxpayers who have a number of properties in various countries and may be reluctant to dispose of their overseas properties (or otherwise make those properties unavailable). Instead, the case may well apply to those who have been visiting the UK for a number of years without establishing residence here, perhaps at the point where they move to the UK on a more permanent basis. It may also be of relevance to those coming to the UK for employment who give up their overseas home, for example by renting it out.

One interesting question for those seeking to meet the test of 'only home' in order to qualify for split-year treatment will be the extent of the break that they must make with their overseas home in order to be said to have ceased to have a home in that jurisdiction. Individuals will also need to consider at what point 'available accommodation' in the UK can be considered a home.

HMRC guidance is of little assistance here, the only clue being at RDR3, para A27:

> 'The main difference between the term "home" for SRT purposes and available accommodation is that accommodation can be transient and does not require the degree of stability or permanence that a home does.'

However, the degree of permanence needed for accommodation to be a home cannot be great, since the law regarding the second automatic test contemplates a 'home' when a property is available for as little as 91 days. See para **7.14** for more discussion on this topic.

### Can a home overseas become 'accommodation'

**[8.17]** As well as the line at which accommodation becomes a home, there is also some question over the point at which a property overseas which an individual has used as a home ceases to be a 'home' and whether the property can cease to be a home even if the individual occupies it – in effect 'available' accommodation in the overseas location (although there is no such concept of overseas available accommodation in the SRT).

HMRC guidance suggests that, in HMRC's view, once a property has been an individual's home, it is difficult for it to cease to be their home. RDR3, Annex A gives us little help on this subject, beginning at A10 with the un-elucidating:

'A home will remain an individual's home until such a time as it stops being used as such by them.'

However, there are two paragraphs which deal with a home ceasing to be a home, both of which appear to set the bar quite high:

First, at A17:

'If an individual moves out of their home completely and makes it available to let commercially on a permanent basis it will not be their home during the period it is let unless they or their family retain a right to live there. This can happen, for example, where the rental agreement permits the individual to use the property or part of the property as living accommodation.

**Example A9**

Ivan left the UK to work in Germany. He lets the flat he previously lived in to a tenant on a two-year lease. After 18 months he was made redundant and returned to the UK. The rental agreement on his flat gave exclusive use of the property to the tenant so Ivan arranged to stay with relatives and friends until the lease expired. For the period his property was let it is not his home.

However, if the rental agreement had allowed Ivan to use the flat and he had stayed there when he visited the UK it would have remained his home throughout.'

HMRC guidance appears to suggest that any access to a property which has once been occupied as a home will maintain that property's status as a home, However, there may well be circumstances where the nature of the arrangement is such that the property has ceased to be a home in spite of some degree of continued use or occupation. It is tentatively suggested that, in the case of Ivan, if the flat is genuinely let on a commercial basis (or even if is made available to friends or family who use it as their home) and Ivan only stays there from time to time, it would not be his home (even if the lease provided for the right for him to stay). However, those looking for certainty will want to take account of HMRC's view of the law here and will need to make their property genuinely unavailable to them if they wish to avoid a protracted discussion or even possible litigation.

The other mention of a home ceasing to be a home is at A19, again requiring an individual to make no use of the property:

'If an individual completely moves out of a property and makes no further use of it whatsoever it will no longer be their home.'

The example given here (Example A10) is of an individual who decides to sell his property and puts his furniture into storage. The property ceases to be his home from the date he puts his furniture into storage. This is a very unrealistic example, since very few people would be prepared to pay for storage of their furniture before they have sold their property (ie when there is no need to do so) and many would prefer to leave a property furnished until it is sold. A better view is that the property ceases to be the individual's home once the decision is made to sell it, provided he has moved out all, or at least the majority, of his personal effects. Simply keeping one's furniture at a property, either to avoid paying for alternative storage or to facilitate a sale should not, in itself, be sufficient for the property to remain an individual's 'home'.

**Example 8.7: Boris**

Boris is German, but has been spending increasing amounts of time in the UK in recent years. He has a house in Hamburg but also maintains a flat in London which he uses as his home when in the UK. He is not resident in the UK in 2016/17.

In July 2017 he decides that he will move to the UK full time. His London flat is smaller than his property in Hamburg and is already furnished. However, there are some items of furniture in the Hamburg property that Boris prefers and he arranges for these to be shipped to the London property. The shipping takes one month, so the furniture leaves Hamburg on 7 July but does not arrive in London until 7 August. He arranges to put the Hamburg property on the market on 5 July.

On 9 July Boris packs his personal possessions from his Hamburg home and moves into his London flat. He does not agree a buyer for the Hamburg house until 1 September and the sale is completed at the end of October 2017.

At the end of October, just before the sale is completed, Boris returns to Hamburg to arrange for his remaining furniture to be put into storage and spends one night at the house.

There are a number of dates on which Boris could be said to cease to have a home in Germany – the date he moves out with his personal possessions, the date the sale is agreed or the date the sale is completed.

The most appropriate date seems to be 9 July when Boris, having arranged for the flat to be sold and his furniture to be shipped, leaves the flat with his personal possessions. However, the HMRC guidance would suggest that the fact that he keeps furniture there and spends one further night there would be sufficient for it to continue to be considered his home. Boris might choose to file his tax return on the basis that the property in Hamburg ceased to be his home on 9 July, but he will need to be aware that HMRC may seek to argue that it remained his home until it was finally sold at the end of October. If HMRC is correct, this may result in Boris failing to meet the sufficient ties test for the overseas part of the year and failing to meet the conditions of Case 4. He would then be taxed as a UK resident for the full tax year. His position would have been strengthened if he had chosen to put his furniture into storage and had not spent another night at the property, but this would, of course, have had associated costs.

In the real world, moves between countries are likely to be far more complex than those envisaged in HMRC guidance, and individuals and their advisors will need to make judgements about the degree to which an individual needs to sever their connections with a property for it to cease to be their home. In the above example, it seems likely that Boris would cease to think of the Hamburg property as his home on the date he moves out (ie 9 July). However, those looking for certainty would need to be mindful of the limits of the HMRC guidance. It will also be important to keep evidence to demonstrate the date on which the move took place.

## Can a home become a 'holiday home'?

**[8.18]** Noting the comments under para **8.17** above, it would seem that, based on HMRC guidance, it would be impossible for something that is a 'home' to become a 'holiday home'. This does not seem to be the correct interpretation, since a property must be able to change its use. Furthermore, if HMRC accept that a holiday home may become a home (see example A11) then it must be possible for a property to make the transition the other way. However, the difficulty with a home becoming a holiday home for the purpose of the split-year test would be determining the date on which this happened. An individual who is maintaining a property as a holiday home might, after all, be expected to leave some personal effects – clothing, toiletries – in the property.

Anyone wishing to rely on this approach would need to document their decision very carefully and would want to make some clear break on a particular date – perhaps moving the majority of their belongings to their new home and documenting this with evidence – eg receipts for van hire, removals company etc.

In RDR3, para A20, HMRC state 'a holiday home is where an individual spends time for occasional short breaks, and which clearly provides a distinctive respite from their ordinary day to day life.' So, moving to the UK, making the UK one's day-to-day base and returning only to the overseas property for 'occasional short breaks' should be enough to turn a home into a holiday home from the date of change.

One alternative might be for an individual to let their property as furnished holiday accommodation (or make it available for letting). There would then be no question that to the extent it is their home, it is only a holiday home, since it would not be available for the majority of the year.

An individual wishing to keep a property available and claim that it is a holiday home will need to be aware of the HMRC view about the difficulty of a property which has once been a home ceasing to be so and may need to be prepared for lengthy negotiations.

## Sufficient ties

**[8.19]** Assuming that the individual meets the 'only home' part of the split-year test, there is a further condition. The individual must also consider the 'sufficient ties' test in relation to the overseas part of the tax year – in other words, in relation to the part of the tax year ending with the day before that on which he begins to have an 'only home' in the UK.

For this purpose, the number of days which an individual can spend in the UK, relative to the number of UK ties, is reduced according to the formula in *para 47(7), Sch 45, FA 2013* (reproduced in para **8.15**) above. This formula requires the number of days in the sufficient ties tables to be reduced by a number of days based on a pro rata of the total days allowed for a full tax year.

The reduction takes place based on the number of whole months which fall before the day on which the individual begins to have an only home in the UK. A 'whole month' for this purpose is defined in the 'interpretations' section in *para 145, Sch 45, FA 2013*:

'"whole month" means the whole of January, the whole of February and so on, except that the period from the start of a tax year to the end of April is to count as a whole month.'

This means there is effectively no difference to the number of months left in the tax year for someone starting residence at the beginning of March or the beginning of April, since 1–5 April will not be a complete tax month.

The HMRC guidance, very helpfully, contains a table (Table F) at RDR3, para 5.26 showing the number of days which should be substituted in the tables depending on when in the year the individual arrives.

*Table F*

| | Day before satisfying only home or having a UK home tests is | | | | | | | | | | | |
|---|---|---|---|---|---|---|---|---|---|---|---|---|
| | 6 Apr to 30 Apr | 1 May to 31 May | 1 Jun to 30 Jun | 1 Jul to 31 Jul | 1 Aug to 31 Aug | 1 Sep to 30 Sep | 1 Oct to 31 Oct | 1 Nov to 30 Nov | 1 Dec to 31 Dec | 1 Jan to 31 Jan | 1 Feb to 29 Feb | 1 Mar to 5 Apr |
| For 15 substitute | 1 | 2 | 4 | 5 | 6 | 7 | 9 | 10 | 11 | 12 | 14 | 15 |
| For 45 substitute | 4 | 7 | 11 | 15 | 19 | 22 | 26 | 30 | 34 | 37 | 41 | 45 |
| For 90 substitute | 7 | 15 | 22 | 30 | 37 | 45 | 52 | 60 | 67 | 75 | 82 | 90 |
| For 120 Substitute | 10 | 20 | 30 | 40 | 50 | 60 | 70 | 80 | 90 | 100 | 110 | 120 |

The number of days in Table F can then be substituted for those in the tables in *paras 18* and *19, Sch 45, FA 2013* and used to determine whether an individual meets the sufficient ties test for that part of the year.

If the individual is resident under the sufficient ties test for the period before acquiring an only home, he will not qualify for split-year treatment and will be automatically UK resident for the full tax year (even if he acquires an only home late in the UK tax year).

In considering the ties which an individual has with the UK under the test, it is only necessary to consider the ties which he had in the period *before* he began to meet the 'only home' test – any ties acquired later in the tax year can be ignored. This is confirmed by the example of Olan, Example 37 in the HMRC guidance (para 5.29), and seems the better view, since an individual who is starting to have an only home in the UK is likely to acquire UK ties in the latter part of the year.

'Example 37

Olan has been working for his employer in Germany for the last five years. He had no UK ties and was not resident in the UK. On 1 June 2013 Olan moves to the UK to look for work here. He rents out his flat in Germany on a two year lease, from 27 May 2013.

He arrives in the UK and stays in temporary accommodation while he finds a flat to rent. He signs a 12 month lease on a flat in London on 1 July 2013.

He starts UK employment on 22 July 2013 and remains in the UK for a further two years.

Olan receives split year treatment for 2013-14 as he meets the Case 4 conditions:
- he is non-UK resident for 2012-13
- he started to have his only home in the UK during the tax year and that continued until at least the end of the tax year.
- he had no UK ties from 6 April 2013 to 1 July 2013.

For Olan the overseas part of the tax year will end on 30 June 2013, and the UK part of the tax year will start on 1 July 2013, the day he started to have his only home in the UK.

Note: Olan might also meet the criteria for Case 5 or Case 8 split years, but priority is given to the case where the overseas part is the shortest.'

For those who have not previously been resident in the UK (or who have not been resident in any of the previous three tax years) this means that provided they have fewer than two ties in the overseas part of the tax year they will be always be non-resident under this test, regardless of the number of days they have spent in the UK (see table in *para 19, Sch 45, FA 2013* reproduced in para **2.15**).

### A note about the work and accommodation ties in the split year context

**[8.20]** In the absence of any legislation to limit it, it appears that in applying the work tie part of the sufficient ties test to the 'overseas part' of the year, the individual can work up to 39 days without acquiring the tie – even if that 39 days all falls into, say, three months of the tax year before they become resident in July. This seems very generous and means that, in most cases, an individual is unlikely to have this tie for the overseas part of the year of arrival (although those arriving late in the tax year may still have already acquired it).

Similarly, for an individual to have available accommodation, that accommodation must be available for a period of 91 days during the overseas period – this means that those who come to the UK in the early part of the tax year are unlikely to have the accommodation tie for the overseas part of the year – even where they may have had that tie in the previous tax year.

## Case 5: Coming to the UK to undertake 'full time' work in the UK

**[8.21]** Case 5 applies to individuals who are coming to the UK to work full time. It is markedly different from the previous regime (ESC A11) as previously residence was largely dependent on intentions on arrival; anyone coming to the UK intending to stay for a period of at least two years for employment, whether or not it was full time, would be resident here from the date of arrival.

For individuals coming to the UK late in the tax year, the SRT is potentially more beneficial than the old regime. For example, under the old rules, an individual coming to the UK in the last month of the UK tax year not having previously visited would have been resident from date of arrival if coming for at least two years for employment. Under the SRT, such an individual is likely to be non-resident by virtue of the second automatic test, because he will have fewer than 45 days in the UK in the tax year concerned. So split-year treatment is unlikely to be in point. This is likely to be far better for the non-domiciled taxpayer, who could then potentially have overseas workdays relief for the following three UK tax years and would also only become liable to the remittance basis charge, or become deemed domiciled, if he stayed in the UK long enough for either of these to be in point, from a later tax year.

The legislation for Case 5 is set out in *para 48, Sch 45, FA 2013*:

'48(1) The circumstances of a case fall within Case 5 if they are as described in subparagraphs (2) and (3).

(2)   The taxpayer was not resident in the UK for the previous tax year.

(3)   There is at least one period of 365 days in respect of which the following conditions are met–

(a)   the period begins with a day that–

(i)   falls within the relevant year, and

(ii)   is a day on which the taxpayer does more than 3 hours' work in the UK,

(b)   in the part of the relevant year before the period begins, the taxpayer does not have sufficient UK ties,

(c)   the taxpayer works sufficient hours in the UK, as assessed over the period,

(d)   during the period, there are no significant breaks from UK work, and

(e)   at least 75% of the total number of days in the period on which the taxpayer does more than 3 hours' work are days on which the taxpayer does more than 3 hours' work in the UK.

(4)   To work out whether the taxpayer works "sufficient hours in the UK" as assessed over a given period, apply paragraph 9(2) but for "P" read "the taxpayer".

(5)   Paragraphs 17 to 20 (and Part 2 of this Schedule so far as it relates to those paragraphs) apply for the purposes of sub-paragraph (3)(b) with the following adjustments—

(a)   references in those paragraphs and that Part to year X are to be read as references to the part of the relevant year mentioned in subparagraph (3)(b), and

(b)   each number of days mentioned in the first column of the Table in paragraphs 18 and 19 is to be reduced by the appropriate number.'

(6)   The appropriate number is found by multiplying the number of days, in each case, by—

A/12

where "A" is the number of whole months in the part of the relevant year beginning with the day on which the 365-day period in question begins.

(7)   Sub-paragraph (5)(a) does not apply to the references to year X in paragraphs 32(1)(b) and 33 of this Schedule (which relate to the residence status of family members) so those references must continue to be read as references to year X.'

Thus, Case 5 requires the taxpayer to

• have been non-resident for the whole of the previous tax year;

• have a period of at least 365 days starting in the relevant tax year in which:

–   at least 35 hours a week are worked on average;

–   there are no significant breaks; and

- at least 75% of the days on which the taxpayer works for more than three hours are UK days.
 The period must start with a day on which the taxpayer does more than three hours' work in the UK; and
- have insufficient days in the UK prior to the start of that period to meet the sufficient ties test.

There are no conditions that need to be fulfilled in the next tax year so now only a 365-day period is required rather than a two-year test.

If the conditions are all met and no other case takes priority under the ordering rule, the UK part of the year will start on the first day of the period mentioned above. The full-time work in the UK test is considered in more detail in **CHAPTER 2**, with the definitions and key concepts covered in **CHAPTER 3**. A brief synopsis is included below for ease of reference.

The employee must work at least 35 hours a week on average. In determining whether this is met:

- the calculation ignores any days on which the employee also does more than three hours' work outside the UK, so is likely to exclude most travel days into the UK on which the taxpayer also works;
- days spent on 'reasonable' amounts of annual leave and parenting leave are taken out of the calculation, as is sick leave. An adjustment is also made for any non-working days embedded in periods of annual leave, but not for non-working days more generally or bank holidays; and
- a gap of up to 15 days between employments may also be subtracted, subject to a maximum number of 30 days being subtracted in any tax year.

The combination of these requirements and especially the treatment of bank holidays may make contracted hours of exactly 35 hours insufficient to meet the 35 hours per week on average test. This may mean that Case 5 is not available, at least from the anticipated start date. The following example illustrates this.

### Example 8.8: Guido

Guido is an Italian national who has been working in his family's shoe manufacturing business in Milan for some years. He is asked to move to the UK during the summer of 2013 to start work with an associated business for a period of up to two years.

Guido starts work in the UK (on a standard 35-hour working week, seven hours a day) on 2 September and remains working in the UK on a full-time basis until December 2014. It is agreed thereafter that he will divide his time between the UK and Milan for a further period of three months. After that he will return to Milan full time.

Guido has the following business trips back to Milan during his first year in the UK:

6–14 October 2013

18–21 November 2013

28–31 January 2014

10–14 March 2014

18–25 May 2014

23–30 June 2014

On each return trip to Milan he travels by air, and this involves more than three hours' work-related travel overseas on both the outward and return journey (although all travel undertaken at a weekend is in addition to the 35-hour week he has otherwise worked).

He also takes the following holidays over the same period:

23–31 December 2013 (inclusive of bank holidays)

1–3 January 2014

14–21 April 2014 (inclusive of Easter bank holidays)

4–22 August 2014

He works the bank holiday in August, as he is keen to catch up after his long break earlier in the month.

Guido's average working week from 2 September may be calculated as follows:

*Step 1*

Guido has disregarded days on all working days in Milan, including the business travel days even where this falls on a weekend since he has more than three hours' work-related travel and the location of the work is overseas. Therefore travel days are disregarded days even if he undertakes no work on arrival in Milan. This means he has 33 disregarded days.

*Step 2*

Guido calculates his net UK work hours.

In September he has 21 days x 7 hours = 147 hours

In October he has 17 days x 7 hours = 119 hours

In November he has 17 days x 7 hours = 119 hours

In December he has 15 days x 7 hours = 105 hours

In January he has 16 days x 7 hours = 112 hours

In February he has 20 days x 7 hours = 140 hours

In March he has 16 days x 7 hours = 112 hours

In April he has 16 days x 7 hours = 112 hours

In May he has 15 days x 7 hours = 105 hours

In June he has 15 days x 7 hours = 105 hours

In July he has 23 days x 7 hours = 161 hours

In August he has 6 days x 7 hours = 42 hours

He also has 7 hours for 1 September 2014

So, in total, Guido has 1,386 UK work hours on his regular workdays.

*Step 3*

Days in the reference period = 365 less 33 disregarded days, less 30 days of holiday (seven in December less two bank holidays, three in January less one bank holiday, six in April less two bank holidays and 19 in August, including four non-working days embedded within a block of leave) = 302 days

*Step 4*

302 divided by 7 = 43 'weeks'

*Step 5*

Divide 1,386 by 43 = 32.23.

As this is less than the required 35 hours per week on average, Guido will not be regarded as full-time working in the UK from the date of his arrival and so Case 5 is not available from 28 September.

If another period was considered as the law requires – perhaps the 2014 calendar year – he could still be regarded as UK tax resident for 2013/14 by virtue of having a qualifying period of 365 days of UK work. He would only need one day of such a period to fall into the tax year concerned for it to make him tax resident for that year. This means that Case 5 could apply, but from a later date. In these circumstances it is likely that Case 4 or Case 8 would give an earlier start to the split year. See para **8.03** above for the priority of the cases.

It may be difficult to predict on arrival in the UK whether or not a taxpayer will meet all the requirements for a 365-day period of working full time in the UK, especially if he has a role that encompasses duties being performed outside the UK. It should, however, be easier to confirm whether or not the sufficient ties test has been met for the pre-arrival period, as the number of permitted days are subject to pro-rata limits depending on the date on which work started in exactly the same way as they are under Cases 4 and 8. Again, Table F provides an easy point of reference for the number of days that can be spent in the UK, depending on the number of ties that the taxpayer has here before arrival – see para **8.19**. Although the table is headed 'Day before satisfying only or having a UK home test is', it is also intended to apply to cases where full-time work in the UK starts, as para 5.30 of HMRC's RDR3 guidance specifically cross-refers to it.

It may be particularly difficult to determine at the end of any given tax year whether or not a period of UK work is likely to be sufficient to meet all the requirements to establish a 365-day period of UK work: Although the taxpayer does not need to file his tax return for the year until the following 31 January and so, in theory, has until this date to determine whether or not this test is met, for practical reasons he may need to make an initial assessment of when he became tax resident and even file his tax return prior to that date.

**Example 8.9: Stefan**

Stefan arrives in the UK on 23 December 2013 to start an 18 months' assignment to the UK. He starts work that week but does not work any bank holidays and only works his contracted 35 hours per week with no overtime. He takes no 'extra' holiday other than the bank holidays, as he is keen to get established in his new role. This working pattern is expected to continue for at least a 365-day period.

For each month in the January to March period he has two days working in Poland that involve travel to/from the UK. This means that both of those days have to be disregarded in the calculation.

If Stefan checks his position at the end of March, he will find that he has a period of 104 days of which some six are disregarded and he works 462 hours in total in the period concerned. If the 98 days are divided by seven to arrive at a number of deemed weeks then there are 14, which taken across the 462 hours he has worked would equate only to 33 hours per week on average. It is impossible to tell until he has worked in the UK for the full 365-day period whether or not he will meet the 35 hours per week on average requirement, but it appears unlikely, unless he is able to increase the hours he works to compensate for the effect of bank holidays. Preparing this sort of estimate may give him an opportunity to revisit the hours he is actually working and possibly extend them, so that by the time the full 365-day period is considered he meets the required average of 35 hours per week.

Of course, few internationally mobile employees will work exactly the hours they are contracted to do and most would anticipate averaging more than 35 hours per working week with no difficulty. Proving that they have done so may be more challenging, and it is likely that detailed records will be needed to support claims of working hours, especially where substantial overtime is involved, and the employer does not routinely capture that information because no extra pay is involved. Chapter 7 of HMRC's guidance RDR3 is concerned with record-keeping and suggests that a detailed work diary and supporting travel documents are the minimum that are likely to be needed. See **CHAPTER 13** for further details.

It will be noted that the test is not a mirror image of Case 1; for example, there is the requirement for 75% of workdays (as defined) to be spent in the UK before the conditions for full-time work in the UK are met. This is consistent with the third automatic UK test (covered in **CHAPTER 2**), but it is interesting that a quarter of an individual's workdays may be overseas before that disqualifies him from meeting the full time work in the UK test, whereas more than 30 UK workdays will prevent an employee from being regarded as working full-time abroad under the third automatic overseas test and the 30 day limit is prorated for Case 1 depending on when the taxpayer leaves the UK.

## Case 6: Coming to the UK and ceasing full-time work overseas

**[8.22]** Despite the broad title given in the legislation to Case 6, Case 6 can only apply to individuals returning to the UK after a non-resident period of less than five tax years (the law requires the taxpayer to have been non-resident in the previous UK tax year, but to have been UK tax resident at some point during the four UK tax years preceding that in order for Case 6 to apply). *Para 49, Sch 45, FA 2013* sets out the conditions that have to be met in order for Case 6 to apply, and they are as follows:

'49(1) The circumstances of a case fall within Case 6 if they are as described in subparagraphs (2) to (4).

(2)　The taxpayer–

(a)　was not resident in the UK for the previous tax year because the taxpayer met the third automatic overseas test for that year (see paragraph 14), but

(b)　was resident in the UK for one or more of the 4 tax years immediately preceding that year.

(3)　There is at least one period (consisting of one or more days) that–

(a)　begins with the first day of the relevant year,

(b)　ends with a day that–

(i)　falls within the relevant year, and

(ii)　is a day on which the taxpayer does more than 3 hours' work overseas, and

(c)　satisfies the overseas work criteria.

(4)　The taxpayer is resident in the UK for the next tax year (whether or not it is a split year).

(5)　A period "satisfies the overseas work criteria" if–

(a)　the taxpayer works sufficient hours overseas, as assessed over that period,

(b)　during that period, there are no significant breaks from overseas work,

(c)　the number of days in that period on which the taxpayer does more than 3 hours' work in the UK does not exceed the permitted limit, and

(d)　the number of days in that period falling within sub-paragraph (6) does not exceed the permitted limit.

(6)　A day falls within this sub-paragraph if–

(a)　it is a day spent by the taxpayer in the UK, but

(b)　it is not a day that is treated under paragraph 23(4) as a day spent by the taxpayer in the UK.

(7)　To work out whether the taxpayer works "sufficient hours overseas" as assessed over a given period, apply paragraph 14(3) but with the following modifications–

(a)　for "P" read "the taxpayer",

(b)　for "year X" read "the period under consideration",

(c)　for "365 (or 366 if year X includes 29 February)" read "the number of days in the period under consideration", and

(d)　in paragraph 28(9)(b), as it applies for the purposes of step 3, for "30" read "the permitted limit".'

(8)　The permitted limit is—

(a)　for sub-paragraphs (5)(c) and (7)(d), the number found by reducing 30 by the appropriate number, and

      (b)    for sub-paragraph (5)(d), the number found by reducing 90 by the appropriate number.

(9)    The appropriate number is the result of—

A x (B / 12)

where—

"A" is—

      (a)    30, for sub-paragraphs (5)(c) and (7)(d), or

      (b)    90, for sub-paragraph (5)(d), and

"B" is the number of whole months in the part of the relevant year after the 365-day period in question ends.'

Thus, for Case 6 to apply the following conditions have to be met:

- the taxpayer must have been non-UK tax resident for the previous tax year under the automatic overseas test by reason of full-time work abroad but resident in the UK for one or more of the four tax years immediately preceding that year;
- there must be a period during the relevant year for which he meets the criteria for full-time working abroad. This period starts at the beginning of the tax year and ends with a day on which he did more than three hours' work overseas; and
- during this period, he must have met the 35 hours or more on average working hours requirement and had no significant break from overseas work. He must also have stayed within the 30 UK workday and 90 UK day limits pro-rated for the number of whole months in that period. Where there is a gap between employment this may be deducted from the period. Where the gap exceeds 15 days, the deduction is limited to 15 days. Where there is more than one gap between employments, the maximum number of days that can be subtracted in making the sufficient hours calculation is the annual limit of 30 as pro-rated to the 'permitted limit'. Again, there is a handy reference table in the HMRC guidance at para 5.37 (Table G), which is reproduced below.

*Table G*

| | UK part of year starts on | | | | | | | | | | | |
|---|---|---|---|---|---|---|---|---|---|---|---|---|
| | 6 Apr to 30 Apr | 1 May to 31 May | 1 Jun to 30 Jun | 1 Jul to 31 Jul | 1 Aug to 31 Aug | 1 Sep to 30 Sep | 1 Oct to 31 Oct | 1 Nov to 30 Nov | 1 Dec to 31 Dec | 1 Jan to 31 Jan | 1 Feb to 29 Feb | 1 Mar to 5 Apr |
| X – permitted limit on days where you can work more than 3 hours in overseas part of the year or maximum number of days which may be subtracted from the reference period on account of gaps between employment | 2 | 5 | 7 | 10 | 12 | 15 | 17 | 20 | 22 | 25 | 27 | 30 |

| | UK part of year starts on | | | | | | | | | | | |
|---|---|---|---|---|---|---|---|---|---|---|---|---|
| | 6 Apr to 30 Apr | 1 May to 31 May | 1 Jun to 30 Jun | 1 Jul to 31 Jul | 1 Aug to 31 Aug | 1 Sep to 30 Sep | 1 Oct to 31 Oct | 1 Nov to 30 Nov | 1 Dec to 31 Dec | 1 Jan to 31 Jan | 1 Feb to 29 Feb | 1 Mar to 5 Apr |
| Y – permitted limit on days spent in the UK in overseas part of year | 7 | 15 | 22 | 30 | 37 | 45 | 52 | 60 | 67 | 75 | 82 | 90 |

For taxpayers who want to apply Case 6 to tax year 2013/14, *para 154(5)(c), Sch 45, FA 2013* provides that the test of the taxpayer's prior year non-residence should be whether or not 'the taxpayer was working overseas full-time for the whole of that year' under the former rules rather than meeting the third automatic overseas test – see RDR3, para 5.33, which refers back to HMRC 6. Alternatively it is possible to elect (under *para 154(3), Sch 45, FA 2013*) for the SRT rules to apply for this purpose – see also para **2.24**.

Where Case 6 applies, the taxpayer will become UK resident from the end of the period on which he satisfies the overseas work criteria. This will be a day on which he does more than three hours' work overseas. This may have some surprising consequences; for example, a taxpayer who decides to work part time towards the end of his overseas secondment, may find that he becomes UK tax resident from the point at which his hours reduce, rather than from any subsequent date of arrival in the UK when he might acquire a UK home. Similarly, an employee on international assignment who chooses to take a holiday on completion of the assignment, rather than returning home immediately, may nevertheless find that he becomes UK tax resident again as soon as his full-time working abroad stops.

The calculations for satisfying the overseas work criteria are such that a taxpayer may have a number of periods in the tax year that would qualify as the overseas part of the year. *Para 53(7)(b), Sch 45, FA 2013* provides that, if this is the case, the overseas part ends on the last day of longest of these periods. This may work to the advantage of the returning taxpayer although it may not be beneficial to an accompanying spouse who returns to the UK earlier in the year. This latter point is considered in the next section.

# Case 7: Arriving in the UK as a partner of a taxpayer within Case 6

**[8.23]** Case 7 applies only to an individual whose partner meets the Case 6 conditions. In fact, such a partner may fall within both Case 6 and Case 5. Although Case 5 will take priority in terms of deciding the date on which residence starts for the working spouse, because the working spouse still meets the Case 6 conditions, HMRC have specifically confirmed (see minutes of Joint Expatriate forum on Tax and NICs, 3 July 2013) that Case 7 may apply to the spouse or partner.

Case 7 is set out in *para 50, Sch 45, FA 2013*:

'50(1) The circumstances of a case fall within Case 7 if they are as described in subparagraphs (2) to (6).

(2)    The taxpayer was not resident in the UK for the previous tax year.

(3)    The taxpayer has a partner whose circumstances fall within Case 6 for–
    (a)    the relevant year, or
    (b)    the previous tax year.

(4)    On a day in the relevant year, the taxpayer moves to the UK so the taxpayer and the partner can continue to live together on the partner's return or relocation to the UK.

(5)    In the part of the relevant year before the deemed arrival day–

    (a)    the taxpayer has no home in the UK at any time, or has homes in both the UK and overseas but spends the greater part of the time living in the overseas home, and

    (b)    the number of days that the taxpayer spends in the UK does not exceed the permitted limit.

(6)    The taxpayer is resident in the UK for the next tax year (whether or not it is a split year).

(7)    If sub-paragraph (3)(a) applies, the "deemed arrival day" is the later of–

    (a)    the day mentioned in sub-paragraph (4), and

    (b)    the first day of what is, for the partner, the UK part of the relevant year as defined for Case 6 (see paragraph 54).

(8)    If sub-paragraph (3)(b) applies, the "deemed arrival day" is the day mentioned in sub-paragraph (4).

(9)    The permitted limit is the number found by reducing 90 by the appropriate number.'

(10)    The appropriate number is the result of—
A x (B / 12)
where—
"A" is 90, and
"B" is the number of whole months in the part of the relevant year beginning with the deemed arrival day.'

Thus, the required conditions are that:

- the taxpayer was not resident in the previous tax year and has a partner whose circumstances fall within Case 6 for the UK tax year concerned or the previous UK tax year; and

- the taxpayer moves to the UK during the relevant year so that they can continue to live with the partner on the partner's return to the UK;

- for the period before the 'deemed arrival day' the taxpayer has no home in the UK, or has homes in both the UK or overseas but spends the greater part of the time living in the overseas home, and stays within a pro rata of the 90-day limits for the non-UK part of the year. Again, the 'Y' figures in Table G above show the pro-rated figures; and

- the taxpayer is resident in the UK for the following tax year (which may be a split year).

This case is thus available for an individual whose partner returns to the UK either in the same tax year or in the previous tax year. While Case 7 can apply if the individual returns to the UK ahead of the working spouse but in the same tax year, it does not permit the individual to return to the UK in the tax year preceding that in which the working spouse returns and this may cause difficulties in some cases where the change in location occurs around the end of the tax year.

Where all the required conditions are met, the deemed arrival day is the later of the date on which the individual returns to the UK to be with their partner and the date on which their partner ceases full-time work abroad. So, where the partner returned to the UK in the previous tax year, the deemed arrival date is the date on which the individual moves to the UK.

As with Case 2, where the taxpayer has a home in the UK and overseas, they will need to keep detailed records to establish where they have spent their time in the overseas part of the year. In addition, having a possible arrival date that has nothing to do with when the individual or their partner comes to the UK is likely to cause some confusion. In such circumstances, it would be relatively easy to miscalculate the number of days permitted in the UK prior to that date for split-year treatment to apply. Alternatively, and particularly where the working spouse returns to the UK later in the year, the individual may spend more time in the UK home than the overseas home and so fail to meet the required conditions. This point is considered further, together with an example, in para **4.13**.

## Case 8: Coming to the UK and starting to have a home in the UK

**[8.24]** The final case of the split-year test, Case 8, applies when an individual starts to have a home in the UK during the tax year. This case is likely to be the one of most relevance to HNWIs coming to live in the UK – they are less likely to meet the 'only home' requirement of Case 4 since many will maintain properties overseas. However, the ordering rule in *para 55, Sch 45, FA 2013* means that even those who come to the UK to take up employment and who meet the tests in Case 5 may find that this case applies to them. The case may apply to those coming to the UK for the first time, but also to those who are returning after an absence abroad.

To meet the conditions of Case 8, the taxpayer must meet conditions for three tax years – the relevant tax year (ie the year to be split), the previous tax year and the subsequent tax year.

As a pre-condition, the individual must be non-resident in the tax year prior to the relevant year – this means the previous year cannot be a split year.

Assuming that this condition is met, there are a number of further conditions set out in *para 51, Sch 45, FA 2013*:

'(3) At the start of the relevant year, the taxpayer had no home in the UK but—
  (a) there comes a day when, for the first time in that year, the taxpayer does have a home in the UK, and
  (b) from then on, the taxpayer continues to have a home in the UK for the rest of that year and for the whole of the next tax year.

(4) For the part of the relevant year before the day mentioned in sub-paragraph (3)(a), the taxpayer does not have sufficient UK ties.

(5) The taxpayer is resident in the UK for the next tax year and that tax year is not a split year as respects the taxpayer.

(6) Paragraphs 17 to 20 (and Part 2 of this Schedule so far as it relates to those paragraphs) apply for the purposes of sub-paragraph (4) with the following adjustments–

(a)    references in those paragraphs and that Part to year X are to be read as references to the part of the relevant year mentioned in subparagraph (4), and

(b)    each number of days mentioned in the first column of the Table in paragraphs 18 and 19 is to be reduced by the appropriate number.

(7)    The appropriate number is found by multiplying the number of days, in each case, by–

A/12

where "A" is the number of whole months in the relevant year beginning with the day mentioned in sub-paragraph (3)(a).

(8)    Sub-paragraph (6)(a) does not apply to the references to year X in paragraphs 32(1)(b) and 33 of this Schedule (which relate to the residence status of family members) so those references must continue to be read as references to year X.'

In summary:

•    the individual must not have a home in the UK at the start of the tax year;

•    they must acquire a UK home in the tax year and continue to have a home throughout that tax year and the next;

•    they must not meet the sufficient ties test for the period of the year before they acquired a UK home (see para **8.26** below); and

•    they must be resident in the UK the following tax year and that tax year may not be a split year.

In contrast to the 'only home' test in Case 4, the individual can have another (or indeed several other) home(s) outside the UK. Under Case 8, unlike Case 4, the individual must meet conditions with regard to the subsequent tax year (both with regard to the home and his own continuing UK residence).

Assuming that the individual meets the conditions, the year will be split on the day he acquires the UK home. The 'overseas part' of the year will end on the day before the individual acquires the UK home and the 'UK part' begins on the day it is acquired. This may be an earlier date than the day on which the individual 'permanently' moves to the UK.

## Acquiring a home in the UK

**[8.25]** An individual who is seeking to rely on Case 8 to obtain split-year treatment will need to ask himself two questions. First, is the quality of his occupation of UK accommodation sufficient to give that accommodation the character of a home? And, second, if it is, on what date does the property begin to be a home for the purpose of this test?

For some individuals this will involve the purchase or rental of a new property; for others it may involve reoccupying a property which has previously ceased to be a home (perhaps because it has been let out). For those acquiring a property in the UK for the first time, the date on which that property begins to be their home will be the crucial date for the split-year test. For many individuals the property purchase will be completed and they will move in on the same day. However, for others it will be more difficult to decide the date on which the property becomes their home.

**Example 8.10: Antonia**

Antonia is Italian but her daughter lives in the UK with her English husband, so Antonia decides to retire here.

Antonia finds a property she likes in the UK in March 2017, but delays in the legal process mean that she does not complete the purchase of the house until 15 July 2017. In the meantime, Antonia sells her Italian property (on 30 June), puts what furniture she is keeping into storage and leaves Italy. She moves in with her daughter on 1 July 2017.

As Antonia has no home in Italy or elsewhere between 30 June and 15 July, there is an argument that her daughter's house is her home for the two weeks from 1 July. However, since this seems to have the character of temporary accommodation, a better analysis would be that she does not begin to have a home in the UK until she moves into her house on 15 July.

The position would be complicated further if the property was available for occupation, but Antonia chose not to stay there until, say, redecoration was completed.

HMRC guidance states (at A15 in Annex A) that a home starts to be a home as soon as:

• it is capable of being used as your home; for example, you have taken ownership of it, even if it is temporarily unavailable because of renovation;

• you actually use it as your home.

But it goes on to say:

'If the first point above is satisfied, but in fact you never actually use it as your home, then it will not be your home.'

What is not very clear from this is what an individual needs to do to be considered to have started to use a property as a home. For example, is it sufficient to move furniture in? Does the individual need to stay the night in the property? Example A7 gives some insight:

'Example A7

Aneta moved from Poland to the UK and completed the purchase of her new house on 1 June. Whilst it was empty she stayed with friends, until her belongings arrived. These were moved in by the removal firm on 15 June.

Aneta stayed in her new home overnight that night. However, as she had arranged to have some extensive refurbishment done to her bathrooms and kitchen, she stayed in a local hotel and with colleagues whilst the main works were carried out. She moved into her home on a permanent basis on 15 July.

For SRT purposes we would consider that the house became Aneta's home from 15 June.'

In this example, the property begins to be Aneta's home once her belongings have been moved in and she has stayed there for a single night. What is less clear is whether HMRC would consider it to be her home if she had moved her furniture there but not spent a night. It is tentatively suggested that this on its own would not be sufficient to make a property a home and that an individual must have spent at least one night in a property before it can be considered to be their home.

It seems to be a stretch that a property should be considered an individual's home before he has stayed there, even if his belongings have been moved in. Although he may have an emotional attachment to the property, if he has never stayed there he cannot be said to have 'used' it as a home.

For many, acquiring a home in the UK will not involve the acquisition or rental of a new property, but simply the reoccupation of a previous home. Indeed, the example in the HMRC guidance for this case (Example 41 in para 5.46) involves an individual returning to the UK after a period in Cyprus and re-occupying a property which was previously let out when the rental agreement comes to an end.

'Example 41

Nicola is retired. She is non-resident in the UK for tax purposes having lived in Cyprus for a number of years. She has a home in Cyprus and she also has a property in the UK which has been let out on a commercial basis for the last few years. She has recently become a grandmother and decides that she will now split her time between Cyprus and the UK so that she can see more of her grandson who lives in the UK.

She comes back to the UK and moves into the UK property when the rental agreement with her tenant expires on 4 August 2014. She now has two homes, one in each country.

Between 6 April 2014 and 4 August 2014 when she started to have a UK home, Nicola only spent four days in the UK, visiting her daughter, and therefore did not exceed the limit for days spent in the UK in the overseas period before she started to have the UK home.

Nicola meets the criteria for Case 8 for 2014-15 on the basis that:
- she was not UK resident for 2013-14
- she is UK resident for 2015-16 (Nicola is possibly dual resident in UK and Cyprus)
- she continues to have a home in the UK for the rest of 2014-15 and the following tax year
- she did not have sufficient UK ties to make her resident from 6 April 2014 until 4 August 2014

Nicola does not meet the criteria for Case 4, 5, 6 or 7 split year treatments.

The UK part of the split year starts on 4 August 2014 which is when Nicola starts to have a home in the UK.'

In the HMRC example, the individual (Nicola) reoccupies the property on the same day her rental agreement expires. A more interesting and helpful example would have shown her occupying the property a number of weeks after the tenant moved out and considered on which date the property began to be her home. In the absence of such guidance, it seems reasonable that the property would not be her home simply by being available for her occupation and that she must in fact move into the property and begin to occupy it for it to be her home for this purpose.

There is also a question of when available accommodation in the UK becomes a home – at what point it crosses the line and changes character to become a 'home.' See para **7.07** for a detailed consideration of when 'available accommodation' might become a home for the purpose of this test.

It is worth noting that although the test in Case 8 requires the individual to acquire a home in the UK during the tax year and to have a home throughout that tax year and the next, there is no requirement that it is the same property. An individual could move several times during the period, provided there is no time during which he does not have any UK home.

### The sufficient ties test

**[8.26]** The date on which an individual acquires a home in the UK is critical both because this is the date from which the year will be split, but also because he must be non-UK resident under the sufficient ties test for the part of the year before that date. This part of Case 8 applies in exactly the same way as the sufficient ties test in Case 4, and is explained in detail at para **8.19**.

### The subsequent tax year

**[8.27]** In addition to the conditions which the individual must meet in the year which is to be split, Case 8 also requires the individual to meet tests for the subsequent tax year. The need to have a home in the UK throughout the subsequent year has already been discussed. In addition, the individual must be resident in the UK the following year, and that year cannot be a split year. The split-year treatment is automatic if the conditions are met, so there is no option for an individual to disclaim it. In practice the issue should not arise often, since if the home is kept throughout the subsequent tax year, the individual would need to take up full-time employment overseas, or follow a partner taking up such an employment in order to meet the split-year conditions.

# Options where split-year treatment does not apply

**[8.28]** Where the taxpayer is not eligible for split-year treatment under any of the cases, two alternatives might still apply to ease potential double taxation issues. These are considered in turn below.

### Treaty non-residence

**[8.29]** Where the individual is tax resident in another country with which the UK has a Double Tax Treaty, he may be able to claim that he is Treaty non-resident in the UK up to the date of his arrival in the UK or from the date of departure. This is considered in more detail in **CHAPTER 12** on Double Tax Treaties but for the most part the effect of a Treaty is to limit the UK's right to tax income or gains realised by an individual who is a Treaty resident of the other country.

*Remaining non-resident under the SRT*

**[8.30]** As noted above, split-year treatment only applies to someone who is domestically resident under the SRT. An alternative may be to avoid becoming tax resident in the UK at all by restricting time spent in the UK so as to be within the automatic overseas test or within the limits permitted under the sufficient ties test. For example, a taxpayer with one connection factor – possibly 40 or more UK workdays – could spend up to 182 days in the UK in one tax year without becoming UK tax resident (although this would mean restricting days in the subsequent two tax years). This allows for a significant amount of time to be spent in the UK without becoming resident provided that the taxpayer has limited UK connections and takes appropriate steps to avoid acquiring any more.

## Application to trustees

**[8.31]** The split-year test applies in a limited way to trustees, where those trustees are individuals and they cease to be trustees of a settlement in a split year.

See **CHAPTER 9** for details of the application of the split-year test to individuals who are trustees.

## Special tax rules for taxing income and gains of a split year

**[8.32]** Assuming that an individual meets the tests in one or more of the split-year cases, the tax year in question will be split into the 'overseas part' and the 'UK part'. Broadly speaking, this means that the individual will be taxed as though he is non-UK resident for the 'overseas part' of the year and as though he is resident for the 'UK part'. However, in practice there are some slight differences from the tax an actual non-resident would pay. The rules relating to the taxation of each of the different types of income and gains are set out in *Part 3* of *Sch 45, FA 2013*. It is not the intention of this chapter to set out all of the rules governing the taxation of income and gains in a split-year scenario, but rather to highlight some of the changes from the old concessionary treatment and some of the more unusual elements.

Readers should check the legislation to see if special rules are available; in the absence of any special rules, the individual will be taxed as if they are resident throughout the year.

The codification of the taxation of specific income and gains during the overseas part of the year is very welcome, since there were often uncertainties under the concessionary treatment, particularly given HMRC's discretion over whether to apply the split-year treatment where it resulted in significant amounts of income or gains escaping tax.

Those returning to the UK may also need to consider the anti-avoidance legislation which may trigger a tax charge in respect of certain income or gains which arose before they came to the UK. See CHAPTER 13 for a detailed exploration of this legislation.

## Employment income

**[8.33]** Prior to *Finance Act 2013*, the application of ESC A11 led to the individual being treated as though they were non-UK resident for what would now be described as the 'overseas part' of the tax year, and the legislation was applied on this basis. General earnings which arose in the non-UK resident part of the year and derived from duties performed outside the UK were not generally taxable in the UK.

For the most part, the previous position with regard to employment income has been maintained under the SRT. For example, *para 58, Sch 45, FA 2013* re-crafts *s 15* of *ITEPA 2003* so that it applies to general earnings from the UK part of the split year but so that any earnings from the overseas part of the year that are not attributable to UK duties fall outside the scope of *s 15*. A similar rewrite to *s 26* of *ITEPA 2003* ensures that income related to overseas workdays is only regarded as remittance basis income within *s 26* to the extent it relates to the UK part of the split year.

The position with regard to specific employment income and especially to share awards taxed under the special rules in *Part 7* of *ITEPA 2003* can be more complex and is outside the scope of this work.

## Property income

**[8.34]** Foreign property income is effectively split into two parts during a split year, with the portion arising in the UK part of the year being taxable and the portion arising in the overseas part of the year being non-chargeable. One minor complication, however, is that the profits must be split before deducting capital allowances (or adding back any charges arising under capital allowance legislation). Any adjustment for capital allowances is then made to the UK part of the profits. This is likely to be favourable to taxpayers in most cases. See ITTOIA 2005 s 270(3) – (5) as amended by *para 81, Sch 45, FA 2013*. The apportionment is to be done on a 'just and reasonable' bases, which in many cases will mean time apportionment.

## Transfer of assets abroad

**[8.35]** There are no specific split-year provisions relating to income treated as arising under the transfer of assets abroad provisions. As such, income chargeable under these provisions will be taxable even if it arises in the overseas part of a split year. See para **8.38** below on the remittance of income chargeable under these provisions.

## Trading income and income from partnerships

**[8.36]** Individuals who are self-employed or in partnership, carrying on a trade wholly or partly inside the UK, are treated as ceasing one trade and beginning a new trade when they either become or cease to be UK resident (ie at the start of the UK or overseas parts of the year). Under the old split-year concessions, this would have been treated as taking place at the point where the year was split.

For partnerships, the former treatment is largely preserved by the legislation, in *s 6(2A), ITTOIA 2005*, since the rules are amended to treat a partner as non-resident in the overseas part of a tax year for this purpose:

'(2A) If the tax year is a split year as respects a UK resident individual, this section has effect as if, for the overseas part of that year, the individual were non-UK resident.'

This means any deemed ceasing and re-commencing will take place at whatever date the year is split. As pointed out above, depending on what case the individual's circumstances fall within, this date may not be the same as the date that he comes to or leaves the UK.

The legislation with regard to the sole trader appears to be intended to achieve the same outcome, but may not, in effect, work in quite the same way.

The relevant part of the legislation is in s 17 ITTOIA 2005, as amended by *para 76, Sch 45, FA 2013*:

'(1)  This section applies if–
(a)    an individual carries on a trade otherwise than in partnership, and
(b)    there is a change of residence.

(1A)  For the purposes of this section there is a 'change of residence' if–
(a)    the individual becomes or ceases to be UK resident, or
(b)    a tax year is, as respects the individual, a split year.

(1B)  The change of residence occurs–
(a)    in a case falling within subsection (1A)(a), at the start of the tax year for which the individual becomes or ceases to be UK resident, and
(b)    in a case falling within subsection (1A)(b), at the start of whichever of the UK part or the overseas part of the tax year is the later part.'

In other words, the trade is treated as ceasing and recommencing when there is a change of residence. There appears to be a risk that, as the legislation is drafted, an individual who leaves the UK on, say 1 July 2016 and qualifies to split the tax year from that date, will be treated as ceasing one trade and beginning a new trade both on that date and again on 6 April 2017. This is because the legislation does not treat the individual as becoming non-resident on 1 July – it simply deems this to be a 'change of residence'. As the individual will, in fact, be UK resident throughout that tax year (assuming that they would be), they will then have a further 'change of residence' on 6 April the following tax year – the beginning of their first year of non-residence.

This does not appear to be the intended effect of the legislation, and it is hoped that HMRC will take a pragmatic approach.

## Capital gains tax

**[8.37]** Probably the most significant difference under the new statutory split-year test, as compared to the old concessionary treatment, is for capital gains. The old capital gains tax concession for split-year treatment (ESC D2) was of much more limited scope than the treatment for income tax. An individual could only qualify for split-year treatment for capital gains if he came to the UK having not been resident at all in the previous five tax years, or if he left the UK and had been both not resident and not ordinarily resident throughout at least four of the previous seven UK tax years.

Effectively this meant that for all except those who had been only short-term visitors to the UK there was no split-year treatment for capital gains when leaving the UK and becoming non-resident. There was a further complication even where the treatment did apply since, as split-year treatment was concessionary, there was some concern that if a large gain arose in the non-resident portion of the year, HMRC might consider that the split-year treatment was being used for tax avoidance purposes and so deny the concession.

By contrast, and subject to the temporary non-resident rules (see also CHAPTER 11), the new split-year test applies in the same way to both income and gains; provided that the individual meets the conditions of one of the eight cases, he will be entitled to the special tax treatment. *Finance Act 2013* amends *s 2* of *TCGA 1992* to provide that if an individual qualifies for split-year treatment, he will not be chargeable to capital gains that accrue in the overseas part of the year. Likewise, any losses which arise in the overseas part will not be allowable losses.

However, gains on assets used in a UK trade (which would be taxable on non-resident individuals) remain subject to charge (and corresponding losses will be allowable losses). Gains arising in the non-resident portion of the tax year could still come back into charge under the temporary non-residence rule, if the individual's absence from the UK lasts for five years or less.

This treatment extends to gains chargeable on the remittance basis. *Section 12, TCGA 1992* treats gains chargeable on the remittance basis as accruing in the year that they are remitted to the UK. *Finance Act 2013* amends *s 12* to make it clear that they are treated as accruing in the part of the year in which they are remitted (either the UK part or the overseas part). This would mean that gains which arose when an individual was resident in the UK could be remitted in the overseas part of a split year without a tax charge (subject to the anti-avoidance rules in *s 10A, TCGA 1992* regarding those returning to the UK within five years).

There is also an amendment to the anti-avoidance legislation which treats the gains of non-UK resident close companies as accruing to UK resident participators (*s 13, TCGA 1992*). *Finance Act 2013* amends *s 13* such that an individual qualifying for split-year treatment is only chargeable on gains which accrue in the UK part of a split year.

The position is more complicated and less generous for the anti-avoidance legislation regarding the taxation of gains accruing to non-resident trustees.

*Section 86, TCGA 1992*, which treats gains of the trustees as accruing to the settlor, will continue to apply, and the settlor will be taxable on gains that accrue to the trustees throughout the whole of the split year, but the gain which the section treats as accruing to him will be treated as accruing in the UK part of the tax year.

For *s 87, TCGA 1992*, which treats gains as accruing to beneficiaries who receive a benefit from non-UK resident trustees, until 5 April 2018, the amount of deemed gain on which they are charged is time-apportioned over the tax year and they are taxable only in relation to the portion of the gain relating to the UK part of the tax year. This might give rise to unexpected consequences. Where an individual receives a distribution from a trust in the overseas part of the tax year, he might expect that any gains matched to this amount would not be taxable. However, he will in fact be taxable on a proportion of those gains, relating to the UK part of the tax year. So, for example, an individual who came to the UK on 6 July and for whom the overseas part of the tax year ended on 5 July, might have received a distribution of £1 million in say, May. He might expect this to be tax free, but if the full amount were matched with capital gains, in fact 9/12ths, or £750,000, would be subject to capital gains tax. From 6 April 2018, under the draft legislation published on 13 September 2017 for inclusion in Finance Bill 2018, the time apportionment is abolished. Regardless of when the payment is received in a split year, any gains matched in that year are treated as accruing in the UK part of the year. This change thus brings the charge for beneficiaries in line with that for settlors.

## The remittance basis

**[8.38]** Where relevant foreign income is remitted to the UK during a split year, *s 832(2)(b), ITTOIA 2005* (as amended by *Finance Act 2013*) provides that those remittances are only taxable where the income is remitted in the UK part of the tax year.

*Finance Act 2013* makes amendments to *s 26, ITEPA 2003* to ensure that the remittance basis will apply to general employment income if it arises in a split year and is attributable to the UK part of the tax year (non-UK source employment income arising in the overseas part of the tax year will not be taxable at all – see para **8.33** above). However, remittances of general employment income from a UK part of the year can still be taxable if they take place in the overseas part of the year. So, for example, if an individual left the UK during the tax year and qualified for split-year treatment, he could potentially have a remittance of employment income in the overseas part of the tax year – if he perhaps used that income to acquire a UK investment after leaving the UK.

There is also no provision for a split year for income treated as arising under the transfer of asset abroad rules, and a remittance of this income will be a taxable remittance even if it takes place in the overseas part of the tax year. This applies both to the transferor and the transferee charges. Such a remittance may be made by, say, a foreign company (as a relevant person) investing foreign income from the tax year into the UK before the individual ever becomes resident in the UK.

See para **8.37** above for remittances of capital gains.

## Conclusion

**[8.39]** The new special rules for income and capital gains have the advantage that an individual can have certainty as to his tax position in a split year. However, although it is an easy short hand to think of the individual as 'non-resident' in the overseas part of the year, it is important to refer back to the detail of the legislation in all cases since (as highlighted above) there are a number of occasions where it may not give the result expected.

# Chapter 9

# Trustee residence

## Introduction

**[9.01]** Since the residence of a settlement is dependent on the residence of its trustees and it is very common for such trustees to be individuals, it is inevitable that a change to the residence test for individuals may have an impact on the residence position of trusts.

*Finance Act 2013* also includes some new rules where trustees become or cease to be resident part way through a tax year, with new statutory rules applying to individual trustees who qualify for split-year treatment in the year of their arrival and departure.

## Basic rules on trust residence

**[9.02]** Since 6 April 2007, the rules for the residence of trustees have been the same for both income tax and capital gains tax (the rules were amended by *Finance Act 2006, Schedule 12* and prior to this date different rules applied for income and for capital gains).

For income tax, the rules are contained in *Chapter 2, Part 9* of *ITA 2007* (see *s 69, TCGA 1992* for capital gains).

*Section 474, ITA 2007* treats all the trustees of a settlement as a single person. *Section 475, ITA 2007* then sets out the rules to determine whether or not that single person is resident in the UK:

'(2)  If at a time either condition A or condition B is met, then at that time the single person is UK resident.

(3)  If at a time neither condition A nor condition B is met, then at that time the single person is non-UK resident.

(4)  Condition A is met at a time if, at that time, all the persons who are trustees of the settlement are UK resident.

(5)  Condition B is met at a time if at that time—
    (a)  at least one person who is a trustee of the settlement is UK resident and at least one such person is non-UK resident, and
    (b)  a settlor in relation to the settlement meets condition C (see *section 476*).'

In summary, if all of the trustees are UK resident, then the 'single person' will be UK resident and the trust will be a UK resident trust. If the trustees are of mixed residence and at least one trustee is UK resident, then the trust will only be UK resident if the settlor meets condition C (see below).

A trustee may be treated as UK resident, even if he is not, if he 'acts as trustee in the course of a business which T carries on in the United Kingdom through

221

a branch, agency or permanent establishment' (eg s 475(6) ITA 2007). In other words, a professional trustee or company providing professional trustee services will be treated as UK resident for the purpose of deciding the residence of the trust, if that professional trustee carries on business through a branch or agency in the UK which includes acting as trustee of the relevant trust. These rules are unaltered by the introduction of the SRT and are not considered further here.

## Trustees of mixed residence

**[9.03]** In circumstances where at least one but not all trustees are resident in the UK, it is necessary to determine whether the settlor meets condition C. *Section 476* provides:

'(2)  If—
    (a)  the settlement arose on S's death (whether by S's will, on S's intestacy or in any other way), and
    (b)  immediately before S's death, S was UK resident or domiciled in the United Kingdom,
    then S meets condition C from the time of S's death until S ceases to be a settlor in relation to the settlement.
(3)  If—
    (a)  the settlement is not within *subsection (2)(a)*, and
    (b)  at a time when S made the settlement (or is treated for the purposes of the Income Tax Acts as making the settlement), S was UK resident or domiciled in the United Kingdom,
    then S meets condition C from that time until S ceases to be a settlor in relation to the settlement.
(4)  Further, if—
    (a)  there is a transfer of property in relation to which *section 471* applies,
    (b)  S is a settlor in relation to settlement 2 as a result of that section, and
    (c)  immediately before the disposal by the trustees of settlement 1, S meets condition C as a settlor in relation to settlement 1 as a result of *subsection (2)* or *(3)* or this subsection,
    then S meets condition C as a settlor in relation to settlement 2 from the time S becomes such a settlor until S ceases to be such a settlor.'

In summary, if the settlor is dead and the settlement arose on his death, then he will meet condition C if he was UK resident or domiciled at the time of his death. Prior to the abolition of ordinary residence in *Finance Act 2013*, condition C applied where the settlor was resident, ordinarily resident or domiciled at the time of his death. For settlors who died prior to 6 April 2013, this remains the test. In practice, there are likely to be very few instances in which a settlor was ordinarily resident in the UK without also being either UK resident or UK domiciled.

If the settlor is not dead, or he created the settlement during his lifetime, then he meets condition C if he was UK resident or domiciled at the time the settlement was created. Again, for settlements created prior to 6 April 2013, the settlor will also meet condition C if he was ordinarily resident when the settlement was established.

Finally, the settlor may meet condition C if there has been a transfer between settlements to which *s 471* applies, he is the settlor of the transferee settlement as a result of that section and he is either UK resident or domiciled at the time of the transfer. *Section 470* sets out when *s 471* applies, but broadly it applies to a transfer for less than full consideration or not at arm's length, although this is subject to some exceptions.

The position regarding residence for capital gains tax is identical and is contained in *s 69, TCGA 1992*.

With effect from 6 April 2017, an individual who is deemed domiciled under *s 835BA ITA 2007* is treated as UK domiciled for the purposes of the Condition C test (see the outline of the proposed rules in CHAPTER 15).

## Interaction with individual residence and trustee residence

[9.04] Where the trustees of a settlement are individuals, it will be necessary to determine the residence status of those individuals in order to determine the residence status of the settlement. From 6 April 2013, this will obviously mean applying the provisions of the SRT to each one of those individuals. Since the SRT is not intended to change the residence status of the majority of taxpayers, it is to be hoped that its introduction will not have much effect on the residence status of trusts except where individuals who are trustees come to or leave the UK.

Since the residence of a settlement is dependent upon the residence of the individual trustees, it is not uncommon for those coming to the UK to import a trust to the UK accidentally. For example, where a husband and wife are the only trustees of a family trust and they both become UK resident, this will lead to that family trust becoming UK resident.

Similarly, those leaving the UK can accidentally export a trust in similar circumstances. While, on the face of it, this may seem like less of a problem, it can give rise to a capital gains tax charge under *s 80, TCGA 1992* (see para **9.06** below).

## Residence of trustees and the split-year treatment

[9.05] Prior to *Finance Act 2013*, HMRC practice was to allow the tax year to be split when the residence of the trustees changed, but with regard to the trustees' liability to income tax only (TSEM1461). The concession with regard to capital gains tax (D2) specifically stated that it did not apply to trustees. Where trustees changed their residence position mid-way through a tax year, therefore, any capital gains which arose during the 'non-resident' period would still fall within the charge to UK tax.

This could give rise to difficulties in practice. For example, if an individual and his wife were the sole trustees of a discretionary trust and they became resident in the UK in, say, October 2012, then the trust would be treated as resident in the UK from that date for income tax purposes. However, for capital gains tax purposes, the trust would be UK resident for the full 2012/13 tax year and any gains which arose in that tax year would be within the charge to UK tax. This could be particularly unfortunate since the individuals might not seek UK tax advice until close to the date on which they were due to travel to the UK and might not therefore be aware of the potential impact on any trusts of which they were a trustee until it was too late for them to resign.

Under *Finance Act 2013*, the position with regard to split years has been put on a statutory footing and applies with regard to both income and capital gains tax. Although trustees are treated as one continuing body of persons for the purpose of the taxes acts, in order to determine the residence of that body of persons, where it is made up of a number of individuals, it is necessary to consider the residence position of each of those individuals.

Special rules have been introduced with the statutory residence test to deal with circumstances in which an individual trustee changes his residence position part way through a tax year.

This new treatment is introduced as amendments to the relevant sections in the income and capital gains tax acts regarding the residence of trustees (*s 475, ITA 2007* and *s 69, TCGA 1992*). The rules are as follows:

For CGT, s 69 (2DA) and (2DB) read:

'(2DA) A trustee who is resident in the United Kingdom for a tax year is to be treated for the purposes of subsections (2A) and (2B) as if he or she were not resident in the United Kingdom for that year if—
  (a)   the trustee is an individual,
  (b)   the individual becomes or ceases to be a trustee of the settlement during the tax year,
  (c)   that year is a split year as respects the individual, and
  (d)   in that year, the only period when the individual is a trustee of the settlement falls wholly within the overseas part of the year.
(2DB) Subsection (2DA) is subject to subsection (2D) and, accordingly, an individual who is treated under subsection (2DA) as not resident is, in spite of that, to be regarded as resident whenever the individual acts as mentioned in subsection (2D).'

Subsection (2D) is the subsection which covers a trustee carrying on a business in the UK through a branch, agency or permanent establishment.

For income tax, s 475 (7) – (9) read:

'(7)   Subsection (8) applies if—
  (a)   an individual becomes or ceases to be a trustee of the settlement during a tax year,
  (b)   that year is a split year as respects the individual, and
  (c)   the only period in that year when the individual is a trustee of the settlement falls wholly within the overseas part of the year.
(8)   The individual is to be treated for the purposes of subsections (4) and (5) as if he or she had been non-UK resident for the year (and hence for the period in that year when he or she was a trustee of the settlement).
(9)   But subsection (8) is subject to subsection (6) and, accordingly, an individual who is treated under subsection (8) as having been non-UK resident is, in spite of that, to be treated as UK resident whenever
  (a)   the individual acts as mentioned in subsection (6).'

Again, subsection (6) deals with a trustee carrying on a business in the UK through a branch, agency or permanent establishment.

The wording of the two sets of amendments is slightly different, but the effect is largely the same. Where an individual who is the trustee of a settlement qualifies for the split-year treatment in a given tax year, he is to be treated as though he were not resident in the UK for the whole of that tax year only for the purpose of determining the residence of the settlement of which he is a trustee. However, in order for this treatment to apply, in addition to qualifying for split-year treatment, the individual must either become or cease to be a trustee during the tax year and the period of the tax year during which the individual is a trustee must fall wholly within the overseas part (or deemed non-resident part) of the tax year.

This is an improvement on the previous position and means that in the case of the example above of the husband and wife who came to the UK in October, it would be possible for them to resign as trustees and appoint alternative non-resident trustees and thus prevent the trust ever becoming UK resident. However, in these circumstances, it would be necessary for the resignation to take place before the individuals became UK resident. For this reason it will be critical to be sure of the date on which UK residence starts under split-year treatment (see **CHAPTER 8**) and to be well advised in advance of becoming resident and any associated move to the UK.

The amendment would also allow those who have left the UK and who are treated as non-resident for part of the year under the split-year treatment to become trustees of settlements in the overseas (or non-resident) part of the year without those trusts being treated as UK resident settlements. In these circumstances it will again be critical to have certainty of the date on which the overseas part of the year begins (see **CHAPTER 8**).

The treatment is automatic and not by claim or election so if an individual meets the split-year conditions he will be treated as non-resident for the whole of the split year, for this purpose.

Those who leave the UK and are trustees of UK resident settlements may wish to resign as trustees before leaving the UK in favour of other UK resident individuals in order to prevent the application of the rules in *s 80, TCGA 1992* (see para **9.06** below). However, the split-year rules will not apply to these individuals since they will be trustees for the UK part of the tax year. This is positive, since otherwise it may have been necessary for such individuals to resign before the end of the tax year prior to that in which they left the UK.

For both income tax and CGT there is an exception to the split-year treatment where an individual acts as trustee as part of a business which he carries on in the UK. Such an individual cannot be treated as non-resident under the split-year rules for the purpose of his trusteeship (*s 69(2DB), TCGA 1992* and *s 475(9), ITA 2007*, as inserted by *FA 2013*).

It should be noted that these special rules will only apply where the individual who is a trustee meets the conditions of one of the cases of the split-year test. A trustee who becomes UK resident part way through a tax year but does not qualify for split-year treatment may still cause the trust to become UK resident even if he resigns before arriving in the UK – since he will be resident for the whole of the tax year and thus a trustee whilst resident. The safest course may therefore be for all individuals coming to the UK to consider resigning as trustees before the start of the UK tax year of arrival, where this is possible.

If the trustee fails to resign then, even if he qualifies for split-year treatment, he will be resident for the full tax year for the purpose of considering the residence position of the trust. Whether this is sufficient to change the residence position of the trust will depend on the residence position of the other trustees and the residence and domicile position of the settlor (see paras **9.02** and **9.03** above).

## Migrating individuals and the consequences of importing a trust

**[9.06]** Since the residence of a trust is dependent on the residence position of its trustees, where those trustees consist of individuals it is easy for the trust to 'migrate' when the individuals migrate (see paras **9.02** and **9.03** above).

The well-advised trustee will resign before changing residence in circumstances where a change in his residence will impact on the residence position of the trust. However, in view of the fact that an individual's residence position might change mid-tax year and split-year treatment will not always be available, there may be trustees that find they have taken advice too late to prevent an impact on the trust. Care must also be taken to ensure that resignations are properly effected under the terms of the trust documentation and/or the statutory tests. We have seen cases where the failure of a trustee to effectively resign has led to the trust coming into and out of the UK with disastrous tax consequences.

As with individuals, the tax position of a settlement is connected to its residence. The trustees of a settlement which is not resident in the UK will be subject to tax on UK source income only. Capital gains will not be subject to tax in the hands of non-resident trustees (although s 86 and s 87, TCGA 1992 may act to apportion any gains to the settlor or to beneficiaries in certain circumstances). UK resident trustees, by contrast, will usually be taxable on their worldwide arising income and capital gains. Importing a trust to the UK can therefore have serious potential consequences for trustees, depending upon the assets and income flows within the trust.

It is perhaps a less obvious area of concern but, just as a trust can be imported by individual trustees becoming resident in the UK, so it can also be exported by such individuals ceasing to be resident. However, exporting the trust in this way could lead to the application of the 'exit charge' rules in s 80, TCGA 1992.

These rules apply where the trustees of a settlement become non-resident (or in other words, cease to be UK resident). In these circumstances the trustees will be deemed to have disposed of and reacquired their assets at their market value immediately before becoming non-resident. In most cases this is likely to give rise to a chargeable gain which will be subject to UK tax. There is an exception to this general rule where trustees are carrying on a trade in the UK.

In these circumstances assets used in that trade will remain within the UK tax net and so will not be treated as being sold and reacquired.

*Section 80, TCGA 1992* also presents a problem where a trust has been accidentally imported to the UK, since if the trustees resign after becoming UK resident and non-resident trustees are appointed, this will give rise to an exit charge as described above. There is no provision to rebase assets at the time that the trust first came to the UK, so any capital gain will be based on market value at the time of exit, less the cost of the assets, even where they were acquired, say, ten years before the trust became UK resident.

The residence of the trustees will have no impact on the inheritance tax position of the trust, since liability in this case is based upon the domicile of the settlor and the situs of the assets within the trust.

As well as considering the UK tax position when changing residence, trustees of settlements will also need to be concerned with the tax position in the country to which they are migrating. In some jurisdictions, one resident trustee can be sufficient to bring the income and gains of the trust within the scope of local taxes and the UK is not the only country to impose exit charges on trusts leaving its jurisdiction.

# Dual residence trusts and double tax agreements

**[9.07]** Different jurisdictions have different rules for taxing settlements and it is therefore not uncommon for settlements to be resident in more than one country. The trustees of such settlements will need to consider any double tax Treaty between the two countries in which they are resident in order to determine their tax position. It should be noted, however, that trustees who are resident in both the UK and another jurisdiction will remain UK resident even where they are Treaty resident in the other state under the relevant tie-breaker, see below.

Under article 4 of the OECD Model Treaty, a settlement which is resident in more than one state will be resident under the tie-breaker in the country in which its effective management is situated (referred to as the 'place of effective management' or 'POEM'). This rule is designed to apply to all persons other than individuals and so much of the commentary around POEM relates to companies, as opposed to trustees.

The OECD commentary on article 4 states that:

'The place of effective management is the place where key management and commercial decisions that are necessary for the conduct of the entity's business are in substance made. The place of effective management will ordinarily be the place where the most senior person or group of persons (for example a board of directors) makes its decisions, the place where the actions to be taken by the entity as a whole are determined; however, no definitive rule can be given and all relevant facts and circumstances must be examined to determine the place of effective management. An entity may have more than one place of management, but it can have only one place of effective management at any one time.'

HMRC manuals do not contain much guidance on the meaning of POEM from a trust perspective. However, there is one paragraph in relation to trusts with dual residence in the UK and Ireland (at INTM353600) which gives some limited guidance:

'Criteria for determining the place of effective management of an Irish trust

You need to find out who generally controls and supervises the work of administering the trust. By administering the trust we mean: keeping accounts, conducting correspondence, arranging the trustees' meetings and putting the trustees' decisions into effect.'

The picture from both the OECD commentary and the HMRC guidance which is available suggests that it is not the day-to-day administration of the trust which is key, but rather the controlling decisions with regard to the primary business and administration of the trust. The manuals give no additional guidance regarding what that might involve, but it seems likely that decisions about making, holding and disposing of investments, and regarding the accumulation or distribution of trust income will be key decisions, as will signing off trust accounts.

In the Court of Appeal case of Smallwood (*Re Trevor Smallwood Trust; Smallwood v Revenue and Customs Comrs* [2010] EWCA Civ 778, [2010] STC 2045, 80 TC 536) the place of effective management was found to be in the UK in circumstances where the trustees in Mauritius placed heavy reliance on advice from the UK, in spite of the fact that the advice was followed and implemented from Mauritius by trustees who had the power to reject it. This case may be viewed as exceptional in some ways, since it was an avoidance case (in which the trustees relied on the Mauritius-UK double tax Treaty in an attempt to avoid UK capital gains tax), but it nevertheless demonstrates the importance of having competent trustees who genuinely make the key decisions in relation to the management of the trust.

This was confirmed in the recent case of *Lee and another v Revenue and Customs Commissioners* [2017] UKFTT 279 (TC) [2017] SFTD 826, where one issue for the First-Tier Tribunal was the place of effective management of the settlement. Referring to the Court of Appeal's decision in *CRC v Smallwood* [2010] STC 2045, the President of the First-Tier Tribunal (Judge Bishopp) upheld the taxpayer's submissions that as the test applied by the Court of Appeal was with reference to the criteria laid down in *Edwards v Bairstow* [1956] AC 14, [1955] 3 All ER 48, HL and the long line of authority that followed it, it was not permissible (as HMRC argued) to simply apply the outcome of Smallwood to the facts of the present case. It was, instead, necessary to determine where the most important decisions were taken relating to the governance or management of the settlements. The settlements had disposed of shares which represented nearly all of their assets. This was not a matter of routine trust management — it was necessary to secure the best price for the shares. However, while at a 'purely formal level', the decision to execute the relevant documents was taken in Mauritius by a trust corporation owned by the Mauritius office of Deloitte, on the evidence 'the shots were called in the UK'. The tribunal was therefore satisfied that important settlement decisions were taken in the UK and the trustee board 'merely implemented' them. The place of management was in the UK so that, by operation of the tie-breaker provisions in the double tax treaty, the gain realised on the sale of the shares was taxable in the UK.

The taxpayers were successful on HMRC's alternative argument, that the Treaty was not engaged at all 'because the UK and Mauritius tax different persons'. In the UK, we tax the single and continuing body of trustees (albeit the settlors in a case of this kind ultimately bear the burden), in Mauritius (if there were to be tax at all) the trust is taxed. The First Tier-Tribunal agreed with the taxpayers' submissions that the Treaty concentrates on 'the category of income or gain, and not the identity of the person liable to tax' and dismissed HMRC's argument.

It is worth emphasising that the tie-breaker is only of relevance for the purpose of reading and applying the relieving provisions of the Treaty. So, a settlement which is domestically resident in the UK will remain domestically resident in the UK, even if the tie-breaker results in it being treated as resident in another jurisdiction for the purpose of the Treaty. This is particularly significant as there are a number of places in the Taxes Act where double tax relief under a Treaty is disapplied. For example, where a UK resident and domiciled individual would be apportioned capital gains arising to non-UK resident trustees under *s 86, TCGA 1992*, and the trustees are dual resident and treated as non-UK resident under a tax treaty, for the purpose of this section the fact that they are UK resident is ignored, but the settlor is nevertheless denied double tax relief in relation to any gains arising.

# Conclusion

**[9.08]** The SRT markedly improves the position for trustees. Those who are internationally mobile will still need to be careful to resign as trustees where their own change of residence will affect the residence of the trust. However, following the amendments to the law introduced by the SRT, it should be possible for them to do this and maintain the settlement's existing residence status, even where they do not seek advice until close to the date of their arrival or departure.

# Chapter 10

# Abolition of ordinary residence and Overseas Workday Relief

## Introduction

**[10.01]** One of the questions posed by the June 2012 Consultation Document on the Statutory Residence Test was whether the UK's tax system was excessively complex in having three different aspects – residence, ordinary residence and domicile – to consider in determining an individual's liability to UK tax. The conclusion, following an analysis of the responses to the consultation, was that abolishing ordinary residence as a status would be a significant simplification of the UK tax regime on residence. However, it was recognised that an important tax relief for employees that had been dependent on them having ordinary residence status should be retained.

There was no statutory definition of ordinary residence under the former regime. Hence abolition in *Finance Act 2013* is not achieved by a single section. Instead, *Finance Act 2013* removes or replaces substantially all the rules which depend for their effect on the taxpayer having ordinary residence status. This requires a lengthy schedule of amendments. It also provides the framework for any further amendments to be made by Statutory Instrument. Perhaps the most important amendment was to replace the rules for overseas workday relief. This chapter considers this rule in detail, and also considers, more briefly, some of the other areas of tax affected by the abolition of ordinary residence.

## Ordinary residence under the former regime

**[10.02]** Ordinary residence continues to be relevant for the first few years of the SRT since, under transitional provisions, some taxpayers will still have their liability to tax determined as if the status continued.

As noted above, there was no statutory definition of ordinary residence under the previous regime. Rather, three principles from case law were generally applied to decide whether someone arriving in the UK should be regarded as ordinarily resident. The following extract from HMRC 6 (para 3.2) summarises these:

> 'When you come to the UK you do not have to intend to remain in the UK permanently or indefinitely in order to be ordinarily resident here. It is enough that your residence has all the following attributes.
>
> • Your presence here has a settled purpose. This might be for only a limited period, but has enough continuity to be properly described as settled.

Business, employment and family can all provide a settled purpose, but this list is not exhaustive.

- Your presence in the UK forms part of the regular and habitual mode of your life for the time being. This can include temporary absences from the UK. For example if you come to live in the UK for three years or more then you will have established a regular and habitual mode of life here from the start.

- You have come to the UK voluntarily. The fact that you chose to come to the UK at the request of your employer rather than seek another job does not make your presence here involuntary.

The pattern of your presence, both in the UK and overseas, is an important factor when you are deciding if you are ordinarily resident in the UK. You will also need to take into account your reasons for being in, coming to, or leaving the UK and your lifestyle and habits.'

In general, HMRC would typically accept that someone coming to the UK with the intention of remaining for a period of less than three years should be regarded as not ordinarily resident initially. If he left within three years of his arrival, he would usually remain not ordinarily resident for the whole period of UK residence. However, if he remained in the UK beyond the third anniversary of his arrival he would normally have been regarded as ordinarily resident from the start of the tax year in which that third anniversary fell, unless he had decided in the meantime to remain in the UK beyond the three-year point. If a decision to extend his time in the UK was made before the third anniversary of his arrival, typically ordinary residence applied from the start of the tax year in which that decision was made. In both sets of circumstances, if the individual left the UK before his third anniversary in the UK and disposed of any accommodation here, he would usually be regarded retrospectively as not ordinarily resident.

There were exceptions to the above and, towards the end of the former regime, it appeared that the position was changing, as HMRC sought to link the tests they applied more closely to case law principles. HMRC's stance had always been that buying a UK property or taking on a lease of more than three years would be enough to make the individual ordinarily resident from the start of the tax year in which the acquisition occurred. More recently, HMRC placed greater emphasis on the taxpayer having a settled purpose. Thus in *Genovese v Revenue and Customs Comrs* [2010] UKFTT 283 (TC), [2010] SFTD 1063, HMRC argued that Mr Genovese, who had been resident in the UK since 1995 for employment, had his family with him in the UK, put his children down for school in the UK, and had made an offer to purchase a UK home, had been resident with a sufficient degree of settled purpose to be ordinarily resident. Mr Genovese argued that this was contrary to HMRC's published practice, but the Special Commissioners held that he was ordinarily resident in law. Following the more recent decision in *Tuczka v Revenue and Customs Comrs* [2011] UKUT 113 (TCC), [2011] STC 1438, HMRC argued that having an open-ended UK employment contract was also indicative of coming to the UK for a settled purpose and worked to a presumption of ordinary residence in these circumstances.

It was harder for a UK domiciled individual to claim he was not ordinarily resident on coming to the UK, because HMRC would assume anyone returning home to the UK would be doing so permanently. However, it was possible, if he could establish that his return to the UK was sufficiently temporary, for not ordinarily resident status to apply.

It is apparent, even from the brief summary above, that the tests, especially whether presence in the UK was part of the regular and habitual pattern of the taxpayer's life, were extremely subjective.

From 2013/14, ordinary residence as a status in determining liability to tax has been abolished. However, there are some transitional rules for taxpayers who were previously not ordinarily resident and so fell outside certain charging provisions. For example, those taxpayers who were claiming overseas workday relief in years before 2013/14 on the basis that they were not ordinarily resident in the UK will, under transitional rules, only be eligible to continue to claim the relief if they would have continued to be not ordinarily resident had the status remained in place. This is covered in more detail below, as are other transitional provisions.

# Overseas Workday Relief

**[10.03]** Overseas Workday Relief (OWR) applies to UK resident employees who perform work both in the UK and overseas under a single contract of employment and who are taxed on the remittance basis. Such individuals are liable to UK tax on their earnings for their UK duties in full but are only liable to UK tax on their earnings that relate to their overseas workdays to the extent that these earnings are remitted to the UK.

There are several differences in the application of the SRT Overseas Workdays Relief as compared to previous practice. The following sections first give a brief overview of previous practice and then explain the SRT rules.

### Previous practice

**[10.04]** Under the previous regime, the relief was available to employees who were not ordinarily resident and entitled to the remittance basis. The relief was thus available to both UK domiciliaries and non-UK domiciliaries.

In order to determine the amount of the relief, it was necessary to apportion earnings between UK and overseas duties. *ITEPA 2003* set out the rules confirming how general earnings for UK and overseas duties should be taxed, but it did not determine how those earnings should be apportioned between UK and overseas duties.

HMRC's practice was usually to apportion earnings by reference to UK and overseas workdays. This was set out in Statement of Practice 1/09, an extract from which is copied below:

'Where the duties of a single office or employment are performed both in and outside the UK, an apportionment is required to determine how much of the general earnings are attributable to the UK duties. Apportionment of general earnings is essentially a question of fact, but for many years HMRC has accepted time apportionment, based on the number of days worked abroad and in the UK, except where this would clearly be inappropriate. For example, in the case of an employee with 200 working days in the UK and 50 working days outside the UK, the proportion of general earnings attributable to UK duties would be 200/250.'

As earnings in respect of both UK and overseas workdays would be paid into a single bank account and, of necessity, this bank account would need to be outside the UK in order to permit earnings in respect of overseas workdays to be taxed on the remittance basis, a mechanism was needed for determining the order of remittances to the UK from this mixed bank account. Prior to the remittance basis changes of 2008, the mixed fund rules were more relaxed, and the practice accepted by HMRC was published in a statement of practice (originally SP5/84). This continued in a modified form (SP1/09) following the reform of the remittance basis law from 6 April 2008. This modification was necessary from 6 April 2008 because the remittance basis mixed fund legislation from that date required a strict analysis for each bank account on a tax year basis and by reference to the make-up of the account immediately before the remittance.

SP1/09 is a relaxation of the strict mixed fund law. However, before considering its effect, it is appropriate to note the conditions required for it to apply, which may be summarised as follows:

- An SP1/09 account had to be a newly opened account intended to hold virtually nothing other than employment income of a single employment for a period when the employee was resident but not ordinarily resident. Certain other tightly controlled amounts could be credited, such as proceeds of sale of certain employee-related share transactions and any interest earned on that account only. If all the conditions were met, any number of these types of accounts could be held.
- If any other money was credited to the account, even if that money was entirely cleared out before any earnings were credited, the account would be tainted and ineligible for SP1/09 treatment.
- The account could be in joint names but any spouse or civil partner was not permitted to credit funds to the account (only to spend what was in it!).

The practice only applied to individuals who were resident but not ordinarily resident for the tax year.

If all conditions were met, the mixed fund ordering rules were still applied to any remittances made to the UK, but the analysis of what had been remitted to the UK was deferred until the end of the tax year concerned, rather than being done on a real-time transaction by transaction basis. This thus allowed the employee to access his UK source earnings for the full tax year in considering what was treated as remitted to the UK, regardless of the timing of any actual remittances made. He was only regarded as having remitted non-UK source earnings to the extent that general earnings paid directly into the UK, and general earnings paid offshore but subsequently brought to the UK, together exceeded his total UK source earnings for the tax year.

Individuals who were resident but not ordinarily resident in the UK during 2012/13 and who were already applying the statement of practice to a bank account may continue to apply the practice in the SRT regime for so long as they remain eligible for overseas workdays relief for the tax year concerned. If they prefer, they may use the new statutory special mixed fund rules, but once they do so they will not be able to revert to the SP1/09 regime.

Under the current regime, as is set out below, each taxpayer can only only have one nominated special mixed fund account at any one time. As the law is, therefore, more restrictive than previous practice, most taxpayers who may continue to use SP1/09 are expected to do so.

### The SRT rules

**[10.05]** The SRT regime sets out new conditions for when overseas workdays relief will be available, and for the apportionment of general earnings. Employees eligible for the relief who wish to be able to take advantage of a simplification of the remittance basis rules will need to set up a special bank account that meets the conditions set out in statute.

It should be noted that the SRT OWR is only available to non-UK domiciliaries who meet the necessary conditions. This is because the remittance basis, a necessary precursor for OWR is, from 2013/14, restricted to non-domiciliaries and there are no special provisions extending OWR to UK domiciles who previously could have enjoyed it (except under the transitional provisions).

Individuals who are UK domiciled and who come to the UK for a relatively short period after 6 April 2013 are therefore at a disadvantage when compared with the previous law. HMRC's press release of 11 December 2012 stated that only around 300 such people claimed the remittance basis in 2008/09 and, while this sounds a low figure, the combination of circumstances that could allow UK domiciled individuals to claim overseas workdays relief historically was sufficiently rare for this to be a credible estimate.

The conditions that need to be met in order to obtain OWR under the SRT are set out in a new section in *ITEPA 2003*. *Section 26* previously gave the remittance basis for general earnings of employees who were not ordinarily UK resident. It now gives the remittance basis to employees who satisfy the conditions of *section 26A*. *Section 26A* provides as follows:

'26A Section 26: requirement for 3-year period of non-residence
(1)    An employee meets the requirement of this section for a tax year if the employee was—
(a)    non-UK resident for the previous 3 tax years, or
(b)    UK resident for the previous tax year but non-UK resident for the 3 tax years before that, or
(c)    UK resident for the previous 2 tax years but non-UK resident for the 3 tax years before that, or
(d)    non-UK resident for the previous tax year, UK resident for the tax year before that and non-UK resident for the 3 tax years before that.
(2)    The residence status of the employee before the 3 years of non-UK residence is not relevant for these purposes.'

This effectively allows relief for the UK tax year in which the employee first becomes tax resident (which may be a split year) and for two full tax years thereafter. This is a significant improvement over the previous regime for all non-domiciled employees (and any host employers in the UK) because it offers certainty of treatment, provided the conditions regarding previous periods of residence in the UK are met.

The new provisions also benefit those who would have been regarded as ordinarily resident from arrival in the past. Thus any employee owning a UK property or coming to the UK on an open-ended UK employment contract will be better off under the new regime as neither circumstance will automatically prevent him from qualifying for overseas workdays relief for the first three UK tax years in which he is UK tax resident.

## The calculation of OWR

**[10.06]** When calculating OWR, it is essential to note the distinction between remuneration that is taxed as general earnings and that which is taxed as specific employment income (including termination payments and certain types of share awards such as share options and restricted shares granted to a UK tax resident).

Under the SRT, the way in which the UK element of general earnings is to be determined is set out in *s 41ZA* of *ITEPA 2003*, as below:

'Apportionment of earnings
41ZA Basis of apportionment

The extent to which general earnings are in respect of duties performed in the United Kingdom is to be determined under this Chapter on a just and reasonable basis.'

It will be noted that the precise method of calculation is not set out. Discussions with HMRC during the consultation period have suggested that this is intended to be a workday apportionment unless something else would be more appropriate for a particular receipt, very much along the lines previously set out in the statement of practice.

Some uncertainties still remain as to how this calculation will work in practice. For example, so far neither the law nor HMRC's guidance on the relief (RDR4 of May 2013) have indicated whether HMRC will continue to regard a day on which the duties of employment are performed substantially outside the UK as an overseas workday. The lack of clarity here is a concern as it may affect the records that employees need to keep to demonstrate their working pattern in the event of any future enquiry. RDR4 concentrates on circumstances in which OWR will be available and the transitional provisions. HMRC Employment Income Manual, EIM40103 simply repeats the phrase 'just and reasonable basis' with no commentary. EIM 77020 contains 'Appendix 2: general earnings in respect of duties performed in the UK'. Although this appendix, which explains how to treat days on which work is done both in and outside the UK, is written by reference to the pre SRT regime, in practice it appears that this guidance is still current.

Specific employment income (for example, income from share options) is subject to its own rules and, generally, even before the introduction of the SRT, the law had provided for any necessary apportionment of such income. This continues under the SRT. The law relating to termination payments has been subjected to a more radical overhaul and is considered in more detail at para **10.15** below.

## Transitional provisions for employees already UK tax resident as at 6 April 2013

[10.07] The transitional provisions are found in *paragraph 26* of *Schedule 46, Finance Act 2013* and only apply to individuals who are resident but not ordinarily resident in the UK as at 5 April 2013.

Such individuals fall outside the SRT OWR provisions and instead remain subject to previous practice, giving them the potential to access OWR over four tax years, provided they would have remained not ordinarily resident had previous law and practice continued. The latest year for which such transitional relief is available is 2015/16.

Individuals who were both resident and ordinarily resident as at 5 April 2013 would not have been entitled to OWR for any tax year in which they were both resident and ordinarily resident under the previous regime. However, they are not covered by the transitional provisions and they are eligible to claim the benefits of *ss 26–26A, ITEPA 2003*, to the extent that they have not already been UK tax resident in the three previous UK tax years. The HMRC guidance on OWR (RDR4) has some examples which illustrate this.

**Example 10.1: Yves**

Yves is a French national who came to the UK on 10 January 2013 with an expectation of staying in the UK for no more than three years. He was therefore resident but not ordinarily resident on arrival and will remain so, assuming that he leaves the UK as he anticipates and nothing else happens in the meantime that would deny him this status and the associated relief.

If he leaves at the end of 2015 as planned, he will be entitled, under the transitional provisions, to OWR for the full period.

If, instead he decided to buy a UK property in January 2014, it is likely he would have become ordinarily resident from the start of the 2013/14 tax year under the previous regime (although if he still leaves the UK within three years of arrival and disposes of his accommodation for example by letting it out, he may qualify as not ordinarily resident throughout his stay, with retrospective effect). Under the transitional provisions he would then only be entitled to OWR for 2012/13.

If on arrival he had expected to remain in the UK for at least five years, he would have been resident and ordinarily resident under previous practice, so would have had no relief for overseas workdays during 2012/13. However, there is nothing to prevent him from claiming relief under ss 26–26A for 2013/14 and 2014/15. In these circumstances Yves will obtain more relief than he would have done had he originally been not ordinarily resident in the UK but bought a UK home during his assignment as described above.

# The 'special mixed fund' law

## Introduction

**[10.08]** As noted above, anyone wishing to claim the benefit of overseas workdays relief needs to be paid offshore, claim the remittance basis, and retain that money outside the UK. The cash they receive into their non-UK bank account will be in respect of UK duties (taxable on the arising basis) and overseas duties (taxable on the remittance basis) and the bank account will therefore be a mixed fund for the purpose of applying the remittance basis under the SRT. New rules for such a bank account are contained within *Schedule 6* of *FA 2013* (which largely inserts new *ss 809RA–809RD* into *ITA 2007*) and replace the practice of SP1/09.

## The UK tax benefit available for a special mixed fund account

**[10.09]** The special mixed fund law does not change the tax nature of funds held in the bank account, but it defers the point at which an analysis has to be undertaken when there are remittances or overseas transfers from the account.

A detailed consideration of the normal mixed fund law is outside the scope of this work, but in principle it generally requires the analysis of what is remitted or transferred from any mixed fund account to be done on a real-time, transaction by transaction basis.

In a special mixed fund account the analysis is deferred until almost the end of the tax year and all the transactions over the course of the year are treated as being made in two transactions. First, all UK remittances are treated as a single remittance to the UK made immediately before the end of the tax year, and then all money used outside the UK or transferred to another offshore account is deemed to be used in a single overseas transfer (*s 809RA(2), ITA 2007*).

The effect of this is to simplify the analysis as it is not necessary to work out exactly what is held in an account immediately before any transaction, since the snapshot of the different categories of income and gains only has to be taken at year end. It also helps to smooth out the distorting effect that the timing of UK remittances and overseas transfers can otherwise have, as explained below.

In an ordinary mixed fund account the ordering of UK remittances and overseas transfers matters, because if an overseas transfer occurs before a UK remittance the overseas transfer will use up a proportion of all the different monies in the account, including UK source money that could otherwise be remitted to the UK without additional tax being due. If the transactions occurred the opposite way round, more UK source money may be available for remittance to the UK. The special mixed fund law provides that all UK remittances are made before all overseas transactions, thereby ensuring that all UK general earnings in the account will be deemed to be remitted to the UK ahead of other money, which is likely to minimise any extra tax that has to be paid.

## Conditions to be met in order to qualify as a special mixed fund account

[**10.10**] There are strict conditions that have to be met in order for a bank account to qualify, and a process to be followed before the treatment can apply:

- This type of account is only available to an employee, in respect of a tax year for which he has both UK source earnings and earnings that are eligible for overseas workdays relief (*s 809RA(1), ITA 2007*).
- The account may hold no income or gains other than general earnings from a tax year in which the individual was entitled to overseas workdays relief, specific employment income of such a tax year, interest on the account and the proceeds from the disposal of certain employment-related securities and employment-related securities options. In this latter case, the chargeable event for income tax must also have occurred in a tax year in which the employee was eligible for overseas workdays relief, be an award made when the employee was UK tax resident and the disposal must have occurred as soon as practicable after the income tax event (*s 809RC(6)(7) & (8), ITA 2007*).
- The account may have no more £10 in total in it before the first payment of UK source/overseas workdays earnings is paid into it (*s 809RB(10), ITA 2007*).
- The account must be an ordinary bank account, though it may be held alone or jointly with others (*s 809RB(10)(a), ITA 2007*). For the purposes of this law, an 'ordinary bank account' is defined as 'a cash account in a bank (whether a current or savings account) where sums standing to the credit of the account from time to time represent a debt owed by the bank to the account-holder' (*s 809RB(15), ITA 2007*).
- Although it may be held jointly, it may only be a qualifying account for one employee (*s 809RB(14), ITA 2007*), which will prevent any joint holder from making any deposits into the account.
- If the 'wrong' type of money is credited to the account, it will be a breach of the permitted deposits (*s 809RC, ITA 2007*). If the individual reverses the transaction (by clearing the money from the account) the tainting event is effectively unravelled (*s 809RD*) and may be ignored, provided that:
  - there are no more than two such tainting events in any rolling 12-month period (*s 809RC(4)*); and
  - the reversal happens within 30 days of the individual becoming aware of the tainting event (or within 30 days of the date on which he should reasonably have been aware of the tainting event (*s 809RC(2)*).

The detailed rules here will no doubt mean that it will be very easy to make mistakes and to taint an account by crediting the wrong sort of earnings or other funds to it.

In addition to the conditions noted above, there is a process to be followed in order for the account to be recognised as the individual's special mixed fund. The law does not permit the individual to have more than one qualifying account (s 809RB(13)). This is the most significant change from SP1/09. The single qualifying account dispenses with the need for complex rules governing offshore transfers. In order to facilitate the monitoring of this one account provision, the employee is required to nominate the account by giving written notice to HMRC. The precise details of what is required in the nomination are not specified in the law (s 809RB(7)), but the deadline for making the nomination is 31 January following the end of the tax year concerned. As this is the normal filing date for all tax returns that are e-filed, it is anticipated that the nomination will typically be included on the tax return and in a format prescribed on that return.

The individual may nominate or withdraw a nomination at any time, confirming the effective date as part of the nomination. He may still only have one nominated account at any one time, which will mean some end of tax year housekeeping is required. Under previous practice, the standard advice was to open a new bank account for employment income annually. This was because under the remittance basis mixed fund law, an individual is deemed to remit any current tax year earnings to the UK ahead of prior year earnings in the same bank account, and so continuing to use the same account could block the most tax-efficient use of UK earned income from previous tax years.

Given the administration involved, both with HMRC and in discussions with payroll, in changing to a different special mixed fund account, it may be simpler to clear money from a nominated account at year end into a separate offshore account than to nominate a new account annually, except where a change is required because of a tainting event.

### Example 10.2: Taryn

Taryn moves to the UK from her home in South Africa on 7 April 2015 to take up a temporary assignment in London. She has all of her earnings paid into a bank account in Jersey to facilitate her claim for overseas workdays relief. She is concerned about bringing too much money into the UK so only remits 40% of her earnings during the 2015/16 tax year, although in due course it transpires that her overseas workdays percentage was only 25% (so in principle, she could remit a further 35% of her 2015/16 earnings to the UK).

If Taryn has left this money in the same bank account into which her 2016/17 earnings are being paid, she will be deemed to remit all of her 2016/17 earnings to the UK ahead of her 2015/16 money. If instead she opens a new bank account for her 2016/17 money she will have to nominate that account and advise payroll to pay her into that account if she wants her 2016/17 earnings to be in a special mixed fund account. Taryn may prefer to continue to use the same account for her earnings but to clear her prior year money into a separate account before her 2016/17 earnings are credited to the nominated account.

The date from which the account will be regarded as nominated is the first date on which more than £10 of earnings that are both UK source and overseas workdays related is paid into the account (s 809RB(3)).

Where a third tainting event occurs within a 12-month period, or if a tainting event is not unwound within the 30-day window, the account concerned ceases to be a special mixed fund from the start of the tax year concerned. In this case the employee may nominate a new account, but can only do so from the first date on which the right sort of general earnings is credited to the account. So while it may be possible to correct the position going forward, once an employee has a third tainting event in an account within a 12-month period there will be a period for which any analysis of earnings remitted will have to be done on a transaction by transaction basis.

# Other aspects of the abolition of ordinary residence status

## Introduction

**[10.11]** So far this chapter has been concerned primarily with employees and with the way in which the reform of the law on ordinary residence is likely to affect them. Ordinary residence as a concept has applied much more widely than this in the tax code and this part of CHAPTER 10 considers one other aspect of the tax code that is affected by its abolition and the law relating to the taxation of payments on the termination of employment, which is also affected by the change. For details of other affected provisions, see the previous edition of this book.

Before doing so, it should be noted that, for National Insurance (NI), the concept of ordinary residence has been retained. There is some justification in this, as the definition for NI was always different from the one that applied for income tax and capital gains tax; but it feels slightly odd none the less, given the Government's stated aim of integrating the operation of the two codes over the longer term.

### Transfer of assets abroad

**[10.12]** The transfer of assets abroad legislation is complex anti-avoidance law, set out in *Chapter 2* of *Part 13* of *ITA 2007*. It is not considered in any detail here, but it has the potential to impose an income tax charge by reference to income arising to non-resident entities on anyone who has the power to enjoy income of or who receives a capital sum from that entity as a result of a relevant transaction, or on anyone who receives a benefit from that entity.

The effect of abolishing ordinary residence is to bring more taxpayers potentially within the scope of the law. Prior to 2013/14, this law only applied to taxpayers who were ordinarily resident so that short-term residents were outside its scope. However, from 2013/14 onwards it will apply to all resident taxpayers, regardless of the length of time they are UK tax resident. There are transitional provisions that apply for those individuals who were resident but not ordinarily resident at the end of the previous regime (ie at the end of 2012/13).

Under the transitional provisions, the new rules only start to apply after four tax years of residence, provided the individual would have remained not ordinarily resident under the previous regime. Thus for an individual who was resident in 2010/11 and in 2011/12, the new rules do not apply for 2013/14; where the individual was not resident in 2010/11 but resident in 2011/12 they do not apply for 2013/14 or 2014/15 and where the individual was not resident for 2011/12, they do not apply for years 2013/14-2015/16.

Even where the individual is within the ambit of the regime it may still be possible for him to claim one of the defences against the provisions. Whilst this will improve the position in many cases, the onus of proof is on the taxpayer to demonstrate that the defence is available, which is a less comfortable position than being wholly outside a regime because of not ordinarily resident status.

### Termination payments

[10.13] Any payment that is made on the termination of employment that is not otherwise chargeable to income tax may fall within the law relating to termination payments in *Chapter 3* of *Part 6* of *ITEPA 2003*. This will tax anything in excess of £30,000 unless the employee is entitled to foreign service relief.

Termination payments are a form of specific employment income and have their own set of rules for sourcing any payment received to the period of the service concerned. Broadly, each termination payment is considered across the various tax years the employment covered, and allocated accordingly to UK and foreign service based on the circumstances applying in those years. The level of foreign service relief is significant, because in the right circumstances it will completely exempt a termination payment from tax. In other cases, pro rata relief for the period of foreign service will apply.

For tax years up to and including 2012/13, any year during which the employee was either not resident or not ordinarily resident was regarded as a year that was eligible for foreign service relief. From 2013/14 onwards a tax year will not be eligible for full foreign service relief if the employee is tax resident in the UK and derives any remuneration from UK duties. Instead, employees who are eligible for overseas workdays relief for a particular year will be eligible for foreign service relief for that year, but the relief will only apply to the proportion of the payment attributable to overseas workdays in that year. This will make it harder for an employee whose employment is terminated while he is assigned to the UK to obtain a complete exemption under the foreign service relief provisions.

Prior to the General Election of June 2017, the Government had proposed to abolish foreign service relief for termination payments with effect from 6 April 2018. This proposal was dropped from the truncated Finance Act enacted before the election but now forms part of the Finance Bill 2018 draft provisions published on 13 September 2017, to have effect from 6 April 2018.

## Conclusion

[10.14] The abolition of ordinarily resident status is a significant simplification of the tax code. The retention of relief for overseas workdays and the decision to allow it for all employees who have not been UK tax resident for the previous three UK tax years is a major improvement.

The new form of overseas workdays relief feels much more like an expatriate tax regime, and the decision to exclude UK domiciliaries, whilst unfortunate for them, makes it comparable to tax incentives other governments offer to expatriate employees.

# Chapter 11

# The five-year trap: the anti-avoidance provisions for temporary non-residents

## Introduction

**[11.01]** One of HMRC's concerns with the introduction of the SRT was that the increased certainty which it would bring with regard to someone's residency position would lead to an increase in short-term non-residence as a form of tax planning. In an attempt to prevent such 'tax-avoidance', as HMRC saw it, the anti-avoidance rules aimed at temporary non-residents, such as those in relation to CGT (in *s 10A, TCGA 1992*) were expanded to include particular types of income which HMRC considered to be 'high risk' or easy to manipulate.

In broad terms, the pre-SRT CGT rules operated where an individual had been resident in the UK for four out of seven tax years before departure and returned to the UK within five tax years of leaving. In such circumstances, any capital gains which arose during the period of non-residence were treated as accruing to the individual in the tax year of his return to the UK. There were some exceptions to this general rule, for example for gains on assets acquired after becoming non-UK resident.

Even before the introduction of the SRT, the CGT rules had been extended to cover offshore income gains and there were similar rules covering remittances of relevant foreign income in a period of temporary non-residence.

At the same time as expanding the anti-avoidance rules to include certain types of income, the earlier anti-avoidance rules have been rewritten to unify the language and treatment, and, for CGT, to take account of the changes to capital gains tax in the year of arrival and departure that the new statutory split-year treatment provides (see **CHAPTER 8** for more detail on the split-year rules). In addition, it should be noted that in most cases the exemption from charge provided by double tax treaties is denied.

The SRT anti-avoidance rules are contained in *Part 4* of *Schedule 45, Finance Act 2013*. They only apply to tax years where the year of departure is 2013/14 or later. If the year of departure is earlier than this, the former provisions continue to apply.

## Temporary non-residence

**[11.02]** The SRT anti-avoidance legislation introduces the concept of 'temporarily non-resident' (although the original *s 10A, TCGA 1992* was entitled

'Temporary non-residents', the term was never actually defined and the rules instead applied to those individuals who satisfied the 'residence requirement').

The term is defined in *para 110* of *Schedule 45, FA 2013* and is in fact very similar to the 'residence requirements' in the original *s 10A*:

'110(1) An individual is to be regarded as "temporarily non-resident" if—
  (a)  the individual has sole UK residence for a residence period,
  (b)  immediately following that period (referred to as "period A"), one or more residence periods occur for which the individual does not have sole UK residence,
  (c)  at least 4 out of the 7 tax years immediately preceding the year of departure were either—
    (i)  a tax year for which the individual had sole UK residence, or
    (ii)  a split year that included a residence period for which the individual had sole UK residence, and
  (d)  the temporary period of non-residence is 5 years or less.'

'Sole UK residence' is defined in *paragraph 112*:

'112(1) An individual has "sole UK residence" for a residence period consisting of an entire tax year if—
  (a)  the individual is resident in the UK for that year, and
  (b)  there is no time in that year when the individual is Treaty non-resident.
(2)  An individual has "sole UK residence" for a residence period consisting of part of a split year if—
  (a)  the residence period is the UK part of that year, and
  (b)  there is no time in that part of the year when the individual is Treaty non-resident.
(3)  An individual is "Treaty non-resident" at any time if at the time the individual falls to be regarded as resident in a country outside the UK for the purposes of double taxation arrangements having effect at the time.'

Thus, an individual has 'sole UK residence' if he is resident in the UK and he is not 'Treaty non-resident' – in other words, he is not dual resident and treated as resident in another country under the terms of the tie-breaker article of any relevant Treaty.

In summary, an individual will be 'temporarily non-resident' if, following a period of 'sole UK residence', he becomes either not UK resident or dual resident and Treaty resident in the other country for a period of five years or less. He must also have had sole UK residence for four out of the previous seven tax years before the year of departure (this includes split years for which the individual only had sole UK residence for part of the year).

It is worth noting that, unlike in the original capital gains tax anti-avoidance legislation, the period of five years for which the individual must be 'non-resident' is five calendar years. However, tax years are still relevant for determining residence in the period before departure and in certain circumstances an individual's deemed date of departure may be the start of the tax year (see HMRC's Example 42 reproduced below). The phrase 'five years or less' means that the non-resident period must be **more than** five years if the taxpayer is to fall outside these rules.

When looking at the period of the UK residence, the impact of tax treaties may need to be considered. For example, it may be that the individual's residence changes under a tax Treaty tie-breaker article (because, say, his centre of vital interests moves) at a different time to the start or end of the overseas period under the split-year provisions. In such circumstances, if the individual was, say, Treaty non-resident for one month of the UK part of the split year, he would be considered not to have 'sole UK residence' for that year for the purpose of the legislation. Similarly, if an individual's circumstances were such that he did not meet the split-year tests, but instead claimed Treaty relief for part of a tax year, he would also not have 'sole UK residence' for the purpose of the legislation. This can also have an impact on an individual's deemed departure date for the purpose of counting the five years of non-residence, and can have the odd effect of treating the individual as non-resident before he has left the UK, as evidenced by Example 42 in the HMRC guidance, RDR3.

'Example 42

Max has had sole residence in the UK for the previous ten years. On 22 February 2015 Max moves to Poland and is considered resident there from this point, as well as retaining his UK residence up to the end of the tax year. From 22 February to 5 April 2015 he is treaty non-resident.

For the purpose of this example, Max does not satisfy the conditions for split year treatment in tax year 2014-15.

Max is not solely UK resident from 22 February 2015 but he will remain UK resident for the tax year. As this is not a split year, *Period A* will end at the end of the tax year 2013-14, because that is the end of the last tax year in which Max was solely UK resident. His year of departure for the purpose of applying the temporary non-resident provisions is therefore 2013-14, even though he actually physically left the UK on 22 February 2015. The next residence period begins on 6 April 2014 and Max will begin to be regarded as temporarily non-resident from this point.

Max returns on 26 May 2018 and split year treatment applies.

Max has sole UK residence from 26 May 2018. He is treaty resident for the UK part of the year. His temporary non-residence ends on 25 May 2018. The period of temporary non-residence is 6 April 2014 to 25 May 2018 inclusive, which is less than 5 years and so Max is within the scope of the temporary non-residence provisions.'

If Max had stayed non-UK resident until mid-April 2019, the anti-avoidance rules would not have applied to him, since the period during which he is treated as not UK resident would be more than five years – even though he did not leave the UK until February 2015.

The rules are designed to prevent tax avoidance and so are targeted at those with a history of UK residence who have a short period outside the UK. However, with the inclusion of split years as periods of residence, it would be easy for a mobile employee, say, to find himself within the terms of the legislation, even though he may have been resident in the UK for as little as three calendar years.

### Example 11.1: Hank

Hank is a US citizen who works for a large international bank and comes to the UK in February 2014 to head up a new division. His circumstances are such that he meets the conditions in Case 5 of the split year test (starting full-time work in the UK). Hank stays in the UK for just over three years, before moving to Germany to set up a similar division for the German branch of the bank at the end of April 2017. For 2017/18, he meets the split year conditions for Case 1 (starting full-time work overseas).

After three years in Germany, Hank returns to the US for a year before coming back to the UK in June 2021 to take up a more senior position in the UK banking organisation.

At the time when Hank leaves for Germany, at least four of the seven years immediately preceding the year of departure will be years for which he had sole UK residence or split years where he had sole UK residence for the UK part of the year.

The period for which Hank is not UK resident is less than five full years, so the anti-avoidance rules are likely to apply. Hank will therefore need to consider whether he realised any gains or received any income while resident in Germany or the US which may now become taxable as a result of his return to the UK (2021–22).

# Terminology

**[11.03]** Much of the anti-avoidance legislation (discussed in more detail below) operates by treating relevant income and gains which arose or accrued in the 'temporary period of non-residence' as arising or accruing in the 'period of return.'

The 'Temporary period of non-residence' is defined in *paragraph 113* of *Schedule 45, FA 2013*:

> 'In relation to an individual, "the temporary period of non-residence" is the period between—
> (a)    the end of period A, and
> (b)    the start of the next residence period after period A for which the individual has sole UK residence.'

'Period A' is defined in *para 110* (reproduced in para **11.02** above) as being the 'residence period' when an individual has sole UK residence immediately before a residence period for which he does not have sole UK residence. A 'residence period' (defined in *para 111*) is a period which is either a complete tax year or the UK or overseas portion of a split year (in this context it would, of course, be the UK portion of a split year).

The temporary period of non-residence, therefore, is the period from the end of the last period of sole UK residence to the start of the next period of sole UK residence. Depending on whether an individual qualifies for split-year treatment at the time of leaving the UK, and whether he is dual resident under a Treaty, the period of temporary non-residence may or may not follow tax years (see para **11.02** above). It may therefore include the UK part of the year of departure and arrival.

The 'year of departure' is defined in *para 114* and is the tax year consisting of or including period A (in other words, the tax year including the last period of sole UK residence). As noted in para **11.02** above, this may on occasion be the year before the individual actually leaves the UK.

The 'period of return' is defined in *para 115* as: 'the first residence period after period A for which the individual has sole UK residence'.

The period of return will therefore be the first whole tax year or UK part of a split year for which the individual has sole UK residence. Again, this may or may not be the tax year in which the individual actually returns to the UK (see para **11.02** above). Treating income and gains as arising in 'the period of return' means special legislation is likely to be needed in circumstances where there is a change in tax rate midyear (as happened with the CGT rate in the 2010/11 tax year) to determine the date on which the income/gains is/are treated as arising/accruing.

## The capital gains anti-avoidance rules

[**11.04**] The capital gains tax rules are, in substance, not very different to the previous legislation. *Part 4* of *Schedule 45, FA 2013* substitutes a new *s 10A* and *s 86A* and introduces a new *s 10AA* into *TCGA 1992*.

Where an individual meets the definition of 'temporarily non-resident' (see para **11.02** above) then any capital gains which would have accrued to him during the period of non-residence are instead treated as accruing to him 'in the period of return.'

Specifically, the individual will be taxed on capital gains which would accrue to him directly (ie on personally owned assets) but also on any capital gains which would be treated as accruing to him under *s 13* (as a participator in a non-resident close company) and under *s 86* (as settlor of a non-resident trust), *TCGA 1992*, but see below for more on trust gains. However, *s 10AA* provides that, with certain exceptions, the individual will not be taxed on gains on assets which he acquired during the period of non-residence.

Losses which accrue during the period of temporary non-residence are also treated as accruing in the period of return. However, *s 13* losses are restricted to those which would have been allowable had the individual been resident. They are therefore restricted on a tax year by tax year basis to the level of any *s 13* gains which would have accrued to the individual in that tax year.

Where *s 86* applies and gains which would ordinarily be attributed to the settlor arise in the non-resident period, these are attributed in the year of return. However, because the rules for offshore trust gains would allow such gains to have been attributed to beneficiaries in the interim period (under *s 87*), *s 86* provides that where this has happened, the gain ultimately attributed under *s 10A* will be reduced to the extent that those gains have been already matched under *s 87* but only to the extent that the beneficiaries have been charged to tax on the gains. Effectively, therefore, gains which have been matched on payments to non-UK resident beneficiaries, say, could still come back into charge. Draft legislation published on 13 September 2017 for inclusion in Finance Bill 2018, and effective from 6 April 2018, introduces new provisions for the taxation of settlement gains. This is part of the wider reform of the taxation of non domiciliaries (see **CHAPTER 15**). The proposed new rules increase the scope of the beneficiary charge to include recipients of onward gifts in some circumstances and consequential arrangements are to be made to *s 86A TCGA 1992* to take account of this. In addition the draft legislation proposes the abolition of the matching of gains to non-residents.

If the individual is a remittance basis user, personal foreign chargeable gains which are remitted during the period of non-residence will also be treated as remitted in the period of return (*s 10A(9)*).

With the introduction of the new deemed domicile rules (see **CHAPTER 15**), absent any transitional provisions, an individual within s 10A, who is deemed domiciled in the year of return, would be taxed on foreign chargeable gains realised in the period of temporary non-residence, without the benefit of the remittance basis. Paras 15 and 16, Sch 8 F (No 2) B 2017 provide that for a transitional period only, despite being deemed domiciled, the individual can claim the remittance basis to protect such gains.

# Income tax

**[11.05]** The SRT temporary non-residence rules do not operate to charge tax on a returning individual by reference to all income which arose during a period of non-residence. Instead, when the rules were drafted, certain types of income were identified as being high risk in the sense that large amounts of tax could potentially be avoided by becoming non-resident for short periods. These are:

- Certain pension payments (including lump sums)
- Distributions from close companies (and companies which would be close if they were UK resident)
- Chargeable event gains (in respect of life insurance policies)
- Offshore income gains

In addition, those taxable on the remittance basis who have made remittances of relevant foreign income during their period of non-residence will be treated as having remitted that income in the period of their return. This continues, with some amendments, the provisions introduced in *FA 2008*.

Temporary non-residence rules were already in place for some types of income (eg offshore income gains, pensions, remittances of relevant foreign income). However, *FA 2013* amended the legislation in respect of those particular types of income and introduces new temporary non-residence rules for additional categories of income.

## *Pension Income*

**[11.06]** The previous anti-avoidance legislation on pensions and lump sums was rewritten to make it consistent with the new temporary non-residence rules, but was essentially unchanged. However, some further legislation has been introduced to extend the temporary non-residence rules so that they will apply in more situations.

All the pensions anti-avoidance legislation (new and rewritten) operates in essentially the same way – so that where individuals receive or become entitled to receive amounts during the 'period of temporary non-residence' they will instead be treated as receiving or becoming entitled to receive them during their 'period of return' (see para **11.03** above for definition of period of temporary non-residence and period of return).

HMRC guidance RDR3 provides a list of the pension income affected (at 6.14):

'• Withdrawals from a flexible drawdown pension fund. This replaces and updates the existing temporary non-residence charge. EIM74050 contains detail of the rules.

• Certain lump sums paid under an employer-financed retirement benefit scheme ("EFRB"). EIM15010 contains detail of the rules.

• Certain steps comprising payment of a lump sum relevant benefit (or, for remittance basis users, the remittance of such a lump sum relevant benefit), comprising a "relevant step" for the purposes of the disguised remuneration rules.

• Certain lump sums paid by UK pension schemes in respect of which a charge on receipt is removed by a double taxation agreement. See EIM7040 for more information.

• Certain taxable property deemed income and gains of a pension scheme charged to tax on a scheme member. This replaces and updates the existing temporary non-residence charge. Detailed guidance will be provided in due course and a link to that guidance will appear here.'

## Dividends and other distributions

**[11.07]** These rules apply to dividends and other distributions from close companies (new *s 401C*, *s 413A* and *s 689A, ITTOIA 2005* and *s 812A, ITA 2007*) and to dividends from companies which would be close if they were UK resident (new *s 408A* and *s 689A, ITTOIA 2005*). Again, the rules operate to treat distributions arising in a period of temporary non-residence as arising in the period of return. Prior to 6 April 2016, and the abolition of tax credits on dividends, returnees would have been able to take account of notional tax credits.

The rules only apply where distributions are received by those who are 'material participators' in the company. Material participators are defined in *s 457, CTA 2010*, but essentially are those who, with or without associates, have an interest of more than 5% and those associated with such participators. 'Associate' is defined in *s 448, CTA 2010* and includes spouse or civil partner, parent, child and sibling as well as certain trusts and companies with which a participator has a connection.

Since individuals can be 'temporarily non-resident' either as a result of being non-UK resident for a period or as a result of being dual resident and Treaty resident in another country, the legislation which provides for the taxation of dividends and other distributions is lengthy. For example, an individual who is non-resident in the UK might be taxable in respect of UK dividends during the period of non-residence, but restricted to the level of the associated tax credit (up to 5 April 2016). Such an individual needs to be given credit for the notional tax on that dividend in the year of return (new *s 812A, ITA 2005*).

Alternatively, a UK resident individual may have paid full tax in respect of a UK dividend and received the benefit of the personal allowance – in such circumstances, the dividend would not come back into charge. An individual who is dual resident may be taxable in the UK in respect of a UK dividend, but pay tax at a reduced rate due to a double tax agreement. Such an individual is taxed in the year of return disregarding the Treaty provisions.

However, the overall effect of the various pieces of legislation is broadly the same in all cases, with distributions being treated as made in the year of return and credit given for any tax actually paid or notional tax treated as paid.

Where the distribution is a cash dividend or a stock dividend, the rules will not apply to the extent that the dividend relates to 'post departure trade profits.' Post departure trade profits are defined (in *s 401C, ITTOIA 2005*) as:

> '(a)  trade profits of the close company arising in an accounting period that begins after the start of the temporary period of non-residence, and
>
> (b)  so much of any trade profits of the close company arising in an accounting period that straddles the start of that temporary period as is attributable (on a just and reasonable basis) to a time after the start of that temporary period.'

Similar wording appears in *s 408A* and *s 413A, ITTOIA 2005*, although for foreign companies in *s 413A* the word 'close' is omitted. *Section 812A, ITTOIA 2005* also contains similar wording but here the phrase 'distributing' company is used.

In other words, the rules do not apply to distributions which arise from profits in a period of account beginning after the individual became non-resident or to distributions from profits in a period of account in the accounting period during which the individual became non-resident, to the extent that those profits arose after the start of the non-residence period.

The extent to which a dividend or stock dividend is to be treated as related to 'post departure trade profits' is to be 'determined on a just and reasonable basis.' It is not clear how an individual, especially an individual with a shareholding of just over 5 per cent, would self-assess the extent to which a dividend relates to post departure trade profits.

There will, of course, be some cases where the matter is obvious – perhaps because of a statement in the accounts – but there will equally be cases, particularly where a dividend relates to a period which 'straddles the start of that temporary period', where it is not at all clear.

HMRC promised that detailed guidance would be 'provided in due course' (RDR3 para 6.19). In the absence of such guidance in our first edition we suggested that where dividends relate to an accounting period during which the period of non-residence starts, if there is no detailed information available, an individual should assume that profits accrued on an even basis throughout the year and should time apportion the dividend on that basis. HMRC have now updated their guidance (still RDR 6.19) to say:

> 'HMRC will accept any just and reasonable attribution of dividends to post-departure profits that accords with the facts.'

Our suggestions therefore remain valid.

However, there may be occasions – for example, if exceptional profits arise as a result of the sale of a subsidiary, or similar – where individuals wish to argue that the profits did not accrue evenly. In such cases it will be important to provide evidence to this effect

For non-domiciled taxpayers to whom the remittance basis applies in the year of return, dividends received from non-UK companies and remitted to the UK in the temporary period of non-residence are treated as remitted in the period of return.

### Loans to participators

[**11.08**] A new s 420A has been added to *Chapter 6* of *Part 4* of *ITTOIA 2005* regarding the write off of loans to participators. Where a debt in respect of a loan to a participator is written off during a temporary period of non-residence and the individual would not otherwise be subject to tax, but would have been so subject had the write off occurred in the period of return, that debt is to be treated as though it is written off 'in the period of return'. This includes cases where the loan to the participator is not made during a period of residence (ie even if the loan itself is advanced after the individual has become non-resident).

### Gains from life insurance contracts

[**11.09**] Where a chargeable event gain arises on a life insurance policy during a period of non-residence and the individual would have been chargeable in respect of the gain had he been resident, that gain is treated as income of the individual for the year of return.

There are exceptions for chargeable events on death, gains on which personal representatives or UK trustees are liable (under ss 466 and 467, ITTOIA 2005) and gains which have been taxed on individuals under the transfer of assets abroad provisions. There is also an exception for gains treated as arising on an annual basis on personal portfolio bonds (under s 525, ITTOIA 2005). The rules also do not apply to a policy taken out in the temporary period of non-residence.

Chargeable event gains arise in the year of return if, on the assumption that the individual were resident when it arose, he would have been liable to tax. However, in calculating the quantum of the chargeable event gain, no such assumption should be made. This means that for foreign life insurance policies a reduction will be made under s 528, ITTOIA 2005 to the amount chargeable to tax. This reduction will be based on an apportionment of the gain to the number of days during the policy period for which the individual was non-resident.

### Remittances of income

[**11.10**] Temporary non-residence rules were introduced in relation to the remittance basis in FA 2008. FA 2013 replaces these rules (contained in s 832A, ITTOIA 2005). The revised s 832A provides that where relevant foreign income is remitted to the UK during a period of temporary non-residence, it will be treated as remitted during the period of return.

This is largely unchanged from the previous *s 832A* (apart from the terminology). However, the amended section also prevents double taxation arrangements from giving any relief from a charge. There is no change to this rule and no transitional provisions included within the proposed changes to the taxation of foreign domiciliaries. On these changes in general, see CHAPTER 15.

### Offshore income gains

**[11.11]** An offshore income gain that arises during a period of temporary non-residence is treated in a similar way to a capital gain. See para **11.04** above. However, it appears that there are currently no transitional provisions for offshore income gains realised in a period of temporary non-residence similar to the provisions for capital gains as set out in para **11.04** above.

## Conclusion

**[11.12]** The new anti-avoidance temporary non-residence rules are comprehensive and are likely to apply to many who are absent from the UK for short periods, even where there is no 'avoidance' motive or intention. Care will be needed to ensure as far as possible there are no unexpected tax charges.

# Chapter 12

# Double Tax Treaties

## Introduction

**[12.01]** There will be a number of situations, particularly in relation to split years on coming to or leaving the UK, where a taxpayer may be dual resident and so will need to consult a Tax Treaty in order to determine Treaty residence. In considering the tie-breaker test necessary to determine Treaty residence in the context of the SRT and considering the practical effect of Treaty residence, this chapter takes as its basis the OECD Model Treaty. Readers must check the specific Treaty relevant to their circumstances as that Treaty may differ from the OECD Model.

## Treaty residence – the tie-breaker test

**[12.02]** Assuming that the individual is resident in both the UK and the overseas country under the two countries' respective domestic laws, then it will be necessary to consider the tie-break provision of the relevant Treaty to determine in which country the individual is Treaty resident.

Each Treaty is unique and should be read with care. However, the majority of Treaties to which the UK is a party contain a tie-break clause similar to that in the OECD Model Treaty. The relevant article of the OECD Model Treaty is article 4:

'Article 4 Resident

1    For the purposes of this Convention, the term "resident of a Contracting State" means any person who, under the laws of that State, is liable to tax therein by reason of his domicile, residence, place of management or any other criterion of a similar nature, and also includes that State and any political subdivision or local authority thereof. This term, however, does not include any person who is liable to tax in that State in respect only of income from sources in that State or capital situated therein.

2    Where by reason of the provisions of paragraph 1 an individual is a resident of both Contracting States, then his status shall be determined as follows:

(a)    he shall be deemed to be a resident only of the State in which he has a permanent home available to him; if he has a permanent home available to him in both States, he shall be deemed to be a resident only of the State with which his personal and economic relations are closer (centre of vital interests);

(b)    if the State in which he has his centre of vital interests cannot be determined, or if he has not a permanent home available to him in either State, he shall be deemed to be a resident only of the State in which he has an habitual abode;

(c)    if he has an habitual abode in both States or in neither of them, he shall

be deemed to be a resident only of the State of which he is a national;
(d)    if he is a national of both States or of neither of them, the competent authorities of the Contracting States shall settle the question by mutual agreement.'

So, assuming that an individual is resident in both countries under domestic law, one must work through each of the tests in order until a conclusion is reached. First, one must consider whether the individual has a permanent home in either state. If the individual has a home in both states (for example, he is not within the split-year cases under which he has 'ceased to have any home in the UK' or 'begun to have an only home in the UK'), then one considers the state in which he has his centre of vital interests, ie the country with which he has the most personal and economic connections. If it is not possible to distinguish a country from this test, one looks to the country in which he has his habitual abode and finally to the country of which he is a national.

In considering the 'permanent home' part of the tie breaker, however, it should be noted that an individual may theoretically have a home in both countries for the purpose of the SRT but only one 'permanent home' under the Treaty. In relation to 'permanent home', the OECD commentary states:

'This home must be permanent, that is to say, the individual must have arranged and retained it for his permanent use as opposed to staying at a particular place under such conditions that it is evident that the stay is intended to be of short duration.

As regards the concept of home, it should be observed that any form of home may be taken into account (house or apartment belonging to or rented by the individual, rented furnished room). But the permanence of the home is essential; this means that the individual has arranged to have the dwelling available to him at all times continuously, and not occasionally for the purpose of a stay which, owing to the reasons for it, is necessarily of short duration (travel for pleasure, business travel, educational travel, attending a course at a school, etc.)'

(Commentary on article 4, paras 12f.)

This definition is very similar to the definition of home for the purpose of the SRT. However, HMRC in their guidance (Annex A, para A5) seek to distinguish the two terms:

'A5.    The concept of home as described in this guidance relates only to the SRT. The guidance does not apply for the purpose of applying the residence Article under a double taxation arrangement. Double taxation agreements have additional qualifiers that are not included as part of the SRT and so the two terms do not have the same meaning.'

Nevertheless, in most cases it is suggested that where an individual has a SRT home, he is likely to have a permanent home for the purposes of the tie-breaker test.

The meaning of 'accommodation' for the sufficient ties test is far wider and accommodation will commonly not be a tie-breaker permanent home (eg a hotel room, even if available continuously for 91 days may be accommodation but is unlikely to constitute a tie-breaker permanent home). Nevertheless, there may be occasions where the two are the same and each case should be considered on its own merits.

The interpretation of the tie-breaker tests is not straightforward, especially when it comes to testing the centre of vital interests. This is partly because personal and economic interests can be spread across jurisdictions. In addition, the test can give different results at different stages of an individual's life. For example, family is likely to be a more significant factor for an individual who is married with young children than it is for someone who is single, or married with adult children (for whom the location of the spouse is likely to be relevant, but location of children will be much less so).

Nevertheless, for many individuals who are moving to the UK the point at which they give up a permanent home in their home country or at which their family moves to join them will usually be ascertainable. This may give a different date at which they become UK resident than that under the SRT and, where it gives the taxpayer a better answer, he may wish to claim a Treaty position rather than taking the domestic law outcome.

### Example 12.1: Marie-France

Marie-France moves to London from her native Paris on 30 June 2016 to take up a three-year assignment with a local employer. Although her family are also to move with her, her husband and two young children remain in Paris until September 2016 as she is anxious to avoid any disruption to their schooling and spends much of the summer holiday in France rather than the UK.

Marie-France may well become UK tax resident under domestic law as soon as she starts work in the UK under Case 5. However, she is likely to remain tax resident in France while she retains her home there, is travelling back a lot and her family remain there.

The UK/France Tax Treaty has a similar tie-breaker test to the OECD Model. Applying it to Marie-France, it is likely that she will have a permanent home in both the UK and France but that until September 2016 either her centre of vital interests or habitual abode will be France. Therefore, she is likely to be Tax Treaty resident in France until September 2016 and only become UK Tax Treaty resident once her family move to the UK and she ceases to spend so much time in France.

As the example of Marie-France illustrates, the country in which an individual is resident under the tie-breaker article of a Treaty may alter during the course of the tax year. However, a UK national who has been UK resident for some time is more likely to be UK resident under the tie-breaker than an individual who is non-UK domiciled or a national of another state, has only been UK resident for a short period and is returning to their country of origin. The position will also vary depending on the destination country, since some countries will quite quickly treat an individual as tax resident there while, in others, acquiring such a status will take some time. It goes without saying that an individual must be resident in the destination country as well as the UK in order to be Treaty resident in that country.

It should be remembered that should the individual be resident in their destination country under the tie-breaker this will not prevent their being UK resident under domestic law. So, for example, an individual who is tie-broken to his destination country may remain resident in the UK for the purpose of counting years for the remittance charge in *s 809C, ITA 2007*. However, it will entitle them to be treated as a resident of their destination country for the purpose of applying the Treaty and this may entitle them to relief or exemption from UK taxation on a number of sources of income and gains. Each Treaty is unique in its operation and will need careful study to determine the level of relief available. See paras **12.03–12.06** below.

## Application of the Treaty

[**12.03**] The effect of Treaty residence will depend on the specific Article that applies to the item concerned. The OECD model lists 31 Articles, which include Articles setting out the taxation of business profits, interest, dividends, capital gains, employment income, income from property and government service, amongst others. It also includes an 'other income' Article, which is a feature of most Treaties and typically will allocate taxing rights on any type of income not covered under one of the specific Articles of the Treaty concerned.

Taxing rights may be apportioned between the contracting states, may be allocated solely to the country of residence or country of source, or may be subject to more complex rules, depending on the type of income/gain concerned. To illustrate this, the sections below consider an OECD Model Article that may be taken as indicative of the way in which a Treaty would apply in each case.

Where the taxpayer is Treaty non-resident, the Treaty will normally override the taxation rights as arrived at under domestic law. In some circumstances UK domestic law may prevent the application of the Treaty, particularly in anti-avoidance legislation. In applying some Treaties the UK's remittance basis can introduce an additional complication, as Treaty benefits can be denied where income or gains have not been remitted to the UK. A detailed consideration of this issue is outside the scope of this chapter.

### Exclusive taxing rights

[**12.04**] Where a particular Article grants an exclusive taxing right to either the taxpayer's country of Treaty residence, or the source country for the income, the other contracting state may not tax the item because the Treaty exempts it for that state. An example is the Pensions Article, which will normally allow exclusive taxing rights for the country of residence of the taxpayer, though the taxing rights may instead rest with the country of residence of the pension fund. The OECD Model says:

'Article 18 – Pensions

Subject to the provisions of paragraph 2 of Article 19, pensions and other similar remuneration paid to a resident of a Contracting State in consideration of past employment shall be taxable only in that State.'

Paragraph 2 of Article 19 covers pensions paid in respect of Government service.

So what does this mean in practice for a taxpayer who is dual tax resident in the UK and Switzerland, but Treaty resident in Switzerland, and who is drawing a UK pension? The relevant paragraph of the pensions Article in the UK/Swiss Treaty follows the typical pattern:

'Article 18 – Pensions

1.  Subject to the provisions of paragraph 2 of Article 19, pensions and other similar remuneration paid to an individual who is a resident of a Contracting State, shall be taxable only in that State.'

The taxpayer will need to provide HMRC with confirmation from the Swiss tax authorities that he is regarded as a Swiss tax resident. Assuming that HMRC agree he is Treaty resident in Switzerland, they will issue an NT or no tax code to the pension provider so that the pension can be paid without deduction of tax at source.

It is also common for the 'Other income' Article to give exclusive taxing rights to the taxpayer's country of Treaty residence. This Article does not just apply to types of income without a specific Article, but also to third country income. The OECD Model says:

'Article 21 – Other Income

1.  Items of income of a resident of a Contracting State, wherever arising, not dealt with in the foregoing Articles of this Convention shall be taxable only in that State.

2.  The provisions of paragraph 1 shall not apply to income, other than income from immovable property as defined in paragraph 2 of Article 6, if the recipient of such income, being a resident of a Contracting State, carries on business in the other Contracting State through a permanent establishment situated therein and the right or property in respect of which the income is paid is effectively connected with such permanent establishment. In such case the provisions of Article 7 shall apply.'

## Treaty limitation/apportionment

**[12.05]** The way in which taxing rights may be apportioned under a Treaty will depend on the Article concerned. For example, an interest Article will normally allow interest income to be taxed in the state of residence of the beneficial owner and in the source state from which it is paid, but will set a cap on the maximum tax rate that can be applied in the state of source. A dividend Article will generally operate in a very similar way.

So a taxpayer who is UK tax resident but a Treaty resident of another contracting state may still pay UK tax on his UK source investment income, but the extent to which the UK can tax that income may be limited by the Treaty in force.

It should be noted that where the dividend or interest income is not sourced in the other contracting state, it will not be subject to these clauses, but to the other income Article as explained above.

Similarly, the employment income Article will normally allow for an apportionment of earnings (although in limited circumstances a complete exemption from tax in the Treaty non-resident state may be available). The OECD Model Article says:

'Article 15 – Income from Employment

1. Subject to the provisions of Articles 16, 18 and 19, salaries, wages and other similar remuneration derived by a resident of a Contracting State in respect of an employment shall be taxable only in that State unless the employment is exercised in the other Contracting State. If the employment is so exercised, such remuneration as is derived therefrom may be taxed in that other State.

2. Notwithstanding the provisions of paragraph 1, remuneration derived by a resident of a Contracting State in respect of an employment exercised in the other Contracting State shall be taxable only in the first-mentioned State if:

   (a) the recipient is present in the other State for a period or periods not exceeding in the aggregate 183 days in any twelve month period commencing or ending in the fiscal year concerned, and

   (b) the remuneration is paid by, or on behalf of, an employer who is not a resident of the other State, and

   (c) the remuneration is not borne by a permanent establishment which the employer has in the other State.

3. Notwithstanding the preceding provisions of this Article, remuneration derived in respect of an employment exercised aboard a ship or aircraft operated in international traffic, or aboard a boat engaged in inland waterways transport, may be taxed in the Contracting State in which the place of effective management of the enterprise is situated.'

Under UK domestic law a taxpayer who is UK resident and domiciled will be taxable on all his earnings, regardless of where he has worked on a given day. However, if he is also resident and Treaty resident in, say, Spain, he can use the Tax Treaty to limit the UK's right to tax him. In this circumstance he can apply paragraph (1) of the Employment Income Article to limit his UK tax liability on remuneration to tax on remuneration derived from UK workdays. Article 14(1) of the UK/Spain Treaty is as follows:

'(1) Subject to the provisions of Articles 15, 17 and 18, salaries, wages and other similar remuneration derived by a resident of a Contracting State in respect of an employment shall be taxable only in that State unless the employment is exercised in the other Contracting State. If the employment is so exercised, such remuneration as is derived therefrom may be taxed in that other State.'

So if the employee has 250 workdays, 50 of which are in the UK, the UK will only be permitted to tax $1/5^{th}$ (50/250 days) of his remuneration because that is the extent to which his remuneration derives from exercising his employment in the UK. In the right set of circumstances, Article 14(2) might apply to exempt this income from UK tax altogether, but a detailed consideration of the principles relevant for this is outside the scope of this work.

## *More complex provisions*

**[12.06]** Generally, the (more) complicated alternatives to the above will be found in specific Treaties, as it is the inherent difficulties in two countries reaching a formal agreement that tends to drive the complexity. That said, a typical capital gains tax Article sets out quite complex rules because much depends on the location and nature of the asset concerned. The OECD Model Article reads as follows:

'Article 13 — Capital Gains

1. Gains derived by a resident of a Contracting State from the alienation of

immovable property referred to in Article 6 and situated in the other Contracting State may be taxed in that other State.

2. Gains from the alienation of movable property forming part of the business property of a permanent establishment which an enterprise of a Contracting State has in the other Contracting State, including such gains from the alienation of such a permanent establishment (alone or with the whole enterprise), may be taxed in that other State.

3. Gains from the alienation of ships or aircraft operated in international traffic, boats engaged in inland waterways transport or movable property pertaining to the operation of such ships, aircraft or boats, shall be taxable only in the Contracting State in which the place of effective management of the enterprise is situated.

4. Gains derived by a resident of a Contracting State from the alienation of shares deriving more than 50 per cent of their value directly or indirectly from immovable property situated in the other Contracting State may be taxed in that other State.

5. Gains from the alienation of any property, other than that referred to in paragraphs 1, 2, 3 and 4, shall be taxable only in the Contracting State of which the alienator is a resident.'

Here, it is a question of considering which part of the relevant Article applies and then concluding on its effects.

## Example 12.2: George

George is UK domiciled and a long-term UK tax resident, but in 2013 is sent on assignment to Paris for four years. He remains UK tax resident throughout his assignment, but Treaty tie-breaks to France for its duration.

In year two he is given an award of shares in the parent company of his employing company, which is a quoted US entity. George pays income tax in France on the award, but not in the UK, because at the time of the award and throughout the period over which it is sourced, he was not undertaking any UK duties.

George retains the award for a year and then sells the shares shortly before he returns to the UK in October 2017, when he is still Treaty resident in France.

The relevant Article in the UK/France Double Tax Treaty is reproduced below:

'Article 14 — Capital Gains

1. Gains derived from the alienation of immovable property referred to in Article 6 and situated in a Contracting State may be taxed in that State.

2. Gains derived from the alienation of:
   (a) shares, other than those regularly traded on an approved Stock Exchange, or rights deriving their value or the greater part of their value directly or indirectly from immovable property referred to in Article 6 and situated in a Contracting State; or
   (b) an interest in a partnership or trust the assets of which consist principally of immovable property referred to in Article 6 and situated in a Contracting State, or of shares or rights referred to in sub-paragraph (a) of this paragraph;

   may be taxed in the State in which the immovable property is situated.

3. Gains from the alienation of movable property forming part of the business property of a permanent establishment which an enterprise of a Contracting State has in the

other Contracting State, including such gains from the alienation of such a permanent establishment (alone or together with the whole enterprise), may be taxed in the other State.

4.  Gains derived by a resident of a Contracting State from the alienation of ships, aircraft or railway vehicles operated in international traffic by that resident and gains derived by that resident from the alienation of movable property pertaining to the operation of such ships, aircraft or railway vehicles shall be taxable only in that State.

5.  Gains from the alienation of any property other than that referred to in paragraphs 1, 2, 3 and 4 shall be taxable only in the Contracting State of which the alienator is a resident.

6.  The provisions of paragraph 5 shall not affect the right of a Contracting State to levy according to its law a tax chargeable in respect of gains from the alienation of any property on a person who is, and has been at any time during the previous six fiscal years, a resident of that Contracting State or on a person who is a resident of that Contracting State at any time during the fiscal year in which the property is alienated.'

George's shares do not fall within Article 14(2)(a) because they are quoted shares, and, as they do not fall within any of paras (1), (2), (3) or (4), para (5) will apply and the gain will be taxable solely in France, the country in which he is Treaty resident on disposal. However, para (6) also applies, because George has been UK tax resident throughout the previous six years, and so the UK may charge tax on the gain on his share disposal, as it can make such a charge under domestic law, but only when he returns to sole UK residence. Credit will normally be allowed for French taxes paid on the same gain but, if the UK tax rate applying is higher, George will have additional tax to pay.

If George claims the protection of the Treaty, the gain is likely to be taxed under the temporary non-resident rules in the UK tax year in which he resumes sole UK tax residence. If he does not, he would simply pay capital gains tax on the disposal of his shares when he sells them. This may or may not give him a better answer, depending on other gains likely to be assessed, the availability of capital losses and his marginal tax rate for capital gains tax in the year that he resumes sole UK tax residence. In circumstances where a capital gain is involved, care will be needed to determine whether or not a Treaty claim is likely to be beneficial.

# Conclusion

**[12.07]** The starting point in determining an individual's residence status is the domestic law. Where a taxpayer is UK tax resident under the SRT, a Tax Treaty cannot change this but, where the taxpayer tie-breaks to the other Treaty country, the Tax Treaty can mitigate the UK tax implications.

It is possible that the complexity of the SRT split-year rules may mean that taxpayers decide not to struggle to fall within them, but instead to accept UK residence for a whole tax year and rely on the Treaty tie-breaker for the period of dual residence. In some circumstances, Treaty non-residence may give the same tax result as complete non-residence. However, this will not always be the case (eg with employment income, Treaty non-residence will generally be similar to domestic law non-residence in terms of how earnings are assessed, but can be different where the two contracting states disagree about the period over which a particular item, such as a bonus, has been earned as this may also lead them to disagree about which state has the taxing rights).

Where the Treaty will give a less generous result, the taxpayer may wish to undertake the full analysis to substantiate a complete non-residence position. Nevertheless, tax Treaties will play an important role under the SRT.

# Chapter 13

# Record-keeping

## Introduction

**[13.01]** Record-keeping has always been an essential part of documenting one's residence position. Generally, those seeking to claim that they were non-UK resident have always been advised to keep records of flights (or ferries/trains) in and out of the country (in the form of boarding passes/tickets/passport stamps) as well as detailed diaries of working days in the UK and overseas.

Although in many ways the SRT adds clarity and certainty to the task of determining residence, it does this by imposing a more rigid structure on residence, such that there are now a number of definite lines which, if crossed, will potentially have a significant impact on an individual's residence status. It will now commonly no longer be sufficient to have a record of the number of days spent in the UK (and elsewhere) as there will also be other areas for which clear records will be necessary. Time (including hours) spent working (both in the UK and overseas) is the obvious example, but also the number of days spent in each property and the number of days spent with UK resident children may also be significant.

The HMRC guidance, RDR3, includes some detail of the kinds of records which HMRC consider important as providing evidence for certain purposes – in particular, home, working hours and location, and the sufficient ties tests (see **CHAPTER 7** of the RDR3). It will be essential to maintain as much evidence as possible in a number of areas, but the level and type of evidence needed will depend to some extent on the level of certainty with which an individual might be considered to meet the test – for example, an individual who spends only four days working in the UK is less likely to be required to provide evidence than someone who spends 39 days.

Keeping all of the evidence suggested in the HMRC guidance would prove impossible for most people and a degree of pragmatism may be needed in some cases. However, the more evidence that is retained, the easier it will be to resist any challenge from HMRC (and for HMRC enquiries under the SRT, see para **13.11**). This chapter is intended to explore some of the evidence which it would be advisable to keep for some of the significant tests under the SRT and the relative importance of different types of evidence. Nevertheless, the lists will not be exhaustive and the type and extent of evidence needed will depend on an individual's personal circumstances.

## Days of presence in the UK

**[13.02]** Record-keeping for days of presence in the UK has always been essential. For those who travel frequently or for whom days spent in the UK are very close to a significant limit, record-keeping will be particularly essential. HMRC guidance includes details of records needed for day counting purposes under the 'sufficient ties' test, but in fact most individuals who need to consider the SRT (ie those for whom residence is not totally obvious) will need a record of their travel to and from the UK. The guidance (see para 7.6 of RDR3) suggests the following:

'• In which countries you have spent your days and midnights, for example:
    – your travel details,
    – booking information, or
    – tickets, and boarding cards.
  • If you left the UK to live or work abroad:
    – the date you left the UK,
    – visa or work permit applications, etc. if you had to make them,
    – contracts of employment.
  • If you come to live or work in the UK;
    – the date you arrive here,
    – visa or work permit applications,
    – documentation relating to you taking up employment or ceasing your previous employment.
  • When you were present at your home or homes, or other available accommodation.
  • How long you owned or rent those homes, for example when you purchased, sold or leased those homes.
  • The time your home was unavailable for your use, for example because it was rented out.'

Nowadays it is common for tickets to be provided electronically by email or as downloads and in such cases it should be relatively straightforward to keep a record. In some cases passport stamps will be useful, but EU citizens travelling within the EU are unlikely to have such a record.

Keeping a record of midnights could be done in the form of a diary note, which should be updated as close to the actual dates as possible.

Where an individual spends days in the UK due to exceptional circumstances, they will need some additional records to support this – HMRC actually include details of the records they expect to support a claim for exceptional circumstances in their list of record-keeping requirements for full-time working (para 7.5, RDR3):

'• Time you had to spend in the UK owing to exceptional circumstances:
    – what your circumstances were,
    – what you did to mitigate them where that was possible, for example making alternative travel arrangements.'

Depending on the circumstances which lead to the additional days, an individual may be able to obtain evidence in the form of a doctor's note or a claim to an insurance company. They may have evidence of having to rearrange travel – for example, moving a flight or re-booking train tickets or arranging temporary accommodation. On occasion, the exceptional circumstances may affect sufficient numbers of people so that there will be no dispute and in such cases HMRC usually publish information on their website (for example, as in the case of the volcanic ash cloud in 2010). In such circumstances it will still be advisable to keep a printed record of HMRC published policy.

It is also worth noting that the courts have historically had little sympathy with taxpayers who have not maintained appropriate records. As an example, note the observation of the Special Commissioner in *Barrett v Revenue and Customs Comrs* 2007 SpC 639, [2008] STC (SCD) 268:

> 'Mr Barrett did not have copies of the aeroplane tickets for his trip when he left the UK on what was claimed was a "distinct break" in the pattern of his life. He did not have any boarding pass or similar documents or other evidence despite having paid for high powered advice on leaving the UK for tax reasons. I find this surprising to say the least. I would have expected him to keep any evidence to mark this change and support his case if challenged.'

# Home

**[13.03]** Where an individual spends time in more than one property, or there is a possibility that more than one property could be considered a 'home,' he will need evidence both to demonstrate the substance and quality of his occupation of the property and to demonstrate the number of days he spends there (time spent in the property need not be overnight for the purpose of the 'home' test).

HMRC guidance (at para 7.2, RDR3) provides an extensive list of records which should be kept in order to provide evidence for the purpose of the 'home' test:

'• General overheads – utility bills which may demonstrate that you have been present in that home, for example, telephone bills or energy bills, which demonstrate usage commensurate with living in the property.
• TV/satellite/cable subscriptions.
• Local parking permits.
• Membership of clubs, for example sports, health or social clubs.
• Mobile phone usage and bills pointing to your presence in a country.
• Lifestyle purchases pointing to you spending time in your home – for example, purchases of food, flowers and meals out.
• Presence of your spouse, partner or children.
• Engagement of domestic staff or an increase in their hours.
• Home security arrangements.
• Increases in maintenance costs or the frequency of maintenance, for example having your house cleaned more frequently.
• Insurance documents relating to that home.
• SORN notification that a vehicle in the UK is "off road".
• Re-directed mail requests.
• The address to which you have personal post sent.
• The address to which your driving licence is registered.
• Bank accounts and credit cards linked to your address and statements which show payments made to utility companies.
• Evidence of local municipal taxes being paid.
• Registration, at your address, with local medical practitioners.

- What private medical insurance cover you have, is it an international policy?
- Credit card and bank statements which indicate the pattern and place of your day by day expenditure.'

This is an extensive list, and it is extremely unlikely that many individuals would be able to produce everything on it! These records are intended to indicate either quality of occupation (the property being the emotional centre – flowers, club, family – etc) or time spent there (utility bills, cleaning costs etc). As a result, different records will be significant for individuals with different circumstances.

In some circumstances, the existence, or lack, of some kinds of evidence may prove to be of limited relevance – for example, an individual is unlikely to be registered with a local medical practitioner or be a member of a gym if he only spends 30 days at a given home. In such cases, utility bills may well be of increased relevance, as will evidence from phone bills (including mobile phone bills) and cash machine withdrawals or credit card and bank statements which evidence expenditure in nearby shops/restaurants. Although HMRC suggests retaining records of what it terms 'lifestyle purchases', in practice very few people are likely to keep receipts when they purchase flowers. However, bank and credit card statements may be helpful for reconstructing such purchases if evidence is later required.

Where an individual has a limited presence at a property, evidence of the quality of his occupation is likely to take on additional significance – in order to prove that the property should be considered a 'home' and not merely 'available accommodation'. The nature of this evidence will vary from individual to individual, but in some cases the membership of nearby clubs may be relevant. It is not included on HMRC's list but, potentially, evidence of home improvements or the purchase of furniture may be of relevance in demonstrating that a property is an individual's home (especially where large or expensive items are purchased, since these might demonstrate the degree of permanence needed for a property to be considered a 'home'). Individuals may also find it useful to retain evidence of previous long-term occupation (eg utility bills, etc) since HMRC guidance suggests that it is difficult for a property to cease to be a 'home' when it has once been one.

Although a case about CGT Private Residence relief rather than 'home', the first tier tribunal case of *Regan v Revenue and Customs Comrs (No 2)* [2012] UKFTT 570 (TC), [2013] SWTI 198 is instructive for the kinds of evidence which a court may consider in trying to determine whether a property is an individual's 'home.' In this case, the court looked at where post was sent (putting particular emphasis on correspondence from HMRC), evidence of the appellant's registered address on the electoral roll and whether the appellant entered into any credit agreements from the address as well as considering where he kept his things. In another private residence case of 2015 before the first tier tribunal, *William P Harrison v HMRC* [2015] UKFTT 0539 (TC), the taxpayer owned a farmhouse which he considered to be his main residence and also made main residence elections on several flats, which he claimed to be 'second residences'. He failed in his claims, the tribunal distinguishing between 'occupation' and 'residence'. Although he kept a change of clothes and cooking utensils 'sufficient to function' at the flats, he had no television, telephone or computer and did all his paperwork at the farmhouse. Such things were considered important to make a property a residence. The case of *Mr Paul Favell* [2010] UKFTT 360 (TC) is also similarly instructive. In this case, the individual concerned had not retained any utility bills or similar records and was not therefore able to satisfy the burden of proof that the property which he claimed to be his main residence was indeed occupied as a residence. Although for private residence relief the court was considering a different test from 'home', the HMRC guidance quoted above suggests similar evidence will be used in the latter case.

It will be particularly difficult to provide evidence in cases where the character of an individual's occupation of a property changes (for example, from a 'holiday home' to a 'home' or from available accommodation to a 'home').

HMRC guidance (RDR3, para 7.4) includes an additional note in relation to a 'holiday home' becoming a 'home':

'Where your home has changed from a holiday home to your home, for the purposes of the SRT, the change in occupation could be evidenced by, amongst other things:

- utility bills which may show an increase in usage
- changes you have notified to:
  - local municipal authorities, or
  - the company providing your buildings and contents insurance.'

Although HMRC guidance does not appear to consider that a home could cease to be a 'home' and become a 'holiday home', where an individual wishes to claim that it has done so (see para **8.18**), presumably similar evidence would be useful. Certainly one might expect to notify one's insurance company if the property is to be left empty for prolonged periods. It would also be advisable for an individual to document his intention to change the use of the property and, where relevant, keep records of any requests to redirect mail and other changes of registered address – for example, with banks, on driving licenses etc. Where belongings are moved from such a property, evidence of this – eg van hire, removal company invoices – should also be retained.

Where available accommodation begins to be a home, this is also a qualitative change and useful evidence might include evidence of removal costs – where additional belongings are transferred to the property, or the purchase of (relatively) expensive furniture. Evidence of decorating and other home improvements (either professional or DIY) might also be useful as it may indicate a stronger level of emotional investment in a property. At the point when temporary accommodation begins to be an individual's home, in some cases he may register with a doctor/dentist, arrange for his post to be redirected, and/or take out a subscription to satellite television. However, this kind of evidence may not be available in circumstances where an individual has more than one property which could be considered a home.

# Working hours and location of work done

**[13.04]** Record-keeping for those working full-time abroad or full-time in the UK will be particularly onerous. This will be especially so for those who frequently travel between the UK and an overseas location and perform duties of their employment in both locations.

HMRC suggest (at para 7.5, RDR3) that the following records should be kept by those whose residence status is determined by the automatic tests relating to working full-time in the UK or overseas:

'•   The split in your working life between the UK and overseas, particularly noting days where you worked (including training, being on stand-by and travelling) for more or less than three hours.
•   The nature and duration of your work activities – a work diary/calendar or timesheet is likely to indicate this. You may find that it would be beneficial to ensure your diary is sufficiently detailed, maybe reflecting hours worked and the nature of your work, for example reviewing and responding to emails, meetings, or filing travel claims.
•   Breaks you had from working, for example between jobs, and why
•   Your periods of annual, sick or parenting leave.
•   Time you spend visiting dependent children (those under the age of 18) when they are in the UK.
•   Time you had to spend in the UK owing to exceptional circumstances:
    –   what your circumstances were,
    –   what you did to mitigate them where that was possible, for example making alternative travel arrangements.
•   Your contracts of employment, and documentation/communications which relate to these, particularly to curtailment or extension of these or other changes to them.'

Not all of these records will be relevant to proving that an individual was working full-time overseas or in the UK – for example, an individual who is automatically non-UK resident due to meeting the full-time working abroad criteria will not need to be concerned with the time spent visiting dependent children, since this is only likely to be of relevance for the family tie under the sufficient ties test.

Documentation regarding days spent in the UK will be of relevance for many people who have cause to consider their residence position, as will evidence of days spent in the UK for exceptional circumstances and will not be restricted to those claiming to be non-UK resident by reason of full-time working abroad. Record-keeping for days in the UK and for exceptional circumstances is dealt with under 'Days of presence in the UK' (see para **13.02** above).

For those employed abroad or in the UK, what will be of significance is a copy of an employment contract and any other documentation evidencing an individual's duties and responsibilities, hours an employee is expected to work and details of their entitlement to annual leave, parenting leave and any other leave entitlements. Any time that a new contract is issued, or there are any other changes made to the terms and conditions of an employment, evidence of these changes should be retained.

In addition to this, individuals will need to keep detailed records of their working practices. The level of detail required will vary depending on the nature and pattern of an individual's work. For example, if an individual does shift work and always works an eight-hour shift, it may be sufficient for them simply to record working and non-working days (in the case of non-working days, they may also wish to record whether this represents holiday or other leave). However, for most internationally mobile employees, the number of hours worked will vary day to day and will need to be recorded on a contemporaneous basis. It would be advisable for such individuals to keep a detailed diary and to note down the hours worked at the end of each day. Where individuals work in professions which keep timesheets, such timesheets should be retained (and individuals should aim to ensure that all working time is recorded, or where it is not, a separate record kept). For those who do not have timesheets, any diaries with records of meetings etc should be retained. Expense claims are also likely to be useful for helping to prove the country in which work is performed (ie where claims are made in relation to work travel).

The importance of record-keeping for those working full-time overseas is shown in the case of *Hankinson v Revenue and Customs Comrs (No 2)* [2009] UKFTT 384 (TC), [2010] SWTI 1368. As well as considering the days for which Mr Hankinson was available for work, the court looked at evidence of the work actually undertaken by Mr Hankinson overseas and in the UK. The case demonstrates the importance which will be placed on evidence of meetings attended and diary notes of work actually performed when the position is in dispute.

The three-hour work rule – where a day is counted as a working day where an individual has worked for more than three hours – may require additional record-keeping. For example, if an individual for whom counting UK work days is important responds to emails while on leave in the UK, he will need to record the time spent doing this. He may also, where possible, wish to retain evidence of other (non-work related) activities that day, to support the fact that he did not work more than three hours. This can be particularly important where an individual is responding to emails on a Blackberry® or similar device and could therefore be said to have been 'working' all day, but may in fact have only worked for five or ten lots of five minutes each. The more detailed the records an individual keeps, the easier it will be to respond to a challenge from HMRC that the individual was working.

Where individuals take leave, this should be recorded in their detailed work diary, along with the type of leave (eg holiday, sick leave, parenting leave). If the particular amount of leave an individual takes is unusually long (eg if they take additional leave because of sickness, or to care for children), they may wish to retain some evidence of the reason for this, eg doctor's note or information from a school, day care provider. If an individual has had to apply to his employer for parenting leave, he should keep a copy of the application and any approval of it.

In their more general guidance to residence, domicile and the remittance basis (RDR1), HMRC indicate records that may be required by individuals working in the UK and overseas, to enable them to identify earnings received for duties carried out in the UK. The following are listed as examples of records which may be required (para 12.15, RDR1):

- Business diaries which show where duties were performed and the nature of duties performed.
- Business emails.
- Time-sheets.

- Expenses claims and receipts for the reimbursement of expenses including travel costs incurred during an overseas visit.
- Travel itineraries.
- Boarding cards for flights in and out of the UK.
- Telephone records.

HMRC have provided further guidance during an enquiry into UK work days. In addition to what has been noted above from official publications, they have recommended that records include:

- Hours spent out of the office when in the UK
- Travel time records, eg when the taxpayer arrives at a UK airport and the time taken to travel to the office
- Mobile phone records, noting the purpose of each call which does not relate to work duties
- Records of all travel and the purpose, particularly where paid for by the employer
- Copies of all expense claims and details of the use of a corporate credit card while in the UK, including the reasons for the expense and whether this is linked to private or work affairs

Clearly not all of these will be needed in each case, but this demonstrates the depth of enquiries a taxpayer can expect should HMRC decide to enquire into their UK work days.

## Sufficient ties

**[13.05]** For those who are neither automatically non-UK resident nor automatically UK resident and need to consider their residence position under the sufficient ties test, HMRC provides (at para 7.6, RDR3) a single long list of the records needed. There is no breakdown of which records would be relevant for which test.

Obviously, for anyone needing to apply the sufficient ties test, the day count will be crucial and the evidence needed to support day counts is dealt with above (see para **13.02**).

Leaving aside the evidence of days of presence, the remainder of the HMRC list of suggested documentation is:

- If you left the UK to live or work abroad:
  - the date you left the UK,
  - visa or work permit applications, etc if you had to make them,
  - contracts of employment.
- If you come to live or work in the UK:
  - the date you arrive here,
  - visa or work permit applications,
  - documentation relating to you taking up employment or ceasing your previous employment.
- When you were present at your home or homes, or other available accommodation.
- How long you owned or rented those homes, for example when you purchased, sold or leased those homes.

- The time your home was unavailable for your use, for example because it was rented out.'

In fact, it is difficult to see how some of this evidence would assist in demonstrating that particular ties were met or not met, and some of this evidence appears more geared towards either proving the relevant date in cases where the split-year treatment applies (eg the date you arrive, work permits) or even that there has been a distinct break from the UK (which is no longer of relevance under the SRT).

## Family tie

[13.06] Where an individual has UK resident children, he will need evidence of the time which he has spent with those children – since he will need to spend 61 days with the child in the UK in a tax year for a UK resident child to be a family tie. The only evidence likely to be available in most cases will be the individual's own diary notes. However, for some there may be information recorded in a visitor's book at a boarding school. Where an individual spends a night in the family home, where the child usually lives, this is likely to be assumed by HMRC to mean that they have seen the child on two days. If the child is away or the individual does not see the child for some other reason, they may wish to retain some evidence of this – for example, if the child is on a school trip, there may be letters to this effect. If the child is staying with friends, it may be that a diary note will have to suffice.

Where children are in the UK for education, it will be necessary to retain evidence of their days of presence in the UK to help determine their UK residence (see para 13.02 above). A record should also be kept of school term dates (for example, if these are communicated by letters from the school) and the days spent in the UK outside term time.

Where an individual has a UK resident partner, there will be no need to keep records with regard to children as he or she will already have the family tie.

## Accommodation tie

[13.07] Those who need to consider the accommodation tie will want to retain records to show where they have spent the night while in the UK. A diary note of nights spent in particular properties, updated on a contemporaneous basis, will be a minimum requirement. Any other evidence of nights in particular accommodation may also prove useful – for example, phone and utility bills, evidence of local purchases, dining in restaurants, etc.

Once a property has been occupied for even a single night, it can be considered available accommodation provided it has been available for occupation for at least 91 days (with the exception of accommodation owned by close family), so where there is some doubt, individuals may wish to keep some evidence of the terms on which they were able to occupy the property – if, for example, they stayed with a close friend, they may wish to record that they did not have a key and could not have returned without specific permission. If an individual stays with close family for some of the year and spends other nights in the UK, it will be particularly important to retain records of the accommodation used on other nights in order to demonstrate that their stay with close relatives remains below 16 days. Invoices/bills for hotel or bed and breakfast stays and similar should be retained.

Individuals who have accommodation available in the UK may also want to keep records to demonstrate that it is not their 'only home'. In particular, this may involve retaining records to show that they have a home elsewhere – see para **13.02** above regarding the kinds of records needed to demonstrate that a property is an individual's home. It will also be advisable to keep lease agreements and other documents which demonstrate the terms of occupation.

## Work tie

**[13.08]** Those who perform some duties in the UK either as part of an overseas employment, as a discreet employment (eg where a director post is retained) or as self-employment, will need to retain records of any days of work in the UK as well as records of the days when some work is performed in the UK but it is insufficient to pass the 'more than three hours work' test. For details of the types of records needed to show working patterns, see para **13.04** above.

In fact, of the list of records which HMRC suggest as appropriate for the sufficient ties test, the majority are likely to be helpful for the work tie test, eg work permits. Even though the relevant information for the tie will be days of work in the UK, it will be sensible to retain records of days worked outside the UK as this will assist in proving that the individual was not performing UK duties.

## Country tie

**[13.09]** The country tie means that in addition to keeping a record of the midnights spent in the UK, individuals who spend time in a number of different countries will also need to keep a record of their days in each individual country. The records needed will be similar to those needed to demonstrate days of presence in the UK – ie plane/rail tickets, boarding cards where possible, passport stamps etc. See para **13.02** above.

## 90-day tie

**[13.10]** Assuming that the individual has kept clear records of his days of presence in the UK for the previous tax year (see para **13.02** above), it should be relatively straightforward to demonstrate whether or not the 90-day tie is met.

# HMRC enquiries into residence status under the SRT

**[13.11]** The need for scrupulous records has been demonstrated by the first enquiries which HMRC have raised into residence status under the SRT (at the time of writing three tax return cycles have been completed under the SRT). In this context, HMRC have made it clear that they consider incorrect claims to non-residence one of the significant areas of risk relating to high net worth individuals (see, for example, 'HMRC's approach to collecting tax from high net worth individuals', a report by the Comptroller and Auditor General, 1 November 2016, figure 7 on page 17).

In the writers' experience, enquiries have focussed around taxpayers who work in the UK, looking particularly at those who consider themselves to be working full time overseas but who spend some time in the UK, or those who fall within the sufficient ties test but do not report a work tie. The particular focus has been on days spent in the UK which the taxpayer reports as non-working days.

In their review, HMRC have asked to see all telephone, email and diary records, including timesheets where available. Areas where taxpayers will need to demonstrate no work was done include where another person, for example their PA, reads their emails (so there is a record of an email being read, but is this work by the taxpayer?), meetings which remain in the diary but which the taxpayer did not attend, and taxis booked but not used. Taxpayers should be particularly careful with records relating to working patterns which are out of the ordinary and where work is undertaken out of the office, eg from home.

No doubt we will see additional areas of focus over the coming years.

# Conclusion

**[13.12]** The list of records HMRC expect to see may seem daunting, even if many of them probably seem like common sense. Nevertheless, the fact that HMRC devotes a separate section in their guidance to record-keeping shows that the importance of it should not be underestimated. The enquiries into residence status under the SRT reinforce this.

# Chapter 14

# HMRC guidance and practice

## Introduction

**[14.01]** One of the principal aims of introducing a statutory residence test was to provide certainty over an individual's residence status, as the previous regime had been criticised as too heavily dependent on HMRC guidance. It is ironic, therefore, that HMRC have already produced a lengthy 'guidance note' on the SRT (RDR3, revised version published August 2016). It is natural that advisers will turn to it when considering their clients' residence status and it is also natural, in the light of the judicial review cases concerning IR20, that advisers will question the extent to which they may rely on the guidance.

In addition to guidance, where HMRC may comment on a particular piece of legislation (eg Annex A of RDR3, where HMRC provide their interpretation of the terms 'home' and accommodation' within the SRT), they may also provide a non-statutory code in the form of a statement of practice (eg SP1/09).

## Statements of Practice – SP 1/09

**[14.02]** SP 1/09 was introduced to replace SP 5/84 and both are good examples of where statute required additional clarification. They also introduce a non-statutory code that operates in favour of the taxpayer and, in the case of SP 1/09, instead of the statutory provisions. Both SPs worked in a very similar way, although in the interests of brevity only SP1/09 is considered below.

SP1/09 is discussed in **CHAPTER 10**, and it addressed two aspects of the law not included in the underlying statute. First, it set out a rule for apportioning income between UK and non-UK duties (now replaced by *s 41ZA, ITEPA 2003*, which included this aspect in statute for the first time) and second, it simplified the way in which the mixed fund law applied to certain types of bank accounts.

This second aspect was introduced following the changes to the remittance basis in *FA 2008* to assist employees with overseas workdays determine the UK tax implications of remittances to the UK from the bank account containing their UK/overseas earnings. The practice set out in SP 1/09 has now largely been replaced by *Schedule 6 of FA 2013*, but continues to apply for a transitional period.

SP 1/09 does more than set out HMRC's interpretation of terms in the legislation; it sets out how HMRC will analyse UK remittances from an offshore bank account holding earnings of employees who are entitled to relief for overseas workdays (for a discussion of this, see **CHAPTER 10**). It provides a non-statutory practice that HMRC will apply provided certain conditions are met. In terms of reliance on the statement, a HMRC general note explains:

> 'Statements of Practice explain HMRC's interpretation of legislation and the way the department applies the law in practice. They do not affect a taxpayer's right to argue for a different interpretation, if necessary in an appeal to the General or Special Commissioners.'

Where the taxpayer adheres to the requirements set out in the statement of practice, HMRC will apply it, but they have been known to challenge its use in circumstances where a slight deviation would not appear to have had any serious implications. For example, if a taxpayer had credited the wrong sort of money to an account, but backed it out entirely before any other transactions involving the account, in principle the account should have been untainted by the earlier transaction. HMRC is nevertheless understood to be reluctant to allow accounts to qualify for SP1/09 treatment in these circumstances.

The conclusion to be drawn from this appears to be that anyone wishing to rely on HMRC's practice must follow the terms of it exactly as any deviation may call its application into question. This is a common theme in the context of HMRC's guidance and practice, as explored further below.

## HMRC guidance pre-SRT

[14.03] In IR20 HMRC set out some guidelines, loosely drawn from case law, that would allow taxpayers to self-assess their residence status prospectively, as they would generally need to do under self-assessment. Although it was not awarded any special status formally, it was relied on heavily by taxpayers and their advisors as it was understood to set out an approach that was acceptable to HMRC.

The reliance that taxpayers could place upon IR20 was called into particular focus by the Supreme Court hearing of R *(on the application of Davies) v Revenue and Customs Comrs; R (on the application of Gaines-Cooper) v Revenue and Customs Comrs* [2011] UKSC 47, [2012] 1 All ER 1048, [2011] 1 WLR 2625.

The main contention of the appellants was that, on its proper construction, the guidance contained a more benevolent interpretation of the circumstances in which an individual became non-resident and not ordinarily resident in the UK than was reflected in the ordinary law and that they had a legitimate expectation, to which the court should give effect, that the more benevolent interpretation would be applied to the determination of their status for tax purposes.

HMRC did not dispute that a legitimate expectation could exist, but rather argued that in neither case had the appellant met the terms of its guidance so unequivocally that they were entitled to rely on it.

The taxpayers' second argument was that, even if, when properly construed, the guidance did not contain a more benevolent interpretation than was reflected in the ordinary law, there had been a gradual shift in HMRC practice such that HMRC's settled practice was more generous than the guidance set out in IR20 and that this practice was such as to give rise to a legitimate expectation, to which again the court should give effect. For example, the then Inland Revenue had indicated to various tax advisors that it would accept that an individual could be working full-time abroad while undertaking on-going UK duties without the full-time character of the work abroad necessarily being affected.

The Supreme Court held that it was possible for HMRC to have created a legitimate expectation that its guidance would be applied, and that the guidance could, therefore, effectively extend the law. However, it also held that in order for this to be so, the guidance would have to be so clear and unequivocal and widely accepted and understood that its application in any circumstances would be totally beyond doubt. This placed a very high burden of proof on the appellants that they were unable to meet. In the words of Lord Wilson at [49]:

' . . . whereas, in the booklet [IR20] the Revenue gave unqualified assurances about its treatment of claims to non-residence which, if dishonoured, would readily have fallen for enforcement under the doctrine of legitimate expectation, it is more difficult for the appellants to elevate a practice into an assurance to taxpayers from which it would be abusive for the Revenue to resile and to which under the doctrine it should therefore be held . . . The result is that the Appellants need evidence that the practice was so unambiguous, so widespread, so well-established and so well-recognised as to carry within it a commitment to a group of taxpayers including themselves of treatment in accordance with it.'

At best, therefore, taxpayers could rely on practice that was so clear and so closely aligned to their own circumstances that there could be no doubt that the guidance fitted them exactly and they needed to follow the guidance precisely. This may include seeking guidance on an individual's specific case from HMRC itself if that is the recommendation of the published guidance.

In this context, it is worth noting the 2012 case R *(on the application of Cameron and another) v Revenue and Customs Commissioners; R (on the application of Palmer) v Revenue and Customs Commissioners* [2012] EWHC 1174 (Admin). This case considered HMRC published guidance to seafarers on what would be treated as a day of absence from the UK for the purposes of Seafarers' earnings deduction. The guidance (termed the 'broad concession') was considered to be clear and the taxpayer entitled to rely upon it until or unless it was revoked, withdrawn or altered by HMRC with reasonable notice to taxpayers.

Much has been made of the qualifications introduced into IR20 and its successor HMRC6 as a result of the judicial review case (see also CHAPTER 1). So what of RDR3? This is an important consideration where RDR3 goes beyond comment and provides guidance which appears to go further than the legislation (eg the treatment of notice periods and gardening leave – see RDR 3, section 3.13 and the discussion in para **3.14** – or the switch between accommodation and home – see para **7.14**).

# RDR3

**[14.04]** In their introduction to RDR3, HMRC state (para 1):

' . . . This Guidance Note gives you information about the statutory residence test (SRT), introduced in Finance Act 2013, and how HMRC interprets the legislation in the context of applying the SRT to an individual's circumstances. The guidance should be read in conjunction with the statutory residence test legislation, which forms Schedule 45 to the Finance Act 2013, to gain a comprehensive understanding.'

So the guidance is not a substitute for the law. The same point is made in Annex A. Annex A is concerned with the meaning of the terms 'home' and 'accommodation' and states a further caveat:

'A1. This guidance provides information about how HMRC interprets the term "home" in the context of applying the SRT to an individual's circumstances. It must be read in conjunction with the statutory residence test legislation, . . . to gain a comprehensive understanding.

A2. This guidance is intended primarily to help individuals apply the second automatic UK test . . . to establish their UK residence position.

A3. As the meaning of "home" can vary according to its context, it is not possible for this guidance to provide an absolute definition of the term. What this guidance does is to give indicators outlining the characteristics that a home will generally have. We give some general examples of what a home may or may not be; whether a place is or is not a home will always be dependent on the facts and circumstances of the use by the individual. HMRC may choose to enquire into those facts and circumstances.'

The HMRC guidance in Annex A is helpful as it indicates HMRC's own approach to the interpretation of the terms 'home' and 'accommodation' However, in view of the judicial review findings in *Gaines Cooper*, it is suggested that many taxpayers may not wish to rely on the guidance unless it can be shown to adhere closely to the legislation. Certainly, in applying HMRC's examples to their own specific circumstances, taxpayers are likely to feel most comfortable about relying on the conclusions HMRC give where their case matches that of the example precisely. However, inevitably there will be occasions when taxpayers choose to rely on the HMRC guidance because the law itself is unclear and untested. In doing so, taxpayers are advised to keep detailed records of their conclusions and the rationale for them since contemporaneous records are likely to be of great significance in any future litigation.

In this context, it is worth noting the comments of the Special Commissioner, John Clark, in his decision on Mr Genovese's ordinary residence status ([2009] STC (STD) 373 at [54]). Applying principles derived from case law, Mr Clark concluded that Mr Genovese was ordinarily resident in the UK in the 2001/02 tax year although he noted that this was:

'With some concerns as to the inconsistency with the practice laid down in HMRC's booklet IR20, which I consider myself unable to take into account when applying the common law test.'

Had Mr Clark felt that he could apply HMRC's published guidance to Mr Genovese, the outcome of the case might have been very different. This comes as a salutary reminder for anyone who chooses to rely on HMRC guidance where that guidance extends beyond what case law or statute plainly supports. Such a taxpayer may be putting themselves into a vulnerable position.

Under the SRT this continues to be the case, as the meaning of particular terms may be disputed in the future, and there is no case law to date that would help us understand how a court might interpret the statute. There are a number of examples where RDR3 appears to extend the law or reach a conclusion beyond what can be found in the legislation. A few of these are included here, but this is by no means an exhaustive list.

As noted in CHAPTER 3, HMRC's guidance on exceptional circumstances in Annex B of RDR3 is a good example of a practice that goes further than the related law, but where the taxpayer might claim to have a legitimate expectation of being able to rely upon it. *Para 22(4)* of *Sch 45, FA 2013* only mentions exceptional circumstances in the context of events that may prevent the taxpayer from leaving the UK, but Annex B is more generous:

'**Exceptional circumstances and Foreign and Commonwealth Office (FCO) advice**

B16 Exceptional circumstances will generally not apply in respect of events that bring you back to the UK. However, there may be circumstances such as civil unrest or natural disaster where associated FCO advice is to avoid all travel to the region.

B17 Individuals who return to and stay in the UK while FCO advice remains at this warning level would normally have days spent in the UK ignored under the SRT, subject to the 60-day limit.'

It would be difficult for HMRC to argue that any taxpayer relying on exceptional circumstances in such a case would not be able to ignore up to 60 days spent in the UK, although, since the word 'normally' is included, individuals in this situation still might want to seek a separate confirmation on the point from HMRC.

A further example where the law and the guidance may not be exactly on all fours is in the definition of work and 'garden leave'. Para 3.13 of RDR3 states that work will normally include 'instances where your employer instructs you to stay away from work for example when serving notice'. This is reasonable in the context of the definition of work in *para 26(2), Sch 45, FA 2013*, which states that regard should be had as to whether or not any associated pay would be taxed as employment income. It would be easy to think from para 3.13 that this means that garden leave is therefore included in a period where one is considered to be working and therefore days of garden leave can be treated as days on which more than three hours' work are undertaken. This would be relevant, for example, in determining whether a period of garden leave could constitute a significant break.

A similar issue arises with annual leave. Holiday pay means that annual leave should fall within the definition of 'work' and yet annual leave is specifically disregarded in deciding whether or not there has been a significant break. In other words, the legislation has deemed it necessary to deal separately with the fact that no work is actually performed on these days. There is no such exclusion for garden leave. Therefore, arguably HMRC guidance extends beyond the legislation in including garden leave as work or, perhaps we are reading too much in hoping that its inclusion in the definition of work would prevent an individual on garden leave being treated as though he had a significant break. For a full discussion of this topic and conclusions on it, refer to para **3.14**.

The lack of clear definition of the word 'home' and the centrality of the home to the SRT mean that by necessity RDR3 attempts to fill the gap. It does this by providing numerous examples of what is and is not a home, when a property begins and ceases to be a home and similar difficult areas. Although the examples are helpful in giving us an insight into HMRC's interpretation of the word 'home', an individual will need to exercise caution in applying these examples to his particular circumstances. Where his circumstances are exactly as described in an example or elsewhere, he is entitled to reply on that example as stating HMRC's position. The difficulty comes where the position is similar to one or more examples and he needs to extrapolate in an attempt to understand HMRC's view. As an example of the uncertainty still present, even with HMRC guidance, consider the question of the date from which a property may begin to be regarded as a home if there is a delay in the owner occupying the property. Example A7 from HMRC's Annex A in RDR3 (see **CHAPTER 7** which considers this in detail) suggests that a property would normally have to be occupied for at least one night before it would count as a home; but the guidance itself stops short of stating that. The comments in paragraphs A15 and A18 do not make the position clear. It is unlikely, therefore, that any taxpayer could claim he had a legitimate expectation of HMRC regarding a property as not becoming his home until such time as he had spent a night there, as the guidance on that point is neither clear nor, given the very recent introduction of this regime, could the guidance be described as well-established or well-recognised.

# CAP 1

**[14.05]** If the legislation is unclear and, having referred to the available guidance the position remains uncertain, an individual may contact HMRC for a non-statutory clearance. This procedure is now known as a CAP 1 application. Individuals may, for example, wish to make a CAP 1 application for guidance on the date on which the property begins to be an individual's home where the facts are similar but not precisely the same as in one of the RDR3 Annex A examples (see comments in para **14.03** above).

Individuals must provide detailed information regarding the action (or transactions) being considered, including for example full details of the transaction and the reason for carrying it out. A full list of the information required in a non-statutory clearance application is provided in Annexes A to E of CAP 1 (available on the HMRC website). Provided an individual has given full and accurate information and carries out the transaction as anticipated, he should then be able to rely on any advice given by HMRC.

HMRC's website states that they will normally reply within 28 days. However, HMRC may not answer the query if it does not consider that there are genuine points of uncertainty or if it considers it is being asked to 'give tax planning advice'. HMRC will also not comment on transactions which it considers are for the purpose of avoiding tax.

# Departing from HMRC guidance

[**14.06**] It is possible for individuals to form their own view which may differ from that of HMRC. The recommendation of professional bodies such as the CIOT and ICAEW is that a taxpayer taking a different view should disclose this on the relevant tax return, while in SP 1/06 HMRC note that such disclosure is necessary to protect the taxpayer from a discovery assessment.

> 'It is open to a taxpayer properly informed or advised to adopt a different view of the law from that published as HMRC's view. To protect against a discovery assessment after the enquiry period, the return or accompanying documents would have to indicate that a different view has been adopted.'
>
> SP 1/06 para 18

# Conclusion

[**14.07**] HMRC guidance in RDR3 will be useful to any individual who needs to apply the SRT legislation. However, it is not intended to replace the legislation and the challenge for individuals and their advisors is to resist the temptation to accept it without question.

# Chapter 15

# The New Deemed Domicile Rules

## Introduction

**[15.01]** The origin of the new regime, most of which will be effective from 6 April 2017, can be originally traced to the July 2015 'Technical Briefing on Non-Dom changes': https://www.gov.uk/government/publications/technical-b riefing-on-foreign-domiciled-persons-changes-announced-at-summer-budget-2015.

A Consultation paper 'Reforms to the taxation of non-domiciles' then followed in September 2015: https://www.gov.uk/government/consultations/r eforms-to-the-taxation-of-non-domiciles/reforms-to-the-taxation-of-non-dom iciles. The draft legislation published with the Consultation paper has been superceded.

In December 2015 a Policy paper was issued 'IHT: reforms to the taxation of non-domiciles' with draft IHT clauses. The draft legislation issued with the policy paper has been superceded: https://www.gov.uk/government/uploads/s ystem/uploads/attachment_data/file/484090/151209_publication_v1_4.pdf.

A further Policy paper was issued on 2 February 2016 and updated on 5 February, 'Domicile: Income Tax and CGT' & draft IT/CGT clauses: https://www.gov.uk/government/publications/domicile-income-tax-and-capita l-gains-tax.

Further proposals were contained in Budget 2016 and in August 2016 a further Consultation paper 'Reforms to the taxation of non-domiciles: further consultation' was published: https://www.gov.uk/government/consultations/re forms-to-the-taxation-of-non-domiciles-further-consultation.

Further amended provisions were included in the Finance Bill in March 2017 and revised draft clauses and explanatory notes were published on 13 July 2017.

We set out the proposed new rules, to be effective from 6 April 2017 (see clause 42 of the Finance Bill published in March 2017) and based on the draft legislation published in September 2017. We focus on the deemed domicile tests and the protected settlement provisions. We note that at the time of writing there are likely to be further amendments to the draft provisions.

We also note that on 13 September 2017, HMRC published a draft schedule inserting:

(1)     Sections 87D to 87L TCGA 1992;
(2)     Sections 643A to 643L ITTOIA 2005;
(3)     Sections 733B - 733C and 735C ITA 2007.

The proposed new provisions are intended for the Finance Bill 2017 to 2018 and HMRC say they are 'subject to confirmation at autumn Budget 2017', which is scheduled for 22 November 2017. The draft provisions cover a non-resident disregard, a close family charge and an onward gift charge. We hope to deal with these charges, if implemented, in the next edition.

## The New Regime: IHT and IT/CGT

**[15.02]** In outline, there are now four categories of IHT deemed domicile and two categories of IT/CGT deemed domicile. The IHT deemed domicile rules are:

| IHT deemed domicile | Introduced | Provision in IHTA 1984 |
|---|---|---|
| 3-year rule | unchanged | Section 267(1)(a) |
| Formerly domiciled resident | new from April 2017 | Section 267(1)(aa) |
| 15-year rule | was 17 year rule | Section 267(1)(b) |
| Spouse-election | unchanged | Section 267ZA |

The IT/CGT deemed domicile rules are:

| IT/CGT deemed domicile | Introduced | Provision in ITA 2007 |
|---|---|---|
| Formerly domiciled resident | new from April 2017 | Section 835B Condition A |
| 15-year rule | new from April 2017 | Section 835B Condition B |

The 15-year rules for IHT and IT/CGT differ slightly. IHT deemed domicile applies for (almost) all IHT purposes. The exceptional situations are FOTRA securities and qualifying certificates of Channel Islander/Isle of Man individuals and double tax treaties.

## Inheritance Tax Three Year Rule

**[15.03]** Section 267(1) IHTA provides:

'A person not domiciled in the UK at any time (in this section referred to as "the relevant time") shall be treated for the purposes of this Act as domiciled in the UK (and not elsewhere) at the relevant time if—

(a)     he was domiciled in the UK within the three years immediately preceding the relevant time...'

As noted above, this rule is unchanged. It should be noted that this rule does not impact the SRT and runs on calendar years. The IHT Manual gives an example:

'IHTM13024 - Change of Domicile: Deemed Domicile [Aug 2016]
Example 1 Paula

Paula has an English domicile and lives in England. She retires from work and decides that she wants to live for the rest of her life in Spain. She goes to Spain and takes a Spanish domicile of choice on 31 January 2007. She dies on 1 January 2010 still in Spain.

Because of the deemed domicile 'three-year rule' she is deemed domiciled in the UK at her death and her world-wide estate is chargeable to IHT. Her estate can, of course, claim tax relief for any Inheritance Tax paid in another country.

Section 267(5) IHTA provides:

> 'In determining for the purposes of this section whether a person is, or at any time was, domiciled in the UK, sections 267ZA and 267ZB are to be ignored'.

So the spouse-election domicile and the 3-year rule operate independently: the loss of spouse-election domicile does not give rise to deemed domicile under the 3-year rule. We do not consider the spouse-election rule here as it is unchanged.

## Formerly Domiciled Resident: IHT

**[15.04]** Section 267(1) IHTA provides:

> ' . . . A person not domiciled in the UK at any time (in this section referred to as "the relevant time") shall be treated for the purposes of this Act as domiciled in the UK (and not elsewhere) at the relevant time if ...
>
> (aa)   he is a formerly domiciled resident for the tax year in which the relevant time falls ("the relevant tax year")'

'Formerly domiciled resident' is defined in section 272 IHTA which provides:

> '"formerly domiciled resident", in relation to a tax year, means a person—
>
> (a)   who was born in the UK
> (b)   whose domicile of origin was in the UK,
> (c)   who was resident in the UK for that tax year, and
> (d)   who was resident in the UK for at least one of the two tax years immediately preceding that tax year'.

For (c) and (d) this requires residence throughout the year. Note that even in the years of arrival or departure, where the split year provisions apply, the individual is strictly resident throughout the tax year; it is simply that they will be taxed to income tax and CGT as though they were non-resident in the overseas part of the year.

The domicile start date for formerly domiciled residents is 6 April in the second year of residence. The domicile end date for formerly domiciled residents is 6 April in the first year of non-residence.

## IHT 15-Year Rule

**[15.05]** Section 267(1) IHTA provides:

> 'A person not domiciled in the UK at any time (in this section referred to as "the relevant time") shall be treated for the purposes of this Act as domiciled in the UK (and not elsewhere) at the relevant time if ...
>
> (b)   he was resident in the United Kingdom—
> (i)   for at least fifteen of the twenty tax years immediately preceding the relevant tax year, and

(ii)     for at least one of the four tax years ending with the relevant tax year'

The start date for acquisition of 15-year deemed domicile is 6 April in the tax year after the 15/20 year test is satisfied.

For example, if a taxpayer has been continually resident in the UK from 2002/03 they will be deemed domiciled on 6 April 2017, from 2003/4 on 6 April 2018 and so on.

Once acquired, to lose deemed domiciled status, it is necessary to remain non-resident for 6 tax years, although the IHT implications of deemed domiciled status no longer apply from the 4th consecutive year.

Residence for this purpose is defined in section 267(4) IHTA which provides:

'For the purposes of this section the question whether a person was resident in the UK for any tax year shall be determined as for the purposes of income tax'.

This is superfluous from 2013/14, as the statutory residence test applies for IHT generally (paras 1 and 2, sch 45 FA 2013).

# Children

**[15.06]** The deemed domicile of the long term resident foreign domiciliary has no effect on the domicile status of their children. Therefore, common law rules apply to children unless they then come to be deemed UK domiciled in their own right.

However, the UK resident years count towards the 15 year total even if the individual is under the age of 18.

# IT/CGT Deemed Domicile

**[15.07]** Section 835B ITA provides:

'(1)     'This section has effect for the purposes of the provisions of the Income Tax Acts or TCGA 1992 which apply this section.

(2)     An individual not domiciled in the UK at a time in a tax year is to be regarded as domiciled in the UK at that time if—

(a)     condition A is met, or
(b)     condition B is met'.

IT/CGT deemed domicile applies only for provisions which apply *s 835B ITA 2007*. If a provision refers to domicile but does not apply section 835B, the IT/CGT rules do not apply. The list of provisions is:

Income tax

ICTA 1988: s 266A;

ITEPA 2003: ss 355, 373, 374, 376;

ITA 2007: ss 476, 718, 809B, 809E, 834.

CGT

TCGA 1992: s 69, 86, 275;

TCGA 1992 Schedule 5A para 3;

Schedule 7 FA 2008 transitional reliefs (formerly domiciled residents only): paragraphs 100(1)(b), 101(1)(c) and 102(1)(e);

paragraphs 118(3)(b) so far as having effect for the purposes of paragraph 118(1)(d) paragraphs 124(1)(b), 126(7)(b), 127(1)(e) and 151(1)(b).

### Condition A: Formerly Domiciled

**[15.08]** Section 835B(3) ITA 2007 provides:

> 'Condition A is that—
>
> (a) 'the individual was born in the UK,
> (b) the individual's domicile of origin was in the UK, and
> (c) the individual is resident in the UK for the tax year referred to in subsection (2)'.

This is equivalent to the IHT formerly domiciled resident rule. (See para **15.04** above.) However, there is no equivalent to the grace period of one year. So the domicile start date is 6 April in the 1st year of residence. In that year, a formerly domiciled resident will be deemed domiciled for IT/CGT but not for IHT.

Spilt year rules do not strictly alter deemed domicile, but in practice IT/CGT relief would usually be available in the offshore part of a split year. In addition, deemed domicile is usually irrelevant during that period, so that may explain the absence of a grace period.

The domicile end date is 6 April in a year of non-residence, which is the same as the IHT rule. Again, note that the year of departure, to which the split year rules apply, will not be a year of non-residence (see also para **15.04** above).

The interaction of Conditions A and B should be noted. It is possible for an individual to be caught under Condition B too, which would have implications when they left the UK.

### Condition B: 15 Year Rule

**[15.09]** Section 835B(4) ITA provides:

> 'Condition B is that the individual has been UK resident for at least 15 of the 20 tax years immediately preceding the tax year referred to in subsection (2)'.

This is the equivalent of the IHT 15-year rule.

Section 835B(5) ITA provides:

> 'But Condition B is not met if—

    (a)    the individual is not UK resident for the relevant tax year, and

    (b)    there is no tax year beginning after 5 April 2017 and preceding the relevant tax year in which the individual was UK resident'.

The £90,000 remittance basis charge (introduced 2015/16) has ceased from 2016/17.

## Split Year Treatment

**[15.10]** A tax year for which the individual is UK resident will count in full for the 15-year test even if the year is a split year under the SRT.

There is a mismatch of treatment: for inheritance tax purposes foreign excluded property will be non-excluded property even in the overseas part of the year; however, for income tax and capital gains tax deemed domicile will not prevent the split year rules applying.

## Transitional Arrangements

**[15.11]** Para 16 schedule 1 Draft IT/CTGT clauses published in July 2017 provides:

'(10) The amendment to section 267(1) of IHTA 1984 made by subsection (1)(c) does not have effect in relation to a person if—

    (a)    the person is not resident in the United Kingdom for the relevant tax year, and

    (b)    there is no tax year beginning after 5 April 2017 and preceding the relevant tax year in which the person was resident in the United Kingdom.

In this subsection "relevant tax year" is to be construed in accordance with section 267(1) of IHTA 1984 as amended by subsection (1)'.

This is consistent with the policy that for those who left the UK before 6 April 2017 but would have been deemed domiciled under the 15 year rule on 6 April 2017, the pre-2017 rules (the 17-year rule) will apply.

In relation to settled property, clause 42 FB March 2017 provides:

'(11) The amendment to section 267(1) of IHTA 1984 made by subsection (1)(c) also does not have effect in determining—

    (a)    whether settled property which became comprised in the settlement on or before that date is excluded property for the purposes of IHTA 1984;

    (b)    the settlor's domicile for the purposes of section 65(8) of that Act in relation to settled property which became comprised in the settlement on or before that date;

    (c)    whether, for the purpose of section 65(8) of that Act, the condition in section 82(3) of that Act is satisfied in relation to such settled property.

(12) Despite subsection (2), section 267(1) of IHTA 1984, as originally enacted, shall continue to be disregarded in determining—

    (a)    whether settled property which became comprised in the settlement on or before 9 December 1974 is excluded property for the purposes of IHTA 1984;

(b)    the settlor's domicile for the purposes of section 65(8) of that Act in relation to settled property which became comprised in the settlement on or before that date;

(c)    whether, for the purpose of section 65(8) of that Act, the condition in section 82(3) of that Act is satisfied in relation to such settled property'.

The 15-year rule is not retrospective in that it does not impact on past actions taken.

There is no transitional relief for formerly domiciled residents.

# Protected Settlements

**[15.12]** There is obviously a policy tension between tightening up the foreign domiciliary provisions and collecting more tax on the one hand and not driving foreign domiciliaries to leave the UK permanently on the other. One measure that has been a central tenet of the provisions since they were first anticipated in 2015 is the promise to give trusts created by foreign domiciled settlors before becoming deemed domiciled protected status after the settlor becomes deemed domiciled if certain conditions (set out in para **15.13** below) are fulfilled.

The current proposals provide that trust gains and foreign income of protected trusts are to be subject to tax on distributions to the settlor, or other UK resident beneficiaries (either on general principles or under special new provisions) but are not subject to tax if retained in the trust.

We set out the proposed rules for completeness below, but note that as there are still a number of uncertainties in relation to the precise drafting and scope of the rules, we intend to comment more fully in the next edition, once we have more clarity.

It should be noted that protected trust relief ceases to apply to those who become actually UK domiciled and the relief does not apply to formerly domiciled residents.

# Protected Settlements: Section 86 TCGA 1992 /paragraph 5A Sch 5

**[15.13]** New paragraph 5A(1) schedule 5 TCGA 1992 provides:

'Section 86 does not apply in relation to a year ("the particular year") if Conditions A to D are met'.

### Condition A

Paragraph 5A(2) schedule 5 TCGA 1992 provides:

'(2)    Condition A is that the particular year is—

(a)    the tax year 2017-18, or

(b)    a later tax year'.

Condition B

Paragraph 5A(3) schedule 5 TCGA 1992 provides:

'(2)    Condition B is that when the settlement is created the settlor—

(a)    is not domiciled in the UK, and

(b)    if the settlement is created on or after 6 April 2017, is not deemed domiciled in the UK'.

Condition C

Paragraph 5A(4) schedule 5 TCGA 1992 provides:

(2)    'Condition C is that there is no time in the particular year when the settlor is—

(a)    domiciled in the UK, or

(b)    deemed domiciled in the UK by virtue of Condition A in section 835BA of ITA 2007 [i.e. a formerly domiciled resident]'.

Condition D

Paragraph 5A(5) schedule 5 TCGA 1992 provides:

'(2)    Condition D is that no property or income is provided directly or indirectly for the purposes of the settlement by the settlor, or the trustees of any other settlement of which the settlor is a beneficiary or settlor, at a time in the relevant period when the settlor is—

(a)    domiciled in the UK, or

(b)    deemed domiciled in the UK'

Condition D applies if property is provided by the settlor, or the trustees of any other settlement of which the settlor is a beneficiary or settlor.

## Adding Value

**[15.14]** Paragraph 5A(7) schedule 5 TCGA 1992 provides:

'For the purposes of Condition D, the addition of value to property comprised in the settlement is to be treated as the direct provision of property for the purposes of the settlement'.

Para 5A(7) is new, however, an addition of value will usually amount to providing property indirectly in any event.

One example of when the rule will apply is leaving an interest-free loan outstanding. The official HMRC view is that leaving an interest-free loan outstanding is providing property, although that it not universally accepted.

Definitions: 'Loan' and 'arm's length terms'

"Loan" is not defined, and therefore refers to a simple loan of money.

Para 5B(8) schedule 5 TCGA provides:

'For the purposes of this paragraph a loan is on "arm's length terms"—

(a)    in the case of a loan made to the trustees of a settlement, only if interest at the official rate or more is payable at least annually under the loan;

(b)    in the case of a loan made by the trustees of a settlement, only if any interest payable under the loan is payable at no more than the official rate'.

What is the effect of an adjuster clause?

Arm's length transaction

Paragraph 5B schedule 5 TCGA 1992 provides:

'(1)    Condition B is that when the settlement is created the settlor—
(2)    Ignore—

(a)    property or income provided under a transaction, other than a loan, where the transaction is entered into on arm's length terms,
(b)    property or income provided, otherwise than under a loan, without any intention by the person providing it to confer a gratuitous benefit on any person'.

A transaction between connected persons is treated as 'otherwise than by way of a bargain made at arm's length'.

Loan to trustees

Paragraph 5B schedule 5 TCGA 1992 provides:

'(2)    Ignore ...
(c)    the principal of a loan which is made to the trustees of the settlement on arm's length terms'.

Paragraph 5B(3) schedule 5 TCGA 1992 provides a clawback charge:

Where—

'(a)    a loan is made to the trustees of the settlement by the settlor or the trustees of a settlement connected with the settlor, and
(b)    the loan is on arm's length terms, but
(c)    a relevant event occurs,

the principal of the loan is to be regarded as having been provided to the trustees at the time of that event (despite sub-paragraph (2))'.

There are three types of relevant event. Paragraph 5B(4) schedule 5 TCGA 1992 provides:

'In sub-paragraph (3) "relevant event" means—

(a)    capitalisation of interest payable under the loan,
(b)    any other failure to pay interest in accordance with the terms of the loan, or
(c)    variation of the terms of the loan such that they cease to be arm's length terms'.

It will be interesting to see whether HMRC take the position that the clawback charge applies if the failure to pay interest under sub-paragraph (b) is, for example, one day late.

Loan from trustees

Paragraph 5B schedule 5 TCGA 1992 provides:

(2)    Ignore ...
(d)    the payment of interest to the trustees of the settlement under a loan made by them on arm's length terms,

    (e)    repayment to the trustees of the settlement of the principal of a loan made by them'.

Loan by foreign domiciliary to trustees

Paragraph 5B schedule 5 TCGA 1992 provides:

(5)    Sub-paragraph (6) applies (subject to sub-paragraph (7)) where—
    (a)    the settlor becomes deemed domiciled in the UK on or after 6 April 2017,
    (b)    before the date on which the settlor becomes deemed domiciled in the UK ("the deemed domicile date"), a loan has been made to the trustees of the settlement by—
        (i)    the settlor, or
        (ii)    the trustees of a settlement connected with the settlor,
    (c)    the loan is not entered into on arm's length terms, and
    (d)    any amount that is outstanding under the loan on the deemed domicile date ("the outstanding amount") is payable or repayable on demand on or after that date.
(6)    Where this sub-paragraph applies, the outstanding amount is to be regarded as property directly provided on the deemed domicile date by the lender for the purposes of the settlement (despite sub-paragraph (2))'.

2017 transitional relief

Paragraph 5B(7) schedule 5 TCGA 1992 provides:

'But if the deemed domicile date is 6 April 2017, sub-paragraph (6) does not apply if—

(a)    the principal of the loan is repaid, and all interest payable under the loan is paid, before 6 April 2018, or
(b)    the loan becomes a loan on arm's length terms before 6 April 2018 and—
    (i)    before that date interest is paid to the lender in respect of the period beginning with 6 April 2017 and ending with 5 April 2018 as if those arm's length terms had been terms of the loan in relation to that period, and
    (ii)    interest continues to be payable from 6 April 2018 in accordance with those terms'.

The position is still not clear in relation to a loan to an underlying company held by a trust.

Para 5B schedule 5 TCGA provides:

(2)    Ignore ...
    (f)    property or income provided in pursuance of a liability incurred by any person before 6 April 2017'.

Expenses

Para 5B schedule 5 TCGA provides:

(2)    Ignore ...
    (g)    where the settlement's expenses relating to taxation and administration for a tax year exceed its income for that year, property or income provided towards meeting that excess if the value of any such property and income is not greater than the amount of—
        (i)    the excess, or
        (ii)    if greater, the amount by which such expenses exceed the

amount of such expenses which may be paid out of the settlement's income'.

SP5/92, which gives guidance on previous protected status granted to offshore trusts will provide some useful guidance on the new provisions.

# Protected Settlements: Section 624/628A ITTOIA 2005

**[15.15]** Section 624 ITTOIA 2005 provides that income of a settlor interested trust is treated as income of the settlor.

New section 628A(1) ITTOA 2005 provides:

'The rule in section 624(1) does not apply to income which arises under a settlement if it is protected foreign-source income for a tax year'.

This improves the position for relevant foreign domiciliaries as it is not necessary to pay the remittance basis charge and protected foreign source income (but arguably not capitalised benefits) can be remitted without a charge to income tax.

Section 628A(2) ITTOA 2005 provides:

'For this purpose, income arising under a settlement in a tax year is "protected foreign-source income" for the tax year if Conditions A to F are met'.

### Condition A: relevant foreign income

Section 628A(3) ITTOA 2005 provides:

Condition A is that the income would be relevant foreign income if it were income of a UK resident individual".

### Condition B: originating from settlor

Section 628A(4) ITTOA 2005 provides:

'Condition B is that the income is from property originating from the settlor (see section 645)'.

### Condition C: domicile of settlor on creation

Section 628A(5) ITTOA 2005 provides:

'(5)    Condition C is that when the settlement is created the settlor—
(a)    is not domiciled in the UK, and.
(b)    if the settlement is created on or after 6 April 2017, is not deemed domiciled in the UK'.

### Condition D: domicile in the tax year

Section 628A(6) ITTOIA 2005 provides:

'(6)    Condition D is that there is no time in the tax year when the settlor is—
(a)    domiciled in the UK, or
(b)    deemed domiciled in the UK by virtue of Condition A in section 835BA of ITA 2007 [formerly domiciled resident]'.

### Condition E: non-resident trustees

Section 628A(7) ITTOA 2005 provides:

'Condition E is that the trustees of the settlement are not UK resident for the tax year'.

### Condition F: tainting

Section 628A ITTOA 2005 provides:

'(8)    Condition F is that no property or income is provided directly or indirectly for the purposes of the settlement by the settlor, or by the trustees of any other settlement of which the settlor is a beneficiary or settlor, at a time in the relevant period when the settlor is—
(a)    domiciled in the UK, or
(b)    deemed domiciled in the UK.

(9)    In subsection (8) 'relevant period" means the period—

(a)    beginning with the start of 6 April 2017 or, if later, the creation of the settlement, and
(b)    ending with the end of the tax year'.

### 2017 transitional relief: pre-2017 trust income remitted post-2017

Section 628C(1) ITTOIA 2005 provides:

'For the purposes of applying section 809L of ITA 2007 (meaning of remitted to the UK) in relation to transitional trust income, "relevant person" in that section does not include the trustees of the settlement concerned'.

Section 628C ITTOIA 2005 provides:

'(2)    Transitional trust income" means income—
(a)    that arises under a settlement in the period beginning with the tax year 2008-09 and ending with the tax year 2016-17 ("the protection period"),
(b)    that would be protected foreign-source income for the purposes of section 628A(1) if section 628A(2)—
(i)    had effect for the protection period, and
(ii)    so had effect with a reference to conditions A to E (instead of A to F),
(c)    that prior to 6 April 2017 has neither been distributed by the trustees of the settlement nor treated under section 624(1) as income of the settlor, and
(d)    that would for the tax year in which it arose under the settlement have been treated under section 624(1) as income of the settlor if the settlor had been domiciled in the UK for that year'.

In principle, a receipt in the UK of 2008-2017 income by trustees does not constitute a taxable remittance. This is of limited importance, though it might facilitate UK investment by the trust.

### Minor child of settlor

Section 630A ITTOIA provides:

'(1)    The rule in section 629(1) does not apply to income which arises under a settlement if it is protected foreign-source income for a tax year.
(2)    Sections 628A(2) to (12) and 628B (meaning of "protected foreign source income") have effect also for this purpose.
(3)    Section 648(3) to (5) (relevant foreign income treated as arising under settlement only if and when remitted) do not apply for the purposes of this section'.

This applies a protected trust exemption to the charge on payments to the settlor's minor child.

## Protected Settlements: Section 720/721A ITA 2007

**[15.16]** Section 721(3B) ITA 2007 provides:

'The amount of the income treated as arising under subsection (1) [the amount of s 720 income] is (subject to sections 724 and 725) given by the following rules—

**Rule 1**

The amount is equal to the amount of the income of the person abroad if the individual—
(a)   is domiciled in the UK at any time in the tax year, or
(b)   is at any time in the tax year regarded for the purposes of section 718(1)(b) as domiciled in the UK as a result of section 835BA having effect because of Condition A in that section being met [formerly domiciled resident].

**Rule 2**

In any other case the amount is equal to so much of the income of the person abroad as is not protected foreign-source income (see section 721A)'.

Protected foreign-source income is not, therefore, subject to the s 720 charge.

This relief is an improvement for relevant foreign domiciliaries as it is not necessary to pay the remittance basis charge and protected income is not subject to income tax even if remitted.

Section 721 ITA 2007 also provides:

'(3BA) In a case in which rule 2 of subsection (3B) applies, so much of the income of the person abroad as is protected foreign-source income for the purposes of that rule counts as "protected income" for the purposes of section 733A(1)(b)(i)'.

Section 721A ITA provides the definition of 'protected foreign-source income':
(1)   This section has effect for the purposes of rule 2 of section 721(3B) (cases where the individual is not UK domiciled and is not deemed domiciled by virtue of Condition A in section 835BA) [formerly domiciled resident33].
(2)   The income of the person abroad is "protected foreign-source income" so far as it is within subsection (3) or (4)'.

Trust income

Section 721A ITA provides:
'(2)   The income of the person abroad is "protected foreign-source income" so far as it is within subsection (3) or (4).
(3)   Income is within this subsection if—
(a)   it would be relevant foreign income if it were the individual's,
(b)   the person abroad is the trustees of a settlement,
(c)   the trustees are non-UK resident for the tax year,
(d)   when the settlement is created, the individual is—
(i)   not domiciled in the UK, and
(ii)   if the settlement is created on or after 6 April 2017, not deemed domiciled in the UK, and

> (e)  no property or income is provided directly or indirectly for the purposes of the settlement by the individual, or by the trustees of any other settlement of which the individual is a beneficiary or settlor, at a time in the period—
>
> > (i)  beginning with the start of 6 April 2017 or, if later, the creation of the settlement, and
> > (ii)  ending with the end of the tax year,
>
> when the individual is domiciled or deemed domiciled in the UK'.

### Company income

Section 721A ITA 2007 provides that the income of the person abroad is 'protected foreign-source income' so far as satisfies the same 5 conditions set out in the preceding paragraph, with the necessary amendments that paragraph (b) requires that the person abroad is a company (rather than trustees); and paragraphs (c)(d) are added, as follows.

Section 721A ITA provides:

> '(4)  Income is within this subsection if...
> > (c)  the trustees of a settlement—
> > > (i)  are participators in the person abroad, or
> > > (ii)  are participators in the first in a chain of two or more companies where the last company in the chain is the person abroad and where each company in the chain (except the last) is a participator in the next company in the chain,
> > (d)  the individual's power to enjoy the income results from the trustees being participators as mentioned in paragraph (c)(i) or (ii)'.

If the company is not held in a trust, there is no relief.

### 2017 transitional relief: pre-2017 s 720 income remitted post-2017

Section 726 ITA provides:

> '(6)  In addition, where the tax year in which any foreign deemed income arises is earlier than the tax year 2017-18, section 832 of ITTOIA 2005 does not apply to the foreign deemed income so far as it—
> > (a)  is remitted to the UK in the tax year 2017-18 or a later tax year, and
> > (b)  is transitionally protected income.
> (7)  In subsection (6) ...
> "transitionally protected income" means any foreign deemed income where the income mentioned in section 721(2 [that is, the income of the person abroad])—
> > (a)  arises in a tax year earlier than the tax year 2017-18,
> > (b)  would be protected foreign-source income as defined by section 721A if section 721A—
> > > (i)  had effect for tax years earlier than the tax year 2017-18, and
> > > (ii)  so had effect with the omission of its subsections (3)(e), (4)(g), (5) and (6) [tainting rule], and
> > (c)  has not prior to 6 April 2017 been distributed by the trustees of the settlement concerned'.

# Protected Settlements: Section 727 ITA 2007

[15.17] Identical rules are set out again for the purposes of the s 727 charge (capital sum paid to settlor).

## Commencement

[15.18] Paragraph 39 schedule 8F (no.2) A 2017 provides:

'(39) 'The amendments made by paragraphs 19 to 38 have effect for the tax year 2017-18 and subsequent tax years'.

# Index

High net worth individuals – *cont.*
double tax treaties
coming to the UK, 7.10
leaving the UK, 5.09
establishing UK residence (other than
employees etc)
ceasing to have a home outside the UK,
7.15
home in the UK, 7.14
introduction, 7.11
leaving the UK, 7.20
limitation of anti-avoidance rules, 7.19
long-term consequences of UK
residence, 7.18
split-year test, 7.13
timing of arrival, 7.16
timing of departure, 7.21
when does UK residence begin, 7.13
year of arrival, 7.12–7.16
years of presence in the UK, 7.17–7.21
leaving the UK
conclusion, 5.27
introduction, 5.01
maintaining non-residence, 5.10–5.22
year of departure, 5.02–5.09
year of return, 5.23–5.26
maintaining non-residence
accommodation traps, 5.15
automatic non-residence, 5.11
avoiding automatic UK residence, 5.12
children, 5.21
country tie, 5.22
family, 5.21
full-time working in the UK, 5.17
introduction, 5.10
location of work, 5.20
maintaining UK property, 5.14
spouse, 5.21
sufficient ties test, 5.13
three-hour rule, 5.19
UK property, 5.14
work tie, 5.18
working in the UK, 5.16–5.20
spending time in the UK without
establishing UK residence
accommodation tie, 7.07
automatic non-residence, 7.03
automatic UK residence, 7.04
deemed days trap, 7.09
double tax treaties, 7.10
introduction, 7.02
limiting days in the UK, 7.03
90-day trap, 7.08
UK home, 7.05
sufficient ties test, 7.06–7.09

High net worth individuals – *cont.*
split year treatment, 5.03
travel (coming to the UK)
limiting days in UK, 7.03
spending time in UK without
establishing residence, 7.03
travel (leaving the UK)
country tie, 5.22
location of work, 5.20
three-hour rule, 5.19
year of departure
double tax treaties, and, 5.09
holiday homes, 5.06
introduction, 5.02
spends fewer than 16 days in the UK,
5.07
'sufficient link' with country overseas,
5.07
timing of departure, 5.08
UK home, 5.04–5.05
when does non-UK residence begin,
5.03
year of presence in the UK
introduction, 7.17
leaving the UK, 7.20
limitation of anti-avoidance rules, 7.19
long-term consequences of UK
residence, 7.18
timing of departure, 7.21
year of return
five-year trap, 5.24
introduction, 5.23
timing of return, 5.26
when does UK residence begin, 5.25
HMRC guidance
background, 1.03
CAP 1, 14.05
changes since FA 2013, 1.05
conclusion, 14.07
departure from, 14.06
introduction, 14.01
IR20, 14.03
RDR3, 14.04
Statement of Practice (SP 1/09), 14.02
HMRC 6
generally, 1.03
Holiday home
coming to the UK
employees and self-employed, 6.04
high net worth individuals, 7.05
leaving the UK
high net worth individuals, 5.06–5.07
meaning of 'accommodation', 3.18
meaning of 'home', 3.07
record-keeping, 13.03